T0272604

Disrupted City

ALSO BY MANAN AHMED ASIF

The Loss of Hindustan: The Invention of India

A Book of Conquest: The Chachnama and Muslim Origins in South Asia

Where the Wild Frontiers Are: Pakistan and the American Imagination

Disrupted City

Walking the Pathways of Memory
and History in Lahore

Manan Ahmed Asif

THE
NEW
PRESS

NEW YORK
LONDON

Published in the United States by The New Press, New York, 2024
Distributed by Two Rivers Distribution

ISBN 978-1-59558-907-1 (hc)
ISBN 978-1-62097-363-9 (ebook)

Library of Congress Cataloging-in-Publication Data

Names: Asif, Manan Ahmed, author.
Title: Disrupted city : walking the pathways of memory and history in
Lahore / Manan Ahmed Asif.
Description: New York; London: The New Press, 2024. | Includes
bibliographical references and index. | Summary: "A history of
Pakistan's cultural and intellectual capital, from one of the preeminent
scholars of South Asia"—Provided by publisher.
Identifiers: LCCN 2024005193 | ISBN 9781595589071 (hardcover) |
ISBN 9781620973639 (ebook)
Subjects: LCSH: Lahore (Pakistan)—History. | Lahore
(Pakistan)—Civilization. | Lahore (Pakistan)—Intellectual life.
Classification: LCC DS392.2.L3 A845 2024 |
DDC 954.91/43—dc23/eng/20240405
LC record available at https://lccn.loc.gov/2024005193

The New Press publishes books that promote and enrich public discussion and
understanding of the issues vital to our democracy and to a more equitable world.
These books are made possible by the enthusiasm of our readers; the support of a
committed group of donors, large and small; the collaboration of our many partners
in the independent media and the not-for-profit sector; booksellers, who often
hand-sell New Press books; librarians; and above all by our authors.

www.thenewpress.com

Composition by Westchester Publishing Services
This book was set in Adobe Caslon Pro

Printed in the United States of America

2 4 6 8 10 9 7 5 3 1

Dedicated to Sultan Ahmed Asif (1939–2012)

I am walking in the city, book in hand, asking a question
I am walking in the city, tongue in hand, asking a question
My question
How can anyone answer it
The city itself is a question.

—*Nohay Takht Lahor kay* (Dirges of Lahore City)
by Tabassum Kashmiri, 1985

Contents

Note on Translation and Transliteration   xv

List of Illustrations   xvii

Introduction   1

1. City: Forgetting Lahore   11

2. History: Writing Lahore   65

3. Nation: Making the Nation   115

4. Memory: Making Origins   163

5. People: Making the People   217

6. Place: Walking Lahore   269

Afterword   321

Acknowledgments   325

Notes   327

Bibliography   337

Index   355

Note on Translation and Transliteration

All translations from Arabic, Persian, Urdu, Hindi, Panjabi are mine. All terms are introduced first in italics, followed by the English translation in parenthesis. For readability, I have omitted all diacritics except for marking the letters 'ayn (') and hamza ('), and used -e for the Persian/ Urdu izafat. All dates are in the Common Era (CE). Place-names are specific to the historical period and reflect usage in primary sources—most importantly, "Panjab" and "Panjabi" are the common usage pre-1947 and continues as such in India, while "Punjab" and "Punjabi" are more commonly used in Pakistan post-1947.

All single-word names are pseudonyms in order to protect the privacy and safety of the individual.

List of Illustrations

All Photos © Manan Ahmed Asif

Figure 1.1: Aerial view of Lahore Fort (2001) 1

Figure 2.1: Ruins of a *haveli* (palace) in a
cordoned-off property, outside the Walled City (2015) 11

Figure 2.2: Rang Mahal School, Walled City (2011) 20

Figure 2.3: Punjab Archives, also known as
Anarkali's Tomb (2018) 27

Figure 2.4: Data Darbar courtyard (2023) 34

Figure 2.5: Miyan Mir's shrine (2023) 42

Figure 2.6: Chauburji Gate (2023) 52

Figure 3.1: Badshahi Mosque with Ranjit Singh's
Samadhi (2015) 77

Figure 3.2: Refurbished Lakshmi Chowk with
"Allahu Akbar" inscription (2015) 84

Figure 3.3: Printed map of Walled City (2011) 90

Figure 3.4: Prospectus map of new colony
schemes (2015) 108

Figure 4.1: Pakistan Day celebrations in
Sadr Bazaar (2022) 121

Figure 4.2: Statue of Alfred Woolner on
Mall Road (2011) 128

Figure 4.3: Gated *mohalla* on Delhi Road,
Sadr (2011) 135

Figure 5.1: Minar-e Pakistan (2015)   170

Figure 5.2: Tomb of Aibak (2014)   177

Figure 5.3: View of Patiala Ground from *Hikayat*
offices (2022)   184

Figure 5.4: Advertisement for Nasim Hijazi
novels (2011)   191

Figure 5.5: "Heroes of Islam" print poster for sale
near Urdu Bazaar (2014)   206

Figure 5.6: Ara'in Community Center (2011)   211

Figure 6.1: Commemorative blankets for sale (2014)   223

Figure 6.2: Gate to the grave of ʿIlm Din
in Miyani Qabaristan (2023)   230

Figure 6.3: "Satnam Sri Vahiguru" Sikh
haveli (2011)   242

Figure 6.4: Stairs leading to an entrance to
Lahore Fort (Shahi Qila) (2015)   247

Figure 6.5: Grave of Saʿadat Hasan Manto (2023)   254

Figure 7.1: West bank of Ravi River (2012)   277

Figure 7.2: Schoolboy looking at books (2022)   284

Figure 7.3: A Christian shrine (2014)   291

Figure 7.4: A pathway toward Punjab
farmland (2023)   308

Figure 7.5: Domicile certificate for Sultan
Ahmad Asif, dated September 27, 1967 (2021)   315

Figure 8.1: Ferrying across River Ravi (2023)   321

Disrupted City

Introduction

Figure 1.1. Aerial view of Lahore Fort (2001)

Lahore shimmers in the sunlight. The Walled City is shaped like a clenched fist, with the mostly dry bed of the Ravi beyond. A cloud rolls across the canopy of our Piper PA-28 Cherokee as it flies left to follow the Grand Trunk Road. This is my first time looking at the city from the air as it slowly reveals landmarks to my excited gaze. The plane circles around the Badshahi Mosque, the Lahore Fort, the Lahore Museum, the National College of Arts. The Walled City is immensely dense, with multi-floored houses leaning up against each other, and with narrow, twisting alleys a mere foot or two wide. My hope is to discern some logic that can only reveal itself from above. Instead, the city appears even more inscrutable. No visible alleys or lanes, just a plethora of pigeon coops and kite flyers. No grid, no star like formation, no pattern. Six long roads extend from the fist outward until five of them meet the Lahore Canal, running through the east and south of the city. On the other side, Cantonment and various other planned housing societies and colonies. Down south, nearly endless flat, green land. Our flight plan is not approved for the east, which is protected airspace (owing to the airport and, right behind it, the border with India). The plane slowly turns back toward the highlight: the Lahore Fort.

It was early 2001, and over the years, I have often remembered that flight, even just to remind myself that one used to be able to "see" the city in the winter months. For the slightly over two decades since, for much of mid-December through late January, Lahore is enveloped in a dense mixture of fog and smog. Toxic to breathe and blinding to the eyes. One can see nothing, on the ground or from the air.

I have cleaned, polished, and kept safe a small collection of memories of Lahore. I left the city some thirty years ago. My home is still there and I return to it once a year, usually for periods of a few weeks but rarely longer than that. Every return begins with a careful survey of the familiar (my home) and the unfamiliar (the city). Lahore has rapidly grown in the last thirty years. The metropolitan area has tripled or quadrupled in size, with even larger growth in population. These kept memories provide a necessary function. They are snapshots of moments frozen in time that I can take a quick peek at, as I try to make sense of the new Lahore around me.

Here is another memory. We are on a small motorbike (a Honda 70). Something has happened that has us talking about an impending war with India. I am sitting on the back of the bike and he is driving. As he weaves in and out of traffic, I remember the conversation going something like this:

Him: They want us to hate India but this is all fake.

Me: Yes, what do we care about India! I am not dying for some dictator.

Him: But what if India attacks Lahore?

Me: I can imagine fighting to protect Lahore . . . but ONLY Lahore!

The friend on that bike now lives across the Hudson in New Jersey, and I have never asked him about this conversation or his memory of it. I am not even sure this memory is real, or if what I said is what he said or vice versa. Were we really talking about wars and dying at age sixteen? True or not, the memory remains vivid—I can even count the number of cars we passed over the course of this (short) dialogue. The sense of this memory rests in our deep love for Lahore. My friend and I spent much of our college days skipping class and riding that bike to various parts of the city. We were like tiny explorers, seeking neither goods nor riches, but stories. Barely sixteen, we aimed to start conversations with shopkeepers, hangers-on-at-the-corner, pedestrians, and other bikers about the neighborhood, asking for imaginary or real addresses, wanting to know what was special or noteworthy, soaking up the cadence of speech, chasing the unfamiliar street-turned-cul-de-sac. The great joy, what we incessantly sought and always found, was meeting someone who would narrate the history of that bit of Lahore. I am not sure or cannot remember why we began to do this.

My home was at the edge of the city. My family claimed no special relationship to Lahore. We were not the elite in social, political, economic, or cultural terms for the city. Members of the extended family were scattered around various parts of Lahore, including the old city, but visiting them did not mean much more than moving from one living room to another. I was a lower-middle-class kid kept mostly in seclusion. College changed much of that as, with the help of my friend's motorbike and company, I could move around the city and get to know it.

I recount all this to introduce to you the central preoccupations of this book: the persistence of memory, the circumspection of history, the strange in-between-ness of immigrant and diasporic life, and across all three, the city.[1] Over two decades, for my own PhD training as a specialist in the medieval history of South Asia and then while teaching in universities in Berlin and New York, I read and consumed hundreds of books about "the city." The singular cities—Rome, Paris, Berlin, London, New York, Los Angeles—provided much of my thinking vocabulary, and the scholars, artists, novelists, poets, activists who wrote about those cities gave me the theory, the wherewithal to "see" the city. Yet, much as I loved reading and learning from Georg Simmel, Patrick Geddes, Louis Mumford, and Max Weber, I could not find a way to "see" Lahore. Their "universal" city seemed particularly alien to me.

Once I came to experience Cairo, Mexico City, and Kampala, however, the particular dynamic of a postcolonized city's history and memory became much clearer to me. These were all postcolonized cities, the part of decolonized nation-states that continued to be shaped by the laws, strictures, violence, and undemocratic rule that persisted despite decolonization. I saw Lahore in Cairo. I saw Lahore in Mexico City. I saw Lahore in Kampala. When I heard or read historians of these cities, I could find traces of my own thought intermixed with theirs. There was some common knot here that felt important enough to unravel.

Lahore is a city at least a thousand years old. The history of Lahore, verifiably recorded in texts, goes back to the ninth century. It is also a postcolonized city, existing in a nation-state that only came into being in 1947. As a medieval historian, I understand well the urge to tell the history of this city without it being held hostage to the nation-state that inherits it. After all, even if you know nothing about Lahore, you have heard about Pakistan: a nation often ill-scripted and poorly understood within the framework of terrorism or security or geopolitics going back to the Cold War era. Wouldn't it be easier if I could ignore Pakistan in order to tell the history of Lahore? Yet Lahore's future is tied inexorably to Pakistan, and Lahore's past is dependent on what has happened since 1947.

Lahore is also somewhat unusual in the subcontinent—not least because of its continuous habitation and political importance. It is a city that has remained with the same name: "Lahore." Each time it was destroyed or rebuilt, or each time a new ruler poured resources into casting it in their image, they let the city keep its name. There may be seven or eight ways of spelling Lahore, but there has only been a singular Lahore for more than a thousand years.

In order to write Lahore, I began with walking Lahore. I talked to those who live, struggle, and survive in the city. They gave me perspectives; they directed me to texts, to illegible scripts, to contesting stories, to deep fountains of knowledge. Their insights, suggestions, hints, and remarks shaped my own pursuit of ideas of Lahore. My walking led me to conversations that, in turn, helped me see that there is no singular story of Lahore. Unlike the nation-state that insists on a unique story of origins, and a cohesive, panoptic view of the past, the residents of Lahore saw hundreds of different beginnings and tens of variant histories. After years of walking and talking in Lahore, I turned to the deep historical record of the city. My aim was to combine my experience of walking and being in the city with the experience of finding Lahore in the archive. There was a resonance, I felt, between the fragmentary glimpses of the city in my own individual observations and the fragments of the city preserved in medieval, colonial, and national histories of the city. The city remained beyond their, or my, grasp. At the same time, I distance myself from the all-knowing stance of the modern scholar of the city. I make no claim to knowing, or writing, everything that has existed in or about Lahore. In a very deliberate manner, I am just one among millions and millions, no more a knower, no less a seeker, than anyone else.

One does not easily walk in Lahore, even as an able-bodied male. The difficulty lies in poor infrastructure for walking and a strongly held class- and caste-based opprobrium for city-walking. Men who walk, walk in pairs or more. They walk in specified spaces such as markets, or neighborhood lanes. They congregate at intersections or at the gates and openings of public buildings. Middle-class women walk in pairs toward a destination (a bus stop, a school, a market). Working-class men and women walk to work and toward public transportation. All of this walking is difficult walking. The city constantly threatens in the form of bikes, cars, buses, horns, lack of shade, lack of pavements, lack of resting places. Amid this chaos, you can still find walkers, lingerers, sign-keepers, maintainers of memory.

Walking in and writing on Lahore is also critically informed by my own long immigrant life away from Lahore. As I have walked in various postcolonized cities, I have also heard from others who walk Lahore, either in their dreams or in their minds. Again and again, chance encounters, an aside in a conversation, introduced me to those who remember Lahore in their own condition of generational exile. Lahore haunts New York, Berlin, Chicago, Lisbon, Cairo, and so many other cities where I walked. Walking and talking in Lahore and remembering Lahore as an exiled or diasporic person are the two twinned strands of this book. They informed my practices of reading, of analysis, and of raising questions. Walking taught me a slow(er) hermeneutics, a measured, deliberative approach toward texts: to walk, to listen to stories, to trace the pathways of memory and history in those stories back to historical archives and texts, and finally to return to the walk—in order to think anew. I resist an archaeological or phenomenological approach alone. The holistic, aerial view of Lahore, spectacular as it was, did not afford me any clarity about what I was hoping to see about the city. I was only able to see by walking slowly, by listening carefully, and by following Lahore across dreams and realities.

The book is structured in that experience of traversing a city— especially a new city. I suspect many of the readers of this book will not have been to Lahore or know about its history. As they read, they will encounter strange names, unfamiliar dates, vast swaths of historical context, contestations and turns. I invite you to treat the book as you would a new city. As you walk in a new city, its statues, buildings, their names, the names of the streets and boulevards only slowly impress upon your consciousness. Slowly, over time, you will find the same names repeated and you will learn of their historical embeddedness in the history of the city, and you will have conversations that telescope you into one particular history or another, out of the hundreds such histories in the city. You can rest assured that by the end of this book you will have experienced Lahore.

This book is about ideas of Lahore, its history, the role of memory and violence, and the vexed question of nationalism and state control. It is also a book about the survival of people, and the modes of surviving that enable the making of a people. Thus, the foremost archives for the book are the conversations I have had over the years. From them emerged links to Arabic, Persian, Urdu, Punjabi, and English texts from the tenth century to roughly the late 1980s. As I read these texts—poetry, epics, novels, memoirs, histories, collections of fables, recipe books, occult books, sex manuals, courtroom transcripts—I wove through them the ethnographic, the oral, the observed, the lived-in. My approach is toward a cultural, intellectual, and social history of the city, rather than a linear political narrative. I think about the city and what is visible or invisible, what writing the history of Lahore has signified over the centuries, how the project of "nation-making" is grounded in the life of the city, how the invention of new origins for the memory of the nation took place in the city, how "people-making" by the nation-state is a transhistorical project of its own, and how walking the pathways in Lahore showed me the right approach to writing this book.

What did I find? If you do not know anything about Lahore, or even if you are one of the elite inhabitants of Lahore who know its past intimately, what will you learn from me? One way to answer that question is to tell you what I learned from my own research and process of writing this book, as someone with an expertise in medieval through modern South Asian history and as a native of

Lahore: I learned about the sheer climate peril facing Lahore's immediate future. I learned of the many times Lahore has been destroyed before, by invading armies, fires, floods, and plagues, and I learned how each return of Lahore, as a city, was also a new incarnation of the city. I learned that the next destruction, the one predicted in ten to thirty years, holds no promise or hope of return. I learned how land exploitation is central to the "plan" of the city. I learned that the state sanction of language (Urdu versus Punjabi) has shaped this city to an extent that I could never have previously imagined. I learned that the making of the nation-state of Pakistan was a process initiated and embedded in the landscape of Lahore. I learned that those who live in, and write about, Lahore hold disparate images of the city in their mind. It is as if the city exists simultaneously in parallel realities. I learned that Lahore is a city partitioned from its own past and the current inhabitants of Lahore are themselves partitioned from *their* own pasts. I learned that this partition is just as much due to the political history of the subcontinent as it is the state-imposed hegemony of a specific language, Urdu. There are ghost Lahores in Amritsar and Delhi and Mumbai and Accra. There are ghosts from Amritsar, Delhi, Bombay, Lucknow, Hyderabad in Lahore. I learned that to write the postcolonized city, I need to hear the many different voices of those who live and struggle in the city.

I learned that the rhythm of the dance between history, memory, and the city is set by dreams. In the process of thinking and writing this book, I began to keep a dream journal. A large number of entries contain the word *haveli* (a multistory, multifamily townhouse or mansion). The entry from the morning of December 24, 2020 reads: A walking tour of a giant broken *haveli*, somewhere, built like a Mughal *haveli*, and then on the one side was the *mazar* (shrine). I paid five rupees to enter and tried for a while to pick a place to sit. Then saw a woman putting *soorma* [kohl], and then someone paid for her to put *soorma* in my eyes and dots on my forehead and *mehndi* [henna] on my hand and prepare me as if I was a bride. This is a *sambhali huwi* [protected] city, she told me. I understood her, in my dream logic, as making a reference to my own personhood also now being protected, like the city.

Throughout my diasporic life, I have often dreamt of a city. The city has medieval architecture, some in ruins, some rebuilt in bright modern colors, all of it populated and brimming with life, traffic, noise. My dreams take me to the same building, neighborhood, turns, shops, only some that I can recognize from my own life. There is a home in this dream city, a modern facade to a medieval structure, a floor torn to reveal open space that extends into the horizon. I have never physically been in any such structure but I have dreamt it consistently for decades. I understand this city to be Lahore too. It is where I live.

1

CITY: FORGETTING LAHORE

Figure 2.1. Ruins of a *haveli* (palace) in a cordoned-off property, outside the Walled City (2015)

Lahore has always been kind to me. Going back to my childhood, the city somehow knew what I wanted, was seeking, needed even without knowing, and led me to that book, door, person, sight, smell, that object that I wanted. The examples are too numerous, and I suspect detailing these small miracles (in my perception) would be impossibly tedious to read. Still, it is true that for a long while, something magical could happen in a normal walk or errand, and it reaffirmed my sense of this relationship between my city and me. Sure, I can explain some of such happenings to my way of seeing or being in Lahore. I am slow and deliberate. I hear the rhythm of the city's heartbeat around me. I pay attention to the lungs, the veins, the muscles that are the moving goods, people, and traffic. I gaze at the still parts even as I move in their periphery. But I also want to imagine Lahore as an agent. In the course of my wandering about the city, what appears as serendipity or coincidence is actually an agentive act—the city is reaching out and nudging into existence what I am seeking. Such happenings personify the city for me, as particular a character as one you would find described in medieval texts.

Lahore is also unkind. First, there are the prejudices, the hatred, the misogyny that sparks violence against women, non-Muslims (deemed or otherwise), the poor, and disenfranchised. Then there are the infrastructures of harm and exclusion that have created islands of haves and have-nots—the gated colonies, the car-only shopping malls, the "clearing" of precarious housing by municipal authorities. Further, those who live there (I have immediate and extended family in Lahore) also face profound climate calamity. A dense "smog"—fog and pollution—traps air in a bubble such that for months of the year there is no safe breath to take, and you cannot see past your own outstretched hand. In summer months, high heat and humidity combine to create a feeling not unlike being cooked in a pressure cooker. The regular floods, contaminated groundwater, and lack of clear air presage that by 2030 much of contemporary Lahore will be partially uninhabitable, and perhaps fully so by 2050. A city that has existed for thousands of years may have only a few more left. How does one write about that long history in the face of such ongoing and impending disasters?

Lahore, whether visible in the archive or not, is a city that one can easily imagine having existed for thousands of years. Like many of the oldest continuously inhabited cities of the world, Lahore is rooted next to a major river, Ravi, and at the intersection of long-standing land routes (if you are headed to Samarkand or Baghdad from Guangdong or Fujian, you will pass through Lahore). The geography that surrounds Lahore was once alluvial, fertile, temperate, with major settlements to the east, the west, the north, and the south. A natural city. A sensible city. An open city. For centuries upon centuries, Lahore has been repeatedly destroyed and repeatedly rebuilt—each time growing, shifting, remaking its contours.

My initial intention was to show Lahore's long-lasting significance, what happened to the city, and how it changed over a millennium. However, framed across such a *longue durée*, Lahore seemed to lose any specificity. Of course, it changed. Things change. As I did the archival and ethnographic work on the book, I read about many Lahores, many ideas of Lahore, many who experienced Lahore in diverse ways. Yet it also became clear that there was one particular moment when a profound change took place in Lahore that orients both its past and its future. In 1947, the end of British colonial rule came with the partitioning of regions of Bengal and Punjab and the creation of India and Pakistan. Lahore joined Pakistan (and not India, as many argued for at that time), and much of the diversity and multitude of the pre-1947 Lahore ended with the mass exodus of the city's Hindu and Sikh inhabitants and the influx of refugees from the parts of Punjab now governed by India and beyond. This cataclysmic turn created a new Lahore. Over the next seventy-five years, Lahore would change more and more, but never as radically. After that moment of disruption, it became a city in exile from its own past. A city partitioned not in space, but in time, a city constantly in a state of disruption.

The twentieth century was a century of enforced partitions of cities and states: Bengal, Prussia, Ottoman Middle East, Ireland, Germany, Korea, Palestine, the subcontinent (India and Pakistan), Vietnam, and more. Much, if not all, of the partitions were driven by outsiders, by colonialists, imperialists, nationalists. Lahore fits uneasily in the received accounts of such political partitions. It was not itself physically partitioned. Yet partitioned it was, and partitioned it remains, from its own past.

How do we reinscribe into the city modes of thinking and being that counteract this partition? How do we write across the divided past rather than within it? A deep literary tradition in Sanskrit and Persian provides a fruitful archive for thinking about urbanity and cities (in general) in the subcontinent. Genres, themselves more than a millennium old, capture the contours of experiencing the city through the vantage of travelers, rulers, ascetics, or conquerors. In Kalidasa's *Meghaduta* (Cloud Messenger), I find some evocative glimpses of the city. Kalidasa, writing in the fifth century, composed this Sanskrit *kavya* (lyric poem) to capture the pain of separation between lovers. A lover asks a cloud heading north to take a message to their beloved. As the cloud moves across mountains, valleys, hills, hamlets, Kalidasa describes the abundant natural and physical beauty. The cities shine. The lovely terraces of the mansions of Ujjain, the mansions of Vishala, a piece of paradise on earth with "scented smoke of dressing hair pouring forth from lattice-windows," the "soaring palaces" of Alaka.[1]

From the early eighth century comes another epic tale of movement and wandering: the *Dasakumaracarita* (What Ten Young Men Did) by Dandin, with kings and their cities as a central focus. Not one or two cities of mythical status, but a whole world full of them. Across many of the epics, dramas, and poems in Sanskrit, magnificent cities, full of planned and ordered roads, public waterways, gardens, palaces, courts, and markets, learned people and extravagant beauty abound. The grand cities of Mithila, Ayodhya, Lanka in the *Ramayana* exult in their opulence and order. Cities are the seats of political and sacral power. They exist as the manifestation of sacral order and harmony. They provide the cover of anonymity, but also the announcement of an arrival: the entrance of a nameless traveler, a yogi, into the city gates is often more momentous than the entrance of a rival king into the palace gates.

The genre that most definitively defines Lahore, for me, is the *shahr ashob*—the Persian poetic form that can literally be rendered as "city disrupted." Likely emerging in the ninth or tenth century, *shahr ashob* consists of a long poem or a series of short quatrains that describe the city in a series of vignettes. They contain recognitions of the beauty of the city mixed with recognition of the beauties that live and work in that city—both of which cause tumult, disruption, in the poet and the writer. As a result of the narrator's description, the city, or its beautiful inhabitants, disrupts the interiority of the poet. Mas'ud Sa'ad Salman, a native of Lahore in the early twelfth century, wrote many descriptions of Lahore and its inhabitants in his *shahr ashob* verses. Salman composed these verses while imprisoned far away from Lahore, so the thought of Lahore, and its beautiful young men, inflamed his senses, providing refuge from all that terrorized his present. The memories of Lahore set him on fire, and that is what he expressed in his verses and poems.

Like the city of Lahore, *shahr ashob* also shifts form and meaning. It moves across literary cultures and time. One key shift is captured in its movement from Persian to Urdu in the eighteenth century. Munshi Syed 'Abbas 'Ali's *Qissa-e Ghamgin* (A Tale of Sorrow, 1779) is about the British conquest of the city of Bharuch by the river Narmada, in Gujarat. The poet captures the imminent destruction of the city, its slow and inexorable movement toward that fate. The tumult here is now physical—in the streets of the city, in the panic and movement of the city's inhabitants. Such Urdu *shahr ashob* in this vein would focus on the destruction of Delhi by Nadir Shah, in 1739 (as in Mirza Sauda's *Qasida-e Shahrashob* from 1760, for instance), or the destruction of Delhi by the British in 1857 (as in Tafazzul Husain Kaukab's *Fughan-e Dilli* from 1863).

Other *shahr ashob* would take a civilizational perspective, such as in Altaf Hussain Hali's *Musaddas-e Madd-o-Jazr-e Islam* (Flow and Ebb of the Tides of Islam, 1879). The cities here (Delhi in Hindustan or Córdoba in Andalusia) serve as the backdrop for the unfurling of grave injustices, but the cities also become metaphors for the past that was being destroyed and erased. *Shahr ashob*, as a poetic form for thinking about the city, is able to capture both the immediacy of the sorrow that the poet feels at the destruction, but also "what once was," the past that glimmers from underneath the rubble.

The wandering genre of the *kavya* and the disruptions narrated in *shahr ashob* immerse the listener and the reader in the experience of the city by foregrounding the perspective, limited and volatile as it is, of the poet. That narrator in both genres is in a disturbed emotional state, separated from the beloved, separated from the city, and even worse. Still, the poet must create a full record, a full testimony of their ideas of the beloved or the city. That is the unique pleasure afforded by the poetry—that through their grief, they narrate the space of the city. Hence, separation and exile form a central feature in these poetic works.

Shahr ashob is a model for me to think and imagine the past of Lahore in light of the future it portends. Similarly a *kavya*, like *Meghaduta*, becomes a lens for my approach to Lahore, a city inhabited by nearly 10 or 11 million in the Islamic Republic of Pakistan. Clearly, there is no singular gaze that can capture this multitude. My class, my gender identity, my social status allow for a perspective that may not be uniquely mine nor easily transferable to other experiences. Thus, the particularity of the speaker and my presence in this book and the methodology of movement, of walking, of tracing pathways, of seeing without explanation such that someone else may trace that same pathway and see something completely different.

Yet, this "how to" guide to thinking about the city as a generic subcontinental phenomenon does not fully account for Lahore. We are also embedded in our own particular time and place. Hence Lahore, as the oldest continuously inhabited political and cultural "capital" in contemporary Pakistan, offers particular challenges. Pakistan, as constituted out of the subcontinent in 1947, certainly has much older urban centers—the more than five-thousand-year-old Moenjodaro, or the thousands-year-old Taxila, Peshawar, or Multan—but unlike Lahore, they did not maintain the significance that it has effortlessly carried for more than a millennium.

To think about Lahore is impossible without thinking about Pakistan and the way it has been written and thought in the broader anglophone world. It is a country that "partnered" with the United States in the long Cold War and then the so-called global war on terror. Islam is the bare fact that over-determines history, culture, politics, and society. Hence, whatever the long history of Lahore may be and whatever befell it in 1947, the Lahore I grew up in and the Lahore I am choosing to write about is an example of something called the "Islamic city"—a term invented by French urban historians during the colonization and "domestication" of North Africa in the early 1920s and later taken up for everywhere that Europe saw Islam. The "Orientalist" version (put forward by William and George Marçais, Henri Pirenne, Louis Massignon, and Gustave von Grunebaum) imagined the Islamic city as one with distinguished and static functional parts: the Friday mosque (that would be the Badshahi Mosque for Lahore), the bazaar (Anarkali), the labyrinthine and anarchic narrow alleys (the old city), segregated living (religious segregation but also gender-based segregation between the public and the private realms), and a lack of any controlling urban plan. Later scholars, such as Albert Hourani, Ira Lapidus, and Janet Abu-Lughod, who wrote against such colonial pablum, emphasized networks, relationships, and the existence of "planned cities" since the very beginning of Islam; and they questioned how any city can ever be reduced to just being "Islamic."

The analytical and explanatory models for thinking and knowing the Western city seem inadequate to the task at hand. The subcontinent undergoes a series of conquests by colonial powers beginning in the early eighteenth century. Lahore is conquered by the British in the mid-nineteenth century, and colonial rule reorders and fundamentally reshapes the colonized city. In addition, colonial rulers create their own cities in the colonies, and those new urban centers reorient public and private life across the colony. The modern post-colony inherits the colonial ways of knowing and making the city, with its particular spatio-political arrangement of people, and is unable to create a sense for how a premodern city fits, unless as a prop for the attraction of tourists. Colonial rule shapes not only the present of the city, and its future, but most drastically, its past. It imposes a unitary understanding of religion (as a mark of pre-modernity); it shapes the glossy, developed parts of the city as "modern," to contrast it with the "historic" parts of the medieval city. The postcolonized national state, inheritor of the colonial imagination, embraces "modernization," "development," and other violent measures of keeping history at bay. It gives rise to history as commerce, history as panacea, history as a tourist attraction, with an indifference to the material and social complexities of that very same past. The nationalist state props up mythical inventions of traditions and origins that draw a straight line from deep antiquity to the contemporary nation-state.

Lahore is full of both recognized and forgotten monuments to its own past. Some sites, much known and written about, have stories that are at odds with the historical record. For others, the historical record is itself missing. The material traces of deep history in Lahore offer an opening into the questions of experience, genres of description, colonialism, and Partition that I have detailed above. The "hidden Lahore" also gestures toward serendipities, coincidences, inclusions, and exclusions that may strike the readers as kind or unkind in equal dimensions. In this section, I write the city from the perspective of undoing colonial and colonizing ways of seeing the past that persist in Lahore today.

To write Lahore here, I combine techniques from embedded and situated genres in the subcontinent's literary cultures, such as *kavya* and *shahr ashob*, with lived experiences and histories of the present. This is not romance or the reimposition of antiquity, but a desire to rethink the postcolonized city across ruptures. I write with the idea that I am thinking alongside the inhabitants. I write with the idea that telling these stories about Lahore creates new Lahoris, inside and elsewhere.

I.

Figure 2.2. Rang Mahal School, Walled City (2011)

Rang Mahal is a dense neighborhood inside the Walled City, named after and shaped by a *haveli* (mansion) built by Saʿadullah Khan (d. 1656), who was a *divan* (minister) for the Mughal emperor Shah Jahan. The *haveli* would later become a missionary school. A bazaar, inhabiting the tightest, narrowest lanes bunched up like intestines, swirls around the massive structure, home to fine jewelers and to wholesale kitchen and pantry suppliers with footpaths made with metal grates and corrugated sheets yawning above the head.

Tucked a few steps away from the *haveli*, and within a morass of doors, there used to be a small, stand-alone domed structure with a plaque claiming it to be the grave of Malik Ayaz, who likely perished in 1041. By the late 1980s, the gravesite had been swallowed by a mosque, its walls festooned with encomiums to the Companions of the Prophet. The most prominent space was given to a couplet from Iqbal: *aik hi saf mein kharay ho gaye Mahmud o Ayaz / Na koi banda raha na koi banda nawaz.* Liberally rendered into English, it reads: "Mahmud [of Ghazna] and Ayaz stood in the same line [of prayer] / None remained as bonded, or as providers to the bonded." The couplet came from Iqbal's poem "Shikwa" (Complaint), which he first recited in Lahore in 1909. Iqbal had enigmatically linked in one verse a much more dynamic relationship than prayer alone.

I encountered the structure because Rang Mahal was where "we were from" if someone within Lahore asked about our family. Almost every weekend, I would visit Rang Mahal for *ziarat* or for food or for conversations. It is recorded in Kanhaiya Lal Hindi's 1884 history of Lahore that Ayaz's grave was once embedded in a large enclosure and surrounded by a garden. "This Ayaz is the one who, in the period of Sultan Mahmud Ghaznavi attained the status of his equal as a lover and who rebuilt and repopulated this city of Lahore after it was destroyed in the aftermath of the war with Raja Anangpal," he wrote.[2]

Malik Ayaz is credited as the one who repopulated and founded the city of Lahore in the *'Ibratnama* (Book of Admonitions, 1854) by Mufti 'Aliuddin and Khairuddin Lahori. Ayaz, when he arrived at Lahore in the early eleventh century, considered it a unique space that ought to remain populated until eternity, so he built a fortified structure and took care of the civilians, for he was "good-willed, justice-minded, and a benefactor of civilians."[3] This was well-considered history. Sujan Rai Bhandari's *Khulasat-ut-Tawarikh*

(Compendium of Histories, 1695) also recounts the same history
for Lahore, though he makes Malik Ayaz originally a Kashmiri
who was captured and sold into slavery and taken to Badakshan.
The stories of his beauty reached Mahmud, who purchased him.
Bhandari's take may well have been influenced by the much more
intimate relationship between Kashmir and Lahore during the
Mughal period.

Stretching further back in time, we get to Farrukhi Sistani
(d. 1037), who was a poet attached to Mahmud Ghaznavi's court
and wrote a number of *qasida* (panegyrics) to the ruling elite and
many more dedicated to lovers of those elite. One of the *qasida*
is in praise of Malik Ayaz and Mahmud. Farrukhi has a lament
that was common to lovers then and is still today—the inability
to sleep because you keep seeing the lips, cheeks, and eyes of your
beloved. In this instance, the lament is compared to the love between Mahmud and Ayaz, who are separated from each other.
After a long note of praise of the beloved, Farrukhi tells us that
though Mahmud had many *ghulam* (bonded or conscripted men),
none were like [Mahmud] in bravery except Ayaz (who was "heart
and arm of the king on the day of battle").

Theirs was an especially close relationship, built on mutual love
and admiration. Mahmud showered Ayaz with devotion and
wealth, giving him forty thousand dinar and land grants.[4] At the
end of the *qasida*, Farrukhi reports the parting of the companions: Ayaz leaves Ghazna in darkness to head toward, one imagines, Lahore. It is quite plain here that Farrukhi is portraying
Mahmud and Ayaz as an ideal couple, with the strength of their
love marked by their martial valor and bravery.

Lahore, conquered and destroyed twice by Mahmud, was not
like Ghazna, his capital city, though in poetry it is often referred
to as "little Ghazna." Lahore stretched in a cluster of villages,
estates, markets, and smaller fortifications along the banks of the
Ravi. The city lacked strong defenses, save the river when Lahore
was approached from the north and, from the east, a long and difficult jungle. Mahmud had culled the city of fortification, people,

and material wealth. Malik Ayaz would create new walls for Lahore, and invite intellectuals, administrators, and merchants back to the city. This is why he would become known as the founder of this renewed settlement by the river.

The poet Mas'ud Sa'ad Salman (d. 1121, at the age of eighty) was born in the Lahore that Malik Ayaz built. His father was part of Mahmud's bureaucracy and had served the Ghaznavi sultans for sixty years.[5] Salman himself served several Ghaznavi kings and often at his own peril. He spent thirteen years in prison for disrespecting the sultan's authority—first for ten years during the reign of Sultan Ibrahim (d. 1099), and then another three years under Mas'ud III (d. 1115).

Salman invoked Lahore in his poetry, whether he was living and working there or imprisoned far from it. He wrote about the house that he lived in, his library (and how to make it much bigger), the streets, the markets, the luminaries. *Oh Lahore, how do you lament my absence?* he writes from the prison cell in Dahak. *Without the bright sun, how do you shine?* Calling himself Lahore's favorite son, he asks the city, with the pain of separation, *How do you endure and persevere?*[6] He praised the river Ravi: *O Ravi, if paradise is to be found, it is you / if there is a kingdom come that's completed, it is you / water's so heaven's stream be depleted, is you, / a spring in which there are a thousand rivers is you.*

Salman gave us a sense of his city in a collection of verses included in his compendium as *shahr ashob*. These are short poetic compositions testifying to the qualities of various young men (or "boys") who work in the city or are at private estates, and whose beauty, wiles, or cruelty disrupts the poet's existence in the city. The poet, needless to say, is wildly in love with them. The verses serve a dual purpose. For one, the verses serve mnemonic function—for they bring to the mind of the exiled poet the city that he has lost because of his imprisonment. For another, they reconstruct beloved people from the perspective of separation. Salman, who owned a palace in Lahore, as well as land and villages outside the city, and who bathed twice a day, is now sitting in a small prison cell without water or light: *Not a single white hair was there / when I was put in prison by fate / Such torment and grief is mine / not one hair is black, I state.* In this mood of self-pity and sorrow, the encounters he used to have in the alleys and bazaars of Lahore became a way of remembering his city, and also marking his fall from grace.

The seller of ambergris and of carnelians, and the wine-pourer, and the bazaar-dweller, and the bread maker, the garment dyer, the ironworker, the weapons maker, the carpenter, the gardener, the chemist, the seer, the wrestler, the pigeon trainer, and the bird catcher all show up in Salman's verses. In ninety or more couplets, he describes the *sifat* (qualities) of the beloved with the curly locks, the beloved with a new letter, the beloved with wet hair, with a mole under his eye, the one who fasts, the Hindustani one, the one blind to your suffering, the one with the beautiful voice, the Sufi, the Qalandari, the beloved with the heart of stone, the preacher, the philosopher, the writer, the butcher.[7] These are the common and the extraordinary people of eleventh-century Lahore (the extraordinary made so by the lover's gaze).

They are rendered often in very mundane terms, just a description of the face or body, or a play between their work and their form (for example, the naan maker is bronzed from the heat of the oven). Each description, an encounter in memory and verse, disturbs the poet. He desires to be reunited with these men, yearns for them, recalls their memory, his memory's hold over them. These idealized figures are awash in everyday life, and there is a social world that we can grasp from these small bits of poetry. We can see Salman's material life—his work, his home, his belongings—wrapped up in these verses. He speaks of his teachers, his poet rivals, the nobility who got favors from him, and even lovers who once lay only a bedsheet apart and now are six hundred miles away.

Mas'ud Sa'ad Salman writes about the everyday in Lahore, where sacral and political communities worked in tandem: *O Rooster, I don't know what you do / Neither good deeds nor purity / You*

*have a difficult and tumultuous path / Neither Muslim nor Brahmin /
You are always crowing, seeking attention / With those who pray and
those who don't.* He is showing us a world that resonates even in the
existing political tracts and laws. The edicts of Aibak, the first
governor, or other governors and rulers of Lahore continue to show
remarkable attention to protecting the learned classes (no matter
their faith), and ensuring the safety and support of all religious
communities, both residing in Lahore and those undertaking pilgrimage to the city. Lahore was understood, and protected, as a
city of multiplicities and mutual comprehension.

The Hindustani Lahore of Salman was indeed a vibrant, poly-
sacral space. Aibak cultivated Lahore as a city of poets and intellectuals. One of the other accounts of this early Lahore comes
from Fakhruddin Mudabbir, who wrote his own genealogical
work in the city. Fakhruddin Mudabbir wanted to connect the
families of rulers and intellectuals in Ghazni and Lahore to the
Prophet and the earliest generations of Islam. He was also likely
born in Lahore, since his father was the one who had migrated to
Lahore from Ghazni. He reports that much of Lahore and surrounding cities, such as Jalandhar and Sialkot, were governed by
devotees of Vishnu or Surya, and that the "Muslims" were themselves antagonistically Shiʻa, Qaramati, or Sunni. (Mahmud of
Ghazni would sack Lahore, Multan, and Uch because it was populated by Muslims he considered to be heretics.)

Ayaz belonged to that Lahore where other "Hindu" nobles were
his peers and other bonded elite were his compatriots. He may or
may not have been Mahmud's lover, but he certainly seemed to
have his attention as a confidant and a trusted general. In the late
sixteenth century, Mahmud Lahori would write a *ghazal* (a poem
of seven or eight couplets, often with parallel rhyming end),
Mahmudnama, praising the love Mahmud had for Ayaz: *O
Mahmud, the net of Ayaz's hair / is like a wondrous rope for you to
hold onto tightly.*[8] Yet, by the time Lahoris decided to put a plaque
on Ayaz's tomb, they chose Iqbal's verse that elided all such history
to put Ayaz and Mahmud as "equals" standing in a row of praying

believers. The ambergris seller, the wine seller, the bonded general of Lahore are all reduced to the wishful imaginary of a praying line.

Ayaz's memory cannot be swallowed nor spit out. Over a thousand years, he has lived in Lahore, known but forgotten, unknown but preserved, known and appropriated. The mosque built around him, Iqbal's verses wrapped around him, are meager attempts to resolve him, to make his history digestible to memory. Yet, sometimes it seeps up. The man who built the walls of Lahore overnight. The man who made a king fall in love at first glance.

II.

Figure 2.3. Punjab Archives, also known as Anarkali's Tomb (2018)

Lahore's Anarkali is a very popular and old bazaar. It was always to this bazaar that my mother would take us to buy school uniforms, Eid clothes, or dry fruits. It was a place of life, full of artisans, merchants, shopkeepers the family had known for decades; a refuge from the daily life, a moment to breathe and walk across time, space, and being. When Claude Lévi-Strauss visited Lahore in the early 1950s, he walked this same Anarkali bazaar wondering, "Where could it be, the old, the authentic Lahore?"[9] He had been to the avenues of Lahore carved out from the "ruins . . . of houses five hundred years old" and still smoldering from the "riots of the recent years." Lévi-Strauss, an "archaeologist of space," was adrift, trying to piece together the feel of a city by linking debris and particle into some whole that fit his notion of an "Eastern City."

In the alleys of Anarkali were "wooden buildings that were falling to pieces with old age," with "primitive electric wiring that crossed and crisscrossed," and surrounding it all the din of a "djinn with a thousand arms . . . absent-mindedly practicing on a xylophone."[10] Lévi-Strauss's invocation of ruin in Lahore mimics that of earlier colonial travelers, François Bernier or Jean-Baptiste Tavernier, who also saw ruins everywhere in Hindustan. Their writings were a similar elemental mixture of real and unreal, of life and death everywhere. They also created new fictions to highlight the strangeness, the moral decay, and the dangers in Lahore.

Anarkali had another signification in those colonial accounts—as a woman immured in Lahore.

A twenty-minute walk southwest from Anarkali bazaar ends at an octagonal, whitewashed brick building sitting behind a row of checkpoints and a white bungalow. The complex houses Punjab's Civil Secretariat offices and the Punjab Archives. The building itself is popularly known as "Anarkali's Tomb." A two-storied building with a staircase that used to be inside but is now mounted outside, it has eight anchors and a small domed tower, with (now bricked) eight windows. On the high dome is a finial, where a cross was once installed. It is an oddly shaped building and was once likely covered in glazed tilework.

When you enter, you discover that the high dome makes the structure many times larger, light flooding in from all sixteen windows. At a corner in the east is a small sarcophagus carved from white marble and with the ninety-nine names of God covering the top and sides. Underneath the names, on the inner end, is the inscription, *Majnun Salim-e Akbar* (the one who has lost his senses, Salim son of Akbar) and a couplet in Persian—*If only I could see the face of my beloved once more / until the day of Judgment I will give thanks to the Maker.* Two dates are inscribed on either end: 1599 and 1615, the former supposedly marking the death of the beloved; and the latter, the building of the tomb. The name of the beloved or the inhabitant of the tomb is not inscribed anywhere. We do not know who is buried there.

During Sikh rule in Lahore, in the early nineteenth century, this building was part of the royal palaces. It remained a residence until 1856, even after the annexation of Panjab by the British East India Company in 1849. It was then converted into a site for church gatherings, and the ground was consecrated in 1857 as St. James Church. The building housed the church for the next thirty years. After 1891, with a new cathedral built in Lahore, the congregation moved, and this structure became a storage house for the documents of colonial offices and departments. In the mid-1920s, it was converted into a proper "Records Archive," with the intention of housing all documentary records of the colonial state, as well as the state in Panjab dating back to the seventeenth century.

After 1947, the new state made it a part of the city municipal apparatus. Until recently, it housed the offices of the sensitive departments of the Civil Intelligence Bureau, with metal plates tacked onto the wall under the standard portrait of Pakistan's founder, Muhammad Ali Jinnah, with a series of inscriptions mounted on plates: "He who guards his secrets, attains his goals." "Never a Word About Cypher outside the Cypher Bureau." "Safeguard your Cyphers, Protect Pakistan." "Security, Secrecy, Silence. Protect Them." In the early 1960s, the building was partially opened to the public, and the "Punjab Archives" was established on the premises (where it remains to this day), but if you were a civilian, it was not easy or even possible to visit it. The sarcophagus and the spies made it a strange building to behold and experience.

The real historical cipher in the building is certainly the name Anarkali. Around this name rests a series of interlocked romantic fables, and fantasies of Oriental despotism. William Finch (d. 1613) visited Lahore in 1610 while seeking *nil* (indigo) for his London merchant boss. In his travelogue, he describes the city, as "one of the greatest Cities of the East with streets faire and well paved," with "buildings faire and high" that have "carved windows" and an "ascent of six or seven steps" to the door. He mentions galleries, walks, and a "garden of the King" with almond, peach, fig, mango, and other fruit-bearing trees.[11]

Yet Finch is less concerned with the topography of Lahore than with the life of the ruling Mughal monarch, Jalaluddin Akbar. He describes a series of audience halls where the king rests, meets his nobility, or allows the public to gaze upon him. There were private halls where he lounges with "one hundred" of his women and where the ceilings are, according to Finch, covered in paintings that include portraits of Mughal emperors, their sons, Hindu gods and goddesses—"or rather Devils, intermixt in most ugly shape, with long hornes, staring eyes, shagge haire, great fangs, ugly pawes, long tailes, with such horrible difformity and deformity that I wonder the poore women are not frighted therewith."[12]

Here, Finch produces some of the key tropes that highlight early European travel accounts of Hindustan: the plight of women at the hands of the despotic king or his family, largely by being burned or poisoned to death. In Lahore he describes a tomb for a wife of Akbar, mother of Daniyal, and with whom his other son, Salim, had a "to do"—signifying a transgressive relationship.[13] As punishment, Akbar had her immured in a wall. Salim, after becoming the emperor Jahangir, built a magnificent tomb for her within a garden, a splendid structure with gold inlays. Finch gives her name as "Immacque Kelle, or Pomgranate kernell" (Anarkali).[14]

This is the first instance of any story about a woman named Anarkali. A colonial invention, the story is meant to signify the cruelty of the Mughals as well as their depredations. Finch gives no citation or source, yet his account becomes part of the influential and widely circulated compendium by Samuel Purchas (its first edition published in 1611, the last edition in 1625). The story of Anarkali becomes a totemic part of Lahore for generations of Europeans to come. Notably, nothing of the sort exists in any of the Mughal sources, including all the texts written in and based in Lahore in the seventeenth century. Dara Shikoh, for instance, names "Anarkali" only once, identifying it as a pomegranate garden where Miyan Mir would often go to meditate.

In the nineteenth-century Urdu and Persian accounts of Lahore, the transgression alleged by Finch is either missing or transposed to a love between a prince and a commoner. Anarkali becomes a lowly palace *kaniz* (maid) who falls in love with the prince or the emperor. Nur Ahmad Chishti's 1860 account has her fall in love with Akbar and die of natural causes, after which he builds the tomb. The historian Syed Abdul Latif, in 1892, makes her a servant who falls in love with the prince Salim and whom Akbar, the emperor, observes in the reflection of a mirror smiling at the prince. Akbar immures her in a wall. Another late-nineteenth-century-history, by Kanhaiya Lal, names Anarkali as Nadira Begum, who died of natural causes, and says that Akbar built a tomb for her. Other histories credit this tomb to Jahangir's wife, Sahib Jamal.

Despite these other Lahori histories and stories, the colonial version of Anarkali remained the most popular. A 1913 guidebook produced by Faletti's Hotel, in Lahore, for British or European tourists puts the story succinctly:

Anarkali's tomb is now used as a Record Room for the Secretariat and may be seen by visitors any working day between the hours of 10 and 4. The lady who gave her name, the "pomegranate Blossom," to the part of Lahore that lies between the city and the civil station was one of the favourites in the Harem of Jahangir's father. One day Akbar caught her exchanging glances with his son and forthwith had her buried alive with her head above ground. She died in 1600 and Jahangir in 1615 built a tomb over the place of her lingering death.[15]

In 1921, a Lahori dramatist, Imtiaz Ali Taj, wrote a historical play called *Anarkali*, in which he elaborated, at great length, the crisis of an imperial state when confronted with a pure love between two young protagonists, Salim and Anarkali. In the preface to the 1933 edition, he writes that the story of Anarkali has taken several forms—*dastan* (epic), *drama* (play), *ravaiat* (oral story), and tragedy—but regardless, he understands the story's origins to be *farzi* (invented). Yet as he had heard this story from his youth, he wanted to enact it as a quintessential tale of beauty, love, defeat, and impotency. The play was not an immediate success, but a film was sanctioned in Lahore and another in Bombay. After Partition, two major films, Nandlal Jaswantlal's *Anarkali* (1953, with Nur Jehan) and K. Asif's *Mughal-e-Azam* (1960, with Madhubala), would turn the story of Anarkali from a tomb in Lahore to a tale of doomed lovers that resonated globally.

These films and the continued attention to Anarkali rest almost entirely upon the version created by Imtiaz Ali Taj. That play gave the films their rhythms: the initial falling in love; the crucial role of jealousy among the women of the harem; the role of music and dance as expository of internal passion; the simmering tension between father and son, duty and obedience, empire and subject; and the final choice between love and throne. Taj's play ended with the death of Anarkali and the permanent fissure between Salim and Akbar. The movies, especially Asif's *Mughal-e-Azam*, opted for a happier ending, though still not one of union.

Walk the Anarkali bazaar and you will discover other stories of immurements. Anarkali is not in that state building, she is here in the bazaar. Look at that small jutting segment of an old *haveli* that seems preternatural in its ability not to collapse upon the walkers-by. In there is the secret wall with Anarkali, someone will whisper. Such is the continuing life of the story of Anarkali's immurement, which retains within it the idea of violence toward women.

As a teenager, I had a habit of compiling lists, and over the mid-1980s that included a list of newly wed women reported to have been burned to death by an exploding cooker (oil-based and later gas-based home cookers are prone to sudden bursts of flames). The daily newspaper would carry these as four-line summary items in columns on the back pages. A typical report would contain barely any more detail than the name of the neighborhood and the name of the victim. There were almost never any prosecutions. That same daily newspaper also carried reports of rapes, of murders of women. There was no dearth of proof that the city produced tens of Anarkalis a day.

III.

Figure 2.4. Data Darbar courtyard (2023)

At, or near, the center of gravity of Lahore is a shrine commonly known as "Data Darbar" (also "Data Sahib") It is one of the few points in the city's landscape that has remained fixed since the early twelfth century. Data Ganj Baksh—the lord who gives treasures—is the patron saint of Lahore. In his earthly life, he was ʿAli bin Usman bin ʿAli al-Jalabi al-Ghaznavi al-Hajweri (living in the years ca. 1050–1100), and he came to Lahore late in life and eventually settled after building a mosque. He is buried next to that mosque, and his shrine orients Lahore's civic and public life. This shrine, as well as the Sufi, existed above particular orders or sects; it was an embodiment of the spirit of the city itself as open, welcoming, present, as always there. The travelers, the hungry, the seekers, the kings all have made their way to Data Darbar, for centuries upon centuries. Being but a simple devotee in Lahore, I remember countless visits to distribute alms or to buy particular items (threads, bands, sweets) from the bazaars surrounding the shrine.

What little we know of Hajweri's own time and place comes from his only extant text, *Kashf al-Mahjub* (Rendering of the Veil). I joined a reading group for *Kashf al-Mahjub* in 2011. Since it was originally written in Persian, the reading group convened around a popular Urdu translation. By the time I joined, they had moved on from (or perhaps never covered) the preface of the work, in which he bemoans that two of his previous texts have been "stolen," which is to say someone had borrowed the manuscript, erased his name, and then circulated the text under their name. To prevent future thefts, Hajweri included his own name (and bits of his own history and experiences) throughout *Kashf*. He wrote nine or ten other works on Sufism, as well as his own *diwan* (that book is one of the two stolen works), but none have endured with as much significance as *Kashf*.[16]

The work is a manual or a guide on "how to be a Sufi." It is a text that has been lauded and studied over the last nine hundred years. Though our earliest extant manuscripts date only to the seventeenth century, it has remained one of the most important theoretical exegeses on the history and practice of Sufism from the early period of Islam. It is also one of the most famous texts to have been written in Lahore. It would not be a stretch to say that the reason why Hajweri is the patron saint of Lahore owes in large part to the centuries-long influence of *Kashf.* The shrine and the text each exist because of the other. You read the text and you see a long-lost history. You peer into the shrine and you see other worlds.

Hajweri was prompted to write the book because a devotee asked a series of questions: What were the Sufi orders and the paths of their beliefs? What were their recognized forms of worship and meditation, their key teachings, their hidden knowledges, their ways of praising and worshipping God? The answers to such questions, the book asserts, are necessary because the capacity to research, to investigate, has dwindled or diminished throughout the world. Most believers are passive and do not engage in critical thinking in order to learn the spiritual path. This has thus created a reality counter to *tariqat* (knowledge of the path) that lures those easily led astray.[17] Hajweri wants to lift the veil over people's hearts—like the veil that covers knowledge—and provide clear, easy-to-understand descriptions and definitions of key technical terms and histories of the spiritual orders of the Sufi. *Kashf al-Mahjub* is meant as a history, a manual, a spiritual and political geography, and a guide to the ways and means to support a community. 'Ali Hajweri documents his own expertise by narrating his travels in search of true knowledge across (contemporary) Afghanistan, Iran, Azerbaijan, Uzbekistan, Tajikistan, Syria, and Iraq. He meets ascetics, mystics, and theologians, who teach him ways of being, meditating, and learning. The mode of exposition is dialogic and pedagogic: Hajweri poses questions and then provides answers, often giving explanations and addressing the reader directly. The material world is intertwined with other realms. He has dreams and visitations, in which he meets other learned scholars, prophets, and guides. He asks for their guidance and narrates the knowledge imparted to him.

A worldly text, *Kashf al-Mahjub* exists in various temporalities. Take as an example Hajweri's discussion of a Sufi's wardrobe: he opens by describing the type of clothing that the Prophet and his earliest followers wore, as well as what Moses and Jesus wore, and then moves on to give testimonies from the earliest Sufis in Baghdad in the ninth century. He cites other authoritative texts, discusses debates among groups of believers on what constitutes ascetic life, and concludes with an exegesis refuting the notion that outward appearances (what one wears) are indeed a window into anyone's interior realities. In other words, should it even matter what a Sufi wears? He ends by describing a group of Sufis dressed in *moragha'* (patched, coarse clothes) who publicly ask for alms. Hajweri's teacher, chiding their attempt to elicit sympathy for their poverty, interprets it as being born of the greed of their Sufi teacher, who took disciples he could not provide for, and the greed of the disciples, who are hungry for food without labor.[18] In other words, they are not Sufi at all, even if they are dressed in ascetic robes.

At each point of this short section, Hajweri carefully gives examples and counterexamples. He differentiates between the rich and the poor, the king and the mendicant, and the counterfeit and the pure. His attempt is not to provide a dictum or a direct answer. Instead, he is keen to show the workings of logic, evidence, claims and counterclaims. It is a master class on not only how to answer a question, but to know what question to even ask.

Employing his dialogic and rhetorical approach, he opens with a question, gives several points of view, links the evidence to particular parts of Muslim history but also to histories of Christianity and Judaism, and finally ends with a more immediate and personal anecdote or case study. Although Hindustan rarely shows up in the text and he does not cite any text or tradition outside of the Abrahamic, it is likely he would have known scholars of Sanskrit and systems of asceticism. Much of his critique of outward appearances determining inner value is in sync with the yoga and tantra knowledge systems.

In his exegesis on how one researches what is known and unknown, he uses the word jihad (struggle) and interchanges *muhaqaqin* (those who research) and *mujahidat* (those engaged in the struggle for knowledge). Deep in an esoteric discussion of what can be known about the self (can it know itself by thinking about itself or by examining its action?), he uses direct, everyday examples. He urges the student to think by using real-life problems, such as training a headstrong horse or designing a house. That is, he argues, the key part of self-study and learning. There is a hidden capacity that only emerges via nurturing, direct action, and deep self-awareness.

This extends to a series of chapters on "good conduct," which focus on eating, sleeping, studying, walking, marrying (he is very glad that he married late in life), friendships, and more. Reading this text now, I am struck by its insistence on using evidence and logic for the sake of comprehension and understanding. That and the sheer number of textual citations that he deploys in order to illustrate his own past experience, which is both direct (observations or dreams) and indirect (teachings of his teachers, citations from other people or texts).

These are some of the qualities that have made *Kashf al-Mahjub* such an enduring classic. His own life would later merge with many legends and miracles—such as his "first convert," who, in many versions, is a yogi who challenged Hajweri in a showdown of sacral powers. Thus the yogi performed many miracles in front of Hajweri, who kept on ignoring him (and negating the power of the miracles), until the futility of spiritual combat made the yogi an enlightened disciple. Many such accounts are accretions to his memory, but they point to the vitality of his text's afterlife and the centrality of Hajweri as a figure in the city's own imagination.

Dara Shikoh, the Mughal prince, mentions Hajweri and his text with great reverence in his own history of the Sufis in the early seventeenth century. Shikoh also records one of Hajweri's most popular miracles. When Hajweri first built his mosque in Lahore, the theologians suspected that it was not properly oriented toward the direction of the Ka'aba. So Hajweri invited a group of elite Muslims to pray at the mosque. As they went for the *sujjud* (ritual bow), the Ka'aba physically materialized in front of their eyes. Suitably chastened, the theologians and elites paid their respect to Data and left. Such miracle stories remain an integral part of the ethos of Data Darbar, his shrine, in Lahore.

Data Darbar was always keenly supported by the political rulers over Lahore. Sultan Ibrahim, in the eleventh century, built the mausoleum over Hajweri's grave. Future rulers, even if they were based in Uch, Delhi, or Agra, would continue to maintain and augment his shrine. The new rulers of postcolonial Pakistan did not break from this tradition, either. Starting in the 1970s, under Prime Minister Zulfikar Ali Bhutto, Hajweri's shrine complex was expanded and rebuilt. It was an expensive and long process that continued through the 1980s, when it was supported by the military dictator Zia ul Haq (who hanged Bhutto), and, after Zia, into the mid-1990s when Benazir Bhutto (Zulfiqar's daughter) finished the project.[19] Bloody political rivals united over the course of the thirty years in paying homage to the Sufi intellectual from the eleventh century.

Kashf al-Mahjub will remain salient and important across centuries. It will be used as a pedagogic text with advice, to be read with a guide or teacher who can uncover the multiplicity of meanings. The earliest surviving manuscript dates from the seventeenth century, and the work (and Data Sahib) remains an important part of all Sufi *tazkira* or *malfuzat* (accounts of conversations) literature. The founder of the Sufi Chishti order, Mu'in al-Din Hasan Sijzi (1143–1236), stopped in Lahore to pay his respects and to undertake his own meditative regime at Data Sahib. Upon leaving he composed a verse that remains inscribed prominently at the shrine: *Ganj-bakhsh-e faiz-e 'alam, mazhar-e noor-e Khuda / na qasaan ra pir-e kaamil, kaamelaan ra raahnuma* (The bestower of treasures, the manifestation of the light of God's grace to the world, is perfect-teacher for the imperfect and a guide for those who have obtained completion). His words would influence the production of many new guides to spirituality. By the early twentieth century, there were more than twenty Urdu translations, and many editions of the work were published in Lahore.

In July 2010, two suicide bombers killed themselves and fifty others at Data Darbar. The attack came in the middle of a long string of bombings at Sufi shrines—Rehman Baba in March 2009, Mian Umar Baba in June 2010, Fariddudin Ganj Shakar in October 2010, Sakhi Sarwar in April 2011. The attacks would continue: Shah Noorani in 2016, Sehwan Sharif in 2017, another attack on Data Darbar in 2019. The bombings have changed the character of the places. These sites were once a place to linger, sleep, pray, be suspended upside down for meditation, bequeath stories, claim beloveds, enter trances, and be possessed by ecstatic beings. The walls and cameras, the army and police enacted a surveillance system, and their ever-seeing gaze drove out all the activities that had existed in the shades and shadows for hundreds of years.

Many of my earliest recollections of storytellers came from Data Darbar, and much of the time that I lingered at Data Darbar after the attacks came without any stories. The bombings changed the phenomenology of the place. The last time I visited, I gave my token to one of the men staffing the structure where visitors to the shrine deposit their shoes. He took my 100 rupees (the rate for the shoe service), then looked me in the eyes and said, "There is an order from inside [Data] that you pay more this time." Everyone around us, busy taking or giving shoes, paused. I put my hand back in my pocket to withdraw some more cash. "This time it has to be a blue note," he said, meaning an amount over 1,000 rupees. I gave him a blue note. The worker next to him said to me, "He is not a scammer and he doesn't ask for alms. He only asked because there is an actual message . . ." and gestured to the dome of the shrine. As I was leaving, another man tapped me on the shoulder and said these workers are scammers. I didn't have to give anyone any extra money, he asserted.

IV.

Prince Dara Shikoh (1615–59), son of the emperor Shah Jahan and governor of Lahore, reports in his *Sakinat ul Auliya* (Calmness of the Saints) that the Sufi master Mir Muhammad Miyan (d. 1635) was fond of walking and meditating in gardens. Miyan ji, as he was commonly known, had arrived in Lahore from Sind during Jalaluddin Akbar's rule. He would remain in Lahore for nearly sixty years, and in that time, a host of successive emperors, princes, and ministers would knock on his door (he kept his room locked from the inside). Miyan ji walked everywhere. He had walked from Sind to Lahore and would spend his days taking long walks. He was especially keen to walk in the many gardens and cultivated green patches in the city. He asked that when he died, he should be buried next to some of his disciples outside the city in the southeast. The funeral procession was led by Wazir Khan, who was then the mayor of the city. Dara was in Agra, but writes that Miyan ji came to him in a dream and asked that he perform the ritual prayers for burial. Dara writes this couplet: *I said that I would spend my life describing the pain of separation from him / Alas, that pain took such a turn that my tongue has no power to speak.*[20]

Miyan ji lived near or around the area that was known as Bagh-e Anarkali (the Pomegranate Gardens), near the city walls. Dara lists thirty such places that Miyan ji liked to visit, away from the busy streets and bazaars: a canopy of trees to the south, outside the city walls; one particular tree in Naulakha, with which he often

Figure 2.5. Miyan Mir's shrine (2023)

conversed (the tree would disclose the healing qualities of its flowers, leaves, bark, and so on); the *baradari* (pavilion) of Mirza
Kamran; a certain dome without a door; a pond; a minaret on the
road to Firuzpur; the *beri* tree at the gravesite of Bibi Taj; a small
structure that would eventually be adjacent to his gravesite; a

rosewood tree in the mayor's gardens; a garden in Icchra; another
tree in Icchra, which collapsed at the instance of his death; and
so on.

These sites mentioned by Dara range from built structures,
semipublic or partially inhabited, to public gardens and private
gardens. Miyan ji was certainly known and respected throughout
the city (two Mughal emperors and numerous members of the
royal households were devoted to him), so it is easy to understand
how he had access to these many places. Yet, he was also someone
who shunned these emperors and the attentions of the powerful.
The Lahore that emerges from Dara Shikoh's list is already a
mixture of the old and abandoned, and the new and lively. Miyan ji
sought out places of calm at the southern and western ends of the
city, away from the commerce, the law, and the polity.

In *Sakinat ul Auliya*, Dara Shikoh provides a history of Miyan ji,
his Qadiri *tariqa* (his spiritual lineage back to Baghdadi Sufi Abdul Qadir Gilani), and accounts of his own disciples and teachings, his miracles, and his daily life. Dara writes that Miyan ji
practiced a form of breath control to the point that he could spend
a full night taking only a single breath (Dara reports that in his
eighties, due to age, this was extended to four breaths per night).
As a Sufi, Miyan ji understood the sacral and political worlds to
be distinct, even antagonistic. He kept his distance from the
political rulers. Dara Shikoh, in his devotion to Miyan ji, understood his own work to be a way to understand how sacral power
intersected with political power. He comments at numerous
times in the text on his own capacity to perform the difficult tasks
of meditation, or having dreams and hearing voices that directed
his attention and propelled him further on his spiritual journey.

Dara Shikoh lists a number of miracles performed by Miyan ji.
While Miyan ji emphasized that no one was to speak or write
about any demonstration of his spiritual powers, Dara Shikoh
collected accounts of these miracles from the other disciples of
Miyan ji (who were also hesitant to speak of them). A number of
the miracles were about Miyan ji reclining or meditating under

trees and being visited by snakes that moved around him or wrapped him in coils as a way to pay respect to him. There were other accounts of prophecy, of deliverance from pain and sufferance. Many miraculous deeds concerned Miyan ji's capacity to travel to distant places, often overnight—such as to Jabal al-Nur, a site outside Mecca where the Prophet used to meditate. Miyan ji cured many illnesses, including that of Dara Shikoh himself— the prince had been severely ill as a child and Shah Jahan brought him to Miyan ji to be healed. Miyan ji also spoke with trees, which taught him how to use botanical sources for healing. Once, when Lahore was suffering from a plague, he was able to cure many who were afflicted. There is, however, not a single miracle connected with the conversion of anyone from Hinduism to Islam— perhaps indicating that the sacral landscape of the city harbored no such conviction.

Dara Shikoh was a student not only of Miyan ji; after Miyan ji's death, he would also become a student of the Sufi's main disciple and successor, Mulla Shah Badakhshi, in Kashmir. He would have a beautiful mausoleum built to mark the last resting place of Miyan ji. The structure was made of the same red stone that was used in the building of the fort and the mosque in Lahore. Dara Shikoh would later be executed by his brother Aurangzeb, so he likely did not live to see the site finished. Yet it is luminescent and breathtaking when the sun shines directly on it.

Like ʿAli Hajweri in *Kashf al-Mahjub*, which is cited extensively in *Sakinat ul Auliya*, Dara Shikoh in his own work reveals many secrets that he feels underpin the path of spiritual power and enlightenment. In his *Majma ul Bahrain* (Conjunction of the Two Seas), written in 1655, he brings the esoteric worlds of Hindus and Muslims into a cosmological union. Much of his argument for pathways to the truth build on meditation practices—breathing, suspension of energies, concentration— that link the asceticism of yogis and that of Sufis. The world of Miyan ji was reflected clearly in Dara Shikoh's new cosmology.

A mosque sits at the north of the enclosure that surrounds Miyan ji's mausoleum, and a garden and a graveyard sit at the east. Dara Shikoh also constructed a mausoleum, within the enclosure, for his sister Nadira Begum who died in 1632. The *baradari* has long held a special place for women devotees of Miyan ji, who gather there for sustained meditation and prayers. During the Sikh rule of Lahore, many of the mausoleums would be stripped of their marble and their gold, but not Miyan ji's mausoleum. In popular accounts, Ranjit Singh (1780–1839), the first Sikh ruler of Lahore, was thwarted in his attempts to demarble Miyan ji's mausoleum—a miracle the devotees attributed to the saint's continued presence in Lahore. The Lahore-Amritsar railway line had a stop near Miyan ji's mausoleum called Miyan Mir Station—later renamed as Cantonment Station.

Over time, the mausoleum became the site of an annual 'urs (pilgrimage and gathering) and several other commemorations. A bazaar formed outside the walled enclosure selling devotional items, as did a row of shops dedicated to kitchenware and cooking pots made from baked clay. Miyan ji used only clay plates and cups, and some of the shop owners claim a special relationship to Miyan Mir's *gaddi nashin* (descendants of a saint and caretakers of the shrine). The graveyard attached to the mausoleum became a key site for visitors as well. The 'urs there was known to be a boisterous affair with *daru* (spirited liquor), bhang (cannabis mixed with milk or rosewater), and *chars* (hash or cannabis residue) in easy supply. It was known to be a place where ecstatic behavior—through *samah* (a trancelike state entered via music and/or chanting) or *aseeb* (possession by a jinn)—was commonplace. Consequently, such behavior would attract undesirable attention from the uninitiated or the police who would carry out raids. For much of this history, women were welcome observers and participants in all activities at the shrine, and then they were slowly cordoned off into "women's only" spaces and outright excluded from the mausoleum.

Such policing of conduct is also part of the history of another Qadiri shrine—one that belonged to Shah Hussain (d. 1599), who was popularly known as "Madho Lal Hussain," for his penchant for wearing red and his love for the beautiful Brahmin boy Madho. This shrine was also a place of transcendence where women and men, the old and the young, could act in a transcendental manner—that is, they could escape the gender-based constraints on public behavior. Shah Hussain's poetry was the basis for the musical performances. As at Miyan Mir's shrine, Shah Hussain's shrine was a frequent target of both curfews and police actions.

I visited the shrine of Miyan ji a number of times as a child, but I never went to his 'urs. I had a friend who lived very close to the shrine yet never went there. Since he never brought up the subject, I assumed his family did not believe in Sufis or shrines, and I never mentioned it to him. Miyan ji was one among many "forbidden" sites of the city in the 1980s which the middle class prohibited their young sons (and certainly their daughters) from visiting. It was imagined to be a place where drug-taking or "improper" activities took place. The police were usually nearby to arrest those who seemed "out of place," which is to say they were dressed in jeans or pants. The devotional landscape of Lahore no longer had space for the independent-minded Miyan ji. His memory was tucked away in a corner of Lahore surrounded by middle-class aspirants who rejected his memory. Steel cages and concrete blocks (anti–suicide bomber apparatus) rest prominently next to the door.

V.

Of the thirteen devastations of Lahore that Kanhaiya Lal covers chronologically in his history, the devastation caused by Zahiruddin Babur (1483–1530) comes in at number nine. Lal uses the word *sadhma*, which denotes in Persian a type of collision and its resulting devastation. In 1525–26, Babur destroyed Lahore twice. Babur does not specifically mention Lahore in his memoirs, but in his tabulations of the revenue seized in Hindustan, the amount looted from Lahore (and its environs) nearly matched his plunder from Delhi. For him, Lahore was not a city of political consequence. Once he had taken the riches of Lahore, he abandoned the city and moved with his army farther to the east than any of his Timurid forbears. Lahore would only reemerge as one of the most important cities for the Afghan Suri and the Timurid Mughal kings who followed Babur. Later, it would become one of the capitals of the Mughal imperium and an important waystation on the path to Kashmir.

Guru Nanak (1469–1539) is known and revered around the world as the founder of the Sikh faith. His memory and presence in the landscape of Punjab remains a source of devotion for millions in and outside Pakistan. A small number of verses in Guru Nanak's *kalam* (poetic collection), generally known as the Baburvani verses, contain the only contemporary record of Babur's destruction of Lahore.

In fact, Babur's destruction of Lahore would have vanished from memory were it not for its mention in Guru Nanak.

Lahore, which Nanak describes as "a pool of ambrosial nectar, the home of praise," "suffered terrible destruction for four hours" at the hand of Babur's armies.[21] The verses describe the destruction as a deeply personal calamity: "A wedding party (of sin) has taken the most prized possession (the bride) from the house."[22] The metaphor of the disruption of a wedding marks the destruction of Lahore as a great social crime. The Qazi and the Brahmin (the Muslim and Hindu elite) are the tragic heads of the households that are getting married, with the devil as the officiant of this perverse wedding of force. Babur, Nanak records, was a catastrophe sent by God to Hindustan: "There was so much pain (and slaughter), that people screamed, have you no compassion my lord?"[23] A wedding with the devil, a slaughter like a powerful tiger attacking a flock of sheep, being laid to waste and defiled by dogs, a land made so bereft that no one is left even to pay attention to the dead—these are evocations with which the Baburvani verses capture the destruction of Lahore by Babur.

Even in the glimpses afforded in these short, impressionist verses, Nanak seems to hold Lahore in great esteem. Guru Nanak was born in 1469 in Talwandi Rai Bhoi (now Nankana Sahib), just forty-odd miles west of Lahore. His father, Kalu Bedi, and mother, Tripata, were childless, they say. In the *janamsakhi*—the various collections of stories of the life of Nanak, which were composed around 1604—Nanak moves to Sultanpur to begin working as an accountant. It was at Sultanpur that he first hears the voice of Akal Purakh (the timeless one), urging him to move away from the worldly affairs of bookkeeping and toward the search for Truth.

Prompted by the call, Nanak left his wife, Sulakhani, and his two sons, Lakhmi Das and Siri Chand, for his first *udasi* (separation or exile), heading east around 1505. Alongside his companion Mardana—a musician of the *mirasi* caste—Nanak traveled west to Kurukshetra, Karnal, Panipat, Hardwar, Delhi, Mathura,

Nankmatta, Ayodhya, Lucknow, Kashi, Patna, Gaya, Raj Mahal, Malder, Dhaka, Dhanpur, Kamrip, Dhubri, Chittagong, and back to Talwandi. The next *udasi* took them south to Sirsa, Bikaner, Ajmer, Pushkar, Abu, Ujjain, Bedar, Pongal, Madras, Nagapatti-nam, Ceylon, Sudampauri, and back through Sind and Lahore. The third *udasi*, in 1514, went north to Manasarovar, Tibet, Kashmir, Jammu. The fourth *udasi*, around 1518–22, took Nanak and Mardana to Mecca, Medina, Jerusalem, Damascus, Aleppo, Baghdad, Kabul, Peshawar. Where Nanak walked, in each community he came across, he helped those who could not help themselves. After the fourth *udasi*, having covered the four cardinal directions and having visited the main seats of political power in the world, and the centers of all major religions, Guru Nanak settled with his family and followers in Kartarpur, a mere seventy-odd miles from Talwandi. He died there in 1538.

The great Guru is one among many world-walkers of the subcontinent. Farid Ganjshakar (1179–1266), buried in Pakpattan some 270 kilometers south of Kartarpur, walked to Baghdad, Jerusalem, Mecca, Ghazni. Makhdoom Jahaniyan Jahangasht (1308–84), buried in Uch Sharif some 540 kilometers south of Kartarpur, went to Mecca, Rome, China—around the world. There were also walkers who moved within the subcontinent—such as Dnyaneshwar (1275–96), Lal Ded (1320–92) and contemporaries of the Guru, Chaitanya (1486–1533), Mirabai (1499–1570), Dadu Dayal (1544–1603), and most importantly, Kabir (1440–1518) and Surdas (1478–1581). Nanak moved in their world as they all had moved in his. He met Baba Farid and Kabir—their verses are included the *Guru Granth Sahib* alongside those of Namdev and Ravidas. All of them walked and traveled across vast swaths of territory in Hindustan. If one thinks of Nanak alongside these Hindustani contemporaries, his peregrinations seem almost prosaic. But try imagining him next to his contemporaries outside Hindustan, such as Martin Luther (1483–1546) and Erasmus (1466–1536), and the contrast in world-making comes into sharp relief.

What did Nanak do as he traveled? His miracles are inscribed into the earth, as ponds, streams, and lakes that bear his name and that sprung into existence when he struck the earth with his walking stick, as trees that remain standing to this day, under which he prayed. He was also learning, debating, talking, thinking. He was composing his verses. In the *Adi Sri Guru Granth Sahibji* are thirty-one *raag* compositions of Nanak and the four gurus that succeeded him. Though compiled between 1603 and 1604, these verses speak to the philosophy and sacrality of Nanak, and what would emerge as Sikhi. Nanak's verses are in Panjabi, the language of the region where he was born and where he died. The world-walker spoke in his mother tongue to his followers.

Nanak's Panjab is shaped by Lahore, by Multan, by Sialkot, by the flow of the five rivers Jhelum, Chenab, Ravi, Sutlej, and Beas as they rush helter-skelter across wide plains to merge with the Indus. To the five rivers belong the five Sufi *panj pirs*: Khwaja Khizr, Baba Farid, Shaikh Bahauddin Zakariyya of Multan, Makhdoom Jahaniyan Jahangusht of Uch, and Lal Shahbaz Qalandar of Sehwan. They are all itinerant—traversing both space and time. They can visit you, if you ask with a pure heart, and bring you the message that you seek. If you walk around Pakpattan, Uch Sharif, you will see a poster or two in every shop, in most public places, affixed to any means of transportation, heralding these Sufi masters.

Yet little of Nanak himself is in Lahore. At the end of Delhi Gate in the old city is a *haveli* that is often remembered as a spot where Nanak stayed when he visited the city. A number of wells and small ponds in the city have memories associated with Nanak. There are also mentions of Nanak's visit to Data Darbar. Near the very edge of Lahore, less than a mile from the border with India, is the Pehli Patshahi (First Abode) of Guru Nanak. It is a simple arched structure, next to a set of neem trees where Nanak had rested. The structure was likely built during Ranjit Singh's rule in Lahore. There are no signs marking the site; the only visitors it draws come from the surrounding villages. The nearby tree branches are covered in threads and strips of fabric, the remnants of seekers and believers. A few other sites remain visibly attached to the history of Sikhism or Sikh rule: the birthplace of Guru Arjun, the fifth Guru, or the magnificent Samadhi of Ranjit Singh himself, next to the Badshahi Mosque in the heart of the city. Elsewhere in Lahore, Nanak is sometimes present in shop names, and there used to be a street named after him, but it too has vanished.

Rather, only destruction wrought on Lahore during the Sikh rule of Ranjit Singh remains etched in the city's memory. His shelling of the city reduced much of it to ruins. He despoiled marble and gold from tombs, shrines, and official buildings. He converted elite Mughal quarters to horse stables or warehouses. The Urdu histories of the period say that Ranjit Singh's forty-year reign of Lahore changed the city from one of learned and cultured intelligentsia to one of warlords and deviant public artists and performers. Much of this characterization is driven by the animus of Partition, when Sikhs were blamed for atrocities against Muslims. Nanak's love, the gift of his wisdom and spirituality, are missing from Lahore's history and memory.

VI.

Figure 2.6. Chauburji Gate (2023)

Only the gate to the garden remains. The gate itself is now surrounded by a high metal fence. A metro looms overhead, supported by heavy concrete pillars. This is an island cupped in the smokey grasp of a double-laned road. Across one lane, there is a market of domestic appliances, and across another, a row of tuition centers. Here, on a small patch of green, stands an enormous gate with four towers or minarets. It has long stood here, mournfully watching the city grow around it and the streets uproot the trees that were once its pillars.

It is a square brick two-floor structure. It has a high archway opening and the outer surface is covered in inlaid ceramic panels with floral themes and frescoes. On the west-facing archway, in Persian, a couplet: . . . *this garden in the pattern of gardens of Heaven was founded / and to the mercy of Miyan Bai, this garden was given / by the kindness of the "beautiful lady" of the time.* The couplet was missing an opening passage for nearly two hundred years until the modern restorers added, in the space preceding "this garden," "By the grace of the all-powerful and eternal creator of the universe," in order to remove agency from mere mortals. Above the couplet is a passage from the Qur'an, *Ayat'ul Kursi,* often inscribed to protect one from harm—as well as the date of the structure's construction (1646).

The gate is known as Chauburji (Four Pillars). The gate was one of the entrances to a vast garden intended to rival the one built by Shah Jahan in Lahore—the Shalimar Gardens. Yet, the garden and a large settlement were wiped out when the river Ravi flooded or change its course, leaving only the gate. One of the four pillars was destroyed or fell in the early 1920s and was rebuilt in the 1970s.

A Punjab Tourism board installed after the renovation is meant to inform the visitor about the putative origins of the gate. It says that "local tradition connects Zebinda with Begum Zeb'un Nisa' (1638–1702), the accomplished daughter of Aurangzeb" who "built it and bestowed it" upon her lady-in-waiting, Miyan Bai, "but this is incorrect since Zebun Nisa, born in 1639, was still a child of eight when the garden was founded." The garden was established in 1646, when Zeb'un Nisa' was only seven. Zeb'un Nisa' may or may not have been the benefactor, yet Chauburji remains the only existing Mughal structure sponsored by a woman and dedicated to another woman. This alone makes it an exceptional relic.

Colonial-era photographs show not the small green patch we see today, but a relatively open green space flanked by two large trees. Maps from the same period show a dense graveyard close by, and wide-open space to the west and south. It is easy to see how a garden may once have stretched toward the river Ravi in the west. Walk farther south, and the intersecting road of Chauburji leads to what was once the village of Navakot, where another garden existed alongside a mausoleum. It is also popularly maintained that Zeb'un Nisa' is buried here. That too is contested, and the municipality maintains that it is likely the mausoleum of a male noble, for whom they have one or two candidates. I would note that it remains a much more impossible task for a male name to be effaced or forgotten when attached to buildings and monuments than for a woman's name, considering that women are usually hidden, either by design or happenstance, in history and memory.

By all accounts, Zeb'un Nisa' was a very learned woman who was close to her uncle Dara Shikoh and interested in esoteric and spiritual matters. She composed poetry, and some of it was included in various collections. In her verses, she calls herself *mukhfi* (the hidden), and hence the collection of her verses (*ghazals* mostly) is named *Divan-e Mukhfi* (Hidden Collection). Many of her verses play with that idea of the hidden speaker and speech: *dar sokhan-e makhfi shudam, chon boe-e gul dar barg-e gul / mayel-e deedan har ke darad, dar sokhan benad mera* (I am hidden in words like the scent of a flower in its petals / Anyone who wants to see me must have an inclination for understanding my words).

The poetry draws heavily upon the Sufi and literary roots of the subcontinent, but also upon Arabic and Persian traditions. This early poem gives a good sense of her use of well-established conventions in poetry, such as the doomed love between Layla and Majnun, or between the nightingale and the night blossoms. She frequently inverts the implied gender roles, while also highlighting her own status:

Though, I am Layla's foundation, my heart is like Majnun's in tone
  I would wander in the desert, but shyness chains my feet.
The nightingale, by being my disciple, became a companion of
the flower in the garden
  In the realm of love, the butterfly is also our disciple.
My hidden blood has just become visible
  my color is hidden within me like the color red in henna.
I have thrown the burden of sorrow off my shoulders and onto
time
  now see the blue garment I wear, with two humps on its back.
  I am the daughter of a king, but I have turned towards poverty
  burning beauty and adornment.
My name is Zeb' un Nisa', "the most beautiful woman."[24]

The *Divan* was published in various editions, including one in
1912 by a Lahore publisher. Several authors penned brief biographical notes. Some of these publications mentioned the stories about Zeb'un Nisa' that were circulated by European travelers
to Lahore. There were doubts that she was the author of the *Divan* or wrote much of anything at all. There were also stories of
her being courted by or exchanging letters with men who pined
for her. One suitor who snuck into her garden was surprised by
Aurangzeb and jumped into a vat. Aurangzeb, suspicious that his
daughter's honor was at stake, had burning oil poured into the vat
to see if anyone was hiding in there. The suitor kept quiet, even as
he was burned alive. Other stories spoke of her love for Shivaji or
for Dara Shikoh. In all such stories, she is transgressive and must
be imprisoned or kept in seclusion in Lahore, or robbed of her due
stature (and riches) as a princess.

To counter these accounts, the male Muslim authors of the late
nineteenth and early twentieth centuries extolled her as a learned
princess. They mentioned her sponsorship of poets, calligraphers,
painters, and libraries. How absurd, they wrote, that a woman of
such noble birth would deign to exchange couplets with some

random man in the street of Lahore. Was it such deliberate erasure of her, an unwed Mughal princess who wrote poetry and
dedicated public monuments to her attending lady, that hid her
from public memory? There were other monuments or sites in
Lahore named after, or dedicated by, women, such as Bibi Pak Daman or Dai Anga, or Anarkali. But these are women who were also
literally "hidden"—literally buried in the earth or in a wall. Chauburji, a public monument devoid of its historical relationship to
women, is congruent with how women are represented in the
city's geography: hidden and forgotten.

Chauburji had no clear place among the surviving Mughal-era
monuments in the city. It was not spoken of in the same breath as
the fort or the mosque and garden built by Shah Jahan, or the
baradari or the mausoleums of Jahangir. It was a small island but-
tressed with heavy traffic. After 1947, it became derelict, partly
collapsed, all of its glazed tiles stolen. It would slowly be rebuilt
with ordinary masonry as the neighborhoods around it rose in
prominence. There was a row of colonial-era homes to the west of
it, which would be demolished and converted into shopping plazas.
The cinemas to the east would linger into the 1970s but also became shops soon after. A looping road linked it to the city's preeminent graveyard, Miyani, which remained the only space in the
city not overtaken by the dense urban development.

I never knew, growing up, who had built Chauburji or when or
why. In the landscape of memory, this particular space has remained an anomaly. I never went to Chauburji—the gate itself—
nor ever spent any time at it. In the early 1980s, it was known only
for being the hangout of heroin addicts and drug traffickers. It
was especially forbidden, for a lower-middle-class boy like me, to
visit it *specifically*. We could go to other Mughal sites. There was
also no real path to it, nor any way to linger and observe. Around
you, at all times, was a cacophony of trucks, buses, vans, and trol-
lies on the busy Multan Road. The businesses around Chauburji
were surrounded by rows upon rows of parked bicycles, motor-

cycles, and other transportation. The fence was erected to keep out those deemed undesirable.

It was only when I began to attend a reading group near Chauburji that I began to see it. By that time the dense smog of traffic had permanently rendered the structure into hues of gray and black. Once, as I stood outside the *halqa* (gathering), taking a moment to myself, a fellow reader struck up a conversation with me. The Chauburji, he said, gesturing to it, keeps Lahore upright. They are pillars rather than towers.

VII.

Lahore was a city of gardens. There is a sepia-toned photograph from when I am around five or six holding on to the *pallu* of my mother's sari while she is pushing a stroller with my younger brother. In the foreground are her sister and my father. We are all in Shalimar Garden, which I recognize from the elaborate fountains visible in the background. Even in sepia, it looks green and full of flowers. In another photograph my mother and father stand together, both gorgeous and stylish, in front of one of the side porticos at Shalimar. I imagine it was my mother's idea, given all the time we spent in the various Mughal gardens, the colonial gardens, and the national gardens in Lahore. Her love for gardens and gardening came from her father, who spoke often of the apple orchards and gardens of Srinagar that he had left behind in 1947.

There are several such tiny square photographs from my childhood. In front are usually my parents or aunts. The background is the garden, but in effect, Shalimar is in the foreground in every photograph. In each image, I see other people, a newlywed bride still in red, marking the special day at Shalimar; a tourist from out of town; a delegate of some agency; children running—all are joyfully present. I cannot read the sky in those pictures anymore, but in my mind, it is soft blue with a trace of gold.

Babur's son Mirza Kamran built the first palace and garden in Lahore, on the bank of the river Ravi opposite the city walls, sometime in the early 1530s. The *baradari* there still survives. Abdul Hamid Lahori (d. 1655), the author of Shah Jahan's *Bad-shahnama* (Book of the King), mentions many of the gardens, describing a garden resembling paradise built for the mausoleum of the newly deceased Jahangir (d. 1627; his mausoleum was finished by 1637). Jahangir's wife, Nur Jahan (d. 1645), and her brother Abu'l Hasan Asif Khan (d. 1641) are all located next to the river. The existing garden of Kamran was converted into a funerary garden that surrounded the *baradari* structures and became an important resting place (Shah Jahan would often stop there), as well a model for the many new gardens that were subsequently built.

Shah Jahan, who was born in Lahore, would change the geography of the city with extensive building projects, one of which would be the gardens called the Shalimar to the east of the city. The tomb of Dai Anga in Lahore, Shah Jahan's caregiver, was also centered in a "rest-inducing" garden. Shah Jahan built a garden, also called Shalimar, in Kashmir. Perhaps, this was his way of linking Kashmir and Lahore, which was a major stop on the Mughal court's journey toward Kashmir—Akbar, Jahangir, Shah Jahan, Aurangzeb, and Dara would all spend months staying here in spring. Jahangir also made Lahore his capital. Much of the architecture of that period was washed away in the flood that also destroyed the gardens of Zeb'un Nisa'. Some forty gardens are listed at various times by Lahori. Accounts from the sixteenth century onward mention approvingly the many gardens, orchards, and open green spaces that made up the city.

Chandarbhan Brahman (d. 1670), a secretary to Shah Jahan, praises his native Lahore in his memoir *Chahar Chaman* (The Four Gardens). He sees a Lahore of tall houses, bustling gardens, palaces, and public courtyards ("better than any other city in the seven skies"). The city is filled with intellectuals, merchants, ascetics, Sufis, and poets ("of sweetest tongue"), who all cherish the illustrious gardens of Lahore, which are always in bloom. Prominent among them are the Bagh-e Dilkusha (Garden That Pleases the Heart), Bagh-e Dilameez (Garden that Steals the Heart), the Bagh-e Naulakha (Garden of the Riches), and the garden of Shalimar's Bagh-e Faiz Baksh (Garden that Bestows Immanence) and Farah Baksh (Garden that Grants Joy), which attracted visitors from afar.[25]

The Mughal gardens are frequently invoked in contemporary writings as a personification of Heaven on earth. While this is an important aspect of imagining paradise on earth (much as St. Augustine did with his *City of God*), such readings also end up underselling the invocations of the garden as spaces for rest and recharge, whether to perform the duties of the empire or to simply get away from it all. That is to say, these were ordered spaces for ordered rests for those who kept the world in order. Shalimar was explicitly imagined as a series of linked gardens and wide spaces for rest and relaxation. In 1640, the emperor gave funds for a canal to bring the waters of Ravi to the eastern side of the city. It was this that allowed for the construction of the massive garden complex, and Shalimar was inaugurated by Shah Jahan in 1641–42. It was vast enough to easily accommodate the royal household.

In *Badshahnama*, the magnificently detailed annals of Shah Jahan, Abdul Hamid Lahori describes the creation of Shalimar. It is a story of water, first and foremost. The movement of the river was always unpredictable, and the new canal allowed for the river to be channeled and safely diverted. It also made available rich soil for fruit trees—orange, mango, cherry, pear, apricot, and so on. Yet it is the water that is the most alive in *Badshahnama*'s description of the Shalimar. Water moves across horizontally and vertically in the quadrangles of the garden. Three terraces were built in marble—a garden of joy, a garden of benefit, and a garden of delight—each arranged in eight quadrants with buildings at each end. The canal fed the garden, where pulleys brought the water up to the top terrace (third level), from which it cascaded down. At the center of each quadrant were fountains fed by inlaid channels for water flowing from the terrace above. Fountains were installed on each of the terraces, which sprayed water up to four feet—

some 120 to 150 fountains on each terrace. The fountains were also marbled, as were the palatial rest areas for the emperor and the queen and places where they received the public or the nobility.[26]

In the mid-eighteenth century, when Ahmad Shah Abdali wrecked Lahore, many of the marble and copper inlays were removed and transported away. The buildings must have also suffered extensively, for Ranjit Singh would camp in Shalimar rather than stay in any of the buildings. The remaining structures were also stripped of marble during the period. The adjacent gardens would become *basti* (villages), then towns, and finally neighborhoods of Lahore. Post-Partition, this area was one of the key settlements. Encroachments, rendered here as *galli* (pathway) or *makan* (house), swallowed nearly all the eastern gardens. The walls would be rebuilt retrospectively.

The water stopped flowing as well. The fountains, as described in the nineteenth- and early twentieth-century works, are only occasionally flowing.

In the 1980s, the governor of Lahore, Ghulam Jilani, would give specific attention to Shalimar in order to make a case for it as a World Heritage Site. The beautification whitewashed all the existing structures, but I never personally saw the central fountain turned on except in photographs. It presented a strange sight—a garden designed for flowing, cascading, and springing water, dry. Rain would accumulate now and then, but the main terraces would remain without water, with only patches of verdant green. The boundary walls were used as spaces for hanging out, playing cricket, or a store of bricks from which the city's residents would steal. What idea of the "garden" has survived in the city of gardens?

The various mayors of Lahore and governors of Punjab made sure that some of Shalimar was visible as an artifact of splendor or of Lahore's past grandeur. John Lawrence, the first governor of Punjab, had taken up the public garden as his own initiative to create a colonial resting space. His "Lawrence Garden" would become one of the key models (now renamed Bagh-e Jinnah) for the dictatorship-era governor Ghulam Jilani in the early 1980s. He would create new public parks (such as Race Course Park) but also stop the slow erasure of Shalimar. Yet, neither Shah Jahan nor the Mughals were of great significance to the dictatorship and the version of the garden that emerged from the 1980s was a mixture of picnic spots and sports areas. A number of festivals and processions that had long been a part of Shalimar (for example, the festival of lights and the kite-flying festival) but have been banned since. The public space of the garden has ceded almost total control to the demands of a rapidly expanding city. Middle- and upper-middle-class families now congregate only in shopping malls. Spaces like the Shalimar Gardens, with their low entrance fees, cater mostly to the very poor or itinerant—along with the schoolchildren of nearby public schools.

The connective tissue of gardens and pathways linking Lahore's many villages to its fort has been replaced by cement. You cannot see through cement. It has cordoned off sight lines and created a city full of myopic people. The open garden spaces have been replaced by gated communities, the first instance of erecting cement walls to seclude and to protect the elite. In the 1980s, the military began parceling off all the green and open spaces and enmeshing it in cement and steel. First, the Askari Housing Society for military officers. Next, the Defence Housing Authority, which became its own municipal power, emerged on vast swaths of arable land confiscated, distributed, and redistributed by the military junta. That military gated community needed its own armies of servants, *chowkidars* (security guards), and drivers who couldn't live too far but not too close. As a result, behind the military communities formed the soft settlement of corroded tin, bricks, mud.

As more land was cleared off, parceled out, and built on, as more roads were added, the idea of a city of gardens became a cruel jest. By the 2000s, massive roads circled Lahore, a thick toothpaste of cement and asphalt slathered across neighborhoods. The Ring Road, created for easy access around and through the city, cut through arable land, dairy colonies, satellite townships, gardens, anything and everything. On the north, the Ring Road resembles the canal that once drew water to the city from the Ravi, but now is a cement and concrete river with eight-foot-high walls to keep people out of the motorway. It neatly runs through towns, neighborhoods, communities, slicing them into halves and thirds.

2

HISTORY: WRITING LAHORE

In the Muslim geographical works of the ninth or tenth centuries, much attention is paid to the *bilad* (country or sometimes region) and the *hudud* (the limits) of the known landmass. The historians, geographers, or bureaucrats fashioning such Arabic works were not only describing the ways in which different parts of the Muslim imperium were connected to each other but also explaining how important sites and cities, which were now in *dar al-islam* (Realm of Islam), were part of the Islamic sacral and political supra-structure. The *medina* (city)—both the particular city where the Prophet migrated in 622 and the general or idealized idea of the city—was a key part of delineating a universalist political power. After al-Farabi (d. 950) introduced the theoretical structure of the ideal city in his *Mabadi' ara'ahl al-Madinah al-Fadilah* (Principles of the Opinions of the People of the Virtuous City), investigating and writing cities became an important part of the toolbox of political theory from the late ninth century onward. Thus Medina, Cairo, Baghdad, Damascus, Jerusalem, Cordoba, Isfahan, Samarkand, Nishapur, Herat, and more all had dedicated histories by the thirteenth century.

The Arabic and Persian treatises on cities were centrally concerned with the idea of the political state as illustrated in the physical contours and inhabitants of the city. Cities became exemplars of political theory just as much as the nature of political power—its rise and fall, its ebb and flow—would become visible through the rise and fall of the physical city. The making of new capital cities heralded new political power, the sacking of political

capitals sounded the death knell for the subjugated powers. That
theoretical construct gave incentive to new political powers to
create new cities, just as it gave incentive to those conquering established polities to destroy them. Kings and caliphs were known
through the magnificence of their cities and their cities' orderliness, their adherence to principles of justice and equity, and the
richness of their social welfare.

By the mid-ninth century, the presence of port cities and inland capital cities had become markers of civilization and political
knowledge. Specific attention to cities is found in works from the
mid-ninth-century accounts of Buzurg ibn Shaharyar's *'Aja'ib al-
Hind* (The Wonders of Hindustan), to the late ninth-century geographical text of Ibn Khurradadhbih, *Kitab al-Masalik wa'l
Mamalik* (Book of Routes and Polities), to the mid-tenth-century
history of all known Muslim lands by Mas'udi *Muruj al-Dhahab
wa-Ma'adin al-Jawhar* (The Meadows of Gold and Mines of
Gems). Across such enduring works, order in the political realm—
in fact, in all the realms of the world—is represented by an ordered city, whether within Muslim political control or not.

The cities of Hindustan—Uch, Delhi, Agra, Surat, Ahmad-
nagar, Bijapur, and Warangal—were featured in political, social,
and sacral histories, often with chapters or sections dedicated
to their foundation, their modes of governance, their flora and
fauna, their economic structures, and their notable intellectuals,
courtiers, and merchants. The history of the city was woven into
accounts of kings, regions, and sacral orders. Inversely, the histories of prominent individuals, when written to emphasize their
significance, featured their presence in major metropolises or capital cities. These medieval authors saw the individual, the political
order, and the city to be in sync.

Lahore flickers in and out of sight in a host of histories, travel
accounts, and geographies from the tenth century onward. The
tenth-century Persian geography *Hudud al-'Alam* described it as a
city populous and verdant but without any Muslims. The mid-
eleventh-century historian Baihaqi, writing from outside Kabul,

reported that Lahore was a city in a state of agitation and turmoil in his *Tarikh-e Baihaqi*. The Hindustani poet Khusrau, in Delhi in the late thirteenth century, marked the destruction of the city by the ravaging Mongol armies with the following: *az hadd samana wa ta Laohur / heech 'imarat nah magar dar Qasur* (from the borders of Samana to Lahore / no building remained standing until the city of Kasur). Abu'l Fazl's *Akbarnama*, the late sixteenth-century universal history of the reign of Mughal emperor Jalaluddin Akbar, declared Lahore a city open to all people and renowned for its crafts.

The seventeenth century marked a shift in history writing on Lahore. European merchants, doctors, courtiers, and travelers began to frequent the city and describe it as one of the important capitals of Hindustan to their home audiences. "Lahori Indigo" was one commodity that brought many of these East India Company merchants to Lahore. Access to various Mughal princes and kings was another. William Finch (d. 1613) describes the city as "one of the greatest," as does Thomas Coryat (d. 1617), who praises the wide streets and bountiful gardens. François Bernier (d. 1688) remarks on the beautiful brown women, and Jean-Baptiste Tavernier (d. 1689) welcomes the fine wines of Lahore (he also comments that the women of Lahore have no hair on their body). Niccolao Manucci (d. 1717) is taken with the industry, the shipbuilding timber, and the physicians. William Moorcroft (d. 1825) describes the city's craftspeople. Moorcroft remains buried in Lahore, in the Shalimar Gardens.

Much of this colonizing gaze is twofold—lavishing Lahore with praise while condemning it as decadent or barbaric. Finch is responsible for the apocryphal account of Anarkali as one of kingly excess and degeneracy—forever linking the city to the tragic tale of the immured poor servant woman. Once published and popularized by Samuel Purchas, Finch's account is retold by the other Europeans who write about Lahore. One or another form of violence stalks all accounts of Lahore written by these visitors.

As European philosophers and historians began to write their own versions of universal histories in the eighteenth century—Robert Orme, Edward Gibbon, Voltaire, Immanuel Kant, David Hume, Johann Gottfried Herder, Georg Wilhelm Friedrich Hegel, and Thomas Carlyle—these travel accounts were knitted together into a schematic project. James Mill inaugurated the tripartite division of the subcontinent's history with his 1817 *History of British India*. Mill fractured precolonial past into an "Ancient" Hindu "Golden Age," a despotic Muslim "Dark" Age, and a British "Liberal Age." The central tropes of the dark, medieval Muslim age were despotism, decay, and decadence. As the British colonial rule over Panjab began to take shape, such colonial renderings of the city became more prominent. Lahore in the early nineteenth-century accounts was "a melancholy picture of fallen splendour" with "lofty dwellings" that were "crumbling into dust, and in less than half century more will be levelled to the ground."[1] Debris, ruins, sterile soil are the main features of Lahore in many of the English accounts until the mid-nineteenth-century conquest of Lahore by the East India Company.

The colonial gaze on Lahore would soon accrue into an edifice of its own. John Lockwood Kipling (1837–1911), the founder of a new school of arts and the curator of the Central Museum in Lahore, would insist on collecting and prominently displaying the Gandharan Buddhist relics and monuments alongside objects and artifacts tied to Alexander's campaigns in the region. The "ancient" would take precedence over all other periods of history. Lahore, to him and his son, Rudyard Kipling, was a strange repository of the distant past, divorced from its immediate context. As Kipling Sr. would put it: "On a hot night there is no more fearful place in the world than Lahore. It is hell with the lid on."[2] Kipling Jr. provided his own take in his short story "The City of Dreadful Night" (1885), where sleeping men "lay like sheeted corpses," and "on either side of the road lay corpses disposed on beds in fantastic attitudes—one hundred and seventy bodies of men." It was a literally a city of death.

As a starting point, I collected all the histories of Lahore that I could locate. The intention was obvious—in order to write the city, I had to assemble an archive of writing on the city. I chose formal histories of the cities, the memoirs of those who lived in it or went back to it, the histories of organizing and planning the city, the journals and historians who narrated the city in the immediate aftermath of the Partition. How best to distill away the colonial renderings of the city? How to find the influence, if there was any, of the much longer writing on the city in Persian and Panjabi? These questions forced into relief the problem of writing a history of the city that did not start with the colonial powers but that did employ the formal structures of colonial knowledges that remain dominant to this day.

In her memoir of her family and life, *Meatless Days*, Sara Suleri remembers Lahore as a hard city, demanding "frequent tolls" and "behaving like a mirage."[3] It was a city built "upon the structural disappointment at the heart of pomp and circumstances."[4] I want to note that Suleri's structural disappointment is not the same as the jaundiced eye of Kipling seeing corpses of Lahoris everywhere. Yet, it does need to be marked as a site of violence in the aftermath of Partition. Suleri leaves Lahore, and her family, prompted by being "full of history."[5] This "history" is the dictatorship of Ayub Khan, the brutal war on civilians in East Pakistan, the bloodied creation of Bangladesh in 1971, and, most tragically, the refusal of her father and others to "see" the country that they had made:

> It was not so much the country's severing that hurt as the terrible afterimages we had to face: censorship lifted for a flash, flooding us with photographs and stories from the foreign press of what the army actually did in Bangladesh during the months of emergency that preceded the war. "I am not talking about the two-nation theory," I wept to my father, "I am talking about blood!" He would not reply, and so we went our separate ways, he mourning for the mutilation of a theory, and I—more literal—for a limb, or a child, or a voice.[6]

For Suleri, there was the literalness of the violence that needed to be recognized as such. Likewise, for me. It is not enough to just assemble the "facts" of Lahore as narrated across a thousand years, nor is it enough to point to the colonial fingers for being the scribblers of a hateful paradigm. The excess of one (colonial) cannot override the taint of the other (colonized), or vice versa. Suleri helped me see the "forgetting and remembering" that constituted her own experience of the city, and by extension, mine. What we choose to remember and what we seem to forget was clearly the leitmotif of my Lahore.

I.

Only a few scattered examples survive of writing *about* Lahore as a city. Mas'ud Sa'ad Salman's quatrains about Lahore from the eleventh century are important. The city is glimpsed in various official histories, memoirs, and geographies of the subsequent centuries but nothing that privileges the city above all else. By the seventeenth century, with Akbar's attention on Lahore, there were new buildings, new elites, and new narratives for the city. The new writings remained, however, embedded in the rather singular feature of writings about Lahore: a *public* and *peopled* city.

Jatmal Nahar's *Lahore ki Ghazal*, from the early seventeenth century, is a good example. The poem, in Hindustani, is about 110 lines and principally interested in describing street vendors and the public workers (hair cutters, cobblers, bakers, washers, and colorists). The poem describes the beauties (male and female) of the city and their features. Even when it comes to describing the physical landscape of the city, its gates, its gardens, its markets, its palaces, the poem frames it within the natural beauty of the inhabitants.[7] The people literally make the city.

By the mid-nineteenth century there was another model for writing the city, introduced by the colonial officers curious about the antiquity of cities like Delhi and Lahore, as well Damascus, Isfahan, and Cairo, as compared to European cities. They commissioned ethnographies of material cities—that is, accounts of prominent buildings, landmarks, neighborhoods, and the elite families that inhabited or governed such spaces. In some ways, this was the exact opposite of the existing model of writing about the city, elite and moneyed rather than public and dispossessed. Mirza Sangin Beg's *Sair al-Manazil* (Journey to Destinations, ca. 1821) was the product of the author's colonial employer commissioning him to write about Delhi. Syed Ahmad Khan's *'Asar-al-Sanadid* (The Remnant Signs of Ancient Heroes, 1847; expanded 1854) extended that model for Delhi with a fusion of an "encyclopedia of the city" and a "directory of notable births."

The arrival of colonial rule and the first Urdu printing press, Matba'i Koh-i Noor, which was established in 1849, brought to Lahore the same attention toward writing the city. Charles Raikes, a commissioner in Lahore, asked for a history of Panjab and of Lahore, which would be featured at the 1867 Imperial Exhibition in Paris. The commission landed with Mufti 'Aliuddin, who took the opportunity to finish a work that his father, Mufti Khairuddin Lahori, had begun in 1821. This resulting work, *'Ibratnama va 'Umdat al-Tawarikh* (Book of Moral Exemplars and Basis of Chronicles, 1854), is a momentous history, told with immaculate attention to sources, much of it asking the reader to learn from the decline of Muslim and Sikh political power.

The history is divided first into political spaces, and then into political rule. From a survey of the geography and natural landscape of Panjab, it moves on to Lahore. After a chronological overview, it discusses the main Mughal and Sikh monuments, followed by a history of Muslim rule in the subcontinent from the eighth century to the present. The next section focuses on the rise and fall of the Sikh polity in Panjab and in Lahore. The last section details the customs of the three main communities of Panjab and Lahore—Hindus, Muslims, and Sikhs—covering their saints and their customary practices and traditions such as marriages and funerals, dress, and foods, and concludes with a list of employees of the Sikh polity. It is an intimate account of the city, though the gaze is slightly detached from the fabric of everyday life, as if the text cannot shake the impression that it is being read by foreign, colonial eyes. The descriptions speak at the level of the "collective," or describe details, such as the meaning of certain rituals, in a way that natives would not. Yet, it remains one of the key histories to emerge in the nineteenth century on the city.

With the new ways of narrating the city and the colonial conscription of native scholars for the purpose of cataloging the city come two of the most significant pieces of writing on Lahore. The author of both works, Maulvi Nur Ahmad Chishti Lahori (1829–67), breaks from previous models, which see the city in terms of its geography or politics, and makes Lahore his explicit, and sole, focus. He also picks up the lost thread of writing about the city via its people and combines it with the newer model of a material understanding of the city. He does this in at least his two extant volumes on Lahore: the 1858 *Yadgar-e Chishti* (Chishti's Memorial) and the posthumous 1876 *Tahqiqat-e Chishti* (Chishti's Researches), published by the Koh-i Noor Press.

Maulvi Nur Ahmad Chishti Lahori came from a learned family that moved to Lahore a generation before his birth. His father had worked as a tutor for East India Company (EIC) officials, and eventually settled in Lahore. Chishti would first find employment with Ranjit Singh's administration and then, in 1849, followed his father's example and began working as a Persian and Urdu tutor for EIC officers. One of them, an assistant commissioner of Lahore, asked Chishti to write a book detailing the condition of the houses, shrines, graves, and mosques of Lahore. Chishti accepted the commission and produced a rich social history of Lahore.

Yadgar-e Chishti opens with a history of Lahore, and then turns to specific kinds of public sites and public spaces in Lahore. The first is the shrine, where Chishti describes the processes of how an ordinary Lahori may become a disciple to a particular shrine, how everyday veneration happens at shrines, and how seekers of relief beg for mercy or intercession from the sufi. From the shrine, he moves to the public street, where processions, shopping, celebrations, and festivals occur, drawing all types of religious communities (Hindu, Jain, Sikh, Shi'a, Sunni) and customs and traditions. He is ecumenical in his description, which is always intimate in detail, such as his account of his own curing of a seemingly possessed woman by "the judicious application of a thin branch" (his words).[8]

His other work, *Tahqiqat-e Chishti*, which was left unfinished due to his untimely death, is a monumental work on Lahore. Chishti lists some forty volumes of histories and chronicles that he either purchased or borrowed. In addition, he writes that he walked all over Lahore to interview the inhabitants and get both oral histories and documentary proof via documents and materials in their possession. He often reproduces these conversations and even written accounts in the body of his text. This history of the city has a pronounced ecumenical stance. He starts his account of Lahore outside the city walls, closer to Shalimar Garden, at the joint shrines of Shah Hussain (1538–99) and Shaikh Madho, whom Chishti introduces as "Madho Lal Hussain Lahori." Shah Hussain, a Sufi who was born and died in Lahore, is a unique figure because he eschewed conventional Sufi orders, decried those who were beholden to orthodoxy, consumed wine and intoxicants, sang, danced ecstatically, and often went unclothed. Relatively late in his life, he met and fell in love with a Brahmin boy, Madho Lal, who became his devotee. Their bond was so strong that Shah Hussain became known as Madho Lal Hussain, an amalgamation of their names. After Shah Hussain's death, Shaikh Madho became the holder of his patrimony and was eventually buried next to him, in the same shrine complex. Both were revered figures, and their shrines were the site of pilgrimage for Hindus, Muslims, and Sikhs as well as an annual festival of lights, Mela Chiraghan, which would remain the most important public procession in Lahore for hundreds of years.

The neighborhood of Baghbanpura, where the shrine is located, opens Chishti's sacral geography of Lahore. He next moves to the oldest temple in Lahore, Ganga Parbat. Then to Anarkali, to Miyani Sahib graveyard. Outside and inside the Walled City's gates,

Chishti marks a particularly dense network of codependent communities of faith, listing the miracles, the stories, and the individuals that are associated with each site in Lahore. He is physical in his descriptions, noting the number of steps from the street to the doorstep, charting all the cardinal points for each site and the streets that take you to and from there. He narrates Lahore in a spiral. It begins slightly off-center (outside the walls, at the shrine) but then circles around the old city in an increasingly tight pattern: the neighborhoods such as Basantnagar, Bhoray Shah, Baghbanpura, Garhi Shahu, Icchra, Chauburji, Mozang, Tabla Shah, Qila Gujjar Singh slowly come into view until we are deep inside the interior of the Walled City.

This is not a chronological account of the city, but rather an account of the city as an ecosystem of power and belief. Near the end of the text, a discussion of the etymology of "Shalimar" garden shifts into a discussion of the genealogy that extends from Mai Baghi (a Mughal noblewoman) to Raja Ram Chand, who was the founder of Lahore, to the broader histories of rajahs of Hindustan, to the coming of Alexander, and then Buddha, and from there to the arrival of Islam, and finally to a discussion of Akbar and Shah Jahan as rulers who ruled *be-taussab* (without prejudice). In essence, he devotes considerable attention to describing the multivalent histories of Lahore. His accounts of the lives of Guru Nanak, Guru Arjun, and Ranjit Singh brim with respect, admiration, and love. He narrates all the miracles that Guru Hargobind Singh and Guru Tegh Bahadur performed against the Mughal emperors. At every point in the text, Chishti marks the convergence of the communities that make up Lahore: the Hindu, the Sikh, and the Muslim. He privileges a nonsectarian view of history and a warm recognition of Lahore's diversity.

His Lahore appears populated by *samadhi, mazar, shavala, takia,* and *khanaqa*: in equal measures Jain, Sikh, Hindu, and Sufi holy places. Hence, from his very deliberate opening with Madho Lal Hussain to his pointed remarks about rulers who ruled with prejudice or violence that was enacted on non-Muslim populations, Chishti appears to be writing with an urgency of purpose about maintaining respect across religious differences.

Yet, such a city was already vanishing. This Lahore is a post-1857 Lahore where the EIC and Sikh rule has been replaced by the British Raj. The politics of a starkly divided present, past, and future for Hindus, Muslims, and Sikhs would have been readily apparent to Chishti. Though his language is light and direct, it is not impossible to interpret his work as an antidote against the divide-and-conquer politics of his present, as exemplified by his insistence on recording the love of a Muslim Sufi for a Brahmin boy, or the ways in which Sikh and Muslim piety are connected. Of course, a comprehensive interpretation of *Tahqiqat-e Chishti* eludes us because it remains unfinished (though the lithograph version is still around nine hundred pages).

The post-independence editing and publication history of Chishti's nineteenth-century texts provides a grim coda to the story. The editors of the 1975 *Yadgar-e Chishti* censored his clearly negative comments about a group in Lahore that followed Abdul Wahab, the reformer who laid the foundation of Saudi Arabia. Chishti called it a perilous sect that was leading Muslims astray. The editors replaced that sentence with an anodyne "some unbecoming critique is made of a religious group."[9]

Tahqiqat-e Chishti suffered an even worse afterlife. The two-volume critical edition published in 1964 by Punjabi Adabi Academy rearranged the whole text so that it opens with the foundation of Lahore, the Muslim rule in the subcontinent, and then the Sikh period. All the Sikh and Hindu sites and personages are gathered from across the whole work and combined into one section, placed in the middle of the first volume under the headline "Non-Muslim." Madho Lal Hussain is, thus, now on page 363. This was a philological partitioning with the intention of creating a safer text for consumption in Pakistan: an imbricated knot is unraveled.

II.

Figure 3.1. Badshahi Mosque with Ranjit Singh's Samadhi (2015)

The colonial rulers both remade Lahore and spurred a new dimension in writing about Lahore. Two figures from the late nineteenth century—Kanhaiya Lal Hindi (1830–88) and Syed Muhammad Latif (1845–1902)—are critical for understanding not only the deep history of Lahore but the history of their present. They were both employees, celebrated and honored ones, of the Raj in Lahore.

They both produced accounts on Lahore of deep intimacy—born of long life in the city but also a critical and analytic gaze upon it. Their texts on Lahore endure to this day as the definitive accounts of the city—more perhaps for the history they captured than for the present they inhabited. They are also paradoxical figures in their own relationship to the city and to its past. One a Hindu, the other Muslim, they read the traces of Lahore differently, but each does so with great care and a clear love for the city.

Kanhaiya Lal Hindi worked as an executive engineer for the Raj in the Barge and Development Ministry, earning the title of "Rai Bahadur" for his excellence. He took part in the building of various colonial structures in the city, including the High Court, the Women's Prison, and the Medical School. He wrote a number of educational manuals in Urdu and English and a treatise on morals and ethics (intended for his son), *Gulzar-e Lal* (The Garden by Lal, 1866), which was fairly popular.[10] He decided to write a history of the city at the insistence of his friends, who pointed out he had worked in and around the city for thirty years and knew it better than anyone else. He did not disagree. In fact, he recognized that his technical expertise and deep knowledge of Lahore gave him a great vantage point to think about it as a modern city. *Tarikh-e Lahore* (History of Lahore) was published in 1884 by Victoria Press in Lahore. He had previously published a highly regarded *Tarikh-e Panjab* (History of Panjab), in 1877.

Lal opens with a very brief notice of the early medieval roots of the city, only to mark the existence of the word "Lahore" in some early Persian histories and poetry. Quickly, he moves to the physical city. The book properly starts with the thirteen gates of the Walled City: Delhi, Akbari, Moti, Shah Alami, Lohari, Mori, Bhaati, Taxali, Roshnai, Masti, Kashmiri, Khizri, Yaqi. For each of the gates he provides an etymology, location, and the type of commerce associated with the markets that surround them. The thirteen gates set him up to describe the thirteen destructions of Lahore that immediately follow. Each time Lahore is destroyed,

Lal mentions the nature of the calamity and the resilience of the people of Lahore. The thirteen gates (open, inviting) and the thirteen destructions (by invaders, debilitating) mark the polarity he sees in Lahore, the city that continuously needs to be rebuilt and remade. It is a city marked by survival just as much as it is marked by destruction. The version of Lahore he is living through and writing in, he says, is the apex in the city's long past, and it was built by Ranjit Singh; for this, he is utterly grateful.[11]

The thirteen gates set up the central dichotomy of the book: *androon Lahore* (inside the Walled City) and *beiroon Lahore* (outside the Walled City). After the thirteen gates and thirteen disasters, the book provides an overview of Lahore's present educational institutes, its publications and press, and its people. These three things are the most critical aspects of Lahore's munificence and beauty. In people, Lal describes the *tawa'if* (trained musical performers), the calligraphers, the intellectuals (first Hindu and then Muslim), the poets, the physicians, the notable rich merchants—again first Hindus, then Sikhs, and finally the Muslims. Following this are major settlements and neighborhoods, first those inside and then outside the Walled City. Prominent religious sites—temples, gurdwaras, mosques—are next, and then Lal turns to prominent freestanding structures. In describing the monuments, buildings, and houses, Lal maintains the inside/outside division but also presents a heterogeneous landscape, including ninety mosques and shrines and also ninety temples and gurdwaras. Moreover, the beauty of Lahore lies in the collective strength of its diverse people. Of all of Lahore's many festivals, he presents the example of Madho Lal Hussain's Mela Chiraghan as the most important, where Hindus, Muslims, Sikhs, Christians, and Jain all participate.

When Lal stands and looks at the horizon from Anarkali, it is not just the minarets of the Badshahi or the Wazir Khan Mosque that interrupt his gaze, but also the tall spires of Dina Nath Temple, the Bhagat Ram Bakshi Temple, the Guru Ram Das Asthan, and the Raja Teja Singh Temple. In the process of listing

all these tall structures, Lal stresses how much Lahore's skyline
was shaped by Hindu and Sikh holy places. Similarly, his descriptions of the prominent neighborhood *havelis* and commercial
buildings on the busy thoroughfares of Lahore highlight the infrastructure built by the wealthy Sikh and Hindu patrons of Lahore. The book ends with an account of all that has been built,
improved, or developed by the British colonial state.

A unique feature of Kanhaiya Lal Hindi's history is that it provides details for all the city's key public and commemorated
places—their height and width, their construction materials, the
way in which they are inhabited, and the interior and exterior
views. Sometimes, he lightens the text with interviews, but the text
is shaped by his own technical expertise. When he describes the
colonial sites, he speaks as an engineer, giving exact measurements
in feet and inches and providing details on the sourcing of building
materials. He is proud of the work he himself has done as an engineer, ending his history with the construction of the Medical
School building that happened under his supervision.

Yet the materiality of his prose does not mask the importance Lal
places on those who live there and make the city. In fact, for Lal,
the Hindus, as the oldest inhabitants of Lahore, were the ones who
had kept the core of the city alive across centuries. The many trag-
edies that had befallen Lahore were offset by the many benefactors
of Lahore, many of them Hindus. He gives due credit to the Mughal emperors, Akbar, Jahangir, Shah Jahan, and Aurangzeb, for
building Lahore. Lal also credits Ranjit Singh with bringing prosperity and glory to Lahore that were unmatched in its history. It
was Maharaja Ranjit Singh who rebuilt Lahore to its fullest and
finest glory. It was Ranjit Singh who took his *darbar* (court) to the
shrine of Madho Lal Hussain during the festival of Basant (Kite
Flying). It was Ranjit Singh who rebuilt all the Mughal mosques,
gardens, and the fort that had been destroyed by the invasions from
the north. It was Ranjit Singh who persuaded learned Hindus and
Parsis to move to Lahore—figures such as the father of the renowned architect and philanthropist Ganga Ram (1851–1927).

Ganga Ram would later become known as "the father of Modern Lahore" for his work in building much of colonial era Lahore.

Like Lal, Syed Muhammad Latif was commended by the British with the title of "Khan Bahadur" for his services, first as a translator for Lahore's session judges and then as a member of the city's judiciary himself. His father, Munshi Muhammad Azim, opened the first English newspaper and press in Lahore, the *Lahore Chronicle*, in 1849.[12] Latif, who was conversant in Sanskrit, Arabic, Persian, English, and Latin, was a prolific historian of British India. He wrote his histories in English with extensive quotations from the original source languages along with his own translations. He relied heavily on colonial histories and historians, as befitting his membership in the Bengal Asiatic Society, and liberally inserted Latin phrases in his prefaces. In 1891, he published his *History of the Panjab from Remotest Antiquity to the Present Times* alongside an *Early History of Multan*. In 1892 came *Lahore: Its History, Architectural Remains and Antiquities*, and his final work was 1896's *Agra: Historical and Descriptive*.

Latif understood the British rulers as the *khalifa* (God's Shadow) on the earth. He is clear that with the exception one or two well-meaning rulers in history (Bikramjit or Akbar), the lot of the subcontinent had suffered and would continue to suffer under cruel, despotic rulers who were "slaves of their own sensual appetites," and that the common person lived under a "rapacious, tyrannical and hated" state of affairs.[13] Lahore had suffered terribly under the hands of both the Muslim and the Sikh rulers, but it was the British who had ushered in its golden age. It was only under the British, in Latif's estimation, that Hindus, Muslims, and Sikhs no longer senselessly killed each other. The British were responsible for the peace, the prosperity, the railway, and the telegraph. The purpose of his historical writing was to enlighten the reader (whom he addressed as the "young man" in all his prefatory remarks) about the beauty and brilliance of colonial rule.

Lahore is the city that best exemplifies the greatness of the British. Latif's *Lahore* is a detailed description of all the monuments

and architectural remains of the city, including his careful copy-
ing of all inscriptions and epigraphs (with his own translations),
as well as over a hundred pencil engravings and sketches of buildings in Lahore and a "Sketch Map of Lahore and Its Enviorns," at
a scale of 880 feet to an inch. The book opens with a sketch of
Lahore's history from antiquity to the arrival of the British. Then
he moves to descriptions of the architectural remains, divided
into the "Ancient" and the "Modern" period. Finally, the colonial
city and a section on the Lahore Museum and its holdings. This
new "modern" Lahore, Latif concludes, is the best city, with soil
that can grow "English flowers and vegetables," proof if any was
needed of its divine sanction.

Unlike Lal, Latif is much more circumspect about the everyday
people of Lahore. The inhabitants of Lahore are naive and taken in
by trickery or sorcery. He provides an account from the late sixteenth century where a holy man tricked Lahoris into thinking his
voice could carry from one bank of the Ravi to the other (his son
was hiding on the other side and mimicking his father's voice). Latif pointedly says that with the telegraph, such a feat is now a scientific reality, but no one is interested in learning the science; they
merely think the telegraph is magic. The people of Lahore are too
superstitious. Nor is he interested in marking out the special inter-
religious nature of sacral sites in Lahore. All of the Hindu and
Sikh sacral sites are restricted to a ten-page section at the end of the
"Ancient" section. Latif's *Lahore* provides a new orientation for the
city between its "Muslim" medieval and its "Colonial" contemporary
present. The Muslims of Lahore, Latif holds, must become edu-
cated and modern, just like their new rulers.

Latif's Lahore is a modern colonial city made so by the Brits'
investment in modern education and the creation of new universities. This makes Lahore the most important and vital city for the
future of the subcontinent. The cleanliness and orderliness are another gift from the British, Latif mentions, that has changed the
city. Finally, he says, Lahoris are now learning how to walk in

their city, because the roads have been cleared of debris and have been widened to allow for footpaths and pathways.[14]

Lal and Latif remain unparalleled for their scholarship on a Lahore that had vanished by the end of the 1940s. They captured the creation of the Sikh and British Lahores as it was happening around them. As contemporaries, they represent divergent futures for that same city: one Hindu, one Muslim, one saved by the Sikhs, and one built by the British. These renderings were not of Lahore as a palimpsest but as a series of segregations, in the past, the present, and the soon-to-be future.

III.

Figure 3.2. Refurbished Lakshmi Chowk with "Allahu Akbar" inscription (2015)

Lahore grew rapidly in the late nineteenth century. The population of the city proper nearly doubled between 1881 and 1911. Then it doubled again between 1911 and 1931, followed by another increase, by 45 percent, over the next decade. By 1941, it had become a city of nearly seven hundred thousand people. The presence of the colonial residential quarters for troops and officers, the Lahore Cantonment, the government infrastructure, the educational institutions, and the railway meant that from 1891 onward, there were generally two men for every woman in the city. Much of the working classes in Lahore were Muslim laborers, who came to the city for work. It was a city of migrant workers, migrant teachers, and migrant students. It was a male city, a laborer's city, a railway worker's city, a journalist's city. It was a public city.

New neighborhoods came into being outside old Lahore: Krishan Nagar, Sant Nagar, Ramnagar, Gawalmandi, and the planned community of Model Town. There were new reporters, new presses, new film crews, new sweet shops, and new clothing markets. The Swadeshi (Freedom) fighters, the Communists, the Congress Party stalwarts, the Unionists, the Arya Samaj, and the Muslim League were all enmeshed in the public life of Lahore. It is impossible to get a fully accurate read of the city's mood as people felt it then. Later accounts, such as the memoirs written in the aftermath of Partition, have a post-1947 vantage point and are thus colored by the passage of time. Such memoirs wrestle with the overwhelming sadness of what was to come. The novels of the period report a much more joyful, carefree domain of a male-centered social world.

Shopping, walking, eating, having tea, visiting the gardens were the chief activities of the flaneurs and the tourists. Certain shops and brands of Lahore were known across Hindustan—Bhalla Shoe Co., the clothier Dunichand & Sons, the jewelers Girdhari Lal, the tailor K.L. Mehra, the chemists Jagat Singh and Sons, the Metro Restaurant in the Melaram Building, and the Cosmopolitan Club in the Lawrence Gardens. There were public festivals like Basant, where kites were flown by the thousands from rooftops and from open spaces, and Lahoris competed to cut the strings of other kites (a traditional pastime requiring careful training and highly technical skills).

Those same rooftops were also places of socializing, intimacy, surveillance, romance, and boredom. Many of the old city's houses rose four or five stories, culminating in a small flat square or rectangular rooftop with a short wall that abutted neighbors on two sides and, in the rear, peered onto an extremely narrow alley. Some, perhaps many, of these rooftops contained overgrown mesh cages for pigeons. Breeding pigeons was another popular and technically engrossing "hobby" that consumed much of the male mind's focus. The rooftops were also spaces to dry, mend, and sew clothes, as well as to dry chilis. It was, after the courtyard, a social space dominated by women. This explains the fabled stories of first love across rooftop walls—unrequited and then requited—as well the surveillance of other rooftops, the gossip and rumors of the *mohalla* (neighborhood), and the censure and banishment of young women caught or ensnared in deviant activities, such as falling in love.[15]

Unsurprisingly for a city of mostly young men, the literature of the period is fixated on the sexual life of the city. Lahore was a city of brothels or a city full of "courtesans" (*tawa'if*), who were understood to be loose, licentious women, opening their second-story windows deep into the night, letting the walker know that they can take the narrow, high steps up to the *kotha* (roof) for an evening of song, dance, food and, perhaps later, more sensual and sexual play. Hira Mandi (colloquially taken to mean "Diamond" Market but actually named after the Sikh governor of Lahore, Hira Singh Dogra) looms large in the public imagination, then and now. Many a young man wrote about their first whispered call from a promoter (*dayal*) and the thrill of a first kiss or first sexual experience in their subsequent memoirs of Lahore. The Kiplings (Lockwood and Rudyard) did their best to memorialize this version of Lahore in their artistic, journalistic, and institutional output.

Were all these mere fanciful memories of an unrepentant sex trade, or did they contain the genuine trace of an erstwhile courtly culture that held music (vocal and instrumental) and the celebration of the body (both in motion and at rest) as the highest forms of artistic endeavor? It is hard to tell.[16] Music was public, and there were highly regarded performers and discerning consumers of music in Lahore. In December 1937, K.L. Saigal, one

of the great singers of Hindustan, gave a public performance at
Minto Park in Lahore that filled the park and the streets beyond.
There were also specialized markets: one for drums, one for *ghun-
groos* (anklets with a variety of bells attached), one for reed and
horn instruments.[17]

There were some women in the public sphere—mostly only in
advertisements, at bus stops, or at schools and colleges. The newspapers of the time reveal more than enough condemnation of their
presence. Still, the documentary evidence shows that women went
to movies, ate at restaurants, and walked along busy streets. The
Mall Road was a space for fashionable women to be seen, as were
the cloth markets, the jewelers, and so on. The cinema was more of
a mixed space, but one where "Ladies Only" shows allowed for
the mass consumption of the latest films, some from Lahore's
nascent film industry. The silver screen certainly featured women:
Alam Ara (1931), *Hunterwali* (1935), *Pind di Kuri* (1935), and
Sohni Mahiwal (1946) were some of the huge draws in Lahore's
cinemas. Still, only one group of women—the working poor—
likely made up the majority of women in public spaces, traveling
between houses and neighborhoods. The poor of Lahore appear
infrequently in the writings about this period; poor woman, even
less so.[18]

The city was not formally segregated, but class, caste, and religion did shape one's life and movement in the city. The planned
colony at some distance from Lahore, Model Town, was largely
occupied by professional and merchant upper-class Hindus and
Sikhs. Shah Alami and Begumpura had more lower-class Hindus.
Icchra and Mozang were majority Muslim.[19] Hindu and Muslim households still participated in collective eating traditions
and shared processions for marriage and for funerals. They had
common heroes, like the anti-colonial Hindu witness who,
when asked to declare his caste at the trial of anti-colonial "terrorist" Bhagat Sing (1907–1931), said: "I am a Hindustani by na-
tionality and a slave by birth."[20] Communists and Unionists hung
out together. Lawyers and journalists congregated at the Mall. The

writers, poets, organizers, and politicians who circulated across Panjab and north India sat in communally united living rooms to discuss politics, faith, and friendships. There were marriages across faiths, and there were businesses and households co-owned by people of different faiths.

Not many in Lahore imagined Partition would happen (at all, or in the manner it did) in 1947. Two of the memoirs of this period, from which much of the information above is taken, make this point over and over again. The authors, both of them Hindus from prominent families in Lahore, did not imagine Lahore would be part of Pakistan rather than India. They did not imagine the borders would be permanently closed and that they would not be able to return.

Som Anand's *Lahore ki Batain* (Talking about Lahore) from 1981 and Pran Nevile's *Lahore: A Sentimental Journey* from 1993 are thus "returnee" memoirs. They are written by men born and raised in Lahore and who left in 1947, but who later returned at some point and wrote these accounts after three wars and the creation of Bangladesh in 1971. That is to say, after the possibility of reconciliation or open borders was proven to be a fiction.

Nevile (1922–2018) and Anand (1929–2016) were contemporaries. They call Lahore of the 1930s and 1940s its "golden era," and the descriptions of their return to the city and their conversations with "Pakistani" Lahoris are full of nostalgia for the city of this era—the Lahore where Hindus, Muslims, and Sikhs lived together. They point to the Lahore Resolution of 1940 (which made the case for a separate homeland for Muslims) and the riots of the early 1940s, as moments when the fabric of the city began to tear apart. They write about the hope of a united Panjab or a united India, and when Sikander Hayat Khan or Khizr Hayat Khan Tiwana debated about the Muslim League. They write about the Muslims who helped the Hindus and Sikhs escape West Panjab and the Sikhs and Hindus who helped Muslims escape East Panjab. Even so, they write about their disbelief that the violence was happening. Anand writes that even when he is confronted by Muslim (Pathan) men who show up at their house in Model Town with lists of Hindu households to target, rob, and kill, his father is unconvinced that a pogrom is going on.[21]

They write of Lahore with great love and affection, not only for the city of their youth but for a world that must have seemed impossible to imagine in the 1980s and 1990s. The memoirs contain unique sketches of the city's neighborhoods and public spaces but also profiles of the larger-than-life people who inhabited it, moving between both subjects. What is important in the writings of these evacuees is their claim on the city. These are the Lahoris who lost not only their homes, their belongings, and their loved ones, but their city. It is not mere nostalgia or romance that seeps through these texts, though there are certainly traces of that. It is rather a direct claim of belonging and ownership. This was their Lahore.

IV.

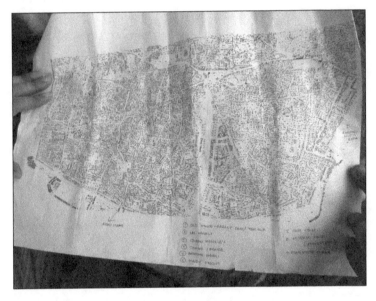

Figure 3.3. Printed map of Walled City (2011)

How did Lahore go from a city largely owned and governed by Hindus and Sikhs to one almost entirely bereft of them? What happened when that 44 percent or 54 percent—the percentages are contested—of Lahore left? What is incontestable is this: In 1947, two-thirds of the residential property in the city was owned by non-Muslims. The taxes and renumeration from the Sikh mercantile community accounted for 46 percent of revenue in La-hore. The Hindu community owned 167 out of a total 215 facto-ries in Lahore. The "non-Muslims" ran thirteen out of 16 colleges in the city, and 70 percent of candidates who sat for exams in Lahore were also non-Muslims. Only two out of fifteen insur-ance companies, and seven out of ninety banks (headquartered or having branches) in Lahore were owned or operated by Muslims. Not one of the twelve hospitals in Lahore was owned or operated by Muslims.[22] Before it became the Muslim city it is now, Lahore was as much a Hindu city or a Sikh city.

"Lahore must go to one State or the other—it cannot be both. But Lahore has been created by all Punjabis and not by Muslims or non-Muslims alone," wrote Evan Jenkins, the last colonial governor of Panjab, to the Viceroy of India, on March 7, 1947.[23] He also added that "Partition solves no problems and does not really make sense." Yet it could be said that the whole subconti-nent was jointly created by non-Muslims and Muslims. Such a fact of a shared history, however, was no longer the motor propelling the subcontinent forward at breakneck speed. It was the exact op-posite: an idea that nothing was shared or co-constitutive between Hindus and Muslims. Yet the Partition Committee continued meeting, collecting petitions and testimonies, all the time know-ing that it was in vain. All hopes of Lahore going to East Panjab or even becoming a "free city" with a common dominion came to naught when the Boundary Commission announced on Au-gust 17, 1947, that Lahore would indeed be in the western half of divided Panjab. Lahore then became wholly Muslim in a flurry of fire and violence.

Lahore ki Yadain (Memories of Lahore), the memoir of writer and journalist A. (Abdul) Hameed (1928–2011), provides a glimpse of the mechanics in Lahore between those called "evacu-ees" (those who left Lahore) and "refugees" (those who came to Lahore). Hameed and his family come to Lahore after 1947 from Amritsar. His family, as they step out of the train onto the station platform, are greeted with sniper rifle shots, and a Muslim League *razakar* (volunteer militia) asks them to crawl out from the station via a side street. "The Hindu-Sikh hoodlums were shooting at us," he recalls.[24] He takes his immediate family to safety in a neighborhood and then returns to the railway station. "I saw scared Hindu, Sikh women and men bundled together in small groups but certainly no Muslim was touching them and they left by train. The trains from Firuzpur (India) on the other hand were coming with Muslim bodies cut into pieces."[25] Hameed reports seeing a wounded Muslim die in front of his eyes. He remembers refugee camps that were overcrowded and filled with injured and dying Muslims.

Hameed's accounts of 1947–48 are more detailed than almost any other memoir by a Muslim man in Lahore during that period. The neighborhood of Shah Alami was burning, Hameed writes, but the mosque was intact (he considers this a miracle). He writes about entering houses abandoned by fleeing Lahoris to find sugar, pulses, rice, and grain still in the kitchen. Cutlery, bedding, furniture, documents are still in place. He enters first one house, then another, then another.

Finally, he decides on one particular house for his family, but he is interrupted by a policeman who claims it for himself.[26] Before Partition, he had been engaged in writing for newspapers and for film. But by mid-1948, he was one of a group of writers, journalists, and hangers-on who gathered at Pak Tea House and Pak Coffee House (the word "India," which had been embossed in cement in the name of both establishments, was replaced by "Pak" after Partition). They swapped stories of atrocities in Amritsar or Jalandhar. They understood it as a coordinated military effort to cull Muslims, known as *muslim kashi*.

In Hameed's memory, there was no violence against the non-Muslim populations in Lahore. The reason for such mercy, he concludes, is that "Muslims do not take up arms against civilians." He gives an example of an old Hindu woman sitting outside the Gawalmandi police station, who told him, "I will never leave Lahore. They say they will kill us. But I will not leave, this is my house."[27]

He writes that she was not harmed by anyone and her house was not looted, but she still disappeared a few days later (perhaps a victim of later mob violence). He contrasts this with eastern Panjab, where "non-Muslims took infants from the bosoms of Muslim mothers to toss them in the air and pierce them with spears."[28] Such anecdotes of individual old Hindu women *not* coming to any harm from Muslim mobs are rife in Muslim memoirs, and it begs the question about who was indeed harmed.

Hameed's family was eventually given an allotment for a house in Lahore's old city. He describes, after moving into the new home, raiding other vacant properties around their house for sugar, clothing, and household items. They and other families always did this at night, away from police detection.[29] A Hindu jeweler lived at one corner. He had converted to Islam in order to spare himself and his shop. He survived, but soon the refugees in the neighborhood made it dangerous enough that he also had to leave the neighborhood. The Muslims of Lahore took care of the newly arrived refugees, while Hindu shops and businesses were occupied and claimed. Bhalla Shoes was replaced by Karnal Shoes.

Much of Hameed's book is an invention of a new Lahore in living memory. Over 370 pages, his Lahore feels much like a fantastic city described in *One Thousand and One Nights*. There is an excess of romance and extravagance about the "Muslim-ness" of the city. He writes about film, theater, radio, writers' collectives, gardens, milk shops, *tongas* (horse buggies), wrestling, breakfast, each of which is imagined to be exclusive to Muslims, each given the golden hue of nostalgia. This Lahore is languid, magical, sometimes unruly. All the while, it surgically removes non-Muslim history from Lahore. This has been the dominant paradigm of writing on the city, especially since the 1970s, by Muslim men from Lahore.

These inventions continue to the current day. A celebrated painter of "Old Lahore," Ajaz Anwar (b. 1946), is someone who has worked tirelessly to preserve Lahore from modern encroachments, state neglect, and worse. His own collected memoirs of

Lahore, *Nain Reesan Shehr Lahor Diyan* (Inimitable Lahore City, 2003), are written in Punjabi and a delightful read. He is also a refugee from Ludhiana. In his Lahore, all the things already mentioned are the key markers of Muslim Lahore: grand and deserted cinema halls, various milk drinks, meat-heavy breakfasts, Volvo municipal buses (which I myself remember from the 1980s), roadside fruit stalls, colorful markets, and moving poetry. Yet it also makes for sad reading. This is a Lahore emptied of its Sikh and Hindu inhabitants. It is also a Lahore where there has been no violence against human beings—only a violence against material artifacts of history. Such is the Lahore after 1947, invented in the 1970s and projected back into the past.

Santosh Kumar's memoir, *Lahorenama* (Book of Lahore, 1983), captures this in a profound way. Kumar, who left Lahore at Partition, returned to seek some of the now invisible markers of Sikh and Hindu life in the city. He goes to the Gita Bhawan building near Lakshmi Chowk, where the verses from Bhagavad Gita, *Yada yada hi dharmasya glanirbhavati bharata / Abhythanamad-harmasya tadatmanam srijamyaham* (Whenever there is decay of righteousness, O Bharata / and there is exaltation of unrighteousness, then I Myself come forth), had been engraved on a plaque. They were erased in the early 1980s.[30] There had been a statue of Lakshmi atop the building, but it had been set on fire at Partition. The Sunehri Gurdwara had disappeared. The Hanuman Mandir had been replaced by an embroidery shop.[31] The temple of Kali had become a house, and its street name was changed from "Kocha Kali Mata" to "Kocha Aurangzeb."[32] Everywhere he turned, Kumar saw the traces of hundreds of years of his own family's history in Lahore erased and forgotten. The sights and sounds of Lahore that Pakistani writers, Hameed and others, take up as their own heritage had been partitioned from the city's Hindu and Sikh history.

My maternal grandfather was entitled to make a direct "claim" at the Central Record Office in Lahore for property and land he had left behind in Baramulla Kashmir. He never felt the need to make that claim because he always imagined he would be able to return to his gardens and his house. My grandmother, some six decades later, would still mention that she had keys to properties that they had left behind. Instead, my grandfather, who before Partition had been coming and going from Lahore for some time and was familiar with the city, purchased a claim from someone else. That property, 350 Lahore Road, was on the outskirts of the city, but in the market center of the Cantonment. It was owned by a Hindu family who fled or was driven out, or perhaps left for another reason. They were not there by the time our family moved in. All the surrounding houses on the street were also homes of Hindu evacuees who had fled.

My mother was born in that house, and it was in that same house that my father, himself a new migrant to the city in 1965, rented a room. They were married in 1969. This house was the doorstep from which I first saw Lahore. My grandfather, much later, would tell me stories of how he had moved away from the old city (where much of his Kashmiri relatives were living then and now) to his new home on Lahore Road. I cannot pretend to quote him, as I was in my early teens at the time and we had already moved away from that house to another, which was closer still to the border with India. I remember him sitting in the tiny patch of green in his semi-reclined rattan chair, saying a darkness had fallen everywhere, and in that darkness people took everything that did not belong to them. He died long ago, and I never got the chance to ask him any questions.

V.

February 10, 1947. "120 Arrested in Lahore," Reuters: "The first fatal casualty since the Moslem League's agitation in the Punjab began over two weeks ago was reported tonight."

March 5, 1947. "30 Killed, 47 Hurt in Riots in Lahore," Reuters: "Police fired twenty rounds into brick-throwing crowds and clamped an eleven-hour curfew on the city."

May 15, 1947. "Lahore Riots Renewed," United Press International: "Twelve persons were killed and more than twenty injured in communal riots that began in Lahore."

May 19, 1947. "Thousands Flee from Lahore," Associated Press: ". . . seeking to escape bomb and brickbat fights between Hindu, Moslem and Sikh mobs, which have caused at least fifteen deaths."

June 17, 1947. "Bomb Damage in Lahore," Reuters: "Fifty-four persons, including eight policemen, were injured when a bomb exploded in the courtyard of a Hindu hospital here today."

June 22, 1947. "Punjab City Swept by Arson, Bombing," Reuters: "From the roof of the Reuters' office in Lahore at sunset smoke could be seen rising along two-thirds of the horizon and fresh fires were blazing in the suburbs about a mile away. About 150 homes were gutted. Death toll at 71."

June 24, 1947. "Walled City Is in Ruins," *New York Times*: "This beautiful city of roughly a million inhabitants has been about one-sixth destroyed. . . . After Saturday's holocaust, which almost razed two crowded business sections . . ."

July 21, 1947. "Rioting in Lahore," Reuters: "Infuriated Moslems stabbed four Sikhs to death after four Moslems had been killed and fourteen injured by a bomb alleged to have been thrown by a Sikh. Moslems then set fire to four homes."

August 15, 1947. "Deaths in Lahore Reach 153 as Flames Sweep the City and Looting Spreads," Associated Press: "Twenty-three shops were on fire in the rich Anarkali shopping center outside the walled city. Five Sikh temples were in flames elsewhere in Lahore."

August 30, 1947. "Screaming Sikhs Raid Lahore Train," *New York Times*: "On the India side of the border the railroad tracks in places were lined with the bodies of Moslems and on which vultures had left their quick and horrible marks. When we passed into Pakistan occasional dead bodies lying in the sand and identifiable by their clothing were Hindus and Sikhs."

September 1, 1947. "Lahore Now City of the Dead, Veritable Civil War in Land of Five Rivers," *Times of India*: "Outside the overcrowded refugee camp hardly any Hindus or Sikh are to be seen, and the few that are visible have a hunted look."

September 22, 1947. "Moslems Attacked in Train and at Amritsar—Hindus Are Killed at Lahore," *New York Times*: "In the Lahore railway station, twenty-one persons were killed when Moslems attacked a Hindu-Sikh refugee train."

September 23, 1947
My Son Bashir Ahmed,

Asalam-o-Alaikum. I hope you have received my previous letter and you are fully safe. With great sorrow it is to be stated that all of our relatives in Sultanpur Lodhi have been put to death. Below is a list of our relatives, including our closest. The sorrow of their deaths is beyond the reach of writing. The names of the martyrs are: 1) Babu Badruddin Sahib 2) Mushtaq Ahmad 3) Firuzuddin (injured) 4) Khair Bibi from your in-laws 5) Azim Muhammad Ul-lah including his wife (Mina) and children 6) Your wife including children 7) Atta Muhammad 8) Daulat Bibi, wife and children except Professor and children 9) Mamun Sahib Muhammad Ibrahim 10) Muhammad Ali 11) Haji Sahiba 12) the son Qaim Din

In brief, no person has survived. Only the wife of Babu Badruddin and two small girls. It is rumored that they are safe. But they have not been able to reach Lahore. Only God knows if they are alive or buried alive. Dear Kalsoom and her younger sister who was betrothed to the late son Saeed Ahmed is still missing. Presumably in the custody of the oppressors or put to death. It is the reality that none of our people there have survived.

Yesterday, 22 September, I went to Sadr Lahore. The people are safe there. Respected Khala is afflicted with a fever and rash for days. Your father, mother and sister are also afflicted with rash. Above all are these days of sorrow. Clouds of grief are everywhere one looks. May God forgive our faults. Ameen. Since you are traveling, and alone, try not to carry this grief on yourself. May God heal these wounds. Ameen.   Continue to write a letter about your safety. Son Muhammad Fazil is content and happy and sends his greetings. Nowadays, I am living in Kissan building. Write to me at the address below. Wasalaam. Khuda Hafiz.

Tajuddin Ahmad Faruqi aka Allah Rakha.
With consideration
MA Mumtaz and Company
Australia Building
McLeod Road
Lahore
23.9.47.[33]

September 30, 1947. "1,000 Indians Die in Flood of Camp," Reuters: "Fearing that even this natural misfortune would be attributed to the Sikhs and Hindus and that trouble would result, the West Punjab Government sent criers with drums through the streets of Lahore's old city on Sunday night to announce that the River Ravi floods were caused by heavy rains in the North Punjab hills and not by sabotage."

September 1947. *Bleeding Punjab Warns* (pamphlet), by communist activist Dhanwantri: "The biggest single case of arson, the setting fire to the big Hindu area at Shahalim Gate (on June 21, 1947) was carried out as everyone in Lahore knows, when a civilian official, Mr. M.G. Cheema, an assistant magistrate of Lahore, personally supervised this operation. A strong Muslim police party and a gang of Muslims equipped with quantities of petrol systematically set fire to the whole bazaar till it was burnt down to ashes."[34]

The facts and figures that have preoccupied historians, politicians, and memoirists since 1947 fail to capture the encroaching drumbeat of disaster that the residents of Lahore must have felt. By the end, if there was ever an end, 4.5 million Hindus and Sikhs swapped places across the border with 5.5 million Muslims.[35] Nearly all of Lahore was engulfed in riots, fires, explosions, and terror, and the streets filled with refugees and evacuees. Those Muslims who survived the massacre on the other side of the border reached Lahore numb and enveloped in clouds of grief. It is impossible to see this destruction. The records insist on reporting casualty totals aggregated by religion—Muslim, Sikh, Hindu—when everyone killed was a Lahori.

Who was what before being killed? Who became something after? The accounts of Partition violence move in a surreal fashion across identities and neighborhoods. Take this slightly altered narrative comingled from several sources:

A Hindu man from Lahore works as a journalist or as a writer or as a publisher. He lives in Model Town or Anarkali or Icchra. His friends, lifelong friends, are also writers, journalists, poets. They eat, drink, hang out. They are Muslims. They live in a semi-bubble of working-class professionals who look with a sardonic gaze at the politicians, the rallies, the demands for separation.

How is it possible, they ask each other, that their city or their lives can be partitioned? Yet a bomb blast on August 9 in a cinema outside Bhatti Gate shakes him up.[36] He rushes to his Muslim friend's house. He does not want to stay outside. The building where they used to print his newspaper, *Bishan Das*, goes up in flames.[37] He confesses to his Muslim friend that he wants to stay in Lahore, no matter what.[38] That friend breaks all contact.

He meets another Muslim friend at Nagina Bakery on August 15.[39] Next to their table, a group of Muslim men chat about who they killed last night. They look at him. He wonders if they will ask him to prove that he is not a Hindu. He learns that his teacher, Professor Brij Narain, the head of the Economics Department at Punjab University, has been murdered by his own assistant. He returns home to Anarkali to find a riot in progress; dead bodies lie on the ground. He runs. He goes to the camp at D.A.V College, where Hindus and Sikhs waiting to be evacuated are kept under guard. He wants to enter but they ask him to prove that he is a Hindu. He shows them the blued tattoo "OM" on his wrist and he is allowed entry.[40] As he leaves Lahore, his remaining Muslim friends hug him and they weep in each other's arms.

The composite account above comes from a series of memoirs written after the Partition. Fikr Taunsvi (1918–87) published his account of leaving Lahore, *Chhatta Dariya* (The Sixth River), in 1948. Gopal Mittal (1906–93) published his, *Lahore Ka Jo Zikr Kiya* (When Lahore Was Mentioned), in 1971. They are both diaries of witnessing violence and destruction, of being confronted by their own friends about whether it is wise to remain in Lahore. Taunsvi tries to imagine converting to Islam, but detests religion too much to follow through. Mittal does not want to live as a *dhimmi* (a protected category under Muslim law) in his own city. Both leave with great reluctance. They describe their last days in Lahore as if they were in a fugue state. They are writers, yet cannot find words for what they saw and felt—the smashing of their gods, the burning of their holy sites, the distance in the eyes of their childhood friends.

Santosh Kumar (1927–2021) came back to Lahore in 1980 and published an account of his visit in *Lahorenama* (A Book of Lahore, 1983). In it, he featured nine photographs taken in Lahore by Govind Lal, a freelance press photographer, in 1947. Kumar introduces these photos as "Burning Lahore." The first is captioned "A horrifying portrait of a burning Lahore at *Batwara* (Partition)."[41] It shows several burnt and collapsed houses. Another photo shows a soldier standing guard in front of bricks and mortar and tendrils of smoke. "Lanes are destroyed but at least we still have guards," reads the captions.[42] The next was taken inside the old city. It shows a small cluster of people in the deep background. The foreground is dominated by rubble and collapsed beams. Another photo shows shops after a fire, with people trying to buttress collapsing roofs with wood beams.[43]

The celebrated photographer of Lahore, Faustin Elmer "F.E." Choudhry (1909–2013), worked for the *Civil and Military Gazette*, and later for the *Pakistan Times*. He sent negatives of his work in Lahore in 1947 to the Bureau of National Reconstruction, which published *Struggle of Independence: Photograph Album, 1905–1947* in March 1970. Only 3 of the book's 238 pages are dedicated to the events of 1947, under the heading "Influx of Refugees." There are no photographs of any destruction in Lahore, no ruins, no fires. Only a single photograph is captioned, "A painful scene of Muslim victims of the Punjab riots in 1947," with no location specified. It shows a mass of bodies in an urban street. All the photographs in Lahore are of refugees arriving on horse carts, bullocks, buses, and trains. "Citizens of Lahore provided relief to destitute refugees," and "All sections of the Lahore public offered their services for the relief of refugees" are the only captions. Most of the eighteen photographs show ordered, clean camps with professional helpers.

Alongside the erasure of the Hindu and Sikh populations of Lahore, the events themselves were sanitized and recontextualized. The atrocities committed on Muslims happened on the other side of the border, and the rehabilitation of the refugee

happened on this side of the border. Most memoirs about Lahore by Pakistani authors will hew to this narrative. The Hindus
and Sikhs, to whom Lahore belonged if it belonged to anyone,
would return to the city in the 1970s and 1980s, and their writings fail to capture the breadth of this erasure. How could they?

VI.

"Care has also been taken to avoid unnecessary details based on fiction and superstition."[44] The necessity of sifting through the various historical accretions to set forth a true, scholarly picture of a city must have been apparent to Muhammad Baqir (1910–93). In 1952, when he published his *Lahore: Past and Present*, he was chair of the Persian Department at the University of the Punjab. His effort was the first scholarly work on Lahore produced by a Pakistani for the new state's new city. As a work of scholarship, it is meticulous and thorough. His method was to reproduce all extant or available sources that explicitly mention Lahore from around the middle of the tenth century to 1952. The book is divided into two parts: "History" and "Description."

He divides Lahore's past chronologically into the Pre-Muslim Period, the Hindu Period, the Muslim Period, the Sikh Period, the British Period, and the Pakistan Period. The Hindus (or non-Muslims more broadly) disappear from history once the book moves out of their period. In this, Baqir mimics the tripartite division of the subcontinental past introduced in the early decades of the nineteenth century by James Mill in his *History of British India*. There, the division broke down into the "Ancient Hindu," the "Dark" Muslim, and the British Liberal. As with Baqir, this progression can only think in exclusions—in the period following the Hindu Period, the "Hindus" disappear as the putative political regime shifts to non-Hindus. Baqir is not merely replicating colonial forms of knowledge; he is creating a new edifice for Pakistan's professional historians to sequester the non-Muslim past of their newly partitioned country.

Baqir's history sets the tone for much of the scholarly work to follow, and not only because it becomes the definitive aggregation of all primary sources leading up to and including the British period. No subsequent historian would care to revisit those manuscripts to re-transcribe or retranslate them. Baqir's method—to select and translate excerpts in order to define the boundaries of knowing Lahore—matches that of earlier East India Company colonial projects. This was the approach of the eight volumes of Henry M. Elliot and John Dowson's *The History of India, as Told by Its Own Historians*, published between 1867 and 1877, which also excerpted and translated selections from a thousand years of the Muslim past in the subcontinent, but with the aim of giving a highly prejudiced colonial perspective of this history.

Writing Lahore in a particular way is a necessary component of the larger nationalist project. An early example is Baqir's quotation from Fakhrudin Mudabbir Mubarakshah's *Adab al-Harb wa'al Shuja'a* (Proper Conduct of War and Valor, ca. 1220s), where Mubarakshah provides an account of the origins of Lahore: "In Lahore, where now stands a mosque, once existed a temple. The Raja ordered an icon be carved from stone and installed with the name 'Sun' as he was a Sun-worshipper and he lived for a long ninety-three years and ruled Lahore for seventy-five years."[45] Mubarakshah, in this account and elsewhere in his work, pays ample attention to Lahore's history before being conquered by Muslim rulers. The presence of a sun temple (very much like the important sun temple in Multan) would indicate Lahore's continuity as a living city prior to Muslim rule. Baqir only glosses over this. In fact, he makes no comment on the quote he has judiciously chosen and translated.

Yet his approach is not to merely present the historical "facts" about Lahore from contemporary sources Describing the conquest of Lahore by Ranjit Singh in 1799, he gives credit to the "Ara'ins of Lahore [who had] approached Ranjit Singh at Rasulnagar and invited him to capture Lahore."[46] This should be read with the contextual knowledge that the Ara'in community had become one of the important caste groups in Punjab after Partition. Later, Baqir assigns blame for the fires in Lahore on March 5, 1947: "As a result of . . . inflammatory propaganda Hindus and Sikhs suddenly burst forth into violent incendiarism. Disturbances started in Lahore and spread all over the province. . . . The trouble in Lahore originated with the taking out by Hindus and Sikhs of a procession. . . . Some 200 or 300 Hindus and Sikhs walked through the bazaar shouting 'Pakistan Murdabad' (Death to Pakistan)."[47] The source Baqir provides for these claims is the *Civil and Military Gazette* from 1950, which was published much later than the event recounted and was certainly colored by the biases of contemporary concerns. In essence, Baqir provides a very specific nationalist slant in a history supposedly aimed at removing inaccuracies and biases.

Lahore is excised and simplified. In Baqir's history, there is no mention of Madho Lal Hussain's presence in Lahore aside from a brief sentence in the section on Shalimar. Nor does he mention Data Ganj Baksh's shrine and history in Lahore. This move away from defining Lahore through its history of devotion and piety that transcended boundaries of sect and creed is also apparent in the scant mentions of any surviving (or historical) temples in Lahore. His Lahore has always been Muslim, and will now look forward to remaining so under Pakistan. Baqir's section on the "Pakistan period" is also noteworthy because he gives an inordinate twenty pages to Muhammad Reza Shah Pahlavi's visit to Lahore on March 9, 1950 (the first dignitary to visit the new country), four pages to the Rawalpindi Conspiracy Case (presenting solely the perspective of the state), and two to the removal of colonial statues, such as that of Governor John Lawrence on August 25, 1951.

A slightly different approach yields another paradigm for writing Lahore. Muhammad Tufail (1923–86) was a publisher and author who began an Urdu literary and criticism journal, *Naqoosh*, in

1948. He would take over as the sole editor in 1951. *Naqoosh* was censored when it published Sa'adat Hasan Manto's short story "Khol Do" in its third issue under the editorship of Ahmad Nadim Qasmi. Under Tufail, *Naqoosh* would become one of the most prominent Urdu journals in the subcontinent, known especially for its "special issues" that compiled across a thousand or more pages new writings or rare, unpublished archival findings.

A special *Naqoosh* issue, titled "Lahore Number: From the Ghaznavids (1014 CE) to the Present Age" came out in February 1962. The full issue is 1,193 pages. It opens with a couple of panoramic shots of Lahore, followed by thirty-six more photos of prominent monuments, mosques, and buildings, restricted to the Mughal or the British period. Tufail introduces the issue in his editorial note. His intention, he writes, is to produce an archival issue more comprehensive than all existing books on Lahore. "All cities are cities, but some cities are protectors of entire civilizations and cultures for those who live in them. Lahore is one such city. *Naqoosh* has attempted to preserve the historical, religious, and cultural heritage of Lahore."[48]

This special issue of *Naqoosh* includes largely unpublished works, commissioned by Tufail from the leading journalists, historians, cultural critics, writers, and poets in Lahore. The first section is organized chronologically—with a series of short essays by various authors—from the tenth century to the beginning of the British period. Later sections include: the monuments of Lahore, Lahore's golden age (Mughal), the Sikh period to the modern period, theologians of Lahore, "Mosques," "Libraries," "Temples" (a short, eight-page section with twelve entries), "Colleges," "Vocalists" and "Singers" (forty-four men, twenty-six women but all Muslim), "Musicians" (over fifty, again all Muslim), "Wrestling Gyms" and "Famous Wrestlers," "Physicians," "Poets," "Writers," "Historians," "Calligraphers," and finally, "Personal Memorials" about Lahore by prominent literary figures.

A recurring motif in this last section is the insistence that "Lahore is the same"—the same, one imagines, as the Lahore before

Partition. Hafiz Jalandhari contributes a poem, "Wohi Lahore!" (That Same Lahore), which includes the line: *zalzalay, aag, aandhian, sailab / laie tashrif aur chal diyay nakam* (earthquakes, fires, storms, floods / came with honor and departed unsuccessful). A small essay near the end, "Chand Khunchkan Manazir" (Some Blood Curdling Scenes) by Ghulam Rasool Mehr, focuses on the Sikh period, depicting it as a terrible evil that befell Lahore. Partition is barely mentioned in the thousand pages.

As a compendium, "Lahore Number" shares much of the framework of Baqir. It is meticulous in writing aspects of the city's Hindu and Sikh past out of its history. It presents a city that has remained the same for over a millennium, even if the city itself was heavily changed by Partition. The listing of notable figures and sketches of the "culture" of Lahore, with a heavy emphasis on music, wrestling, and the literary arts, ordained Lahore as "Urdu" and thus Muslim. Much more powerfully than Baqir, "Lahore Number" would become the encyclopedia for Lahore's past. It solidified the source material for writing the city, turning future authors toward a specific orientation with the city's past. These massive compilations by Baqir and Tufail are matched by the physical erasure of temples, Devanagari and Gurmukhi scripts, and street and neighborhood names, giving birth to a Lahore that is partitioned not only from its past but from those who had built it and lived in it. This last erasure is the lasting epistemic violence on this city.

VII.

Figure 3.4. Prospectus map of new colony schemes (2015)

The city is written in wood, bricks, glass, and cement. It is written in its clusters of buildings, the roads that connect them, its open spaces, and its closed loops. It is written in the movements of goods in and out of the city; its social infrastructure, the availability of air, land, and water; its protection from fire, water, disease; its measures for safety; its reduction of harm. Lahore was certainly burned and rebuilt more than a dozen times over the thousand years of its history, and the loss of life and property was severe each time, but the fires that burned in 1947–48 remain a singular event.

Partition cut Lahore off from the east, where its most significant relationships had existed for a hundred-plus years—with Amritsar and with Delhi. The border sealed it off. It also sealed off Lahore's sources of capital, labor, technical expertise, and infrastructure (mainly, the railway and the Grand Trunk Road). The new Lahore (as with the new state) would need to invent its own supply chains and sources of such resources. The western half of partitioned Panjab (now just "Punjab") would reorient the power base for both the city and the country. The landed elite and the labor force of Punjab would shape the military, industrial, and cultural focus of the new nation-state, and Lahore would be the first site of this transformation. In a 1951 census survey of labor force, Muhajirs (refugees from India) numbered 335,294 out of total population of 632,136.[49] In another decade, the population would grow to 1.2 million.

Lahore before the nineteenth century was a walled city situated next to a wide, flowing river, surrounded by a thick greenbelt with three massive arterial roads—one to Amritsar, one to Multan and one, across the river, to Srinagar. A series of more than thirty villages (some denoted as *mohalla*, some as *-pura*, some as *-abad*) were arranged in a semicircle. Much of everything else was active agricultural land, with some brick and leather industry to the south. The British, their railway, and their Cantonment dictated that this wider Lahore be more closely knit with roads, markets, and public transportation. Planned communities based on "Garden City" models were proposed—and some were successful, such as the Cooperative Model Town Society, founded in 1924.

The Lahore Improvement Trust was launched in 1936 to coordinate and manage the flow of Lahore's population. The "older" townships and the new housing communities were merged (the Cantonment, designed to house active military, remained apart).

After Partition, beyond the influx of refugees, there was an internal migration to Lahore as one of the new country's two cities, even despite its severely crippled infrastructure. New schemes to house the growing population of Lahore were created seemingly on the fly, including the Shadbagh Scheme, Gulberg Scheme, and Samanabad Scheme in the first few years. The city also embarked on a series of institutional changes to its governance in the first full decade after 1947. The Water and Power Development Authority (WAPDA) and the Water and Sanitation Agency (WASA) joined the already existing Lahore Municipal Corporation to manage the city.

The first *Master Plan for Greater Lahore* was finished in 1966, but it wasn't approved until 1973. The plan took a holistic look at Lahore's condition and charted possible sites for its future development—which, it noted, could only occur south of the city.[50] It noted that 52 percent of the residents in Lahore were migrants, and that there was no stable schooling, affordable housing, and health services for the majority of the population. The markets were specialized and unequally distributed. There were major choke points on the arterial roads in and out of the city. The conditions of the roads within the city were poor. There were no pavements, and the majority of deaths were those of pedestrians hit by vehicles. There were only sixty-nine parks and thirty-two cinemas for 1.2 million people.[51] The biggest problem, however, was clear and simple: 89.1 percent of Greater Lahore was private property.

The solutions the master plan offered were to build a new Green Belt (the old one had disappeared after 1947), to create more divisional centers (for municipal administration), to construct thirty thousand more homes geared for small families on small tracts of land, and to diversify the markets so people did not need to travel from one sector to another. The plan recommended the incorporation of *katchi abadi* (or "urban villages," denoting unsanctioned, semipermanent dwellings) into the city with health and sanitation services. This is where the vast majority of the city's domestic and municipal labor lived. The "outskirts" of the Cantonment and south of the city, beyond Model Town, were reimagined as a permanent agricultural zone that would be the future source of food for the city. The plan also recommended a new bridge over the Ravi River to ease the traffic bottleneck, along with a light-rail line circling the city for laborers and workers. In 1975, Lahore Development Authority (LDA) was launched to implement this plan. In order to build new housing, to purchase land, and to provide necessary services, the agency sought funding. The World Bank stepped in.

The World Bank later funded another master plan, titled *Lahore Urban Development and Traffic Study* (1980), which sought to reframe and privatize much of the land outside Lahore. But, in terms of reshaping Lahore, a more consequential move had already happened. The country's dictator, General Zia ul Haq, issued the "Pakistan Defence Officers Housing Authority Order" in 1980. It was a national order to create a housing scheme for the warriors and martyrs of Pakistan's armed forces. The scheme existed outside of any municipal structure, paid no taxes to the city, and was governed by a serving military commander.

In Lahore, this new "Defence Housing Authority" (DHA) superseded the already existing Lahore Cantt Cooperative Housing Society, and set itself up as outside the jurisdiction of the Lahore Municipal Corporation. DHA announced its own master plan, which consisted of nine "phases." Unlike the capital limitations of LDA, DHA did not need to buy any property—it worked by having property deeds transferred to its name by middlemen, who were then compensated by plot allotments in the scheme. In other words, DHA enabled the creation of a highly coercive property mafia. These speculators converted the entire agricultural zone surrounding Lahore into large housing plots that could only be leased and built upon by the remarkably wealthy. All the land acquired in this way belonged to DHA (the property was simply leased to the "file holder"). DHA took much of the property that belonged to the Evacuee Trust Property Board; it gobbled up "urban villages" that consisted of arable farmland. Money came into Lahore (and into Pakistan) from the mid-1970s onward via remittances from the Gulf countries and, after 1979, from the forty years of wars against communism and global terror. This money translated into large, enclosed colonies with gargantuan houses with a sparkling *Masha'allah* (God's Will) sign installed on its facade.

LDA, which already had a Cantonment area outside its jurisdiction, now had to plan outside DHA neighborhoods (called "colonies" in everyday parlance) as well. A new *Integrated Master Plan for Lahore* was created in 1998 and approved in 2004. It aimed to provide a road map for developing Lahore until 2021. It estimated that the population in 2021 would be around 10 million—by 2001, it was nearly 8 million, and today it is around 12 million. The study for the plan found that Lahore had no functioning public transportation. The city's groundwater level (one of the main sources of potable water in much of the city outside the Walled City) was shrinking at 4 feet per year. It was at 15 feet in 1961, fell to below 50 feet in 2000, and in many areas stood below 150 feet in 2022.[52] There was excessive waste and insufficient drainage, and much of the city was in a floodplain. None of the "urban villages" had been incorporated, and municipal services and waste management (sewage as well as refuse landfills) went unmanaged. By the late 1990s, more than three hundred such *katchi abadi* existed in the city. No property taxes went toward LDA, which was unable to coordinate with the more than 150 housing schemes in the city.[53]

The Walled City is the densest part of Lahore. In 1985, there were 285,000 people living in an area of slightly more than one square mile. There were only 22,500 houses, which often had up to seven people to a room. Lanes between the houses were only three or four feet wide. Almost 30 percent of mixed-use buildings were in extreme dilapidation.[54] By 2004, much of that population had moved out of the Walled City to DHA neighborhoods or other schemes. However, commercial warehouses and markets have moved in, making the neighborhood even more congested. Much of the electric infrastructure was installed in an ad hoc manner and exposed, leading to frequent fires in the area (more than a third of all Lahore's fires originated in the Walled City). There were no green areas, no open spaces, and no venues for other forms of recreation.

The 1966 *Master Plan for Greater Lahore* identified forty-eight places of significant historical importance in Lahore that were to be protected as monuments or antiquities. There were only two that were not associated with the Muslim past—the Well of Raja Dina Nath and the Samadhi of Ranjit Singh. The 2004 master plan had 56 sites listed under the Antiquities Act of 1975 and another 104 under the Preservation Ordinance of 1985. Other than the Samadhi of Sir Ganga Ram, nothing from the city's Sikh or Hindu past made it on the list.

The meager planning documents of the municipal government that are available to the public (documents belonging to DHA or private landholding entities are not available) offer a skewed perspective, because they are writing the city in a way that is beyond their control, legally and politically. The Lahore that extends from the 1950s to the present is uniformly about creating wealth for the middle and upper classes. Lahore has been rearticulated as the city of arable land-turned-property-turned-captured wealth by private capital. Their newly built, cordoned, and policed, settlements—such as the Bahria Town—attract buyers and renters for the simulacra of the "foreign" in native soil: the nearly-to-scale replica Eiffel Tower or Statue of Liberty, the mini-malls, the boulevards without trees or grasses, the Arc de Triomphe.

3

NATION: MAKING THE NATION

"Does it serve any useful analytical purpose to make a distinction between the colonial state and the forms of the modern state?" Partha Chatterjee asked in *The Nation and Its Fragments*.[1] The nation-state that emerged in Pakistan certainly acted much as the colonial state had—asserting domination and power over the populace through authoritarian and dictatorial means. The nationalism in Pakistan appropriated all colonial measures for the disciplining and control over its citizenry. It established a canonical version of history—with a heavy emphasis on the classicization of tradition. It created punitive measures to streamline linguistic and ethnic differences into an officially sanctioned whole, and it put the instruments for rethinking the past—archives, history departments, access to languages—out of the reach of the everyday citizen.

Lahore helped trace this nation-making project. This premodern city posed a particular challenge to the new nation. How best to incorporate its long history into the natural arc of progression that the postcolonized nation imagines for itself? Fazlur Rahman, the first minister of commerce and education in Pakistan, commissioned and helped publish, in 1950, the first text to address this quandary. That work, *Five Thousand Years of Pakistan: An Archaeological Outline*, was authored by Robert Eric Mortimer Wheeler (1890–1976), who had recently been the director-general of the Archaeological Survey of India. Wheeler had undertaken excavations in Taxila and in Harappa, and over the course of the 1950s, would do more in Moenjodaro and in Charsada on behalf of the government of Pakistan.

In the book's preface, Fazlur Rahman noted that a cohesive history of Pakistan was a "story . . . worth telling and re-telling in every school and university of the land."[2] The story was deeply colonial. Wheeler set up the colonial dichotomy between Islam and India in this way: he imagined Islam as "a product of the desert and the plateau; of broad, bare horizons, broken if at all by the hard geometry of rocky ranges," and India, he presented, as "swarming, monstrous, sinister, fantastically beautiful [land, within which] lurks the ultimate godhead in the pallid flicker of an oil lamp."[3] These "opposites," he posited, were combined in the artistry of Akbar.

Lahore is a major focus in this colonial telling of history for a new nation. In Wheeler's slim volume of 130-odd pages, Lahore is the only city treated in any great depth (this includes his sections on Taxila, Harappa, and Moenjodaro). He describes in detail eighteen of the monuments, including Old Lahore itself. He describes its "narrow, wandering streets with picturesque impending houses and shops in various stages of decay" as part of its charm and grandeur.[4]

Lahore represents the synthesis that the newborn nation was looking for—it is grand, but the grandeur belongs only to the monuments, which are in disrepair. The text, perhaps inadvertently, also shows the basic fissure in that cohesive story about Pakistan's origins. Wheeler surveys East Pakistan differently. Here, he writes, the architecture is neither Hindu nor Muslim but *Bengali*.[5] While the antiquities discovered within the physical borders of Pakistan could easily be appropriated by the nation as part of its own heritage, "Bengali" as a style, a language, or a history was much more of a threat. The original political argument for separate electorates for Hindus and Muslims in order to protect minority rights is now recast as an argument to have a singular material and monumental history for Pakistan. Wheeler imagines that the Greek and Roman artifacts in "West Pakistan" represent the earliest interactions of this nation with the outside world, while the trace remains of Indus Valley civilization provides an indigeneity to Pakistan's inhabitants.

"East Pakistan" is threatening to these imagined origins because of its larger non-Muslim population and also the presence of a different script. Wheeler barely mentions any sites from medieval Bengal. The real intent of the "Coming of Islam," midway through Wheeler's text, is to skip from the eighth century very quickly to the Mughals. For Wheeler, Lahore becomes a key site for this transition. He wants to glorify Lahore's connections to the north and to early medieval conquerors such as Ghaznavi and Gauri. He notes that the sarcophagus of Qutbuddin Aibak is on an "unworthy side-street south of the Lahori gate in Lahore," and it deserves to be made into a proper monument.[6]

History was the conundrum for the earliest years of Pakistan. The very first war with India, a contest over Kashmir, was fought in 1947–48. Partition created not just two nations but two sworn enemies. Yet the country had to "look" eastward, for on the other side of India was "East Pakistan." How to bring the two wings of this Muslim nation conceptually together? What worked for western Pakistan, an argument about indigeneity and antiquity as Wheeler laid out, was deemed by its new rulers to not work for eastern Pakistan. At the heart of this hesitation was a facile view of Islam that associates the religion with a particular script: the Perso-Arabic script in which Urdu is written. That Bangla did not share this script became a source of immediate suspicion. The next step of national meaning-making was to link the Islam in the subcontinent with the earliest periods of Muslim history, in seventh-century Arabia, but this also isolated the eastern wing of the country, where a Muslim presence and a Muslim state were established centuries after Sind. The nation-state sought a smoother historical narrative.

The new rulers imagined Urdu to be the necessary national neutralizing force against Bangla but also, working similarly, against Sindhi, Pashto, or Punjabi, the languages prevalent in other parts of Pakistan. The bureaucrats and politicians of early Pakistan imagined that Urdu would provide a seamless continuity for the "national movement" and the independent nation. Protests by those advocating for a national role for Bangla and Sindhi were brutally crushed. Since the nationalist argument that Urdu should be the sole language also included the view that it had a primal relationship with Islam and a closer affinity to Arabic (the language of the Qur'an), the protesters were also cast as lacking faith. The religious elite who emerged after Partition made a point to write prolifically in Urdu. Simultaneously, a public case was made for the "un-Islamic" nature of the Bangla script. The presence of Hindu and Sikh ideas or structures was condemned in the vast corpus of Sufi texts in Sindhi and Punjabi.

The new nationalist elite of historians or journalists-turned-historians made a holistic argument for a uniform and seamless story of the origins of the nation. The rule of difference was extended from Hindu subjects and pasts to other minority communities and all possible avenues for understanding the past. The "archivization" policies became instruments for making things inaccessible. Stored documents slowly decayed under a watchful benign neglect. The newspaper archives of Lahore, a city known historically for having the most active press in the subcontinent, were kept in "Anarkali's Tomb" and were burned.

These historians who were charged with writing the textbooks determined a new periodization of the subcontinental past. History began with Islam's arrival on the world stage and it focused on Islam's presence in the subcontinent. The arrival and spread of colonial rule was ancillary to the beginning of the "modern" period (whose starting point was imagined to be Syed Ahmad Khan's founding of a college for Muslims in 1875). This modern moment marked the creation of a new Muslim elite who resisted the Indian National Congress, argued for separate electorates, and succeeded in the creation of Pakistan against all odds. The *most* important years for this nationalist elite were 1930, when Muhammad Iqbal gave his speech on the Muslim minority question, and 1940, when the Muslim League held its convention in Lahore to demand the creation of Pakistan.

In the 1980s, as a teenager, my subscription to the British Council Library in Lahore allowed me to check out three books at a time for two weeks. It took me almost two hours by bus and or a little over an hour by bicycle to get there, and during the summer months (the only time I was able to use the library), it was pure torture in the scorching heat. Logically, I decided to check out the thickest books so I would have the most material at my disposal. The Russian and French novelists soon ran out, and I began to eye the tomes on history. The *Encyclopedia Britannica* sat there in all of its glory.

It was in this encyclopedia that I read about the events of December 31, 1929, when the Indian National Congress held its annual session in Lahore (it had previously done so in 1893, 1900, and 1909). It was at this session that the Congress rejected the promise of "Dominion Status" from the colonial state and instead resolved for "Purna Swaraj" (complete independence). It happened right here in Lahore, I learned. I wrote down this discovery diligently in my "summer reading report," prepared for my teacher to sign when school resumed in September. The teacher punished me for including a "historical error" in my report. As punishment, he made me read out loud in front of the class, the "official history," from a chapter from the Pakistan Studies textbook on the "Struggle for Independence." There was no mention of Congress or Gandhi in that chapter. The teacher was incensed that I had implied that Nehru or Gandhi had ever been to Lahore, or that the Congress could hold a general gathering in the very same city that the Muslim League would hold its convention in 1940.

In my school, I was taught the nationally sanctioned "Two-Nation Theory." The idea was that Hindus and Muslims were two distinct civilizations that had barely coexisted in the subcontinent and that required two separate homelands to survive or prosper. This "Two-Nation Theory" as a defense for the creation and sustenance of Pakistan depended firmly on the work of nationalist historians such as I.H. Qureshi and S.M. Ikram. They wrote the digestible versions of this theory for elementary, middle, and high schools and for colleges and universities. They took on this task of nation-making at the highest level and with the full support of the various governments and the military dictators who ruled Pakistan.

They also were the historians who were called upon to modify the Two-Nation Theory after the creation of Bangladesh in 1971. This depended on excising all that did not fit the assembled truth, including all references to "East Pakistan." This was done in public, in print, with a boldness that declared *their* version of history was the eternal truth. This project was indeed contested by historians such as K.K. Aziz and Mubarak Ali, who helped expose the "homogenous past" of the nation-state to be a lie. Their scholarship, rare as it was, was also embedded in the same streets of Lahore, where traces of Hindu and Sikh histories linger, awaiting recognition.

I.

Figure 4.1. Pakistan Day celebrations in Sadr Bazaar (2022)

Almost immediately after Partition, India and Pakistan jointly made a legal claim for the erstwhile East India Company's official "India Office Library," located in London. The East India Company Library was established in 1801 to contain all the records of the company dating back to its foundation in 1600. After 1867, the library was renamed the "India Office Library" and became the home of the "A" files of governance in British India. The paper-work of colonialism operated on an "A-B-C" catalog system, with the label "A" marking the files deemed important for the colonial establishment in London or Delhi. They were often summarized into the "B" files, which were considered relevant for the local establishment, while the "C" files were considered to be ephemera. The library also contained thousands of Persian manuscripts—the material traces of Mughal governance around which the East India Company constructed its own colonial infrastructure. The library also housed the records for the Raj, which governed India from 1858 to 1947. Britain's former colonies wanted this archive, but the imperial state was not willing to entertain this request. The negotiations lasted until 1974, when the newly independent Bangladesh joined in laying a formal claim to the India Office Library. This resulted in a cessation of all dialogue between the governments of Britain and the governments of India and Pakistan. By the late 1980s, the India Office Library was subsumed into the British Library, and the legal claims disappeared.

Archives remain ambiguous spaces for contemplating the history of Lahore. Lahore, as a city, as a municipal and civic entity, has no official archive. There is no museum of the city itself. No repository contains documentary proof of its working, its happenings, or its inhabitants. The few archives in Lahore are the Punjab Records Archive in the Civil Secretariat building (known as Anarkali's Tomb), the Oriental Library at Punjab University, the Dyal Singh Public Library, and the Lahore Museum. The Punjab Records Archive hold some of the colonial "B" files, while the Oriental Library at Punjab University and the Dyal Singh Public Library has manuscripts and extensive print materials. The Lahore Museum holds some of the illuminated manuscripts and courtly documents. All of them are colonial-era institutions, created largely to serve the ruling elite. Even after independence, there remain barriers of entry to them. The result is that to construct a history of the city, one must turn to memoirs, writings of experience, or self-referential paeans to Lahore's past.

At the level of the nation-state, the same dynamic plays out with much more severe consequences. The archive of the military, the most dominant institution of Pakistan's seventy-five-year-long past, remains inaccessible to the public. Similarly, no political party has a publicly accessible archive (or archive at all). Nor do many of the religious political organizations. The personal papers of any prominent political figure, even a former head of state, aren't submitted to any repository. Important bureaucracies, such as the police, civil services, and water department, do not register their archives for any scholarly purpose. Often, any potential records available are process documents at the municipal or neighborhood level, which are literally policed by the officials working at those agencies. No layer of the nation-state, from the parliament to the local district, offers easy or sustained access to its repositories or documents.

This renders the past inchoate. It makes it impossible for those who use the tools of the historical trade, as well as the actual figures of history, to flourish in the city or in the nation. Instead, there are memoirs and first-person reportages masquerading as "behind the curtain" or "corridors of power" perspectives, written by generals, journalists, bureaucrats, and celebrities. Such a biased, self-referential, and closed ecosystem can only reproduce itself. It emphasizes lone individuals and sinister, unaccountable forces as actors. No one has to ever cite any material evidence; they can just offer hearsay, innuendo, or testimony. It produces a messianic and apocalyptic politics where the hidden world and the empirical world cannot be differentiated.

The question of writing history had already become an urgent matter by 1956. When the British partitioned the subcontinent, they also intended to separate existing archives, but that did not happen. The records of the viceroy went to London, the records related to the princely states were burned, and the imperial records of the colonial state, which were housed in Delhi, became the National Archives of India. The records of the colonial state or other functioning archives were never divided between India and

Pakistan in 1947. The first (closed) meeting of the Pakistan Historical Records and Archives Commission took place in Karachi in 1948. At that meeting, a Central Directorate of Archives was created with the aim of streamlining and preserving the central repositories. Central Record Offices were created in East Bengal, Sind, Baluchistan, and Punjab, modeled on the already existing office in the North West Frontier Province (NWFP).

In 1954, the second meeting of the Pakistan Historical Records and Archives Commission was held in Peshawar, where a survey was presented that highlighted the severe lack of resources and infrastructure for the nation. Not only was the new country without any historical or bureaucratic records to help guide it; it lacked funds and a national vision for such an undertaking. The new state's repeated claims to the government of India, asking it share the indices or catalogs of the archives in Delhi, were rebuffed. In 1955, the commission requested the government of Pakistan to create a new physical building to house the national records and archives. This request did not end up being materialized until 1973 when the National Documentation Center was created.

Already there were concerns about who could access the records. As early as the commission's 1954 meeting, it was clear that the Ministry of Defense would keep its own records. At a meeting of the commission in 1970 in Dhaka, historians complained that the records of the political party, All India Muslim League which was founded in Dhaka (East Pakistan) in 1906, had been seized by Field Marshal Ayub Khan and given to Karachi University (West Pakistan), and that the university would not give access to scholars from East Pakistan. Others mentioned the difficulties in locating the papers of political leaders, national poets, or even the official legislature. Still more were vexed by their inability to access private papers and private libraries, especially given the urgency that scholars felt about archiving and preserving Pakistan's past.[7]

After the creation of Bangladesh, a National Commission on Historical Cultural Research, led by the historian K.K. Aziz, was formed in 1973. The commission held conferences in 1973, 1974, and 1975. There was now a new concern: How does one write the history of "modern" Pakistan—that is, post-1947 Pakistan? Aziz summarized the problems facing the historian of the modern period, namely a lack of independent thought, resources, institutional sources, and professional security, as well as a general neglect for any consideration of historical truth. Most critically, Aziz produced a long list of individuals and organizations whose papers needed to be collected in the National Archives. None would eventually make it there.

After 1971, and the creation of Bangladesh, there was a sharp switch in the national policy on the origins of the Pakistani nation-state. The study of the earliest period of Islam and the arrival of Muslim rule to the subcontinent became the key focus for historical writing. The 1980s saw a new ideology and a turn toward writing the history of Muhammad Ali Jinnah and a small group of men engaged in the freedom struggle. This was enabled by the creation of the National Archives in Islamabad alongside the National Documentation Center. However, both archives were nearly exclusive in their focus on the collections of the nation's founding figure—Muhammad Ali Jinnah. The nation was to look toward the history of early Islam or toward Arabia for their founding principles and rationale.

This was made easier by Pakistan's reliance after 1971 on exporting labor to the Gulf countries—especially Saudi Arabia, Qatar, Kuwait, and the United Arab Emirates. Dependence on the remittances from these workers drove the nation-state to deepen ties to the Gulf states. The remittances also began to reshape the fabric and form of the city of Lahore alongside the rest of the country. New settlements, new colonies, and new homes for the diaspora communities changed Lahore's very municipal structure. A new Defence Housing Association constructed by and for the ruling military elite began the long project of remaking Lahore.

This new Lahore was malleable precisely because it lacked a repository for its many-hued pasts. Its colonial history was locked in government buildings. Its precolonial history was inaccessible owing to linguistic obstacles because of the concerted state effort to curtail and reshape citizens' historical comprehension. This Lahore was not a thousand-year-old city, but a city invented in 1977, or in 1990, or so on. That is to say, the partitioning of Lahore from its past allowed the pouring of concrete onto the city to proceed apace.

The city's own archive disappeared as a result of Partition. Even the formal mandates on the operation of the city infrastructure, whether regarding water, electricity, or waste disposal, were never imagined to be "public" property. Writing the history of the city, as it unfolded after 1947, was given over to individual efforts or to nongovernmental organizations. Lahore's incomprehensibility was made alluring or magical by reinvesting in the tropes of a city of jinns or a city of lights or a city of culture. Chasms grew between the history of Lahore, the memory of its expelled population, and the everyday life of its inhabitants. The repositories of public memory—museums, archives, libraries, colleges and universities, cinema halls, theaters—slowly eroded away under successive military regimes.

II.

The only public statue left in Lahore stands on the Mall Road adjacent to Punjab University's pharmacy school. It is of a European man, dressed in coat and gown and clutching a book in his right hand. The plinth identifies him as "Alfred Woolner, 1878–1936: A Great and Beloved Leader." There used to be numerous statues of figures associated with the British Raj in Lahore, all of which were either relocated or destroyed after 1947. Woolner survives, even if Woolner Road, Woolner Hostel, Woolner Hall, and the Woolner Minerva Club do not. There is also the Woolner Sanskrit collection housed in the Punjab University Oriental Library, which has some eight thousand manuscripts acquired by Woolner during his time in Lahore. He arrived in 1903 to serve as principal of the Oriental College, Lahore, as well as the registrar for Punjab University. A scholar of Sanskrit, Persian, Prakrit, and Pali, he would go on to found the Panjab Historical Society (and its journal) as well as the Linguistic Society of India.

Lahore was physically transformed, like many cities under colonial rule. There was a new planned city (the "white town"), a new cantonment (for the military garrison), a new "model town," a new house for the governor, a new railway station, a new telegraph and post office, a new jailhouse, a new police headquarters, new bridges, and new hostels. Yet Woolner's still-standing statue also serves as a reminder of how drastically the colonial

Figure 4.2. Statue of Alfred Woolner on Mall Road (2011)

understanding of education, knowledge, and archives changed Lahore from 1849 to 1947—the almost hundred years that the British ruled over Panjab and Lahore.

The educational institutions created in Lahore in the second
half of the nineteenth century provide another stark reminder of

how colonial rule shaped the city. The British conquest of Lahore in 1849 came fairly late in the history of the subcontinent's colonization. The East India Company had already been a military occupier, settler, and administrator in Madras and in Bengal for a hundred years. Lahore's transformation began immediately after the city came under colonial rule. First there was the Medical College (1860), then came the Government College (1864), the Mission College (1866), and after that, Forman Christian College, the University College Lahore (1869), Punjab University College and Oriental College (1870)—which would combine to become Punjab University in 1882—Aitchison College (1886), King Edward Medical College (1888), Islamia College (1892), Kinnaird College for Women (1912), and Lahore College for Women (1922).

The project of transforming Lahore was undertaken by British scholars of Persian, Sanskrit, and Arabic more than it was undertaken by governors, commissioners, and officers such as Henry Lawrence, John Lawrence, Robert Montgomery, and Charles Aitchison. Gottlieb W. Leitner (1840–99), Marc Aurel Stein (1862–1943), and Woolner were three key figures in remaking Lahore's relationship to its past. They created forms for thinking about history, and for how language and the past are linked, and they created new venues for the dissemination of their thinking. All three of them were also known as intrepid walkers, and incorporated walking into their research and teaching.

Aurel Stein walked (with a camera and a set of indigenous collaborators) much of Kashmir in order to conduct research for his study of *Rajatarangini*. Leitner and Woolner walked through Lahore. Leitner had come to Lahore in 1864 to run the new Government College. He understood that the task of educating the natives of Panjab meant incorporating aspects of their existing educational system while building new forms of thinking. He found that there was "blind veneration for dogmatic thinking" and no sense of causation or chronology among his students. To remedy that problem, he founded Anjuman-e Punjab, a research society for promoting the study of history and cultural knowledge. The Anjuman opened a free public library and a free reading room. It also laid the foundation for the Oriental College, which would subsequently be headed by Woolner. The aim was to "revive" the study of Sanskrit for Hindus and Arabic for Muslims under the notion of a lost "classical" knowledge.

When he arrived in Lahore, Leitner also noted that there were more than eighty schools that focused on Arabic or Persian, and twenty-five schools on Sanskrit, but none where the new sciences of Europe were being taught. This observation fueled his drive to establish a new university. He wanted to promote the diffusion of European sciences—importantly, history and philology—in the "vernacular" language (that is, Urdu). He also wanted to encourage the indigenous elite to fund and support this educational endeavor.

In 1871, Leitner would write, together with Muhammad Hussain Azad (d. 1910), a history of Islam in Urdu, called *Sinin-e Islam* (A Chronology of Islam).[8] The book was intended mainly to be read by *maulvis*—a then common designation for teachers in the *maktabs* (Persian language school) and the *madrasas* (Qur'an or theology schools). Its aim was to "modernize." Leitner had proposed a three-volume work, but only the first volume was published. It focused on world history until the end of the "classical" period, in the thirteenth century. In the work, Leitner and Azad argued that Islam (and the teaching of it) needed to be integrated into world (or universal) history. They highlighted the historical commonalities between Judaism, Christianity, and Islam. Their main interest was in promoting a sense of rational thinking about history and to give readers the tools to mediate between divine rights and a political structure in which causation was driven by human actions.

Like Leitner, Woolner was devoted to improving historical consciousness among the colonized. Woolner founded the Panjab Historical Society in 1911 and established the *Journal of the Punjab Historical Society* that same year. The society would become the Panjab University Historical Society in 1932. The first issues of the journal carried articles on Jahangir's tomb, the Lahore Fort, the shrine of Data Ganj Baksh, and the Lahore Museum's collections. Woolner was key in promoting the study of Sanskrit texts as well as linking scholarship on Sanskrit between Europe and British India.

Like Leitner, Woolner emphasized the development of the philological sciences, such as the study of manuscript culture and the histories of languages, as well as the retrieval of lost or marginalized texts. The journal certainly privileged European perspectives when it came to the history of the peoples of British India. The visitors and travelers from Europe to Hindustan received the same level of historical attention as did the control of territories, the wars and "revolts," and the fates of princes and rajas.

With Partition, the Punjab University became, de facto, the oldest university in Pakistan (the University of Dhaka was established in 1912). The need for new universities for the postcolonial state was readily apparent. In the first few years after Partition, new universities were created in Karachi, Peshawar, and Quetta—all modeled on the colonial system of centralized "board exams" and the necessity of teacher training in higher education. These new universities created new disciplinary programs in history, but the focus on deep history slowly started to fade as the new nation-state took precedence. The study of Sanskrit, Hindi, and Gurmukhi was brought to an end at Punjab University after Partition (though in the 1980s, it was revived in some places in Lahore). Woolner's collection of Sanskrit and Prakrit manuscripts would remain untouched for decades.

The Pakistan Historical Society was founded in Lahore in 1950 at the behest of Fazlur Rahman, the minister of education and commerce. It began publishing the quarterly *Journal of the Pakistan Historical Society* from Punjab University in 1953. The aim of the journal and society, according to Fazlur Rahman, was to "start seriously the work of re-writing the history of Islam." The focus was explicitly on early Islam, and Philip K. Hitti (a

Columbia-trained, Princeton-based historian of early Muslim conquests), was the guest of honor at the inauguration of the journal. This was a history meant to highlight "the glorious conduct of Muslim rulers under the guidance of Islam" outside the subcontinent. In its first twelve issues there were a hundred articles, only twelve of which were on the medieval period in Hindustan—mostly on Akbar. The vast majority were focused on the Umayyad and Abbasid periods. Leitner's earlier project of "universalizing" Islamic history had found resonance in the postcolonial vision of a geography partitioned in space and in time from its Hindu neighbors.

Two new organizations concerned with the writing of history followed the Pakistan Historical Society. The Asiatic Society of Pakistan, in West Bengal Dhaka, was founded in 1952 with the aim of being akin to the "Asiatic Society of Bengal in undivided India"; the Historical Research Institute was founded at the University of Punjab in 1960. The latter organization published the quarterly *Journal of the Research Society of Pakistan* (West Pakistan) beginning in 1964—with the aim "to be modern," as well as to remain "classical," with a special emphasis on the geography of West Pakistan. Historian S.M. Ikram was the journal's chair.

Many prominent archaeologists, historians, philologists, and numismatists—such as A.H. Dani, Yar Muhammad Khan, Hussainuddin Rashidi, Iftikhar Ahmad Ghauri, Muhammad Bashir Hussain, Nabi Bakhsh Baloch, M. Kabir, and S.M. Jaffar—were published in these journals. Yet there was a decided focus on the history of Islam outside the subcontinent, even if the bulk of such scholars' work concerned the textual and material histories of polities in West Pakistan before Partition. The journals covered the Muslim polities in Syria and Iraq, or on contemporary "freedom fighters." Perhaps it was a "safer" choice of topics, or perhaps the arrival of Pakistan's first military dictatorship in 1958 reoriented the writing of history for Pakistan.

With its history inscribed across different languages—Arabic, Panjabi, Prakrit, Persian, Hindi, and Urdu—Lahore was rarely a subject of these history journals. Just as the colonial institutions, organizations, and societies responsible for accessing history or conveying it to the general public imposed their logic of civilizational difference on the city's past, so did those who took over after independence. The new nation-state, and then the military state, preferred a vision of Pakistan fissured from Hindus, Hinduism, or anything remotely non-Islamic, non-Sunni. The journals are a clear archive of this conscious project of political forgetting. Much of Lahore's past certainly was never remembered again.

III.

When I was around fifteen years old, I had a friend who lived in a small colony in Sadr Cantonment. His house was exactly midway between our school and my home, so on our way back from school on our bicycles, it was a convenient daily stop, an opportunity to keep talking and grab a snack. His home was among several others, all with faded yellow paint on the outside walls and a small door set a foot or higher from the ground. The entrance to the complex was gated (there used to be parts of a wooden gate on the left side, but it went missing the last time I visited). The ledge over the gate had a string of Devanagari characters along with a year: 1938. There was a broken arch, at the exact point, which once had presumably the same words written in English. The only thing visible was the letters "BHA" on the left and "ING" on the right. For many months, I passed the gate with only a cursory glance at the script. Though no one had said it, I knew that lingering in front of the gate was not a good idea. I could not read (nor learn how to read) Devanagari in Lahore. I knew that the Devanagari script was "Hindu," and that a "Hindu" was a person who was trying to stab me in the back (per my social science textbook).

Then one day, I decided to try and read the sign. I sat perched on the bar of my too-big-for-me bicycle and tried to figure out how भ corresponded to "bh." A man who was walking by came over. "You will need to learn the Hindi alphabet if you want to read that," he

Figure 4.3. Gated *mohalla* on Delhi Road, Sadr (2011)

said. I asked him if he knew it. "No, but I know that those two are the characters *O* and *M* to make the sacred sound 'OM.'" He pointed to the top left of the pillar supporting the arch where ओम was carved in red. "The *O* or the *M* are not in 'BHA.'" He laughed, patted my head. "This is the Bhagwan Bhawan complex," he told me. There used to be a Bhagwan Das Chemist in Lahore. Perhaps this sign belonged to them or was meant for their employees, I would later surmise.

"There is a *baoli* (pond) that way and a *mandir* (temple) that used to be active until the 1960s," he said, pointing to his left. I would later ask my friend to accompany me to the pond. He would refuse. I could not ask my mother about it (even though she grew up just a few minutes away), because my friend was Christian and I was also not supposed to stop and eat at his home. So I went in search of the *baoli* alone and never told anyone because they might imagine that I had sympathies toward the Hindus. The *baoli* (then dry) had a small cluster of trees nearby, and I made a new friend who would later introduce me to other indecipherable and inaccessible parts of Lahore. All of this I had to keep to myself, so as not to get into trouble. At the same time, much of this history was a secret simply because I could not read the script or because I did not know what a *baoli* was, or who this Bhagwan Das was. The building, the pond that I was trying to hide from my family was unknowable to me anyway.

The British colonial state began its rule in Lahore in 1849 with a question mark regarding the language of governance and the language of the city and the Panjab as a whole. There was already an ongoing debate about what the appropriate language of British rule should be in India. Since its inception, the Mughal state had used Persian as the language of governance and bureaucracy. Persian existed seamlessly with other regional languages, such as Bangla, Marathi, Urdu, and Panjabi. There was also a robust translation and recreation project that moved texts and ideas across Sanskrit, Braj, Persian, and Hindustani. But the British colonial state began its rule in the mid-eighteenth century with an entrenched notion that there were two civilizations in the subcontinent, each with its own script and its own languages. All of the languages that used the Nagari script were "Hindu," and all of the languages that used the Perso-Arabic script were

"Muslim." Once the languages were sorted into their respective faith groups, the question of language became one of managing populations. English would need to become the language of state apparatus, and it was up to the "Hindus" or the "Muslims" to equip their respective communities for participating in colonial activities. Such division between orthographic and devotional communities, and the promise of English, would become the most salient feature of colonial rule, and remains a centralizing idea to this day.

The colonial state's earliest assessments of Lahore held that the general populace in the city used Panjabi as its main language and only used Persian as the language of administration. Notably, the British imagined that the Sikh elite (including Ranjit Singh) were unlettered. This was a common trope attached to a number of princely states that were conquered over the first half of the nineteenth century. Panjabi, with its rich tradition of epics, poetry, and history, was also largely conceived of as an "oral" language, ill-suited for the working of the state.

In his 1882 *History of Indigenous Education in the Panjab: Since Annexation and in 1882*, G.W. Leitner put the matter clearly: while Panjabi was understood by everyone and Persian and Sanskrit were studied and used in Lahore, the Europeans were focused on making Urdu the language of the courts and of public life. The role of Urdu as "the lingua franca," as Leitner termed it, was fundamentally an inconvenience for everyone in Lahore. Yet the allure of government jobs and the "modern" economy was enough to create a new "Urdu-first" stratum of society in the city.

In 1865, there was only one Urdu school in Lahore among more than eighty Persian or Arabic ones (and among twenty-five or so Sanskrit ones). Muhammad Hussain Azad, who would go on to write *Sinin-e Islam* in 1871 with G.W. Leitner, gave a speech in 1867 on the history of the Urdu language. He presented Urdu as a perfect commingling of Sanskrit, Hindi, and Persian. To him, it was the central language with which to approach history and

poetics.[9] Azad was himself a refugee of the post-1857 British destruction of Delhi, and it is likely that Urdu was as foreign to
him as Panjabi.

By 1882, the colonial imposition of Urdu had changed Lahore
radically. There was now a significant European settlement in
the city. Nur Ahmad Chishti, who wrote two of the most important histories of Lahore, reported, in 1880, to having taught
Urdu to more than two thousand British officers. According to
Leitner's 1882 survey, there were nearly seven thousand schools
with 160,000 students across all levels in Panjab receiving
instruction in Urdu or English. By the turn of the century, Urdu
would dominate Lahore. Over 80 percent of the newspapers were
in Urdu. This was for a total population of some 1 million with a
4 percent literacy rate.[10]

While the creation of the Oriental College, and later Punjab
University, was aimed expressly toward reviving the study of
"classical language"—that is, Arabic, Persian, and Sanskrit—the
colleges' founders imagined these languages as belonging to some
idealized past. The present was divided along religious lines among
Hindi, Urdu, and Gurmukhi. Later, this vision—that Urdu, which
was written in the Perso-Arabic script, constituted some inimical
relationship to Muslim identity—would be the unifying feature in
the demands for separate electorates in the subcontinent. This was
the vision despite the reality that only a very small minority
among those who were fighting the British colonial state for
independence counted Urdu as their primary language.

Pakistan, once created, was split geographically into two wings.
In the east was partitioned Bengal with majority having Bangla as
the central language. In the west was a partitioned Panjab, Sind,
Baluchistan, and the North Western Frontier Province with no
single majority language overall. Thus when Muhammad Ali Jinnah, the founding governor general of Pakistan, traveled to
Dhaka in East Pakistan and declared that "the state language of
Pakistan is going to be Urdu and no other language," it came as a
shock to the newly liberated Pakistanis. Protests followed. First, in

the early 1950s, the students in Dhaka demanded the inclusion of Bangla as an official language for the nation-state. This led to riots led by the religious right in West Pakistan (again, based on the logic that Urdu was prima facie more "Muslim" than Bangla). Next, in 1960s, the Sindhi students in Karachi protested the diminution of resources allocated to their language. At each point, the state reacted with violence.

The contestations over language were not merely a question of representation after freedom from colonization. The Panjabi, Sindhi, Pashto, and Baluchi literary cultures represented strong claims to a prior world of letters, of belonging, of knowing the world, one that colonialism had worked to erase over its centuries-long hold over the subcontinent. How could the independent state do the same? The protests highlighted the question that if Pakistan was to be a Muslim state, why did it need Urdu to be the language of the state? Azad's argument for Urdu's antiquity may or may not be correct, but that is not the argument that Jinnah (a non-Urdu speaker) set forth in his Dhaka speech. His case there was simpler: that one nation required one state language.

Lahore was a city that could once speak in Sanskrit, Hindavi, Persian, Arabic, and Panjabi, and now it was unable to understand any of that heritage. Nestled within the old city and across neighborhoods such as Baghbanpura, Krishnagar, Harbanspura, Rajgarh, Ramnagar, and Bhagatpura were many inscriptions: on signs, marble posts, name plaques on houses, felicitations to gods, devotions to family genealogies. All these were rendered mute for there were no readers. Lahore was inscribed with Persian, Hindi, Panjabi, but almost none of it was decipherable by the people who inhabited the city. Unreadable, these scripts haunted public spaces.

A deliberate process of slow erasure, obliteration, and suppression emerged over the decades after Partition—the easiest strategy was to put a huge "Allah o Akbar" sign over an inscription in Devanagari or Sanskrit or Gurmukhi. Sometimes the year inscribed into the building's edifice was replaced with "1947"—effectively giving the structure a new date of birth. Similarly, the temples,

gurdwaras, ghats, and ashrams that used to dot Lahore and contained within and around them signs written in Devanagari and
Gurmukhi were slowly (and somewhat systematically) removed,
first from access and then from view.

Persian fared no better in Lahore, despite being one of the languages of everyday life and governance for a millennium. The vast
array of inscriptions on monuments and shrines dotting Lahore
were adorned with Qur'anic verses to make them palatable even
if no one could understand what they even said in the first instance. The Persian manuscripts joined the Sanskrit and Panjabi
manuscripts in sealed archives and collections. There were resources commissioned for translations into Urdu from Panjabi or
Persian, but they tended to focus on creating an imagined Urdu
"canon." The Panjabi *Hir* of Waris Shah, the Panjabi *kafi* of Bulleh
Shah, the *mela chiraghan* of Lahore, with its veneration of Shah
Hussain's Panjabi, were just as inaccessible as the Persian poetry
of Sa'ad Salman of Lahore or the Arabic of Fakhruddin Mudabbir.

IV.

The first prime minister of Pakistan, Liaquat Ali Khan, made his inaugural trip to the United States in May 1950. He was given an honorary doctorate of law at Columbia University, after which he spoke about the challenges facing the "poor and backward" peoples of his new nation. His concerns were clear: settling the 7 million refugees, establishing an economy, building an army, and training a bureaucracy. Seeking assistance on that last concern, he met with the Rockefeller Foundation. In February 1951, Pakistan announced the establishment of a Center for Pakistan Studies at Columbia, with a commitment of $250,000, to be paid over ten years (adjusted for inflation, that was $2.5 million). Liaquat Ali Khan was assassinated in October 1951, but his vision continued. By 1954, a number of visiting scholars from Pakistan had positions at Columbia. Ishtiaq Husain Qureshi (1903–81) was one of the two prominent historians in that earliest group.

Qureshi was a medievalist trained at Aligarh and Cambridge. He was a refugee to Pakistan who lost all his books and belongings in a fire caused by a riot in Delhi in 1947. After he migrated to Pakistan, he was appointed to the University of Punjab's Department of History, but was soon called for national service by his friend and colleague Liaquat Ali Khan. Qureshi served as the minister for refugees and rehabilitation and then the minister for education before resigning and moving to Columbia for the next six years. He returned to Pakistan in 1960 to become the vice chancellor of the University of Karachi. He would become one of the key architects of the ideology of the new nation-state, using his profound expertise in the early medieval period to produce synthetic histories of the establishment of Pakistan over a thousand years.

The clearest articulation of his idea of why Pakistan was inevitable, destined, wanted, and necessary is in the last pages of his 1962 history, completed while at Columbia. At the end of *The Muslim Community of the Indo-Pakistan Subcontinent (610–1947): A Brief Historical Analysis*, he writes that the Muslims had lived on the subcontinent for thirteen hundred years with little or no contact with the Hindus, from whom they were different in every way, including with regard to culture, outlook on life, fashion, cuisine, furniture, and domestic utensils. The political nation-state of Pakistan was a logical consequence of this centuries-long alienation, felt as a whole by these unified "Muslims." This particular story was certainly part of Muhammad Ali Jinnah's speech in Lahore in 1940, but Jinnah was not a medieval historian who had studied the history of Muslims in the subcontinent since the seventh century. For Qureshi, the story was history.

Qureshi used to think otherwise. In his doctoral dissertation-turned-monograph, *The Administration of the Sultanate of Delhi*, published in 1942 in Lahore, he concluded with a paean to the accommodation of Muslim rulers, writing that the "Hindu population was better off under the Muslims than under Hindu tributaries or independent rulers" and that there was "fairly free social intercourse between the two peoples." Partition reshaped Qureshi's understanding of medieval history. As a civil servant, an administrator for the educational system of the newly minted Islamic Republic, Qureshi helped create a new framework for the history of Pakistan in the subcontinent. His own particular focus, in this project of nationalist history making, was to focus on language and education.

Broadly speaking, education was paramount among the varied pressing questions faced by the new nation after the formal end of colonization. A series of national gatherings were held in Karachi and Lahore in the first three years to articulate a cohesive national strategy for education: the first Conference on Education (in Karachi in 1947), the first Pakistan Science Conference (in Lahore in 1949), the first All Pakistan History Conference (in Karachi in 1951) all proclaimed the urgency of creating a national Urdu cultural repository. Qureshi, speaking at the first history conference, remarked that British colonial rule was predicated on their control of education and the role of textbooks in shaping colonial discourse. For Pakistan, the need was to articulate an "Islamic" form of citizenship, and Urdu was considered the indigenous language most suitable for this project. Qureshi explicitly relied on the colonial ideas of "modernization" for his insistence on Urdu, pointing out that the British had championed Urdu at Delhi College, which was established in 1825.

The colonial project of shaping Lahore by indigenizing Urdu that began the twentieth century was, in the second half of the century, nationalized across Pakistan. Qureshi showed great admiration for the monolingualism of Japan and the Soviets' subordination of various cultures to the Russian language. The use of Urdu as a repository for Islamic history and as a means of preserving national identity and culture was sometimes put forth as anti-colonial, sometimes anti-Western, but it was often self-affirming. In 1967, Quershi said that he bows his head in shame when he hears two Pakistanis speaking in English when they should be speaking in Urdu. In the same lecture, he claimed that there were more writings on Islam in Urdu than any other language—far greater in volume, he claimed, than in Arabic, Persian, or Turkish. Those who were agitating for Bangla, or Punjabi, Sindhi, or Baluchi were actively promoting anti-Islamic ideas, inspired in his estimation by the proximity of those other languages to Sanskrit.[11]

The student protests over Bangla, which began almost as soon as the Urdu-only policy was announced in 1948, continued throughout the 1950s. Under the dictatorship of Ayub Khan, other forms of inequity between the eastern and western halves of the country, in terms of resource extraction, allocation of federal funds, taxation, and representation, would emerge as political problems. There was a clear sense in East Pakistan that the nation-state had a fundamental inequity across its two west and east "wings." One clear source of evidence for this was in the project of history writing. Qureshi, and other major historians based in West Pakistan, continued to cast doubts on the Muslim nature of their fellow citizens in East Pakistan.

In the general understanding of historians, the immediate cause of the War for Independence of Bangladesh in 1971 was the result of its first major election, in December 1970, in which the Awami League party, led by Mujibur Rahman, emerged victorious. That party won 167 of 169 seats in East Pakistan—and consequently an outright majority in the 313-seat election. Instead of handing over power, the military, under General Yahya Khan, declared martial law and launched a punitive campaign of murderous violence in Dhaka in March 1971, known as Operation Searchlight. Among the victims were numerous historians of Dhaka University, such as Santosh Chandra Bhattachariya, Abul Khair, and Giasuddin Ahmed. This deliberate culling of intellectuals in East Pakistan has never been acknowledged by subsequent governments of Pakistan—nor has the wider killing and displacement of millions of East Pakistanis from May to December of 1971. Bangladesh became independent on December 16, 1971.

Almost immediately, Pakisani leaders staged a conference in Lahore for the intellectuals and historians of this "new" Pakistan to declare an ideological vision for the state. It was organized by the Punjab Textbook Board from December 27 through 29, and Qureshi was among the conference's speakers. He rearticulated his vision of history, which was predicated on the idea of an unbroken Muslimness going back thirteen hundred years. He reiterated that while the Muslims of the subcontinent were not of the same ethnicity or race, those in the western part of the subcontinent shared a set of common cultural and devotional markers. This unity, which was there from the very first Muslim community in eighth-century Sind, was still there in 1971 Sind. This would need to be the new basis of national history post the creation of Bangladesh.

The issue, he said, was that the Muslims of Bangladesh had fallen victim to the prejudices of language and culture. Language, in fact, was Qureshi's central target. He claimed that Bangla, which had also been written in Perso-Arabic script during the early modern period and had taken some of its vocabulary from Persian, had been forcibly shifted to a Nagari script and filled with Sanskrit and Hindi words by the Hindus. The Indian state, in his conspiratorial estimation, had initiated this policy of using Bangla script so that the Bengali citizens of Pakistan would become "Hinduized" through their love of Bangla. The other reason, Qureshi provided, was the prominence of communism in East Pakistan and the importation of atheism and secularism—all factors that had robbed it of its claim to Islam as a religion.[12]

Qureshi summarized his theories on history, language, and education in his 1975 book *Education in Pakistan: An Inquiry into Objectives and Achievements*. In retrospect, the formation of Bangladesh was for him the result of the failure of Pakistan's education policies (which he was partly responsible for, though he does not mention that). The "language riots" were not about language but about the removal of "Indo-Muslim culture" from East Pakistan. Again, it was the Perso-Arabic script that carried the "culture" of Islam for him. The dominance of a language, such as Bangla or Hindi, which did not use the Perso-Arabic script, meant that "Muslim Bengal" had turned "its face away from its Muslim past" with a "corresponding weakening of loyalty to Islam."[13] His solution was to tie Islam and Pakistan even more closely—to argue for the uniqueness of the geography of (West) Pakistan to an imagined geography of Islam.

The template set by Qureshi would soon become the official discourse for Pakistan's ideology. A new field called "Pakistan

Studies" would be invented and enforced as a compulsory subject in all schools and universities. New generations of historians would be trained to speak about Pakistan's connections to the Arab world, to the origins of Islam in Sind, to Muhammad bin Qasim, to Arabic, to triumphalism, to prophecy. Qureshi's legacy is the primacy of Urdu and the ideologically motivated writing of history.

V.

Shaikh Muhammad Ikram graduated from Lahore Government College in 1930 with an MA in English literature. While he had only come to Lahore four years earlier (from Lyallpur, some seventy miles west of Lahore), he was well entrenched in its cultural life. He edited the college literary magazine, contributing sketches and essays. He spent time memorizing and reciting the poetry of Rumi and Hafiz and, most consequentially, he became part of a small circle of young students who visited the poet Muhammad Iqbal at his residence in Lahore.

Iqbal, who used to teach at Government College, was a living icon among Lahore's young students, famed for his poetry, his philology, and his attempts to systematize Persian metaphysics. Iqbal was, by all accounts, an attentive and kind teacher and mentor to these young men. Ikram mentions that their conversations revolved around the poetry of Ghalib, Hafiz, and Goethe.[14] He does not mention any conversations on the question of the subcontinent's independence or the issues that Iqbal introduced in his 1930 address to the All India Muslim League in Allahabad—namely, the creation of a "Muslim India within India." Iqbal died in 1938 and was buried in Lahore. In 1940, also in Lahore, the Muslim League would announce its demand for Pakistan.

After his graduation, S.M. Ikram (as he was known and published) took the Indian Civil Services (ICS) examination to acquire a position in the civil bureaucracy working for the British colonial state. He then undertook two years of training at Oxford University, and in 1933 returned to British India with an appointment as an assistant commissioner in the Bombay district. At the time of Partition, he was a collector, a very high rank for a native official in the ICS, and decided to migrate to Pakistan. He was appointed as deputy secretary in the Ministry of Information and Broadcasting and would hold several high-profile civil service appointments in Pakistan until his death in 1973, including as head of the Historical Research Institute in Punjab University, Lahore.

His earliest published books were driven by his interests and training in literature and literary criticism. He did this work while employed as a civil servant, keeping up a healthy correspondence with writers and intellectuals. His first book, published in 1936, was on the poetry of Ghalib. His next two books, however, were histories—*Ab-e Kausar* (Water of Kausar) and *Mauj-e Kausar* (Waves of Kausar)—initially published in 1940 from Mercantile Press in Lahore. "Kausar" is the name of a river in Heaven, according to Muslim tradition. The volumes were thus intimations to his Muslim readers of a future glory. With the publication of *Rud-e Kausar* (Stream of Kausar) in 1944, the *Kausar* works formed a trilogy.

By 1947, not only had the trilogy's entire first print run of one thousand copies sold, but he had produced two more editions and expanded the book from seven hundred pages, across two volumes, into fifteen hundred pages, across three volumes. Over the next twenty-five years, Ikram would revise and expand these volumes in six subsequent editions. This trilogy would become the most consequential history for the new state, and Ikram one of the most important historians of Pakistan. It became part of BA and MA curricula, and sponsored editions were published by religious or social organizations.

How did a literary scholar become such an important nationalist historian? Why did a bureaucrat become one of the most visible historians for the new state? Knowing the "how" requires a closer look at his key works, and knowing the "why" prompts an examination of the ecosystem within which he flourished. More directly, the answers to these questions illuminate the very nature of the nation-making project undertaken by the state after 1950. The works of S.M. Ikram created a seamless blend of a thousand years of history and contemporary nationalist concerns—written in a lexically sophisticated Urdu that itself aimed to universalize a substratum of public intellectuals as the true foundational figures for the state. It was the high literary annex to the everyday language of journalists and popular Urdu novelists.

Ikram's publications in 1940 announce their project in the titles. The first volume, *Ab-e Kausar*, is subtitled "The Religious and Intellectual History of Hindustan's Muslims from the Ancient Period to the Beginning of the Nineteenth Century," and the second volume is subtitled "The Religious and Spiritual History of Islamic Hindustan: Medieval Period from the Beginning of Akbar's Reign to the Decline of the Islamic State." There is an explicit turn toward theological actors (jurists, preachers, advisers, and Sufis) and toward a prose style that is free of wordplay, emotional manipulation, exaggeration, and storytelling.

Rather, he aimed to base his writing on historical criticism. The footnotes are few but careful and largely based on colonial historians and primary sources in Arabic or Persian. The language is sparse, clean, with short sentences. He privileges a "common sensical" interpretation—pointing out that if a Persian history notes that a thousand temples were destroyed and a thousand madrasas or mosques erected in their stead, then this claim is clearly physically impossible and an exaggeration.

The political history for Ikram begins with the conquest of Sind under Muhammad bin Qasim in early eighth century. That event marks not only the formation of the Muslim state but also Muslim history for the subcontinent. As his work proceeds by dynastic rule, he interpolates the actions of the religious elite connected with the royal courts and those undertaking the process of peaceful "Islamization"—the Sufi orders. Further, political questions concerning governance, justice, and welfare are tied to the religiosity of the ruler. Victories and defeats become manifestations of the divine plan. The decline, when it comes for the Muslim Mughal rulers, appears alongside a revival in Islamic thought and practices that is led by Shah Waliullah Dehlawi (1703–62).

Thus, the framework of a new scientific history is underpinned by a commitment to the virtues or glory of Islam. Ikram fashions an idea of civilization that may not be diametrically split between Hindu and Muslim, but it certainly is removed from any notions of coexistence. Furthermore, the idea of Muslim civilization is tied to being Sunni, with pointed references to how Shiʿa polities (Safavid Iran, for instance) may have influenced the early Mughal polity or how specific Shiʿa ideas may have infiltrated the orthodoxy. The revival of Shah Waliullah was properly a Sunni-led one, and was taken up by calls for a political dimension to the idea of jihad. In other words, Ikram presents in Urdu a cohesive conservative tradition for modern urban Sunni Muslims.

As part of the new nation's Ministry of Information and Broadcasting, Ikram commissioned and published an edited volume, *Saqafat-e Pakistan* (Pakistani Culture), in 1956. In the preface, he again made the point that part of the current territory labeled "Pakistan" was the site of Muhammad bin Qasim's state in the early eighth century. To corroborate this origin claim, he cited the fact that Lahore, Peshawar Multan, and Sonargaon (near Dhaka) were central to the early Muslim political rulers. Further, while many of the Mughal capitals and cities were now in India as a result of Partition, he was heartened that the new nationalist Indians were already distancing themselves from the Mughal period. That is, Ikram felt it appropriate that the politics of a "Muslim civilization" was anathema to the Republic of India because it held true to the logic of Partition.

Thus, he said, it will remain up to Pakistan to uphold Muslim culture and civilization for the entirety of the subcontinent.[15] This civilizational heritage, Ikram notes, is available exclusively in Urdu. There was a necessity, he wrote, for a unifying language.

This unity is not lexical, but it exists in the stories that circulate across Bangla or Punjabi. He cites the versions of Yusuf and Zulaikha, Layla and Majnun, and the romances of Amir Hamza that are common to most languages, but which, he claimed, were most present in Urdu. For Bangla, his logic was especially skewed: what he labeled as "Muslim" content in Bangla, such as the *Saif ul Malook* epic, he claimed was actually initially written in the Perso-Arabic script and only later moved into the Devanagari based script. Thus, it was important, he wrote, that as Pakistan flourished, Bangla ought to return to the "Perso-Arabic script," and to its "Muslim" roots.

It was this appeal to a unifying scriptal and civilizational claim that drove Ikram to prominence among the state and intellectual elites. He was granted a fellowship to spend a year at Columbia University in 1953. He returned again in 1958 and 1961 as a visiting professor in the history department. In 1964, he published an English summary of the *Kausar* trilogy as *Muslim Civilization in India*, cowritten with the Columbia history faculty and his sponsor, Ainslie T. Embree (1921–2017). The aim was to cater to an American undergraduate audience. The conclusion, provided foremostly to the Columbia students, was that "Islamic religious inheritance" was the defining characteristic that led to the Partition. Across his many Urdu and English publications, bolstered by his bureaucratic and international appointments, Ikram's version of Pakistan's history would attain a near-hegemonic status. His claim, premised on his reading of history, that the Muslim revival was counterrevolutionary and beholden to the religious elite as the true leaders of the civic society became the ideological foundation for Pakistan.

VI.

Through the eyes of Khurshid Kamal Aziz, Lahore reads like a city built by an enchanted *pari* (fairylike invisible being). He was writing about the Lahore of the early twentieth century, but doing so in the early 2000s, when dictatorships, organized crime, industrialists, and rentier capitalists had reduced Lahore to an archipelago of gated societies in a sea of impermanent townships. Then there was the series of suicide attacks starting in 2006, which created an even harsher layer of the city's segregated geography, with cordons and checkpoints. Aziz's *The Coffee House of Lahore: A Memoir 1942–57* came out in this blasted Lahore.

He called the Lahore of the 1920s "the most highly cultured city of North India," with a string of glamorous sites: Gymkhana Club, India Tea House, India Coffee House, Regal and Plaza Cinemas, the Mall, "bordered by tall trees and wide footpaths," Faletti's Hotel, the Arab Hotel, Lorang's, Stiffles, Anarkali, Nagina, Ferozsons, and Narain Das Bhagwan Das. "The skyline was soothing. Nature's green was the dominating color of the city. Breathing was easy, and so was enjoying life."[16] This Lahore, with its abundant social and public venues for talking, drinking tea or coffee, dancing, and listening to lectures by the great Rabindranath Tagore or Muhammad Ali Jinnah, was a magnet for the Left, the Progressives, the Indo-Soviet Friendship Society, the artists, and the poets. Aziz gives a list of about two hundred luminaries who were regulars at the India Coffee House, and the memoir consists of profiles of some fifty of them.

Aziz (1927–2009) came to Lahore in 1942 to study at the Forman Christian College. His father, Shaikh Abdul Aziz, was a barrister trained in London (he roomed with Muhammad Iqbal) and had made a critical edition of Waris Shah's *Hir*. His family had lived on and off in Lahore, though their generational home was in Batala, Panjab. His grandfather was a medical doctor in service to the British in Panjab and later to the princely state in Bahawalpur. Aziz transferred from Forman Christian College to Government College to complete his BA and MA, where he studied history, English, and political science. He went on to study in Manchester, England.

Aziz is one of the central figures of dissent against Pakistan's nationalist historiography, or the Urdu-prose version of Islamic history that was championed as the state ideal by I.H. Qureshi and S.M. Ikram. Aziz never really found an institutional home inside Pakistan. Instead, his working life was spent in London, Khartoum, and Heidelberg (with a brief stint as "Deputy to the Official Historian of the Government of Pakistan" in 1961–63). His output, over fifty books, focused on Muslim history from the eighteenth century to the post-1947 period. He produced bibliographies, chronologies, handbooks, primary documentation for key individuals and organizations, collected works of political leaders, and essays on history, politics, art, and culture.

He returned to Pakistan, in 1973, at the behest of Prime Minister Zulfiqar Ali Bhutto, to head a new historical research commission. The aim was to provide the country a new historical basis after the bloody civil war and independence for East Pakistan. The moment was short-lived, as Bhutto was deposed in 1977 by General Zia ul Haq. Aziz fled Pakistan, having burned his papers in fear that the dictator would use them against him. He returned only in 1987, after Zia ul Haq's death, and spent the rest of his life standing in public opposition to the nation's dominant ideas regarding its historiography. His final publications, in the late 2000s, were autobiographies and family histories. It is in these books that he launched and developed his critique of the nation-making project undertaken by the post-1971 Pakistani state.

The nationalist project was most persuasively presented in *The Ideology of Pakistan and Its Implementation*, published in 1959 by Justice Javed Iqbal, who was the son of Muhammad Iqbal. The book was a direct response to the edicts, or prompts concerning state ideology, that the then reigning military dictator, Field Marshal Mohammad Ayub Khan, had issued. In Javed Iqbal's argument, the ideology of Pakistan could only be understood through the lens of Islam, which "cements us as a nation," and the state should have one language, Urdu, with the Bangla script being converted into the Perso-Arabic script.[17] Historiography, Javed Iqbal wrote, should focus solely on Islam's distinction from Hinduism (and communism). The nationalist project only hardened after 1971, the same year that Javed Iqbal issued a revision and expansion of his book. During the subsequent dictatorship of Zia ul Haq, much of this intellectual edifice was ported into the legal infrastructure; history was banished as a subject and replaced by "Pakistan Studies," which combined ethno-nationalism with majoritarianism.

Aziz's life's work was a dissent against this ideology. History was the domain through which he launched his critique. The "most astonishing act of self-abnegation" to him was the abandonment of Persian and Panjabi. This had rendered hundreds of years of the past completely illegible to history. Further, the archives are missing, he wrote in *The Pakistani Historian* (1992)—they were either taken by the British, or left behind in India as a result of Partition, or later destroyed by the dictators. Also missing was any critical bone in the journalists, bureaucrats, and state-appointed historians who churned out the vast majority of histories. The history journals were full of hagiographical or fantastical accounts of the past.

Aziz contended that Pakistani historians were beholden to the state, that their aim was to defend the state's self-proclaimed enemies: Hinduism and communism. This aim rested on an idealized Islam, and the sole function and feature of history writing was to defend this Islam. In *The Murder of History in Pakistan* (1993), he traced the material infrastructure by closely examining sixty-six school textbooks written (mostly by the Punjab Textbook Board) for students in grades 1 through 14. These textbooks, he concluded, demonized Hindus, glorified conquerors, and cultivated unfailing support for the state's military elite and rulers.

He turned to the city, and to memory, in order to show the shallowness and the errors in the dominant nationalist history. His Panjabi heritage became the site from which to launch a new project, late in life, of reclaiming the past from the nation. He traced the biography of his own family going back three generations from Batala to Lahore in *The Coffee House of Lahore, a Journey into the Past: Portrait of a Punjabi Family, 1800–1970* (2005), and *Autobiography*, vol. 1, *1927–48* (2006). These books highlighted the multiplicities of languages, of intermixed social worlds, of Hindu and Sikh friendships, of political fealty (to native rulers), and disobedience (to nationalists).

There is a commitment in these works to telling the stories not of great men and women but of ordinary people. This lesson, he writes, was given to him by his friend Zaheer Kashmiri in Lahore, after he took Aziz to a film showing "labourers, street vendors, tonga drivers and the louts of the locality." Zaheer described them as "the unwashed whom you have never met. They are the people for whose freedom the Congress, your Muslim League, and my [Communist] Party are struggling. And you have never before met these people whom the whole problem is about. You talk about the independence and the future of the country but you don't know the people who live [here]."[18] By looking very closely at the margins of his own existence, as he would do, and finding the stories of those who inhabit the same social space as him, Aziz highlighted a critical deficit in history writing by post-independence historians of Pakistan.

This trilogy of books provided an antidote to the top-down, nationalist, and xenophobic histories of the era in which he lived. Aziz offered in these memoirs a focus on the intimate and the domestic, on the relationships between close friends, between parents, and between siblings, and on the disruptions that colonial and state violence would have on these lives. "The autobiographies and biographies are the only writings which bring history, literature, and society together," he wrote.[19]

Aziz noted that none of the important political and cultural figures of Pakistan had produced autobiographies or even left behind their personal papers, rendering their legacies specifically vulnerable to manipulations by later generations. This led him to, where possible, create documentary archives for specific notable individuals, in an attempt to preserve others' papers and finally to write his own history and that of his family. Aziz's emphasis on Panjabi, as his heritage, as the language of his past, but also as the repository of the social history of Punjab in texts such as Waris Shah's *Hir*, was another direct critique of the dominant ideology. He localized the history—moving its focus away from the nation-state and from Urdu, and toward the self and toward Punjabi.

The centrality of the city was crucial. In his description, Lahore's culture was the "joint handiwork of non-Muslims and Muslims," and "Hindus and Hindu political groups had built public spaces for people of all communities."[20] There was a Lahore where his father, Abdul Aziz, could chat about Rumi with a member of the Sikh royal family in a bookstore near Anarkali owned by a Hindu. This vanished almost overnight through intense violence, as Lahore burned for weeks during the mass exodus of the Sikh and Hindu population from Lahore. The history constructed in its aftermath deliberately wrote such intertwined lives out of the past.

VII.

Hindu ki bas eik khasusiat: Baghl mein churi, moen par Ram Ram. It was 1983 and the teacher read the line with a sneer. I was in General Zia ul Haq's Lahore and my ninth-grade social sciences teacher was explaining how Hindus could never be trusted, as they were the hidden enemies of Muslims in places like Lahore and Sind. Our teacher, a history enthusiast, was delighted to field my hesitant question: "Sir, why are Hindus never to be trusted?" "Because they will betray your trust," he replied, "just as they betrayed the Muslims, again and again, during colonial times."

"Class, what is the 'Two Nation Theory'?" the teacher asked, and then launched into an explanation: "Hindus and Muslims are two separate civilizations that existed side-by-side without any cultural, religious, or economic overlap. Muslims were a minority. Muslims were persecuted by the Hindus, who often joined forces with the British colonial powers. Our leaders Quaid-e-Azam Muhammad Ali Jinnah and Allama Muhammad Iqbal created this nation to give Muslims a safe haven. Let me give you an example. The British had conquered all of India, but Pakistan was unconquerable. Sind, Punjab, NWFP, and Baluchistan were independent for a hundred years after Plassey! The first to fall was Sind, as the British conquered it in 1843 when a Hindu traitor, Seth Naomul Hotchand, betrayed his Talpur lords and sold his people to the British. Soon after, they had Punjab, they had everything."

I went home and asked my mother about the class lesson. She translated the idiomatic line the teacher had used: "The Hindu has only one characteristic. He conceals a knife at his side, even as his lips intone his devotion to Ram." I remember wanting to see or speak to a Hindu, to corroborate or disprove this assessment, but I knew no such individual. The city itself held only the bare traces of a "Hindu" place-name, or some legend about a boarded-up building that once belonged to a Hindu merchant, or a strange spiral shape buried in the horizon subtly announcing itself as a being, once upon a time, a temple. Lahore, once the city of Madho Lal or Chandarbhan, had disappeared even from memory as a city of Hindus.

Many years later, while engaged in archival research in Sind, I heard mentions of a Hindu "traitor" named Seth Naomul Hotchand (1804–78). He was a wealthy merchant of Karachi who was a close ally of the rulers of Sind, the Mirs of Talpur. However, he was declaimed by others—some of my interlocutors were devout nationalists—as someone who had "betrayed" Sind by allying himself with the British. The colonial East India Company (EIC) would conquer Sind and Karachi in 1843. It was his treachery, the nationalists proclaimed, that had led to the fall of Sind.

Curious, the next time I was in a Karachi bookstore I asked the storekeeper for recommendations about Sind, and was given a small edited volume, *Sind Khamoshi ki Awaz* (Sind the Voice of Silence, 1994), by the historian Mubarak Ali, which included an essay, "Was Naomul a Traitor?" In starkly revisionist form, the essay resisted all calls to declare Hotchand a traitor to Sind. Instead, it methodically laid out the ways in which the colonial state created a division between minorities and the majority, how the EIC used its funds to capture Hotchand's trade network across the Indian Ocean, and how the Muslim rulers also alienated Hotchand by failing to protect his elder brother from a religious mob.

These details of the story were illuminating to me, but what was more remarkable was that Dr. Mubarak Ali presented, in an inhospitable postcolonial Pakistan, the precarity and violence that was always present for a visible and prominent minority such as the Hindus. I found it to be a remarkably clear-eyed and brave piece of writing, even more so considering that it was originally written at the height of a public uprising against the dictatorship of Zia ul Haq, under the Movement for Restoration of Democracy in 1983.

"I wrote it by hand and published it myself," he told me. There were no venues for a young historian at that time to publish. Ali was born in Tonk (Rajasthan) in 1941. In his memoir, *Dar Dar Thokar Khaye* (1996), he describes migrating from Tonk to Hyderabad (Sind) in 1952, losing not only his house and belongings but a way of life. Ali began his MA in history at Sind University in Hyderabad in 1961, and began teaching there as a lecturer in 1962. In 1970, he went to London and from there to Ruhr Universität Bochum, Germany, for his PhD, which was on the Mughal period. When he returned in 1976, he began teaching at Sind University again. His time as a professor was short-lived and difficult because he did not enjoy any political patronage. Eventually driven out, he moved to Lahore in the mid-1980s and never held any further position in an academic institution.

This ostracization from academia allowed him (or forced him) to become an independent public historian (or "people's historian," as he is often called) who focused first on the history of Sind and then on medieval history. His earliest works are remarkable for their attention to women and lower-caste communities. Since the very beginning, his writings focused specifically on the question of history writing itself—on *tarikh* (history)—and what it meant for this postcolonized society. He recognized how national histories embellished their pasts, the weight of an ideological frame, the tendency to spout majoritarian dogma. In contrast, he wrote in simple, direct Urdu, and in his extensive history books, he would quite often include lengthy discourses on historical evidence, modes of history writing, and the necessity of a bias-free and rational mode of inquiry.

He wrote quickly (he was writing to eat, as he explained), and tried his best to control the means of his production by self-publishing. By various counts, he wrote nearly a hundred sole-authored books in Urdu and English. Also, beginning in 1999, he was the founding editor of a quarterly journal, *Tarikh* (History), which is now nearing its ninetieth issue. Where K.K. Aziz focused on Punjabi and autobiography as a means of dissent, Ali made historical consciousness his central object of study.

Across the breadth of his works are a number of significant studies. *In the Shadow of History* (1993) and *History on Trial* (1999) are based on his columns for national or regional newspapers. Others, such as *History and Philosophy of History* (1993), *The Tragedy of History* (1993), and *Hidden History* (2005), are composed of short essays. His work is intended to question national ideology, to seek alternative explanations for the causes of historical events (alternative to the theological ones, at least) and to pay attention to the social dimensions of history.

I began to visit him in his house in Lahore about ten years ago. He had lost his vision before we first met, and when my own work on Sind was published, I was eager to gain his approval, or at least his acknowledgment. He received me graciously, and over many meetings I came to learn about the ethos that had governed this historian's momentous output. He remains staunchly anti-dictatorial and anti-establishment in his outlook. His education in Germany had alerted him to the danger of a complacent or collaborationist intelligentsia. He saw a parallel in Pakistan, a country with a right wing led by journalists, bureaucrats, and historians who had worked to support an anti-minority, anti-civilian ruling elite.

The military, he said, is not separate from Pakistan's civil society. It is formed from it and by it. The sons of everyday Pakistanis join the military in droves, and then these soldiers retire to join the civic society in bureaucratic, corporate, and entrepreneurial roles, forming another layer of the civil-military society. Thus, it was analytically important to think of the social world in Pakistan as co-constitutive whenever the subject of a struggle between the military and the civil society arose. History, Ali asserted, was the clearest domain where the civilian and military segments converged—in their joint yearning for a golden past, for conquering heroes, for Sunni majoritarianism.

Dr. Mubarak Ali, who at this writing is now in his early eighties, is a unique figure in Lahore. His house is a gathering spot for a range of political and academic cohorts. He is occasionally feted by his long-standing students and admirers. Yet, he lives alone in a small house under an imposing bridge. As the bulk of his output is in Urdu, the anglophone elite remain unaware or uncaring about his concerns. His name is known yet unknown. A subject himself of the Partition of the subcontinent, his life's struggle to articulate a critical analytic for history remains niche. In another volume of memoir, *Meri Dunya* (2014), Ali takes a survey of his own historical writing and asks, of what utility were these many volumes? The only wealth he has acquired, he recounts, is his writings, for they attest to the clarity of a historian constantly at the margins of political and social powers.

Returning from his home, I crossed a cluster of railway lines through a small underpass path, walking alongside an open sewer. It was late evening in December and the narrow street was crowded with bicycles and cars. As I walked, with only an inkling that I was heading toward Gulberg, I saw a small child walking alongside me, clutching a set of books. "What are you studying?" I asked him.

"I am heading to the madrasa," he said.

"What will you study there?"

"It is the history lesson today," he offered, and hurried off into the narrow alley away from me.

4

MEMORY: MAKING ORIGINS

Memory can be a site of dissent when history is presumed to be a site for constructing a unitary national collective. There are memories about Lahore, about its origins being older than a millennium. To remember them now is to recognize that stories, myths, legends can contain narratives contrary to the acknowledged or accustomed history. Lahore, like many other cities of Hindustan, has a specific origin story embedded in its most ancient epics and histories. In this origin story about Lahore, Rama and Sita had two sons, Lava and Kusha. Lava founded Lahore and Kusha founded Kasur (a town some thirty miles south of Lahore). Some believe that a small structure sequestered inside the Lahore Fort is a temple to Lava. This origin story marks Lahore's relationship with *Ramayana* and also with particular strands of veneration. It anchors the city in a different time and cosmology than the Muslim one. The continued memory of this origin widens the narrow tunnel of history toward a Muslim Lahore.

I would never have known this particular origin story if not for another storyteller. I never knew the story of *Ramayana*. A chance encounter with an Urdu novel by a "rebel" woman author (as marked by the newspaper accounts I read in the mid-1980s) opened that vein of history and memory for me. The tale of the god and goddess, Ram and Sita, is recounted in a slim novel of Partition and its aftermath, *Sita Haran* (The Abduction of Sita, 1960) by Qurratulain Hyder (1927–2007).

Hyder's *Sita Haran* revolves around Sita Mirchandani. Born in Hyderabad and a refugee to Delhi, Mirchandani marries a

Muslim man from Ayodhya and with him has a child. But, at
the beginning of the story, the marriage is in trouble and she is
separated from both of them. Mirchandani has a PhD from Columbia, where she completed a dissertation on evacuees from
Panjab. In the novella, Mirchandani constantly crosses, or trans-
gresses, borders. Embedded in that movement across Sind, Panjab, and Sri Lanka are vignettes that tell the story of Sita and
Ram from the *Ramayana*. In one journey, Mirchandani recounts
the origin stories for Sind (Bharata, Ram's half brother, laid its
foundation) and Sehwan (Maharaja Shibi from the *Mahabharata*
laid the foundation of this holy city in Sind). In another,
Mirchandani remembers her grandfather telling her stories
from the *purana* (histories).

The novella links Mirchandani and Sita as characters: they are
both in exile from their husbands; they face the hurtful gaze of
others who condemn them for their independence, for learning,
for knowing; and they are both punished by the men in their life,
in the name of honor or love.

After finishing *Sita Haran*, I turned to Hyder's magnum opus,
Aag ka Darya (River of Fire, 1959), for more of her intoxicating
vision of the deep past of the subcontinent. Hyder had migrated
to Pakistan after Partition but moved back to India in 1961. The
dictatorship of Ayub and the toxic nationalism of the period may
have been the reason.[1] *Aag ka Darya*, a grand epic, revolves
around two characters—Gautam and Champa—who first meet
across a river in the fourth century BCE. They go on to meet
again and again, in the forms of their own recurring avatars—
first in fifteenth-century Bengal, then at the end of the sixteenth
century, at the end of the eighteenth century, in the nineteenth
century, and finally during the present day. The latter-day (rein-
carnated) forms of Gautam and Champa trace the memories of
their earlier selves.

Throughout that spiral timescape runs "the river." Sometimes
that river is the Ganges, sometimes the Ravi, and sometimes the
Indus. What it represents, for Hyder, is an idea of Hindustan that

unites people over and over across centuries. I had never read anything so profoundly knowing in my young life, and it was only
later that I discovered that the version I had purchased and read
had been censored.

Hyder articulated a truth in her fiction that was composed of
everyday experience. Her memory, described in her novels, is the
resistance against the ongoing commemoration of Islam in her
Pakistan. She was writing *Aag ka Darya* in a nation-state actively
erasing a common past for the people of India and Pakistan.
Hence, she wrote it as history. Here is how she defined the idea of
a Hindustan that was not partitioned by faith:

> What was Hindustan? He had never thought of it consciously. He
> was just used to the Hindustan where he had been born. Where his
> ancestors had kept on being born for the last seven, eight hundred
> years. In this Hindustan were fields of mustard greens, well-water
> wheels, temples to mother goddess Sita. Hindustan was that hill
> where he went with his father, and where in the veranda a fat, B.A.
> educated priest sat, whom his mother had given ten rupees for a
> blessing. Hindustan was that workshop in Itawa where the wall-
> perched caretakers of a dark-smeared shrine had fed Kamal an or-
> ange from Batol. Hindustan was the old mother of the chauffeur
> Qadeer who showed up at Mirzapur's station in a yellow dress with
> clay toys for Kamal. Hindustan was those Civil Lines streets where
> the dog-boys of people walked their dogs in the evenings. Hindu-
> stan was the old chef, Haji Basharat Hussain, who, when Kamal
> had gotten the pox, took off his two-ply hat and got on one leg and
> cried out: Goddess, forgive, please leave this small child, I am beg-
> ging with both hands in front of you goddess. This old Muslim
> man begging in front of Sita, he was Hindustan. And those
> mothers, aunties, women of the household were also Hindustan.
> Their intimate language, their sayings, songs, rituals, old stories,
> passed down from the Mughal times about the Raja from Ayo-
> dhya, Dasharatha, with his wives Kausalya and Kaikeyi. [Hindu-
> stan was] the stories from Hindu *purana* and *devshala*.[2]

This is an immense counter-history. Her examples of a "lived-in" Hindustan are not based on theological or civilizational difference, nor does any character confess any alterity for either faith. Hyder listed an array of commonplace and well-understood practices, feelings, and sights. I could easily find parallel, almost verbatim, examples in the memoirs of Lahore. Som Anand, who lived in Model Town in Lahore, wrote about his Muslim chauffeur praying to save his Hindu charges. Nur Ahmad Chishti described Muslim devotees at the temple of Kali Mata. Hyder was articulating the truth of such a conjoined Hindustan, and doing so in the aftermath of a bloody Partition and during a period of military dictatorship. She was making the case for an idea of Hindustan that had been violently erased, discarded, and deemed treasonous to evoke by the authorities. She was accordingly condemned, first by the male literary elite in the press, and then by various authorities. The novel itself was dismissed as flat, predictable, unoriginal, and in spite of all that, too cerebral to be entertaining fiction.

Hyder, after moving to India, reinterpreted and "transcreated" (as she put it) the novel into English as *River of Fire* (1998). It was received with much acclaim. She would continue to publish and write in India on her idea of Hindustan, including with a remarkable combination of memoir, fiction, and history called *Kar-e Jahan Daraz hai* (The Endless Task of This World; the first volume was published in 1977 and the second in 1979). Her works are duly celebrated and acknowledged in India and around the world, but her departure from Pakistan also represents a shunning of her worldview by the country's elite. It heralded an end to any lingering memories, in Pakistan, of a river that united.

In September 1965 came the war between India and Pakistan at Lahore's border, and just five years later, West Pakistan started a bloody civil war against the eastern wing of Pakistan. If political forgetting—the deliberate erasure of shared histories across the border—was once an astute tool for Pakistani nationalism, it was

now not enough. Indeed, new forms of commemoration were created. Already, in the 1950s, the agitation against Ahmadis had
created pressure on the nation-state to begin carrying out a litmus
test of faith and enforcing new borders within the nation. The
creation of Bangladesh and Pakistan in 1971, as well as the wars
with India, fundamentally retooled what story was required for
"a homeland for Muslims."

The state commemoration was in direct contrast to the memories evoked by Hyder. To create this new Pakistan, officials turned
to new origin stories, consecrated by a "classicization of tradition,"
as Partha Chatterjee calls it, and a new politics of commemorative
remembering. The origins of Lahore were not in the *Ramayana*,
these new stories asserted. Rather, Lahore was founded by a
Ghaznavi or Aibak or Ayaz—outsiders to the subcontinent and
Muslims. Pakistan was not hewn from Hindustani limestone. It
was founded by Qasim, a warrior and conqueror from Syria.

These were not altogether "new" arguments. Since the early
nineteenth century, the colonial rule of difference was already a
prominent political force. The premise was that Muslims were outsiders to the subcontinent—hence, unfit to rule and unfit to claim
belonging, but fit to be deposed and punished by the liberating,
liberal British regime. Hundreds of colonial soldier-scribes, Orien-
talists, governors-general, lords, and viceroys spilled a tremendous
amount of ink on this idea, making it concrete with maps, histories, dictionaries, ethnographies, censuses, and so on.

This was made new by a set of Muslim male intellectuals,
writing in Urdu, in Pakistan. They deployed the same methods
(philology and history) and genres (historical romance) as the
English colonizers to resituate the origin of Pakistan. They turned
to public commemorative remembering in order to create a new
righteous past. They claimed as history what memories of a united
Hindustan would have contested as being untrue. They not only
claimed the origins of the nation in Arabia as history, but they
helped the state formalize it via holidays, celebrations, monuments,

special issues of newspapers and journals, novels, caste histories, and personifications of national character—such as the *ghazi* (warrior).

This dyad of forgetting and remembering, begun in the early 1960s, gained nation-making status in the early 1970s, and created a whole new country by the early 1980s. Memory and history did not stand in contrast or contention with one another—the makers of the new nation worked in sync to enforce new origins—erasing a temple here, building a mosque there, condemning a Hindu ruler here, celebrating a Muslim conqueror there, denigrating a language here, valorizing a script there. There was a new investment in a list of the "Heroes of Islam," with historical figures stripped bare of their contexts and complexities and instead made into patriarchs of families and castes, poster boys for the post-Partition generations.

Lahore plays a pivotal role in this commemorative remembering. It is the print capital, the center of Urdu publishing, with a robust infrastructure of newspapers and magazines and a cultural and religious elite. It is a seat of ethnic Punjabi domination in the new Pakistan. It is not possible to tell the story of Lahore without linking it to this national project. Journalists, writers, and columnists who were at the forefront of creating these new origins for the nation were all embedded in Lahore.

I was the generation that grew up in the early 1980s, and who was taught the Punjab Textbook Board school textbooks that proclaimed a new Arab origin for the nation. We were asked to make dioramas featuring the conquest of Debal, in Sind, by Muhammad bin Qasim, the first citizen of Pakistan, in 711–12. Teachers read aloud from the textbook and we, the students, repeated the "facts" of this pantomime of history. It was routine, a banal fact of daily school life. Everyone performed their roles dutifully. I was not taught about Lava and Kusha, nor was I ever given a chance to read about Rama and Sita. That is how a nation forgets.

In order to tell this history of commemoration and forgetting, I retraced the formative people and events of these national projects. I visited the small offices of monthly magazines and the showrooms of publishers. Publishing was also the geography of the city. I began my walk in Patiala Ground where many magazines had their offices, walked down McLeod Road where many printers held shop, up the Mall Road where many organizations rented rooms in ornate *havelis*, behind the Postmaster General, and into the Urdu Bazaar, which was the center for paper, ink, glue, printing, and distribution for nearly the whole country. These walks took place over the course of many years, as fragments of the history revealed themselves in different interviews. The walks also followed the history of dissent—the history of authors, such as Hyder, who were brave enough to remember.

I.

Figure 5.1. Minar-e Pakistan (2015)

Mukhtar Masood served as deputy commissioner of Lahore, among other positions, and headed the building of the Minar in the 1960s. The Minar-e Pakistan (Tower of Pakistan) was a monument created to represent the Muslim ideals of statehood, he wrote in his 1973 memoir of the project.[3] The tower was commissioned by Ayub Khan, then military dictator, in 1959, and it took ten years to complete. It was built to commemorate the site of the Lahore Resolution in 1940 in Minto Park, and was intended to create a new monument for Lahore in a locale central to the sites of the seventeenth-century Badshahi Mosque, the Lahore Fort, and the open spaces extending to the Ravi in the northwest. The architect who won the commission, Nasreddin Murat-Khan, was himself a Dagestani refugee who came to Pakistan in 1950.

Masood migrated to Pakistan in 1948. He became a civil bureaucrat and served two of Pakistan's longest-serving military dictators. His reflections, as a member of the ruling civilian elite, on the Minar provide a key vantage point in discerning the state's ideas about its immediate history. Masood was typical of this earliest generation of civilian autocrats. He was an Urdu-speaking Sunni Muslim. He had studied at Aligarh University, where his father had been a professor, and he flourished in Pakistan, eventually retiring as a federal minister. This was more or less the background of all the elites who were put in charge of constructing the majoritarian perspective for the new nation-state.

His book is a combination of memoir, potted history of "Islamic civilization," and essays on various architectural sites. From the Sumerian to the Egyptian, monumental architecture has a distinct relationship to power and to posterity. The minarets of mosques, especially from Umayyad Damascus and Jerusalem, represent a claim to piety and access to the divine. But the key antecedents for the Pakistani Minar are the victory towers of the dynasties built in Ghazna and Ghur in eleventh- and twelfth-century Afghanistan. These towers marked victories and conquests, and were seen as massive testimonies to the sacral powers gifted by God to the rulers. They were covered with verses from the Qur'an and were intended to reflect the specific relationship between people, the past, and God. The Minar of Pakistan needed to display political power the same way that the victory towers of Afghanistan did.

Masood marks the relationship between the victory towers of Ghazna and the Minar of Lahore through the material he used.

The base of the Minar represents the conqueror Shahabuddin Gauri, assassinated in the hills of Potohar in 1206 on his way back from sacking Lahore. Masood felt that this particular moment recognized the clear distinction between the Hindus and Muslims as different civilizations. The text of the Lahore Resolution from 1940, which was inscribed at the base of the tower, signifies the culmination of history from the early thirteenth century. Ghur's blood spilled in Hindustan sparked the struggle for a separate homeland for Muslims in the subcontinent.

The Lahore Resolution of 1940 demanded a free, "independent state" for the geographically contiguous areas where the Muslims were the numerical majority. These were the North Western and Eastern Zones of British India. Muhammad Ali Jinnah, the leader of the Muslim League, the political party seeking the Resolution, stated in Lahore on March 22, 1940, that "the history of the last twelve hundred years has failed to achieve unity and has witnessed, during these ages, India always divided into Hindu India and Muslim India. The present artificial unity of India dates back only to the British conquest and is maintained by the British bayonet, but the termination of the British regime, which is implicit in the recent declaration of His Majesty's Government, will be the herald of the entire break-up, with worse disaster than has ever taken place during the last one thousand years under the Muslims."[4]

Jinnah's speech underlined that the political question of electorates and sovereignty rested on a timeline of disharmony and disorder. The history of the subcontinent, and by assumption the history of the city in which he was standing, was predicated on the disordered history of "two different religious philosophies, social customs, and literature[s] [that] neither intermarry nor interdine together, and indeed . . . belong to two different civilizations which are based mainly on conflicting ideas and conceptions." The very end of that sentence provided the kinetic force to all that had ever happened and would happen: the two define themselves on conflicting ideas, mainly of each other. This would become an elaboration of the "Two-Nation Theory" upon which the call for a separate political nation-state would be articulated in the 1946 elections.

The speech also had a specific cultural aspect. Jinnah says to the one hundred thousand assembled:

> It is quite clear that Hindus and Mussalmans derive their inspiration from different sources of history. They have different epics, their heroes are different, and different episode[s]. Very often *the hero of one is a foe of the other*, and likewise their victories and defeats overlap. To yoke together two such nations under a single state, one as a numerical minority and the other as a majority, must lead to growing discontent and the final destruction of any fabric that may be so built up for the government of such a state.[5]

His argument was that history for these different peoples has different origins, and the stories that emerge are mutually, and reciprocally, antagonistic. This is the birth of the "Anti-Other" national story. Masood's memoir of the tower being built to commemorate the Lahore Resolution crystallized these stories and consecrated the divergent sources of histories. In crediting the victory towers of Shahabuddin Gauri as the ideal form for Minar, he put the origins of Pakistan on a timeline of warfare—Gauri was engaged in prolonged conflict with the Hindu ruler of Delhi, Prithviraj Chauhan.

Upward from the base of the Minar, each step of the stairs in his telling a literal step in the progression of history, Masood continues assigning dates to each step: 1510s, the "towers of skulls" erected by Babur; 1670, the mosque built by Aurangzeb Alamgir. Then, Masood says, there was a gap in time until 1857, the year of the anti-colonial revolution against the British East India Company. In 1868 came the foundation of a separate university for Muslims in Aligarh—in contrast to the Hindu University in Benares. In 1906, Lord Minto (the governor general of British India who would give his name to the Mughal gardens in which the Lahore Resolution would be passed) met a delegation of Muslims asking for separate universities and electorates. In 1917, the freedom fighting Khairi brothers asked for a division of Hindustan at the Stockholm Socialist Conference. In 1939, three possible names were discussed for this future Muslim polity: Pakistan, Bang-e Islam (Call of Islam), and Usmanistan. In 1940, the Lahore Resolution was finally approved. In 1944, the Hindu nationalist party Akhil Bharat Hindu Mahasabha demanded that all Muslims of the subcontinent be forcibly reconverted back to Hinduism (based on their argument that all Muslims in India were forcibly converted to Islam). Finally, for Masood, the next two years marked the elections, leading up to which Muslim students traveled across the subcontinent asking for votes for a separate electorate.

His essay ends with a Persian verse from the fourteenth-century Sufi Hasan Sijzi: *It is a tale of love, such that cannot be contained in one notebook.* Much certainly goes unmentioned. Masood does not mention the violence of Partition. He does not mention that the very grounds of Minto Park, Lahore, were where refugees were resettled in August 1947. He does not mention the violence that spread through Hindu and Sikh houses, shops, markets, temples, and gurdwaras. He does not mention the religious elite who led the agitations for rejecting Bangla as a language and who declared Ahmadis non-Muslims at this very same Minto Park. Nor elsewhere, or anywhere, does he mention that the eastern half of Pakistan was subject to military invasion and the massacre of civilians in order to be reborn as an independent Bangladesh, and that one of the largest crowds in support of the Pakistan army gathered at Iqbal Park (née Minto Park). He does not, in his staging of history, place any event, text, memory, or person in what would become East Pakistan, in 1947, and Bangladesh in 1971. This is a history that stretches from Gaur to Lahore and Lahore to Gaur.

In the weaving of particular moments and personae, the twin projects of commemorative remembering and political forgetting take concrete shape. Massood's memoir is just one among many texts to create a collective memory that resolves, or rather cements, the identity of a twice-partitioned nation-state. Tellingly, Masood posits that if 1947 had not happened, the Muslims of the subcontinent would be doing menial, caste-sanctioned jobs like "cutting grass" rather than "driving in cars." A particular teleology, faith, and class would create a seamless version of history that culminates in the victory tower. Caste and language—his text is celebrated, then and now, as an exemplar of Urdu prose—would underscore the violence of 1971.

I first began to go to Iqbal Park in the late 1980s to play cricket. It was hallowed ground. The top cricketers of the country would assemble there, often to play open matches. My uncle had told me that this was the park where Pakistan's first cricket team, led by A.H. Kardar, would practice. The team itself was partitioned, with half of the players choosing to remain in India as the Indian cricket team. Mir Elahi, the older brother of my maternal grandfather, was a member of the native team of British India and chose to join the Pakistan cricket team. He would do his net practice at Minto Park in the early 1950s. My own sense of this personal history would always cloud my eyes at the park. I cannot recall ever consciously looking at the victory tower.

Iqbal Park in the late 1980s remains in my memory as a moment frozen in time. Cricketers I worshipped as gods playing next to me. The blue sky filled with colorful kites of all sizes, and the park filled with men hanging on to the strings. I remember lectures delivered (perhaps impromptu) on histories of kite flying, pigeon tending, swing bowling, *beedi* smoking, cross-dressing, bhang drinking, ecstatic dancing. In my memory of Lahore those afternoons, and a very few evenings, seem to last three hundred years.

II.

A small side street off Anarkali bazaar leads to a yellow structure whose construction began in the 1970s and ended in the 1990s. The structure is labeled "Mausoleum of Sultan Qutb-ud-Din Aibak. Died at Lahore in 607 AH 1210 AD." The street used to be known for the many publishing houses that rented rooms, storefronts, and basements there. At some point in the 1960s, it was renamed "Aibak Street." Before that, the mausoleum was simply an elevated platform with a brick edifice on top of it, without a roof or any walls.

Histories of the eighteenth century mention that a domed, marbled structure did exist at this gravesite, and that there was some notion of an annual pilgrimage. Yet there is no indication that people visiting the gravesite understood it to be the last resting place of Aibak. The domed structure was dismantled while the Sikhs ruled Lahore, and new homes and houses were constructed on the site. Whether Aibak's physical remains ever rested in Lahore or not, this particular grave had disappeared from public view by the late nineteenth century. The British colonial administrators "discovered" the grave in the basement of a law practice in the early twentieth century.

In the early 1960s, poet Hafiz Jalandhari, who wrote the lyrics to Pakistan's national anthem, appealed directly to the military dictator Ayub Khan for Aibak's tomb in Lahore to be reconstructed. To make his case, Jalandhari wrote a poem that described an

Figure 5.2. Tomb of Aibak (2014)

afternoon siesta near the site of the abandoned, forgotten tomb in Anarkali, where he dreamt of heroically galloping across fields: *"This highest of kings, now rests in the basement of a rich Hindu lawyer / Even his loved ones forgot him in a short time / So is the warrior buried under this mound of dirt."* The appeal to Ayub Khan must have worked, because in the late 1960s the houses were cleared out, and the gravesite was marked for the construction of a mausoleum.

It is odd that a powerful king such as Aibak would disappear from view, especially so in Lahore. The city was where the earliest histories and genealogies of Muslims were written in Hindustan. Fakhruddin Mudabbir, who lived in Lahore (he called it a city full of historians and libraries), consulted a thousand books to write his own *Shajara-yi ansab* (Tree of Genealogies). He presented it to Aibak around 1206. Another historian, Tajuddin Hasan Nizami, also dedicated his history, *Taj ul Ma'athir* (Crown of Glories), to Aibak. Much of *Taj ul Ma'athir* is a compilation of accounts of Aibak's sieges and routs from Ghazni to Multan, Delhi, Ajmer, Gwalior, and other sites. Aibak was not only a powerful warlord, he was beloved of historians and poets—two communities that a king can count on for posterity's grace. Aibak's patronage and his famous royal library were key components of Lahore's intellectual life.

Aibak's Lahore was full of possibilities and conflict. It had already been more than a century since Ghazni and Lahore were linked as cities under the same monarch (Mahmud of Ghazni). Aibak would play an important role in continuing the development of the city. Lahore and Uch were two of the most visible Muslim centers at the time, although neither had a Muslim majority. Many scholars migrated there, perhaps in the hundreds or thousands, from Western or Central Asia to seek new patrons in Hindustan. Contemporary accounts tell of poets, historians, theologians, jurists, merchants, and traders who had come to Lahore and Uch over the course of around half a century, making the cities important emerging capitals of ideas and polities. Lahore was nearer to the trade network that stretched across the subcontinent. Uch, closer to the sea, was also part of the Indian Ocean trade network. Both these cities were hubs of institutional memories, full of libraries and universities. They were also spaces where the question of religious coexistence was paramount for the ruling elite.

Aibak was in Lahore only briefly. He was part of the elite "bonded" conscripts (known as *turk* in the contemporary Persian sources, *banda* or *ghulam* later). They were military commanders who had spent the previous forty years establishing the Shansabani polity, with its capital in Ghur, which stretched across current-day Afghanistan to Bangladesh. Aibak was bonded to Shahabuddin (d. 1206), who ruled alongside his brother Ghiyasuddin (d. 1203). He was also Shahabuddin's son-in-law. Much of Aibak's life was spent expanding the Ghurid polity from his base of operations in Lahore at the behest of his master and king. What we know of Aibak comes largely from the historians he gathered in Lahore: they recalled him being exceptionally generous. His title was *lakhbaksh*, one who gives away millions.

The Shansabani repeatedly conquered Ghazna, the capital of their rivals, and eventually Ghiyasuddin and Shahabuddin would destroy Ghazna in 1173, ending the Yamini-Ghaznavi dominion (ca. 998–1186) over Khurasan and what is now northern Punjab. Starting in the 1190s, they led campaigns against the cities of Peshawar, Lahore, Multan, Uch, Delhi, Ajmer, and Gwalior, and against the remnants of the Yamini-Ghaznavi rulers, but also the Chaulukyas and the Chahamana, who formed the central-northwestern polities. Lahore's destruction and conquest in 1185 was a key part of this overall military strategy to create a base of operation farther east in order to attack Delhi. Shahabuddin would launch his campaigns against Prithviraj Chauhan in 1191, and then 1192 from Lahore.

In some modern accounts, Shahabuddin becomes the "first" Muslim king of Hindustan (in contrast with the Prithviraj Chauhan, the "last" Hindu king he defeated in 1192). Others would give that moniker to Aibak since he was crowned king in Lahore after Shahabuddin's death at the hands of Ghakkar assassins near the river Jhelum in 1206. Aibak, who was in Delhi when he received the news of Shahabuddin's assassination, rushed to Lahore, where he took the title of sultan. He remained in Lahore for the next four years and died after falling from his horse while playing polo and getting crushed. Once buried, Aibak largely disappeared. Though many more generals, princes, and kings would become part of Lahore's fabric, Aibak would become less than a memory.

The memory of his master Shahabuddin suffered a similar fate. The historians closest to him described his murder occurring near Damyak, where a team of assassins overpowered the guards and stabbed the praying Shahabuddin six or seven times (per the historian Nizami). The body of the slain Muslim king was taken to Ghazna for burial. Firishta, recounting the same event from early in the seventeenth century, inflated the number of stab wounds to twenty-two, but also maintained that his remains were taken to Ghazna. Yet another memory persisted.

A few years ago, while walking on Aibak's street toward Anarkali, I came across a small children's book at a shop display: *Shahabuddin Gauri* by M. Ramzan Gauhar. The cover, featuring a bearded man, mounted and armored, brandishing a curved sword, against the backdrop of a temple, was entirely ordinary, and I was motivated to pick up the book because I just happened to be standing across the street from the tomb of Aibak, one of Gauri's generals. The book become infinitely more attractive as soon as I turned the title page to find it dedicated to the "Benefactor of Pakistan Abdul Qadir Khan . . . who gave Pakistan pride by building an atomic bomb and made our dear nation an equivalent atomic power to our enemy." The author began by noting that the recent military dictator, Pervez Musharraf, had maligned the "father of the Islamic Atomic Bomb," colloquially known as A.Q. Khan, with accusations of corruption because he had "spent a 100,000 from his own pocket to create a magnificent mausoleum over the decrepit grave of Shahabuddin Gauri." In his preface, the author described how Gauri was the "first founder" of Pakistan, citing Mukhtar Masood's book *Aawaz-e Dost*. In another note, he clarified that Muhammad bin Qasim had laid the foundation of the "Two-Nation Theory," and by dying on March 15, 1206, Shahabuddin Gauri had given the soil of Pakistan the necessary strength with his blood such that it would emerge in 1947.

Off the Grand Trunk Road, some forty miles toward Rawalpindi, is Sohawa, from where you can turn right toward the village
of Kot Dhamiak. The road is now called the Shahabuddin Gauri
road. Just a short drive past the village, off to the right and nestled
amid farms and a girls' school, is Shahabuddin's tomb. It is strik-
ingly beautiful terrain—as if a giant had clawed the earth and then
tried to smooth it. Just twenty miles to the northwest is Mangla
Dam, built in the 1960s on the river Jhelum. The region, named
Potohar Plateau, derives its cultural memory, language, and identity from the ancient networks of the Jhelum and Indus rivers. Histories of the region began to emerge in force once Islamabad was
chosen as the site to build a new capital city for Pakistan in 1959.

A more recent history of the region, *Tazikra-e Auliya-e Potohar*,
published in 2010, details the lives and miracles of 120 famous
notables and Sufis of Potohar. Under the entry for Shahabuddin,
it describes how a prominent Sufi had a dream in December 1987. In the dream, Syed Habib Shah Bukhari saw an assembly of glowing (holy) figures. It was explained in the dream
that they were gathered around Shahabuddin's grave. A few days
later, Bukhari's transportation broke down outside Sohawa, and
he began to walk to his destination. Halfway there, his attention
was suddenly drawn to a cluster of trees. He walked over and
immediately recognized that this was the same site from his dream.
On March 5, 1988, Bukhari organized the first public commemoration of Shahabuddin's death. A.Q. Khan was himself a de-
scendant of Shahabuddin, and when he learned of the existence
of this gravesite, he took it upon himself to finance the construction of a permanent tomb in 1994.

A.Q. Khan was besotted with Shahabuddin. Through the early
1980s and 1990s, he was in charge of the Khan Research Lab at
Kahuta (near Islamabad), working to develop a nuclear bomb.
(India had tested its own nuclear device in 1974 and Pakistan
would conduct its test 1998.) Further, India tested its first short-
range ballistic missile in February 1988 and called it "Prithvi I."
A.Q. Khan would then name Pakistan's first medium-range

ballistic missile "Gauri I" in April 1998. A wooden replica of the missile was installed in front of the mausoleum, and more replicas were installed across town and cities of Pakistan (the most preferred location was near town squares). The one outside Lahore Railway Station is almost ten meters tall.

I met with Raja, who owns land and lives near Kot Dhamiak. He told me a slightly different history when I visited the mausoleum. In his telling, the inhabitants of the local villages had always known of the existence of the grave—which was located on a natural elevated platform and was around twenty feet long. The villagers used it as a meeting point, and it was known simply as "Gauri ki Qabar" (Gauri's grave) but without any understanding of the historical personage. Yet, the intellectuals and elders of the region knew this to be the great conqueror of yore. The torrential rains of 1971 washed away part of the embankment, exposing the remains of Shahabuddin from one side, prompting an effort to preserve this gravesite. A local historian then wrote a letter to the national Urdu newspaper informing the public that the conqueror of Hind was lying in an exposed grave. That column got the attention of the federal minister for information, Sher Ali Khan Pataudi. The Pataudis also claimed descent from Shahabuddin, so he arranged for the grave to be reconstructed and a marble plaque installed. Up to this point, as Raja told the story, we were still within the domains of a local legend and a local history. A.Q. Khan was the new champion of the mausoleum who would make this a national origin myth.

In 1988, A.Q. had been incensed that India had called its missile "Prithvi I." He had a driver, a man local to the area named Sardar Rashid. He had informed A.Q. Khan that the Shahabuddin's grave was known and existed in the region. A.Q. Khan then asked to be introduced to a local historian who confirmed this account, even showing a letter from the mayor of Kabul that there was no grave of Shahabuddin in Afghanistan. A.Q. had the site transferred to Pakistan's archaeology and heritage department, and had the mausoleum installed on the site in 1994–95.

The marble plaque outside the mausoleum now presents a triumphant narrative: "This is the place of Shaheed Sultan Mohammad Ghori's Martyrdom, Conqueror of Hindustan and Founder of the Muslim Empire in Delhi." The marbled exterior is of a nondescript "Central Asian" style and, during my visit, there were no visitors to the site. The marble plaque at the head of the grave had a short poem on one end ("Even his loved ones forgot him in a short time / So is the warrior buried under this mound of dirt"), signed by "Major General Sher Ali." On the other end of the plaque, there was a citation from Juzjani's thirteenth-century history attesting to the fact that Shahabuddin was killed near Dhamiak. Sher Ali Khan Pataudi and his wife are also to be buried in the same complex.

The two (hidden) graves and their subsequent mausoleumification attest to the potency of historical memory as a form of rehabilitation project. The nation, the region, the city—all can deploy figures and symbols from the deep past in order to assert a history. There is little to differentiate the dreams of a revered social figure from those of a poet or a chagrined nuclear scientist. There is a need to find the threads that connect these sites, memories, and histories. I felt, in my visit to Shahabuddin's tomb, an intense familiarity with the stories I would hear at other instances to new sacral histories of Pakistan associated with other warriors such as Muhammad bin Qasim. Notwithstanding the slippery timelines, there was an attention to citational authorities (dreams and letters function in the same way) and to the unique concerns of the present. Qasim or Aibak or Shahabuddin are plucked from history to become the heroes Pakistan needed in the 1970s or in the 1980s or in the 1990s—each moment making its own particular twist upon the past. The answer to the question of how and why such "heroes" are needed at all by the ruling and governing elite takes us deeper into the city and the past.

III.

Figure 5.3. View of Patiala Ground from *Hikayat* offices (2022)

In 1987, a popular Urdu monthly magazine, *Hikayat*, published in Patiala Ground, Lahore, began releasing a new serialized book with the evocative title of *Ayubi, Ghaznavi, aur Muhammad bin Qasim Pakistan mein* ([Salahuddin] Ayubi, [Mahmud] Ghaznavi, and Muhammad bin Qasim in Pakistan). A light satire, it was written by Inayatullah (1920–99), the editor, publisher, and leading author of *Hikayat*. The conceit was that these three "Heroes of Islam" were bored in their post-death Paradise, so they petitioned God to send them back to Earth to see how the Muslims were doing. They were sent to Lahore. Back on Earth, they were confronted by incompetent cops, greedy politicians, and (physically) weak Muslim men. They also encountered ghosts of Muslim soldiers who had died in various campaigns and were bereft because no one remembered them, and guardian angels grown jaded from keeping an eye on the citizens of Lahore, its wayward youth, its rampant culture of drug use and sexual deviance. The book's conservative denunciation makes for grim reading now, despite its supposed light touch.

My mother was especially taken by this story when it began its run. She found the first few installments gripping enough, but once the story moved to "everyday" encounters in the city of Lahore, she thought it imperative that I pay attention. I was, at that moment, trying to plot a way to raise money for my first pair of "American blue jeans" (brand Jordache), which represented something cool and unattainable to me. Their cost marked their class, but also their anti-normative potential against the popular baggy *shalwars* that most Pakistani men wore. In one segment of *Ayubi*, Muhammad bin Qasim, who died as a teenager in the early eighth century and remains as such in posterity, encounters another young Lahori, also a teenage boy, who is wearing tight blue jeans. Inayatullah presents this encounter with jeers and slights toward the Lahori boy, who is weak and feminine, who masturbates too much, and has no love for his country. Inayatullah portrays the Muslim hero Qasim as left wondering if, had he had such a "feminized" youth in his army, he would have been able to win even a single battle. My request for money to buy blue jeans was rejected, and the resulting "conflict" left a series of lingering questions in my mind, foremost among them: Why was Muhammad bin Qasim, some Syrian from the eighth century, ruling my daily life in Lahore?

Inayatullah founded *Hikayat* in 1970 and, by the early 1980s, it was one of the most popular Urdu monthlies in the country. In

1976, he also created the Tahrik Takmil-e Pakistan (Movement for the Fulfillment of Pakistan), an organization with the aim of creating a more robust Muslim youth culture. By the time of his death, he was the author of over two hundred books, ranging from reportage to novels (domestic, social, military, historical). Unlike the other novelists engaged in the national project of inventing stories of Muslim warriors, he was himself a military man.

In the Second World War, he went to the Burma front with the British armed services and was taken as a prisoner of war by the Japanese. After 1947, he joined the Pakistan Air Force, and after his retirement, began his literary career in Lahore. He worked with Shorish Kashmiri and the monthly *Siara* for a while. The 1965 war between India and Pakistan turned him into a war correspondent, and he collected oral histories with frontline soldiers, which were serialized in the *Siara* digest. By the early 1970s, he was the most prominent Urdu writer focusing on armed conflict, with books about war and military men in conflicts with India: *BRB Bahti Rahay gi* (The BRB [Canal] Will Continue to Flow, 1965) and *Badr Se Batapur Tak* (From Badr [the first war of Muslim Community in 624] to Batapur [battle in 1965], 1968). In these "reported" accounts, Inayatullah showcased everyday soldiers performing almost in a superhuman capacity against their "Hindu" opponents.

Inayatullah frames *Badr Se Batapur Tak* as an actual crusade. He depicts the soldiers as constantly invoking the wars and battles from the earliest history of Islam up to the Crusades against the Franks. Their heroism against their Hindu enemy is likened to the exploits of anti-Crusader heroes in Syria or Jerusalem. As these are supposed to be oral histories, Inayatullah produces a sort of pidgin Urdu in which an "illiterate soldier" recounts his precise grasp of the centuries-old conflict between Hindus and Muslims, including appropriate references to the history of Islam. In florid, often lurid, language, Pakistani Army soldiers from many different fronts, though chiefly from Lahore's border with India, narrate their struggle as a long-existing one against armies of apostates and nonbelievers. The young ("his mustache had not fully come," reads one description) are the key demographic for Inayatullah and feature as infantry or air force pilots in many of the accounts.

These young, "illiterate" soldiers lack proper military gear and sometimes operate even without direct command, but they have aid from hidden, supernatural sources because of their faith and their belief in Allah and protecting angels. This hidden "advantage" manifests itself in their preternatural endurance after being injured, their skin that is seemingly impervious to direct bullets or shrapnel, and their ability to sow confusion among the enemy ranks or to become invisible as pilots, jeep drivers, or tank operators.

In *Pak Fizaia ki Dastan-e Shujaat* (The Heroic Tales of the Pak[istani] Air Force), he collected accounts from both the 1965 and 1971 wars. In a chapter detailing a dogfight in the skies over Lahore, he describes the city's streets filled with spectators, who cheer every twist and turn of the air battle between four jet fighters. At the story's end, after the Indian planes have been destroyed, the people rush to recover the severed head of a pilot.

But all crowds are not equal in Inayatullah's works. Where the Lahori crowds are staunch defenders against Hindus, their fellow citizens in Dhaka are not. In *Hamari Shikast ki Kahani* [The Story of Our Defeat, 1974], which was written as a defense of the Pakistani military as well as the "Two-Nation Theory," Inayatullah portrays the (then) Pakistani citizens in Dhaka as secretly Hindu or at least with loyalties firmly tied to India. West Pakistan, he argues, had been cleansed of Hindus by the Partition of 1947, but East Pakistan had retained its Hindu population, which had become the intellectual elite and were influencing, or "brainwashing," Muslims. The Pakistani citizens of East Pakistan, according to Inayatullah, were alienated from the idea of Pakistan and responsible for the "defeat" of the Pakistani military in 1971. He also blamed women's liberation (or attempts thereof) for the "deviancy" that existed in public life. Perversely, he blamed Shaikh Mujibur Rahman, who was the leader of the Awami League and, later, the first prime minister of Bangladesh, for the murder and rapes of non-Bengali women. He said this in the face of documented atrocities carried out by the Pakistani military against Bengali citizens during the war of independence for Bangladesh. Inayatullah defended the Pakistani military by arguing that the Indian commandos were masquerading as the Bangladeshi Liberation Army.

Inayatullah wrote over a dozen very popular historical romances—one on Mahmud of Ghazna in *Dastan Iman Farooshon Ki* (Tale of Those Who Sold Faith), and one on Muhammad bin Qasim, *Sitara Jo Tut Gaya* (The Star That Broke). Many of Inayatullah's historical romances began with a complacent and directionless Muslim youth who needs to be martialized or militarized. The sentiment would prove very popular after the Soviet invasion of Afghanistan in 1979. The resulting pivot in U.S. foreign policy to support a guerrilla war through Pakistan's military dictator, Zia ul Haq, created a robust patronage pipeline for elevating intellectuals who touted state policy. Inayatullah's books were heavily promoted by the military and by the Jama'at-i Islami (an Islamic organization founded in 1941 in Lahore). His books prominently featured the same Urdu epitaph: "Those born dancing to drumsets do not have the strength to hold swords and defend the faith."

His novels, Inayatullah himself argued, are invested with a realism that other historical romances do not possess, as they are too *filmi* (cinematic) and their portrayal of military tactics is inaccurate. He offers his novels as a corrective, based on national and international historical sources but also informed by contemporary military strategy. Within the novels, he cites Arabic and Persian sources and provides long excerpts from histories. This claim to "history," or rather to a history that is more correct than the other popular historical novels, is central to the appeal of the novel.

Inayatullah pushed forth the idea of a Muslim polity in his "historical" work, even though he was not trained as a historian and did not know any of the languages necessary for archival work.

The claim of historical accuracy allows his readers to let go of any inhibitions and surrender to the romantic and fanciful elements in the books. For Muhammad bin Qasim, a figure about whom we know very little, Inayatullah invents a profound interiority. Qasim is never tempted by deviant sexual urges, by displays of miracles, or even by claims to political power. Qasim is docile toward his superiors, whose motives remain occluded to him. Qasim as a hero of the 1980s is a perfect military recruit, eager to do the bidding of his commanding generals and lay his life down for the state.

As a publisher, Inayatullah introduced a strict color and design template for all his books—khaki color (to match the colors of the military) and a singular image of a flag or a woman's face. His other books—thrillers, true crime, romances—would all share the same aesthetic, blending together his histories, historical fiction, and social dramas. The "hero" traverses these many genres, escaping the "past" as an intellectual exercise and becoming part of everyday contemporary life. In this way, a satirical novel about Muhammad bin Qasim in modern-day Lahore was a logical extension of the blending of history and a social program to shape Muslim youth.

IV.

By 1984 I knew most of the libraries in Lahore—well, those that I was aware of. As a young teenager, I had permission to take a variety of buses, vans, or tongas to visit these libraries and borrow books (I would lie that these books were related to my curriculum). Punjab Public Library sat hidden behind the Lahore Museum and off Mall Road. My first few times there, I was too intimidated to go inside but I also didn't mind, as the structure—another *baradari*, but this one built by Wazir Khan in the early seventeenth century—was so beautiful and peaceful that I would remain happily seated on a bench in front of it for hours. Once I got over my fears and made my way in, I would sit in the Urdu children's section or go to the reading room, where one could sit and read for hours. It cost money to check books out, although I don't remember ever taking a book out. There was also the British Council Library—my English was barely existent—where I would go to look up its encyclopedias. The Military Cantonment Library was right next to the grounds of my school. You had to be a member of the armed forces to gain access, and I would lie that my father was in the military, when he was actually working as an electrical engineer in the Gulf. That library was usually empty.

These were all sites across Lahore that I would visit at least once every two weeks. Yet the bulk of my reading happened much closer to home in my neighborhood's many lending libraries. Located amid the other shops selling everyday goods, such as cos-

Figure 5.4. Advertisement for Nasim Hijazi novels (2011)

metics or shoes, these storefronts stocked pulp novels. They also
sold the monthly Urdu "digest" magazines (*Siara*, *Hikayat*, *Urdu*,
Pakeeza, *Khwateen*, among others), each issue a mixture of essays,
short stories, and excerpts, some in translation. These were geared
to an audience older than I was at the time, although I read them

all. My own demographic had the "Imran Series," pulp detective stories with a young secret agent as the protagonist. At the lending libraries, you could open an account with a deposit (I remember it being ten rupees) and then, for one to three rupees, you could check out one book for three nights. There were some incentives to return the book early and to borrow more than one volume, but the details escape me now.

The digests and the serials were generally the same size (eight by five inches) with brightly colored covers. The most attractive covers belonged to the historical romances, specifically the romances set in key moments in the history of Islam that featured larger-than-life portraits of (mostly ethnically Arab or Turk) men as warriors and kings. These were as ubiquitous as the digests or even the daily newspapers, with well-regarded authors driving sales. They promised to make their readers better Muslims as well as patriotic Pakistanis. They did a lot more, in fact, to shape ideas of masculinity, national origins, and belonging for their (presumed if not actual) male readership. If the building of monuments such as the Minar or the tombs of Gauri and Aibak are one aspect of reinscribing history, then the construction of specific ideas about the past via populist reimaginations of distant warriors and conquerors is another key to unlocking the memory-history complex.

The materiality of producing novels, digests, and newspapers shaped the urban fabric of Lahore. Urdu Bazaar, which abutted Anarkali, was a marketplace of published material, especially books in Urdu. The ladderlike series of parallel lanes connecting two central arteries were home to paper suppliers, ink vendors, composers, calligraphers, publishers, and book warehouses. Al-Qureish, Dastan, Naqoosh, Qaumi, Maqbool, Shaikh Ghulam Ali & Sons, Ferozsons, Shujah were publishers located in Urdu Bazaar and on Railway Road and McLeod Road—the main arteries from the Lahore Railway Station toward the heart of the colonial city on Mall Road. These publishers came into prominence by reproducing Urdu fantasy novels such as *Tilsim Hoshruba* and *Fasana-e Azad*, which had been published first by Naval Kishor Press in the late nineteenth century.

By the early twentieth century, Lahore's publishing landscape had many major Arya Samaj (Hindu proselytization group founded in 1877 in Lahore), anti-colonial, anti-caste, and Khilafat-oriented presses. They required a rejiggering of the language and the creation of new communities of readers. The publishing houses would increasingly focus on delivering enchanting, captivating Urdu stories, written in clear and concise prose, aimed at uplifting the moral and historical imagination of the "youth." The political and the historical were intimately linked, such as in Qaumi Kutab Khana's 1940 publication of a collection of poems, editorials, and articles called *Tipu Sultan*. This volume was edited by the publicity secretary of the All India Muslim Students Federation, who organized a "Tipu Sultan Day" in Lahore.

Journalists were the driving force in rethinking Urdu prose, and in many ways, inventing a stylistic grammar for a new age. Unlike the scholars of the previous generations—Shibli, Hali, Sharar—these journalists were determined to shape the social, the political, and the historical into a new modern idiom. The products themselves were meant (sometimes exclusively) to be consumed by young readers who needed to be enticed by alluring plotlines, titles, and covers. Sadiq Hussain Siddiqui, Aslam Rahi, Nasir Ahmad Jama'i, and Maqsood Shaikh were some of the better-known names with their own takes on these heroes of Islam, but the landscape of Urdu "history" novels in 1984 had been constituted some forty years earlier in Lahore by two journalists, Jafri and Hijazi.

Syed Rais Ahmad Jafri was born in Khairabad (near Sitapur, Uttar Pradesh) in either 1907 or 1912 (accounts differ) and received his education first at Darul Uloom Nadwatul Ulama in Lucknow and then at Jamia Millia Delhi. As a young man, he would take up the cause of Khilafat—the movement to prevent the British Empire from eliminating the Ottoman sultan's position as a *khalifa* (a shadow of God) with control over the holy cities of Mecca and Medina. First, he wrote a well-acclaimed biography of one of the founders of the Khilafat Movement, Maulana Muhammad Ali Jauhar, and then he became the editor, in the early 1930s, for the Khilafat's mainstay newspaper, *Daily Khilafat*, published from Bombay. From that perch, he would write and publish nationalist, anti-colonial, and anti-imperial works—but always with an eye to creating a new archive for Urdu readers.

He would rewrite the Urdu romances of the 1800s, such as *Tilsim Hoshruba* and *Fasana-e Azad*, published by Shaikh Ghulam Ali & Sons, as well as the histories of the Umayyad dynasty, the Abbasids, the Crusades, the Ottoman Empire, the 1857 Revolution, the Khilafat Movement, and so on. Many of these histories ran into multiple volumes, with each volume near or over five hundred pages. His real strength was in writing biographies and profiles of political figures, such as Muhammad Ali Jauhar, Muhammad Ali Jinnah, Muhammad Iqbal, and many of Jafri's comrades, teachers, and fellow anti-colonial figures.

He also compiled "primary documents" for the purpose of writing future histories. In a note titled "Where Was I on August 14th?," published in *Siara* in August 1964, Jafri wrote that he was forced to migrate to Pakistan because his work was being censored. He eventually settled in Lahore, in Tagore Park, where he edited the newspaper *Zamindar*. From the 1950s onward, he dedicated himself to writing and publishing Urdu texts. He produced translations of the life of the Prophet and the sayings of 'Ali bin Abi Talib (the Prophet's son-in-law and nephew). By the time of his sudden death in 1968, at Lahore Railway Station, he had authored over two hundred books.

His historical novels are responsible for his continuing impact. *Hajjaj bin Yusuf*, *Shahabuddin Gauri*, *Alauddin Tughluq*, and *Harun al Rashid* were some of the more popular and important. A clear influence on him (and other authors of Urdu historical romances) was the Lebanese journalist and novelist Jurji Zaidan (1861–1914). Zaidan was the editor of the prominent Cairo-based magazine *al-Hilal*, but his true fame came through his popular historical novels. His 1902 *Hajjaj bin Yusuf* was translated into Urdu in 1919. Zaidan's novels stressed their historical accuracy, as evidenced by their footnotes to contemporary literary or historical texts. In a similar vein, Jafri, while conceding that *Shahabuddin Gauri* was a "roiling tale" presented as a *roman* (romance), also attested that it was "free from lies." At several points in this adventure story, the reader would see a slim footnote with a brief reference to a text, with maybe an added sentence or two on historiography.

The central task of the novel, according to Jafri, was to construct a Muslim imaginary that was not subsumed by a colonial paradigm of inferiority. To reinvigorate the history of Islam, the novel ought to hold military commanders and warlords as key figures and make them into infallible kings and *ghazi* (those who triumph in war). Many of these historical novels have a similar structure. They are narrated from the perspective of a character who is ancillary or marginal to the titular historical subject. Their didactic intent comes through in speeches and in long descriptions of character. At the same time, brisk dialogue and sharply written action set pieces mark the novels' adventurous spirit. In the case of *Shahabuddin Gauri*, that marginal character is a soldier who volunteers to fight in Shahabuddin's Hindustan campaign. He falls in love with a Muslim woman and, later, with an elite Brahmin woman, and the love triangle (as well as the political history of campaigns and palace intrigues) gives the plot its appealing, propulsive nature.

However, no one, including Jafri, managed to write the pedagogically inclined, rollicking historical adventure as well as Nasim Hijazi. Muhammad Sharif, born in 1914, would take the name Nasim Hijazi (literally, "the air from Hejaz") during his school years—on the contention that his caste family was Ara'in, a people who claimed descent from the Arabs from Hijaz, who, in turn, arrived in Sind with the armies of Muhammad bin Qasim in the early eighth century. Hijazi got his start as a journalist in Quetta before joining newspapers in Karachi and later Rawalpindi. From 1953 to 1966, he was the editor of one of the most influential dailies published in Lahore, *Kohistan*. By the time of his death in 1996, he may have been the Urdu novelist with the highest print sales. In his own estimate, by the mid-1980s his more than twenty historical novels had gone through nearly fifty editions (and that's only counting the official ones), with each edition carrying a print run of two to three thousand copies.[6]

A.Q. Khan wrote in the glossy magazine *Maktab Islamabad* in April 1988 that in his young age the very first historical novel he read was by Nasim Hijazi, and after reading it, he never read any other genre of fiction. Dramatically, he recounted, his eyes were wet with tears from the emotional impact of the novel. He asked every young man in Pakistan to read these books on the golden ages of Islam. In that same issue, Abu'l 'Ala Maududi, the founder of Jama'at-i Islami, also called Hijazi's novels the perfect vehicle for the proselytization for Islam. That the top nuclear scientist and the top religious leader of Pakistan both praised Hijazi already tells us about his importance. From the 1950s through the 1980s, Hijazi remained a close interlocutor with the highest echelons of military and civil power—figures such as General Ayub Khan; civil servant Qudratullah Shahab; the third prime minister of Pakistan, Muhammad Ali Bogra; General Hamid Gul; A.Q. Khan; and author and journalist Mumtaz Mufti. His novels were the foundation of this immense political and cultural influence.

Hijazi attended Islamia College in Lahore, and it was to Lahore's Qaumi Kutab Khana, on Railway Road, that he sold his first novel, *Dastan-e Mujahid* (Tale of the Soldier), which was published in 1943. In the preface to *Dastan-e Mujahid*, Hijazi takes a swipe at the "art for art's sake" crowd and the "progressive" writer crowd who had dominated the Urdu sphere since the early 1930s. Unlike those writers, Hijazi intended his novel as a tool kit or a pathway for young Muslims who wanted to resurrect their golden history. He would follow up with 1944's *Insan aur Devta* (Man and God), which focused on the history of "Shudra" (untouchability). This was a cautionary tale, in which Hijazi warned Muslims that they too would be massacred by upper-caste Hindus. *Muhammad bin Qasim*, perhaps Hijazi's most celebrated novel, came out in 1945.

Hijazi changed the form and texture of the historical novel that his contemporary Jafri had made popular. He focused on the military history of Islam's earliest conquests in the eighth century, in the Indian subcontinent and on the Iberian Peninsula. In these novels the clashes between Islam and Hinduism and between Islam and Christianity took place within clear and sharply delineated moral frames. Unlike Jafri, he made the main historical protagonists the central characters and would often have romantic storylines intersect with their warrior lives. Gone, as well, was the propulsive plot à la Jafri, driven by events alone.

Hijazi embraced world-building—writing in minute detail about the natural landscape, the built environment, and the urban cities. He also included his own exposition, interjecting into the plot long discursive passages that directly addressed the reader on the ethical or moral questions that lay behind the conflict at hand. He used Hindustani Muslim names for main characters, even if the historical characters had Arabic names. This, he wrote, brought the figures closer to the life of his readers. He also centered the "woman in peril" as a pivotal plot point—the female character would stand in for the nation that needed to be protected. Hijazi used simple, direct prose—as a journalist would—explaining the what, when, where, and how, and then giving the reader a clear sense of the stakes and outcomes.

His *Muhammad bin Qasim* is an excellent example. First published in 1945, it was reissued several times and adapted for television in the early 1990s. The novel focused on the arrival of Muslim armies on the shores of Sind in 712 and the conquest of Raja Dahir's Brahmin kingdom. Hijazi had already introduced Muhammad bin Qasim as a character in *Dastan-e Mujahid*, and in *Muhammad bin Qasim*, he gave the general's story its full breadth as a model for the young Muslim man engaged in the anti-colonial struggle: the teenage conqueror was a fearless war-rior and a kindhearted administrator who believed in giving his life up for the cause of Islam without questioning his superiors. *Muhammad bin Qasim*'s plot hinges on the rescue of kidnapped Muslim women, first from pirates in the Indian Ocean and then from the Brahmin ruler in Sind, Raja Dahir. Qasim defeats Da-hir, rescues the women, claims land for the Muslims, and installs an ordered realm of Muslim governance.

The necessary ingredients of Hijazi's novels—the romance of a young hero, the threats against a Muslim woman's "purity," the adherence to a cause or a just ruler, the embrace of self-sacrificing violence, the promise of rewards in the afterlife—were also the political script of Zia ul Haq's dictatorship. The ongoing jihad in Afghanistan, against Russia, was dependent on a vast pool of young Pakistani men who would volunteer to fight for a just cause. Hijazi was a propagandist for a universal version of the same.

V.

The Muslim hero did not have a natural birth. None of the histories written prior to the colonization of the subcontinent reflect an emphasis on a military commander or soldier as a "hero." The notable figures—those to be emulated or revered or learned from—were prophets, kings, sages, ascetics, ministers, lovers, farmers, poets, and historians. The birth of the Muslim hero came after the birth of the Muslim villain and the birth of the anti-Muslim hero in colonial discourse.

In the 1940s and 1950s, Hijazi and Jafri could see a clear reason for writing historical novels championing a Muslim hero. They gestured back to previous writers such as Shibli Nomani and Abdul Halim Sharar as formidable influences on their decisions to embrace the genre of historical fiction. They also relied on works by historians, written in Persian or Urdu or Arabic or English, to give their fiction its historical veneer. Hijazi's and Jafri's books found ready publishers and certainly a wide and prominent readership. But their influences were not all positive. They were also responding to the negative pressure of colonial politics and the making of a new "Hindu history." Heroes and antiheroes were central.

The colonial state prepared the ground for this antagonistic history. The governor general of India, Lord Ellenborough, made an infamous "Proclamation," in 1842, to the "Princes and Chiefs and People of India." This was near the end of the first Anglo-Afghan War. The EIC's army had just sacked Kabul and Ghazna. The proclamation concerned the "gates of the temple of Somnath, so long the memorial of your humiliation," which Ellenborough had wrenched from Mahmud of Ghazna's tomb in Kabul. Ellenborough had this proclamation read out loud and circulated throughout British-held territories. The EIC claimed to have returned, from India to Kabul, the gates, restoration for the insult and aggrievement at the hands of Muslims eight hundred years ago, when they destroyed Somnath and had these very gates moved to Ghazna.

Just a few years before, in 1838, EIC political agent Thomas Postans had visited the site of Somnath and declared that "like everything of a historical character in India, the Hindus themselves are totally ignorant respecting the interest which attaches to Somnath, and certainly in and near the spot, the fact of Mahmud's invasion, startling though it was, is quite unknown, and the building itself looked upon it in its ruined state without the slightest approach to respect or interest of any kind." The gates, of course, were not the gates of Somnath, nor was "Somnath" a historical injury that had occupied the minds of the colonized Hindus for eight hundred years. Yet Ellenborough's central idea of a historical injury that awaited a just reprisal became the most valuable cause for the aggrieved of Hindustan and later India and Pakistan. The antihero, Mahmud, and the destroyed sacred site, Somnath, would become totemic in the subsequent 150 years. In 1992, the destruction of the Babri mosque in Ayodhya (which many argued was the birthplace of Ram) was preceded by a cross-country rally that began in Somnath.

This colonial project relied on history. Thomas Postans and other soldiers of the EIC would go from region to region, court to court, and write archaeological notes, epigraphic studies, narrative accounts, and histories, detailing the destruction and misdeeds of Muslim rulers. Their histories rested on the textual and archaeological source materials from the Muslim "Dark Ages." Alexander Dow's 1768 rendition of Firishta's *Tarikh* (ca. 1612) gave Edward Gibbon the portrait of Mahmud that he included in his

Decline and Fall of the Roman Empire. Mahmud is a "zealous Mussulman," "cruel and inexorable," destroyer of "many thousand idols." Gibbon includes Mahmud in his entry on "Turks," which moved on to discuss the Seljuk empire, which would conquer Jerusalem and set the stage for the First Crusade. Thus the conqueror of the idols is connected to the conquests of the Holy Land. Gibbon was followed by other British historians who knitted this particular history of calumny and terror, such that, by 1850, Mahmud is just one among the colonial pantheon of antiheroes, which included Muhammad bin Qasim, Shahabuddin Gauri, Firuz Shah Tughluq, and Aurangzeb Alamgir, but really any and every single Muslim ruler. From the colonial perspective, all were intent on turning Hindu places of worship into mosques and destroying Hindu society at large.

A politics of anti-Muslim heroes would proliferate in this colonial framing of Islam as a "religion by the sword, for the sword." The colonial wars of the nineteenth century, within and without the subcontinent, against Muslim-led polities provided a steady stream of opponents who were demonized as despots and charlatans. In the colonial imagination, their contemporary political map of the world (whether related to the Mughal, Qajar, or Ottoman empires) will always be tied to an ahistorical framework where Islam (and Muslim rulers) signified a rupture in the progress of time because it represented a freezing of history. The colonized Muslim subjects experienced these same colonial histories in two binaries of either guarded praise or explicit condemnation.

Some European histories that were produced from new translations of the Qur'an (such as George Sale's 1734 translation) or based on newly edited and printed Muslim histories, such as those by Tabari (d. 923), Masu'di (d. 956), Ibn Khaldun (d. 1406), and Ahmad Maqqri (d. 1632), provided in the view of the colonized Muslims a "sympathetic" or generous portrait of Islam or of Prophet Muhammad (☙). These included Goethe's *West-östlicher Diwan* (1819), Thomas Carlyle's *On Heroes, Hero-Worship, & the Heroic in History* (1841), and Samuel Parsons Scott's *History of the Moorish*

Empire in Europe (1904). More common, however, were the histories that attacked Muslim history and needed to be refuted, such as those of Vincent Smith, William Muir, even H.G. Wells.

Syed Ahmad Khan (1817–98) wrote a series of histories of places and people that would reshape the way history was written for colonized Muslims. His *Jam-e Jam* (1839) and *Asar al-Sanadid* (1847) were rebuttals to and engagements with the developing European sciences of philology and history. He would also be among the first intellectuals to create critical editions of Persian and Arabic historical texts. He would encourage Altaf Hussein Hali to write and publish *Musaddas-e Madd-o-Jazr-e Islam* (Epic on the Ebb and Flow of Islam) in 1879. The poem was in large part inspired by the loss of Andalus, a synecdoche for the loss of Hindustan.

Another protégé of Khan's was Shibli Nomani (1857–1914), who would write a number of biographies of early Muslims (inspired by Carlyle's model). The most prominent of these would be his 1899 *Al-Faruq*, a biography of the second caliph, ʿUmar bin Khattab. He also wrote on Ghazali and Aurangzeb, and composed a *sira* of the Prophet. Shibli emulated European "scientific" practices (inspired by Leopold von Ranke, he incorporated footnotes, bibliographies, and critical philology), but also linked his efforts to Ibn Khaldun and other Muslim historians.

Finally, the publisher and author Abdul Halim Sharar (1860–1926) helped popularize the genre of the Urdu historical novel. He wrote a total of twenty-eight historical novels, eight social novels, twenty-four biographical works, twenty-one histories, two dramas, four collections of poetry, and eight translations into Urdu, and he steered ten different journals at various points of his life. In his first novel, *Malik Aziz Varjana* (1888), he sought to counter the ways in which Walter Scott's *The Talisman* (1825) had portrayed the history of the Third Crusade and of Salauddin Ayubi. *Ayyam-e Arab* (1898), *Flora Florinda* (1899), *Fatiha-e Andalus* (1915), and *Zaval-e Baghdad* (1916) were some of his other novels that focused on the "golden age" of Islam or were set during the Crusades.

Starting in 1900, Sharar began working on a series of biographies and histories that were tied together, again, by a focus on the early period of Islam and on the coming of Islam to the subcontinent. In 1907, he began to serialize a history of the Muslim arrival in Sind, published in his journal *Dil Gudaz*. The completed work, *Tarikh-e Sind*, was a two-volume history of Sind focused on Muhammad bin Qasim, the young conqueror who led the Arab army in 712.

The Uprising of 1857 and the destruction of Delhi—but also the resulting migration from Delhi to other cities such as Awadh, Lucknow, Rampur, and Lahore—would prompt Muslim writers to renew their attention to writing the city, especially in the *shahr ashob* (city disrupted) genre of melancholic reflection. A classic of the genre from that period is Sharar's *Hindustan mein Mashraqi Tamaddun ka Akhri Namuna yaʿani Guzishta Lucknow* (The Last Example of Eastern Culture in Hindustan or Past Lucknow), which was serialized in *Dil Gudaz* between 1913 and 1920. Sharar utilized the *shahr ashob* form to describe Lucknow, the city of his ancestors and his own life, in the aftermath of 1857.

This account of Lucknow opens with a history of its founding and political rule, then moves on to chronicles of its language, literature, poetry, sports (wrestling and various animal fights), music, dance, food, clothing, architecture and housing, social gatherings, and public festivals. *Guzishta Lucknow* offers an account of the civilizing process, and also captures the ways history has a claim on the present. When he describes the practices of *khattati* (calligraphy—but understood more broadly as encompassing all the arts of bookmaking), he links the origins of the craft in Islam's earliest moments and then brings it forward to his present by embedding its skill in biographies of prominent Muslims.

In Sharar's history, a new calligraphic form of *nastaʿliq* came to Hindustan with the conquests of Mahmud of Ghazna. Lahore was the first major site for training students in this new form, instructing them on how to make perfect curves, smooth strokes, and elegant points. Where *nastaʿliq* is tied to Mahmud, Sharar ties *naskh* (another style of calligraphy) to the patronage of Sala-huddin Ayubi. In doing so, Sharar traced the specific historic origins of everyday craft to certain historical figures from Muslim past before providing genealogies of teachers and students, masters of practice from his contemporary present. Such reworking of historical memory linked Lucknow's patrons and artists to the deep Muslim past.

Shibli and Sharar provide models for how history and memory could be effectively engaged in the twentieth century. Each inspired an approach to writing a version of the Muslim history that was stripped of colonial excess but that, in turn, was made palatable for the general public through simple language and emotive narrative structures. The task of the historian-novelist was to create a Muslim history and a Muslim public. The emotional language of the novel, whether mired in nostalgia or resentment, mimicked the political language of the Muslim present. For Sharar, valorizing a distant Muslim hero helped cauterize the wounds in the contemporary Muslim psyche. Hijazi would replicate these very same efforts half a century after Sharar when he wrote about the need to "awaken" the urban Muslim youth of Pakistan to the challenges facing them, but with key differences. For one, Sharar was explicit that women constituted part of his audience. Hijazi took his audience to be largely, if not solely, male. Sharar was engaged in reflection at the civilizational level (the Muslim question); Hijazi, at the national level (the Pakistani question).

VI.

My ninth-grade history textbook was published by the Punjab Textbook Board in Lahore under Zia ul Haq's "Pakistan Studies" curriculum. It opened with chapters on geography and climate before turning to the all-important "Advent of Islam." We were introduced to Muhammad bin Qasim as the "first citizen" of Pakistan, who conquered much of the land that is today associated with Pakistan and was thus the founding figure. My school was a Catholic school, and we sat in unfinished rooms next to the oldest church in Lahore—the St. Mary Magdalene Church, consecrated in 1857. Many of my teachers were Christian. Yet the textbook they taught us was fixated on the heroes of Islam and of the "Pakistan Movement."

Neither Lahore, nor the beautiful, massive cathedral in whose shade we all played, nor our Christian and Hindu teachers had much purchase in the world created by the textbook. Instead, the "Hindu" in the textbook served the role as a duplicitous adversary best exemplified by the history of Muhammad bin Qasim and his defeat of the Brahmin Raja Dahir, son of Raja Chach of the kingdom of Sind. Partition was portrayed as a primordial conflict between Islam and Hinduism, and novels, monuments, and these textbooks were the means of explaining this conflict's past.

As a "citizen in the making," I was relatively protected in mid-1980s Pakistan: I was male, Urdu-speaking, denominationally

Figure 5.5. "Heroes of Islam" print poster for sale near Urdu Bazaar (2014)

Sunni, partly Punjabi, aspirationally middle class, living in Lahore (Punjab). In the textbook's worldview, I was an insider, whereas my teachers were outsiders (being Christians). Yet, they were the ones who had to organize "Dress Like Muhammad bin Qasim Day" and tell us about the "Muhammad bin Qasim Appreciation Society."

Muhammad bin Qasim entered the Muslim imagination as the antihero of other discourses. The EIC conquered Sind in 1843, and a number of histories of Sind were produced by the soldier-scribes of the Company. The Persian history *Chachnama* became the most-cited text for the EIC political agents, who saw in it the concrete historical proof of "Hindu slavery" and of Muslim rule by sword and domination. Written in the city of Uch Sharif in the early thirteenth century, *Chachnama* purported to be a translation from Arabic of an eyewitness account of Muhammad bin Qasim's campaign in the early eighth century.

By the 1920s, "Muhammad bin Qasim Day" in Sind, in Uttar Pradesh, and in Panjab was celebrated as *Yaum al Fath* (Victory Day)—generally, on the eleventh day of the month of Ramadan. The Anjuman-e Himayat-e Islam (Organization for the Solidarity of Muslims) in Lahore and the Anjuman-e Nao Musalmanaan-e Sind (Organization of the New Muslims of Sind) in Hyderabad championed Muhammad bin Qasim Day as a riposte to "Shivaji Day," at that time celebrated by the Arya Samaj and the Hindu Mahasabha parties.[7]

Bal Gangadhar Tilak (1856–1920), one of the key figures in the anti-colonial struggle, had organized the first Shivaji Day, held in April 1896 in Maharashtra as part of the Shivaji Raja Memorial Festival. Shivaji Day spread across Bombay, Gujarat, and even Sind. These celebrations were organized as public processions, and by the mid-1920s they were held in Delhi, Lucknow, and even as far as Dhaka. Shivaji Day was observed to remember, in the words of Tilak, "the memory of Shivaji, who struggled hard to raise the Hindu nation from its miserable plight in the time of the Mogul domination."[8] Tilak argued that Shivaji should be remembered across India to remind the Hindus that they were not "effeminate Asiatics," as the British had portrayed them, but were capable of collectively asking the British for representation. The celebration included poems, lectures, and rituals. The processions, when they went through Muslim neighborhoods, would inevitably lead to street violence.

The past was imagined as a series of attacks and counterattacks, crystallized in a present where everyone felt constantly in a state of war. Be they intellectuals or activists, these men were busy defending Islam or Hinduism across time and space. If Shivaji Day was celebrated by the Arya Samaj or Hindu Mahasabha, then Muhammad bin Qasim Day needed to be celebrated by the proponents of the Khilafat Movement or, later, the Jama'at-i Islami. Khwaja Hasan Nizami (1878–1955), a prolific writer on Muslim history and Sufi thought, was one such proponent of the Muhammad bin Qasim Day—largely as part of his efforts to counter the Arya Samaj.

He wrote about the lives of Sufi saints, about resistance against the British, and about conquerors, and he often participated in public debates in Delhi, Lucknow, and Lahore. In 1924 he wrote extensively on Islam's arrival and questions of conversion. In 1927, he commissioned a hagiography of Muhammad bin Qasim in Bhojpuri (then called Purabi) because he felt that the inhabitants of Awadh were listening to the *Ramayana* as it was recited in their villages when they should be listening to the recitations of the *Qur'an*. To make them proper Muslims, he prescribed learning the life of the conqueror of Hindustan. For another commission, issued from Lahore under a "History of the Rise of Islam" series, he produced another biography of Qasim.

Established scholars of Islam, and journalists like Sharar, were also moved to produce histories of Muhammad bin Qasim in the 1920s and 1930s. While written in Urdu, these works were explicitly labeled history, and the pages were formatted according to Western printing conventions: footnotes appeared at the bottom of the page rather than in the right and left margins; citations to texts and sources likewise were at the bottom of the page, numbered and written in full; there was a bibliography at the beginning or end of the text. These histories were meant to push back against British colonial and Hindu nationalist accounts of Islam's arrival, portraying Muhammad bin Qasim as a benevolent figure or stressing that he engaged in just governance. In addition to this public work, scholars of Islam or history were also keen to rescue the sources back from colonial misuse: *Chachnama* itself was translated repeatedly into English during this period—first in 1900 by Mirza Kalichbeg and then by U.M. Daudpota in 1930.

These turn-of-the-century texts and debates did not end with Partition. The historic antagonism, once activated, continued to hold sway. Muhammad bin Qasim Day or Victory Day in Sind led to the Raja Dahir Day among Sindhi nationalists, who did not feel they were given equal rights or representation in their newly independent country. The national politics of the linguistic supremacy of Urdu produced in the early 1950s the movement for Bangla in East Pakistan, and was one of the main causes for the crisis of 1970 and the creation of Bangladesh in 1971.

Similarly, the Punjab-based military elite marginalized the Sindhi language, crushing Sindhi and Baluchi calls for autonomy and rights in the early 1970s. Raja Dahir Day was one symptom of this fractured national narrative. Many prominent Sindhi intellectuals wrote their own books, historical novels, and plays on the Arabs' colonization of Sind under Muhammad bin Qasim. These books were often censored or were shared only among small networks of like-minded readers.

In 2005, I was interviewing some Sindhi activists in Jamshoro who gave me photocopies ("photostats") of novels and pamphlets questioning Muhammad bin Qasim as the "first citizen" of Pakistan. In the same trip, I interviewed a former minister of education who happily detailed plots and funds to create a Muhammad bin Qasim Literary Society in Sind in order to combat other ideas of national origins. The minister was a key member of the Jama'at-i Islami, yet was not aware of the activities of the Jama'at in the late 1920s in Sind to promote Muhammad bin Qasim Day. Nonetheless, he was considerably moved that the young people of Sind did not take a Brahmin Raja as their hero.

In Lahore, Muhammad bin Qasim remained uncontested and popular. There was no counternarrative to the state's vision of him as a founding figure. The proliferation of novels created a vast echo across the cultural sphere. Daily newspapers were just as likely to invoke him for the sake of commentary as they were to invoke a contemporary politician or social figure. He was a paragon of virtue, bravery, and masculinity. Children's stories about him were available on TDK cassette tapes, which we listened to with great delight. The national television network, Pakistan Television (PTV), aired dramatizations of his conquest of Sind.

Where Gauri and Ghaznavi had once held sway, Muhammad bin Qasim now represented the post-1971 Pakistan—which was uncontestably *West Pakistan*. As noted by the 1959 *Report of the Commission on National Education*, which established the textbook boards that would dominate my life, the "area which first came under Muslim dominion" from the eighth-century conquest of Muhammad bin Qasim "was the major part of the present West Pakistan."[9] Noting that "the magic is gone," the commission, which included the historian I.H. Qureshi and the physicist Abdus Salam (1926–96), recommended that the national character be developed by giving citizens heroes to look up to and emulate. Tragically, Abdus Salam would himself become the nation's pariah and be banished as an outsider.

VII.

Figure 5.6. Araʾin Community Center (2011)

Just down the street from where Tagore Park once stood, 5
Montgomery Road was the address of the office of the Jat-Pat
Todak Mandal of Lahore—a local branch of Arya Samaj—which
was invested in "eradicate[ing] the Caste System from amongst
the Hindus."[10] The Mandal, made up of "independent harijans
[farmers] of Punjab," had eagerly invited Dr. Ambedkar to address

its annual convention in May 1936 and to publish the speech he was slated to give. But the Mandal's leaders decided to "postpone" their gathering when they saw that Dr. Ambedkar was making specific critiques of key Hindu texts. Dr. Ambedkar withdrew and published his "not delivered" speech himself, which he titled "Annihilation of Caste."

I first read it as a pamphlet in Urdu, with "Lahore" inscribed boldly on the cover. One summer afternoon I, along with a friend, went looking for the Jat-Pat Todak Mandal office. We went up and down (Robert) Montgomery Road—which forms a triangle with (James) Abbott and (Donald) McLeod Roads. Robert was a bureaucrat who put down the 1857 Uprising in Lahore, James was a signatory on the Treaty of Lahore, and Donald was a governor of Punjab. All three were instrumental in creating colonial Lahore. There were no signs or labels for the Mandal. The national project of heroic leaders had erased all histories of caste and community from the Lahore of the 1980s, even as the names of the colonizers remained on the streets. Tagore Park had disappeared after Partition into an unnamed semicommercial triangle on McLeod Road.

The national heroes were not just in novels, on cassette tapes, on television, or celebrated in monuments. They were also in our blood. My neighbor, a young teenager, proclaimed himself a pure-blood member of the "Awan" caste, descended from the Arabs of Damascus, and maybe even from the Prophet's family, and perhaps from the army of Gauri. I asked him how he knew all of this, and he showed me a card that the Lahore branch of the Awan Society had given him. At the branch, you could get yourself registered, get verified as belonging to the caste group, and, perhaps most importantly, find marital connections for your loved ones. The national heroes—Gauri, Ghaznavi, Muhammad bin Qasim—were the literal origins of these blood lineages.

In thick histories of Awan or Ara'in or Rajput or Jat communities, identity was formed through the creation of an imagined past; through myths of kingship, kinship, and warrior origins;

through parables of social exclusiveness; and through a recognized need for education, economic and social improvement, and the patriarchal ideas on the position of women. They included citations from colonial texts, from the colonial census, from Arabic and Persian histories and genealogies, and from newspapers; and, working in tandem with oral narration, they provided the technical tools for the representation of an "imagined" community, their *qaum* (nation).

Muhabbat Hussain Awan's *Awan Tari'kh kay Ainay Mein* links the Awan community to the direct descendants of 'Ali and provides a listing of key Awani figures, from the history of the nationalist movement to the Indo-Pak war of 1965. Sardar Sher Muhammad Khan Gandapur's *Tarikh-e Pashtun* reaches into the time when jinn and fairies roamed the earth and traces the history back to the Gauri sultanate of the tenth century. Abdal Aziz Ismail Martika's *Tarikh Awkhai Memon Biradari* connects the Memon community's history to the tribes that existed in Sind before the arrival of the Arab armies.

Mukhtar Ahmad Mateen's *Tarikh-e Jatan* was commissioned in 1982 by the Society for the Welfare of the Jats (Karachi). The book is dedicated to the "brave and proud Jat soldiers who conquered Scandinavia and changed the name of Cambria to Jatland." It goes on to trace a line from Noah, through the Aryans, the armies of "Muhammad b. Qasim" (here quoting a Persian history), the Rajputs, and the Sikh regime in Punjab. In the section titled "The Qualities of the Jat," it references the colonial archive: "According to Easton, author of *The Castes of Punjab*, Jats are a very important *qaum*. In the census of 1919, they numbered three times the Rajputs. They are landowners and land cultivators. They are honest, hard-working, quick and cunning."[11] The book features a list of the prominent Jats who participated in the national struggle, as well a list of those who attained a modicum of political or cultural status.

Another caste group—the Ara'in—created their own link back to Muhammad bin Qasim's army, specifically the recruits from

Syria who accompanied him to Sind. It was *Salim al-Tawarikh*,
written in 1919 by the Sufi Muhammad Akbar Ali Jalandhari,
that put forth the main claim for the Syrian descent of the Ara'in
community, which it explains using Arabic and Persian histories,
along with cultural observations such as the way in which the
Ara'in tribe of Sind maintain the customs of their Arab homeland. The "homeland" in this case is repeatedly called "Ariha/Ari-
hah," the former of which is a northern summer resort in Syria,
the latter the Arabic name for the biblical town of Jericho in the
West Bank. In one short chapter, it jumps quickly from the time
of the Prophet to the rule of the Abbasids. Much more attention
is paid to "Awakening the Nation," "Stopping the Progress of
England in India," "The Ill-Effects of Ignorant Religious Practices," "The Paths to the Betterment of the Nation," "National
Character," and "Education."

Salim al-Tawarikh was intregated as the first half of a new work
titled *Tari'kh Ara'in*, published in 1963 and written by Ali Asghar Chaudhry. Chaudhry had previously published a number of
historical novels (*Amir-e Andulas, Doshiza-e Arab, Akhari Jahaz,
Akhari Charagh*). After thanking the president of the All-India
Ara'in Conference, held in March 1947 in Bijnaur, for the impetus,
Chaudhury provides the reasons for the reissuing of the earlier
history and for why he needed to update it with contemporary
information. This was done both in order to incorporate new information on the history, but even more importantly, to create a
new list of notables. These Chaudhry added as a final chapter
with biographies of "Our Thinkers, Soldiers, Traders, Industrialists, Scholars, Doctors, Religious Scholars, Writers"—all meant
to inspire and uplift the community.

Next, he lays out a mandate for a Constitution for the Association of Ara'in Pakistan, which would gather together "all sharif
[upper-caste], intelligent, brave, hard-working community members, so that their collective force would lift everyone in the community." The last lines of the history contained a much more
evocative plea: "The Ara'in *qaum* (nation) is *sharif* [upper-caste],

hard-working and of Arab descent. They are the true *mujahid* (warriors) of this nation. However, we are not united, nor organized. Whether you write Mian, Chaudhri etc. before your name, please write "Ara'in" after it. So that by seeing the word, from East to West, from Peshawar to Karachi, we can recognize ourselves."[12] The lofty genealogy, the luminaries, the arguments based on colonial archives, the exultations to communal betterment remain as identifiable as in any other similar communal history.

The first edition of *Tarikh-e Ara'in*, published in 1963 by the Lahore press Ilmi Kitab Khana, had no illustrations on the cover. Neither did the second edition (1966), which introduced very few changes in the structure or the content. The third edition (1973) expanded the list of notable Ara'in by many orders of magnitude, but the content was left mostly untouched. The great transformation, however, occured in the fourth edition (1977), which ballooned to a thousand pages. It is in this edition that the three prongs of Ara'in identity—Sword, Scythe, Qur'an—were established.

The preface to the fourth edition explicitly argued that Pakistan has entered its own decline (modeled after the declines of Muslim fortunes in centuries past), and the way out of the tailspin is through jihad. Chaudhry opens with praise for Zulfiqar Ali Bhutto ("he claimed to be a Rajput but likely is an Ara'in"), but also notes that Bhutto deviated from the path of jihad. It is now the task of Zia ul Haq (the most prominent Ara'in, according to Chaudhry) to take the burden of jihad and the burden of a divided nation (Chaudhry repeatedly invokes a prayer that East and West Pakistan should be reunited by force), and to call upon the Ara'in community to lead from the front. Muhammad bin Qasim's history receives extensive treatment, with hundreds of pages devoted to his exploits, statements, and heroic qualities.

The Ara'in, like many other caste communities, shed their "menial roles" and insisted on being warriors and nobility. These genealogical histories assembled lists of notable members spanning hundreds of pages, focusing on Pakistani military figures or civil bureaucrats, and sometimes even politicians. The local offices maintained marriage rolls and gave out small loans, but really their main function was to preserve their imagined caste purity. That this same focus emerged under the Zia ul Haq regime is no accident—and neither is the fact that many of the most prominent figures of Zia's Sunnification efforts were members of the Jama'at-i Islami who are also listed in Chaudhry's list of notables.

My paternal grandfather was a farmer who migrated to a small patch of land in the Sahiwal district. My father left his village to seek his own new world in the city of Lahore. He discarded the name "Chaudhry," which tagged him as a lowly field farmer, and appended "Ahmed," a nondescript city name. Later, he added "Asif" to his name in honor of his primary school teacher in the village, who was a poet. In many ways, he escaped into urban anonymity and out of caste placement. My fellow high school classmates would declare their caste identity—Ara'in or Rajput or Malik or Awan or Sayyid—with great pride. They insisted that I too provide my family names to place me in their hierarchy. My mother's family name of "Butt" placed us as Kashmiri, but that was not enough. Where were the notables of my caste groups? Who were the family heroes that I could bring to the show-and-tell?

5

PEOPLE: MAKING THE PEOPLE

I went to Lahore shortly after Salman Taseer's assassination in early 2011. I needed to get something for my phone and went to Hall Road, where all such things are purchased. The wide road is made narrow by layers and layers of street parking, interspersed with small cart vendors, massive displays of electronics outside shops, and a traffic jam that I can remember starting in the early 1980s. At the far end of Hall Road is one of the oldest graves in Lahore. It belongs to Shah Ismail (who lived ca. 1020–50), and it's in an elevated structure supported by two trees. The building stands precariously, the vast garden and endowed land that was once part of the complex encroached on or sold away. No one really visits or pays attention to it. That day, early in the afternoon, a procession had blocked the entire road. There were banners, some flags, and a few microphones mounted on the backs of pickup trucks. The procession was a protest against the arrest of Taseer's assassin, who was a member of Taseer's own security detail. At the moment of his death, Taseer was the sitting governor of Punjab, and one of the most important politicians in the country. The air was filled with slogans against him. I could find no way of getting around or through the mass of protesters. So I meekly walked alongside the procession on the crowded pavement.

Arguably—and I would certainly argue it—even in the long history of calamitous events in Pakistan, Taseer's killing is pivotal. Pakistan's first prime minister was assassinated in October 1951. The first *elected* prime minister was hanged by a military dictator in 1979. That same military dictator died in a mysterious plane crash in 1988. The daughter of the hanged prime minister, elected prime minister herself, was assassinated in 2007. Against that backdrop, the assassination of the governor of Punjab, in the city of Lahore, at the hands of his own bodyguard would appear unlikely to make even the list of top five calamitous events. I only fully realized the significance of his assassination while walking alongside the procession as it slowly moved down Hall Road and toward Mall Road, where it would eventually end in front of the Lahore High Court. The mood in the crowd of young men was jubilant and ecstatic. Intermittent chants in the name of the Prophet, peace be upon him, were followed by curses on the state.

In 2011, as a response to waves of suicide bombings in the city, almost all the religious sites were manned with military snipers or gunmen in visible positions against the skyline. Military checkpoints were set up, requiring you to show an ID to pass through. Police rapid-response teams (alternately called "Shaheen," "Dolphins," etc.) patrolled the streets. The protests on Mall Road or *dharna* (stoppage) at key government sites in the city were almost exclusively sanctioned by the state. Such protests were, in other words, orchestrated by the state, funded largely by trade or merchant guilds, with a roving list of usual targets—the United States, Israel, India. These protests were different from genuinely public attempts to raise awareness against an injustice—those "public protests" were brutally banned by successive military regimes.

A few days later, the major newspaper the *Daily Jang* carried a special section, spanning eight colored pages, on the poet Muhammad Iqbal (1877–1938) and the idea of Tahafuz-e Namoos-e Risalat (Protection of the Sanctity of Prophethood). Nine theologians, all men, had given speeches at a seminar, building on the ways in which Iqbal, considered the national poet of Pakistan since the early 1980s, had provided a framework for the violent response to any (perceived or otherwise, implied or stated) insult or blasphemy. Two verses by Iqbal were emblazoned across the spread in red letters: *ki Muhammad say wafa to nay to hum tarey hain / yeh jahan chiz hay kiya, loh o qalam teray hain* (If you are faithful to Muhammad, I am yours / this world is nothing, the [primordial] pen and tablet are yours). I had heard the same verses chanted repeatedly in the rally in support of Taseer's assassin.

It is this wide consensus on a politics of veneration of the Prophet, predicated almost exclusively on a threat against the idea of Pakistan, that marks Taseer's assassination as a singular event in the history of Pakistan—this is a Prophetic Pakistan. This is a project of people-making in its singular devotion to the Prophet. This phenomenon is diverse in its sources, and it cuts across sectarian faith leaders, political leaders, civil bureaucrats, journalists, authors, television personalities, elected officials, and everyday citizens. It is all-encompassing and it cannot be reduced to "Islamization" or any notion of abstract Islam. This politics of defensive veneration is not visible in any other Muslim-majority country in the world. It is not a textualist, originalist, orthodox, or heterodox argument about religion. It is barely an "argument"; rather, it is an absolute position that calls for extraordinary extrajudicial violence against anyone accused of "blasphemy" across urban and rural Pakistan.

It is not that the state prohibits the violence that occurs in the name of blasphemy. In fact, the grounds for civil violence are enshrined in the constitution under its "blasphemy laws." These laws protect the sanctity of the Prophet, his immediate family, Qur'an, and Islam generally. Transgressing these laws is a capital offense. They allow for unregulated violence against any other person based on hearsay, innuendo, misinformation, or political or economic benefit. Thus, a sort of live-wire, people-centered power exists in Pakistani society, which can resort to violence at a moment's notice. This is the making of the "good Muslim subject" for Pakistan.

Lahore is a critical site in this history. It tells two stories. First is the Lahore where the infrastructure of the Prophetic Pakistan was nurtured and developed, and from where it became national politics. A politics of violence emerged from a city that was itself a site of extraordinary violence before and during Partition. That unforgettable yet unspeakable violence informs the state and the city. It organizes civic and civil life, business hours, traffic patterns, and how a person can walk or even just exist in the city.

Lahore is where Zia ul Haq held his public floggings and beatings. Lahore is where that same dictator declared, "If you hold a protest meeting, I will put everyone behind bars," and threatened to close all newspapers for five years.[1] Lahore is also where classrooms, private residences of professors, and press offices were regularly raided by the "student wing" of Jama'at-i Islami under Zia ul Haq—a cadre of domestic shock troops. Any defiance of this particular idea of religion under Zia came under direct attack. Mela Chiraghan, which had given the city its moniker "City of Lights," disappeared from public view. (Later, Basant, the kiteflying festival, would also disappear.) Joy, spontaneity, and collectiveness would become suspicious activities even as righteous, wounded anger, and bile would form the basis of public commemorative acts.

There is another story that Lahore tells: that of Lahore as the site of protest *against* violence, and *against* oppression. Lahore, the city of dissent. I had grown up reading and thinking in that Lahore. I had imagined that to be the true spirit of Lahore, that anti-dictatorial, anti-patriarchal, pro-freedom-of-expression Lahore. After all, this is a city of colleges and universities, of free thinkers and poets, a city of revolutionaries such as Bhagat Singh. That exact same street, where I walked alongside supporters of the governor's assassin, was also a site of violence, in February 1983, against protesters for freedom of the press, for the rights of women, and against juridical structures prejudiced against women.

There is a particular history of leftist and feminist movements in Lahore, one that nurtured me when, as a young student, I sat in community discussions at Shirkat Gah center, or attended progressive reading circles (my introduction to Rosa Luxemburg's debate with Lenin and Marx), or helped comrades who had been forcibly abducted and tortured by the dictatorial regime. Asma

Jahangir's law office was a particular node for making new connections with like-minded people, as was the Dyal Singh Trust
Library's reading room, as was the small bookstall next to the
Lahore Museum, as was the sports store at the corner of Mall
Road next to the publisher Ferozsons, as was the perch outside
the physics building at FC College. Much of that earlier period
seemed incongruent in 2011—a history of some other city and not
the one that I was walking.

The two Lahores sometimes clash in the same physical space.
When, in 2011, I visited the Dyal Singh Trust Library, established in the early twentieth century, it was almost empty except
for a small group of local madrassa students clustered around a
desk. The library is an immense resource in Lahore, holding rare
materials and providing an open reading room. I asked for their
manuscript catalog, which is a handwritten ledger documenting
about 1,200 of their print, manuscript, and lithograph holdings
from Lahore's Sikh era. The library's holdings are especially
strong in the history of the leftist and anti-colonial authors. I was
there, as I usually was, to consult some of their books on the comrades of Bhagat Singh, the Lahori freedom fighter. The catalog is
a slim bound volume with lined notes. Each page is divided into
columns—Number, Author, Book, Topic—the last of those
headings incorporating a note on the contents. For example, "Entry 295, Ganesh Datt Sharma, *Pandit Lekhram*, 'On that Pandit
Lekhram whom the Muslims killed.'"

As I made notes of books or pamphlets I wanted to get from
the holdings, I turned to the very last page of the catalog. A patron had used the blank space of the final page to compose his
own long letter to the library. It was titled, and underlined,
"Suggestion":

Islam describes the philosophy that every Muslim should respect
the religion of non-believers as well. However, it also discourages
the statues, sculptures. Because of the fact at the advent of Islam
"KHANA KAABA" was absolutely cleared and all sort of idols

were broken by the sacred order of the Holy Prophet Muhammad (peace be upon him). In view of the above stated factor, I suggest that the statue of Late Dyal Singh [Sardar Dyal Singh Majithia (1848–98)] may please be placed in Museum Hall, the Mall Lahore. Any place regarding literature, Islamic studies, may be cleaned from idols, statues. Signed, Ch. Saeedudin Bhatti.[2]

No such statue is to be found at the Dyal Singh Trust Library, nor anywhere else in Lahore. The letter was dated May 17, 1983, just a few months after the women of Lahore endured baton strikes to their heads, from Lahore's policemen, in order to ask for their own freedom.

I.

Figure 6.1. Commemorative blankets for sale (2014)

The book was suddenly everywhere: in the living rooms of my friends and extended family, in newspaper columns, at the book stalls. It was 1987. The author, Qudratullah Shahab (1917–86), was barely known to me. My mother had read and often cited his previous book, *Maan ji* (Mother, 1968), as a classic in Urdu prose.

Another teacher had given me a novella, *Ya Khuda* (O God, 1948), describing it as an exemplary account of Partition. I had skimmed both, unimpressed. This book was *Shahabnama* (The Book of Shahab). It was a memoir, which the author had stipulated could only be published after his death. Its publication was a sensation.

The newspapers that I read daily—*Jang*, *Nawa-i Waqt*, *Dawn*, *Friday Times*—were full of columns by the most prominent intellectuals, novelists, and playwrights in Pakistan's Urdu cultural world—Wasif Ali Wasif (d. 1993), Mumtaz Mufti (d. 1995), Ashfaq Ahmad (d. 2004), Bano Qudsia (d. 2017), A. Hameed (d. 2011)—extolling the virtues of the book and the significance of the author. *Shahabnama* was published by Sang-e Meel Publishers in Lahore. It was slightly over 1,200 pages yet priced at an unbelievably low 250 rupees. A first edition in July 1987 was immediately followed by a second edition in December, and the book has never been out of print; it is in now in its twenty-seventh edition. The publisher calls it "one of the most popular books in Pakistan."

Qudratullah Shahab was a bureaucrat. He came to Lahore in 1937 and attended Government College, studying for his MA. He stayed in Lahore until 1941, when he took the Indian Civil Services exam and was selected. His first posting was in Bhagalpur, Bihar, and he would remain in Bengal and Odisha until 1947. Upon joining the Civil Service of Pakistan after Partition, he was posted to Kashmir and then to the Ministry of Information in Karachi. In 1954, he became the private secretary for Governor General Malik Ghulam Muhammad. This was his introduction to the highest echelons of political rule in Pakistan—and he remained part of, or adjacent to, this world for the rest of his life.

Then he served as private secretary to the next governor general, and later president, Iskander Mirza, and was retained in that capacity by the military dictator, Ayub Khan. He was an ambassador to Holland, and worked for UNESCO, the Foreign Ministry, and the Ministry of Education. Zia ul Haq made him the head of the Association for the Propagation of Urdu in 1980. For over forty years, no matter the form of government, civil or military, Shahab was very close to the most powerful men in Pakistan.

His stature and his influence explain why *Shahabnama* became an instant cultural phenomenon. It also prompts the question: What is it that allowed him to keep his position and influence even as the office holders he served were toppled, exiled, or hanged, as the country fell apart and dictatorships flourished? Over my years of research and interviewing people, the most frequently cited book, which purportedly contained the "true explication of Pakistan," was *Shahabnama*. It has a hidden history, one prominent intellectual leaned in to tell me, his eyes narrowing to judge my response. Pakistan did not come into being in 1947, he said. It was ordained long ago by the Prophet himself. This book is the proof.

Shahabnama is explicitly about power, and much of it revolves around a *Forrest Gump*–esque conceit of a "simple" man who keeps finding himself always present at historic moments. How he remains "pure" and unaffected by the corrupt and powerful that surround him owes to two factors. The first is the Prophet, who comes to him in a dream when he is in tenth grade.[3] Shahab causes the visitation through his recitation of a *darud sharif* (incantation of formulaic praise). His devotion to the Prophet in his childhood was sparked when he was six or seven years old. His Hindu friend had referred to the Muslim faith and the Prophet with a slur. Shahab, incensed, grabbed a stone and swung it into the child's face, breaking his front tooth.[4] This incident, he writes, ensured his lifelong devotion to the Prophet. In a similar vein, a later encounter with a Brahmin made Shahab believe in the power of recitation (it had protected him from the Brahmin's black magic), which he then maintained as a practice for the rest of his life.[5] Much like the childhood awakening described by Nasim Hijazi, these early experiences of Hindu hate proved to the young believer the necessity of devotion to the Prophet.

These experiences would lead Shahab to the second factor behind his ability to remain pure among his fallen contemporaries and

devoted to his cause: his correspondence with a hidden (or invisible) being called "Ninety" (*Shahabnama* is dedicated to his
mother, wife, children, and to "Ninety"). By this moniker, he
means "a ninety-year-young fakir," who had entered into an epis-
tolary correspondence with Shahab early in his career as an ICS
officer. The letters from Ninety would manifest as if by magic
inside books, in his pockets, or out of thin air in his hands. The
inverse would occur when Shahab wrote Ninety back. That is, his
responses would materially disappear after he wrote them. The
condition of the continued correspondence was that he could not
"keep" any of the letters he received.

The correspondence was in English and maintained throughout
his life. It provided Shahab with (occult) information, guidance,
and presumably a moral and ethical framework for his political
work. This invisible spiritual guide, in Shahab's reckoning, would
keep him insulated from the travails of power as well as in the good
graces of the powerful. It was, in other words, his own private su-
perpower. As an example, he shares his story of staying at a possessed bungalow (haunted by a Hindu woman, naturally), where
the poltergeist and Shahab spend weeks engaged in a struggle for
domination.[6]

A veneer of spiritualism envelops *Shahabnama*. It is a sanctified
and orthodox spiritualism, as the source of it is clearly identified
with the Prophet. Shahab also cites a number of texts on mysti-
cism, written by Sunni ulema, which he studied in his life. The
book ends with his own collection of verses from the Qur'an and
recitations. Underneath this spiritual veneer, however, are two
significant formulations for understanding the political history of
Pakistan. The first is a naked devotion to elite structures of power.
Shahab grants full "humanity" to those who are at the very top,
regardless of their means of arriving there. His is not a paean to
democratic rule or the will of the people.

Rather, he believes in the righteousness of those who are en-
trusted to govern over the people. He speaks for them, renders
them sympathetically, and gives examples of how he was the key

to their successes, and how his failure to prevent them from harming themselves led to the failures of Pakistan. This self-aggrandizing, even as he dismisses himself rhetorically, makes him into a swashbuckling character in the book. At one point, he is an undercover agent in Israel, and at another he is figuring out the key to nuclear domination.

Equally significant is the hatred in the text for Hindus, Sikhs, Ahmadis, and any political minority that one can imagine. As an Urdu stylist, Shahab uses strings of florid adjectives to depict his revulsion at their skin, their smell, their food, their conduct, and their demeanor. These are scattered throughout the text. Even in a fabulous encounter from his days in pre-Partition Lahore, where he ostensibly falls in love with a Hindu girl named Chandarvati, he writes about her using greatly violent language.[7] He wishes to smash her head in and cut her into pieces simply because he likes her. When she dies from tuberculosis, he is sorrowful, but there is little doubt that the entire episode is a figment of his imagination.

Shahabnama confirms, if not inflames, prejudices toward the religious Other, while asserting that a hidden, secretive spiritual order is devoted to the protection of Pakistan against political and mystical forces. In the Zia ul Haq military dictatorship of the late 1980s, this was a clarion call to rearticulate the ideology of Pakistan from a body politic to a *body spiritualis*. Shahab's associates, acolytes, and followers—Ashfaq Ahmad, Wasif Ali Wasif, Mumtaz Mufti, Bano Qudsia—propagated the idea that Shahab was a figure of political and mystic credentials during his life and after his death.

To give one example of this network of intellectuals and propagandists who surrounded Shahab, we can look at Mumtaz Mufti. In 1948, Mumtaz Mufti became an assistant editor for *Istiqlal*, a monthly magazine of the Punjab government. From 1949 through 1965, he worked as an intelligence officer for the Pakistan Air Force; as a producer for Radio Azad Kashmir, which was set up as a propaganda unit; as the information officer for the Kashmir publicity director; as the assistant for Qudratullah Shahab, who was then the secretary to President Ayub Khan; and, later, as the assistant director for the Ministry of Information. After he retired in 1966, he continued to write for Radio Pakistan, producing over 150 radio plays, as well as for television and various journals. He also continued publishing his own novels and travelogues until his death in 1995. He wrote *Labaik* (1975), which depicted Shahab as a spiritual master during his hajj, and then wrote the Shahab biography *Alakh Nagri* (1992). In these books he presented Shahab as a divinely guided bureaucrat—the sole righteous man amid a corrupt and immoral system.

A vast ecosystem enshrined Shahab. His devotees all held prominent positions at Radio Pakistan and Pakistan Television, and were part of a wide Urdu press network that were able to disseminate their words and their thoughts across the length and breadth of Pakistan. They were hyper-nationalist and had close ties to both the bureaucratic and the military states. In their writings, their TV shows, and their radio broadcasts, all of which were massively popular, they promulgated a specific type of Prophetic thought about Pakistan's future. Building on Shahab, they offered a triumphant vision of a Pakistan destined to emerge successful as the only truly global Muslim power—the Prophetic Pakistan.

II.

ʿIlm Din was born in Lahore in 1908. He is buried in the Miyani Sahib graveyard. The largest billboard in the cemetery is dedicated to him. It contains an artistic representation of him, smiling and wearing a Western-style jacket and shirt. He is clean-shaven, except for a slim mustache. His name appears as "Ghazi ʿIlm Din Shaheed." The *ghazi* and the *shaheed* denote his special status as a warrior for God and a martyr. On the billboard is inscribed a snapshot of his life:

> The great lover of Rasul (ﷺ), Ghazi ʿIlm Din Shahid, killed with multiple stabs of a knife a Hindu author named Rajpal who published insulting words against the Holy Prophet. For this he was sentenced to death by the English Session Judge Streethain on 22 May 1929. Quaid-e Azam and Allama Iqbal supported his case. On July 17, 1929, the verdict was upheld by the High Court and the appeal dismissed and on 31 October 1929 he was hanged in Miawali Jail.

His grave, built as a shrine, has several marble plaques, one of which asks: "Did you not witness the masses who gathered for his funeral to know what happens to those who insult our Prophet?" The November 16, 1929, front page of the *Daily Inqilab* from Lahore declared that a "sea of 400,000 Muslims" had participated in

Figure 6.2. Gate to the grave of 'Ilm Din in Miyani Qabaristan (2023)

the funeral procession. His memory in Lahore continues to be supported by a host of merchant guilds and state and religious organizations. The pantheon of Ghazi Shaheeds, those who followed in the footsteps of 'Ilm Din by killing a blasphemer, has grown exponentially over the last thirty years in Pakistan.

'Ilm Din's legacy is not only extrajudicial violence but also the colonial laws that emerged around his particular case. Those laws were the colonial state's response to the late nineteenth-century wars between Christianity, Hinduism, and Islam. Panjab as a site for Christian proselytizing flourished after the colonial conquest of Lahore in the mid-nineteenth century, though the American Presbyterian Church's foreign mission had been present in Uttar Pradesh and Panjab since 1833. There was a visible and vocal presence of missionaries in the major cities of Panjab—Amritsar, Lahore, Lyallpur—alongside a robust print production of Christian polemics against Islam, Hinduism, and Buddhism in Urdu, Hindi, and Panjabi.

Many of those Christian presses were based in Lahore. Episcopalian, Anglican, Apostolic, and other denominations had been bringing missionaries from across the world, often from New York, New Jersey, and Pennsylvania, to Panjab and Sind since the mid-nineteenth century, including figures such as George Bowen (1816–88), Hervey DeWitt Griswold (1860–1945), and Henry Martyn Clark (1857–1916). Overlapping with these missionary efforts were Muslim and Hindu reformists who were producing their own critiques and exultations, such as Swami Dayanand's *Satyarth Prakash* (The Light of Truth, 1875) and Muhammad Qasim Nanautavi's *Qiblanuma* or *Hujjat al-Islam*. Mirza Ghulam Ahmad (1835–1908), the founder of the Ahmadiyya movement, was also a critical presence in these debates. These were ticketed and staged public events, for their carnivalesque atmosphere, often lasting up to two weeks.

One such polemic, *Rangila Rasul*, was published in Lahore in 1924 by an author with the pseudonym Swami Pandit Champoti M.A. The publisher was Rajpal & Sons, owned by Mahashe Rajpal, who had started the press in Anarkali in 1912. Rajpal was a member of the Arya Samaj, and the group was reportedly the driving force for the publication of *Rangila Rasul*. The pamphlet, some sixty pages long, was written in a satirical or mocking tone and focused on marriage, and polygamy in particular. It contrasted the conduct of the Prophet (citing various recent Urdu biographies) against Hindu religious and political leaders from Shivaji onward. Readers understood the pamphlet as a response to similar "attacks" by Muslim writers on Arya Samaj and the Hindu faith.

After protests against the pamphlet's publication broke out, the British colonial state arrested Rajpal and sentenced him to two years' imprisonment for inciting religious hatred. Later, the sentence was overturned. In the meantime, Muslim authors responded to the text with their own pamphlets, notably *Muqaddas Rasul bajwab Rangila Rasul* (The Honored Prophet in Answer to the Debauched Prophet, 1924) by Abu'lal Wafa Sanaullah Amritsari. This reply was lauded by all prominent religious scholars as an apt and full response to the pamphlet. But the public was not satisfied.

In 1927, two attempts were made on the life of Rajpal, though he escaped injury. The assailants were arrested and sentenced to jail. As a result of continued agitation, the colonial state modified Section 295A of the Indian Penal Code by passing the "Scurrilous Writings Act" in September 1927, which made any insult to religion a criminal offense. 'Ilm Din, who lived not far from Rajpal's shop, walked in and stabbed him three times with a knife on April 6, 1929. The killing of Rajpal enshrined a new turn in politics in the subcontinent—manifested not simply as self-motivated violence against a blasphemer but also as direct fealty to the Prophet. 'Ilm Din's act created his own hagiography in which his path to martyrdom was illuminated by prophecies and visitations. Pakistan itself would become a product of such direct visitations and prophecies.

Violence against the state and offenses against the Prophet were intricately linked.

The August 2011 issue of the monthly *Nazariya-e Pakistan* (Ideology of Pakistan) published an excerpt from the memoir of former interior secretary Chaudhry Fazl-e Haque, which described the reasons for Muhammad Ali Jinnah's return from England to India to lead the Muslims:

One evening, I was strolling on the lawn of my house in London when I smelt a unique fragrance. First, I thought it was a temporary phenomenon but the fragrance continued to prevail in the air. I could not understand as to what was the source of that fragrance. I decided to go to sleep. I could not sleep for quite some time. During sleep I saw a holy personality in my dream. The holy personality addressed me: *I am Prophet Mohammad (PBUH). I order you to go to India and lead the Muslims to their destiny.* After the dream I awoke and started preparation for my return journey to India.[8]

Versions of this account have long circulated in popular media—pinning the very foundation of Pakistan to the appearance of the Prophet. A suitable summary appeared in a column from September 10, 2011, penned by Syed Siddiqui for the *Daily Jang* and titled "Fate (Prophecy) in the Creation of Pakistan." He narrates the various prophecies recounted to Jinnah, Hasrat Mohani (1875–1951), Ashraf Ali Thanwi (1863–1943), and Muhammad Iqbal, all of whom predicted or ordained the creation of Pakistan.

The role of the state, both in the vision of this column and in the state's own conception of itself, was to protect Pakistan as a country with a unique relationship to the Prophet. By the 1970 elections, the first in Pakistan, both the "secular" party of Zulfiqar Ali Bhutto (the Pakistan People's Party) and the religious party of Maulana Mau'dudi (Jama'at-i Islami) were using the same concept to indicate their commitment to a sacral-orientated Pakistan: Nizam-e Mustafa (The Order of the Prophet).

This concept became the dominant and most politically expedient paradigm (whether in the social, communal, or economic sphere) throughout the 1970s, and with the arrival of the military dictatorship of General Zia ul Haq, it became the sub-rosa constitutional credo. In 1986, under General Zia, the Pakistan Penal Code was further amended to sanctify the "blasphemy laws," including Section 295C:

Use of derogatory remarks, etc., in respect of the Holy Prophet. Whoever by words, either spoken or written, or by visible representation, or by any imputation, innuendo, or insinuation, directly or indirectly, defiles the sacred name of the Holy Prophet Muhammad (peace be upon him) shall be punished with death, or imprisonment for life, and shall also be liable to fine.

This legislation—unique in the Muslim world—had been a central demand of political parties since independence. In late December 2010, Salman Taseer, the governor of Punjab, publicly articulated his support for rethinking the role of 295C in Pakistan in light of a then current case against a Christian woman, Asiya Noreen, who was accused of blaspheming against the Prophet. An opinion column, "Ki Muhammad se wafa tu nay" (If you are faithful to Muhammad) by Mushtaq Ahmed Qureshi appeared on January 1 in the *Daily Jang*. Qureshi opened with a description of a social setting (a funeral) where some sober men were gathered, discussing the affairs of the day:[9]

> One asked a relative arriving from Lahore, what has happened to your Governor in Punjab that he is giving speeches against *khatm-e nabuvat* (Finality of Prophethood)? Another relative asked a *maulana* (cleric) sitting nearby, "Can you tell me why the issue of 'Finality of Prophethood' is so severe that the religious cleric simply throws a person out of Islam for it?" The maulana replied, "The only thing I know is that without faith in the 'Finality of Prophethood' no one can be a Muslim and this is God's command."

It was a shame, Qureshi wrote, that even though the governor of Punjab knew that he would die one day and be judged for his words, he was pandering to the non-Muslim world and speaking about repealing the "blasphemy laws." At the end of the column, Qureshi cited, with great praise, a couplet by the renowned Urdu poet Muhammad Iqbal: *Ki Muhammad se wafa tu nay to hum teray hain / Yeh Jahan chiz hay kiya, Loh o Qalam teray hain* (Be faithful to Muhammad and I am yours / This world is nothing, the Tablet and Pen are yours).

Three days later, on January 4, 2011, the governor of Punjab, Pakistan, Salman Taseer, was assassinated by his own bodyguard, Mumtaz Qadri, in Lahore. The defenders of 295C, various mercantile and religious organizations, gathering under the banner of "Tahafuz Namus-e Risalat" (Protection of the Honor of the Prophecy), publicly declared Mumtaz Qadri a *ghazi* (warrior) and, after his hanging in 2016, a *shaheed* (martyr).

III.

Mirza Shabbir Baig Sajid is now in his mid-eighties. His mass of white hair was pushed tightly under a black baseball cap, and he was sitting hunched over by the window, in a brown *shalwar kameez* (trousers and shirt). His right hand rested lightly on a file folder set on his lap. After a small awkward silence in which I was unsure how to proceed and he looked like he didn't want to speak to me, a halting conversation began. He had taken a bus that morning from outside Kasur to deliver an Urdu short story he had written to a local editor. He liked my questions about the short story. It is titled "Kuffara" (Absolution), and it is about a husband who has to pay the penance of performing a custom that is non-Islamic, he told me.

We were meeting in the offices of *Hikayat* magazine in Patiala Ground. Outside I could hear a group of children playing cricket. I asked him about his career as a writer. "I was around ten at the time of the Partition," he told me. "It was like a tornado that carried me to Lahore in a bus full of refugees. Our bus was stopped and attacked by a group of Sikhs." He rattled off a series of curses. Then he took off his baseball cap and bent his head to reveal a gash on his neck.

"Here and here." He slowly took his arm out from his shirt, showing another deep cut that had healed in an irregular line above his elbow. "They got me with the kirpan twice and cut me deep and flung me outside. This was right at the border of Lahore. I walked during the daybreak. The Sikhs hate us Muslims and I hate them. They destroyed Lahore before they destroyed my family."

He had no nostalgia for a pre-Partition Hindustan. It was a time of sorrow and fear for him, and the violence he recounted was his only birthright. I was shaken by his words and by the force of his recollection. "What happened once you got to Lahore?" I asked him.

"I became a young apprentice to Agha Shorish Kashmiri and I dedicated my life to the pen."

Born in Amritsar, Agha Shorish Kashmiri (1917–1975) was a poet, journalist, freedom fighter, and later a publisher. He joined the Majlis Ahrar-ul Islam. It was an organization that was founded in 1929 to mobilize against Mirza Ghulam Ahmad (1839–1908), whom it deemed a false prophet—a central tenet in Muslim faith is the belief in the finality of Prophet Muhammad (ﷺ) as the last Prophet—and against his followers, the Ahmadi, deemed non-Muslim. In 1934, the Majlis led processions in Lahore demanding that the Ahmadi be declared non-Muslim. Kashmiri joined the Majlis and spent more than five years in jail, in Lahore, under the Defence of India Act in the late 1930s and the early 1940s for his anti-Ahmadi activities. He also worked on the Lahori paper *Zamindar*, another fervent supporter of the anti-Ahmadi cause.

On January 1, 1949, Kashmiri launched a full-color weekly from Lahore called *Chattan* (Rock). Baig Sajid was the assistant editor under Shorish Kashmiri until his death. Kashmiri imagined the magazine as one dedicated to the cause of Islam. He printed on the cover of each issue the motto for the magazine, a couplet from Iqbal: *Agarche but hain jamaat ki astinun main / mujhe hai hukm-e-azaan la ilah-a-illallah* (Though idols are hidden in the sleeves of those standing for prayer / I am commanded to proclaim there is no God but Allah)—giving *Chattan* an anti-establishment credo. *Chattan* was priced low in order to maximize its outreach, used bicolor paper, simple prose, and featured interviews and profiles of prominent political and counterpolitical members of society. It became immensely popular. Kashmiri kept his focus on anti-Ahmadi politics, arguing that there were those who hurt Islam within Pakistan. In *Chattan's* pages were arguments marking Ahmadis as a political community that had conspired to create Pakistan out of India in order to have its own independent state, which, it claimed, was going to be set up in Kashmir. The idea of an Ahmadi "fifth column," nourished and developed by *Chattan*, would eventually define Pakistan's legal and social treatment of this minority.

In early 1953, the Majlis returned to the streets of Lahore demanding the ouster of the Ahmadis in federal government. They were joined by the founder of Jama'at-i Islami, Maulana Abu'l 'Ala Maududi (1903–79). The disturbances led to the imposition of martial law in Lahore. Maududi and Kashmiri were arrested and incarcerated. *Chattan* continued to publish regular reports that claimed Ahmadis were secretly working from within to poison the Pakistani Army and the civil bureaucracy with their propaganda. Maududi subsequently wrote a pamphlet, *Qadiani Masla* (The Qadiani Problem), which laid out his case for an organized political movement that would champion a declaration of the finality of Prophethood as an ideological necessity for Pakistan.

Chattan continued to aggressively mobilize public opinion against the Ahmadis, labeling the agitation against them as "Tehrek-e-Raast Iqdam" (the Righteous Movement). Kashmiri made a fresh bid at fanning anti-Ahmadi hatred in the mid-1960s. He began to argue that the Ahmadis were, in fact, Zionists. By using terms such as *Mirza'il*—an amalgamation of "Israel" and "Mirza" (title of the Ahmadi community's founding leader, Mirza Ghulam Ahmad)—and *Ajami Israel* (Eastern Israel), Kashmiri relied heavily on anti-Semitic and anti-Jewish notions to associate Ahmadis with a conspiracy to dominate the whole world. Thus, *Chattan's* earlier insistence that Ahmadis were a political community had metamorphized into an anti-Semitic theory that they ran an international cabal.

Articles published in *Chattan* included lists of Ahmadi bureaucrats and businessmen—"secretive," "conspiratorial" Ahmadis who were planning to bring about the demise of Pakistan. Ayub Khan's dictatorial regime was generally lenient toward the magazine, as Kashmiri was a close friend of Qudratullah Shahab. Shahab would also write in his memoir about the supposed Ahmadi infiltration of Pakistani state bureaucracy, which he suspected and resisted. He would also incorporate anti-Semitic elements in his works. Still, the street turmoil caused by *Chattan* proved too much and Ayub Khan ordered the magazine to cease publication in 1967 and Kashmiri was jailed, once again, for inciting violence.

Similarly, Kashmiri's other literary friends—Ashfaq Ahmad, Bano Qudsia, and others—became visible and vocal advocates of his mission. In newspapers and on TV and radio shows, they made a point to publicly proclaim their belief in the finality of Prophethood. *Chattan* was also heavily supported by various merchant organizations from Lahore that were especially keen to keep the anti-Ahmadi and finality-of-Prophethood politics at the heart of the city. Major streets were frequently disrupted, markets shut down, and demonstrations were held at key state buildings.

After 1971, *Chattan* also blamed the creation of Bangladesh on Ahmadi conspiracies. It portrayed Mirza Muzaffar Ahmad, President Yahya Khan's economic adviser, as the source of the grievances that East Pakistanis had developed against West Pakistan. On October 18, 1972, the magazine published a cover story that "exposed" India's plans to divide Pakistan into many states. Along with Bangladesh, these included Sindhudesh, Khalistan, and an Ahmadi state in Baluchistan. During these years, *Chattan* turned to lobbying Zulfiqar Ali Bhutto against Ahmadis. Bhutto, then the prime minister of Pakistan, had already received a glowing profile in the magazine's December 4, 1967, issue for publicly declaring that Ahmadi were non-Muslims. Although the government briefly jailed Kashmiri in August 1972 for provoking anti-Ahmadi violence, his agenda was clearly ascendant.

Kashmiri died in 1975, but *Chattan* did not stop its anti-Ahmadi campaign. By then, Kashmiri's supporters had conferred the title of "Mujahid-e-Khatm-e Nabuwwat" (Soldier of the Finality of Prophethood) on him. Zulfiqar Ali Bhutto passed a constitutional amendment on September 7, 1974, to officially declare Ahmadis as non-Muslims. *Chattan* published cover story after cover story "exposing" the presence of Ahmadi spies in the government, as well as an Ahmadi "conspiracy" to control the whole world in collaboration with Jews. The July 12, 1982, issue featured a cover photo of Zia along with a self-explanatory caption: "Qadiani [Ahmadi] Activities and the Role of the President." Inside the issue was coverage of an International Khatm-e Nabuwwat Conference in London and an article "exposing" an Ahmadi "conspiracy" against Pakistan's nuclear weapons program. Substantiating the article's claims was a quote from Dr. Abdul Qadir Khan, who is believed to be the program's founder. *Chattan* published its final issue in 1990.

"Kashmiri was a great man," Baig Sajid told me that day in Patiala Ground. "He led the fight against Ahmadi, and *Chattan* was the weapon we used. Though we were not alone. To make this a land of the Prophet, all of us did work." He started listing prominent publishers and publications from Lahore who were allies in this fight against Ahmadis. *Siyara Digest, Urdu Digest, Hikayat, Naqoosh*—they all had a "Rasool Number" (Special Issue on the Prophet) that provided the reading public with thousands of pages of testimonials, narratives and exegises on the life of the Prophet. The "Rasool Number" of *Naqoosh*, for instance, took ten years to complete and was published in four volumes, each more than eight hundred pages. "I worked on a few of those Rasool Numbers. This was our struggle with the pen, to bring back the unique nature of the Prophet to this new nation. It is a nation that was prophesized *by* the Prophet. It exists to safeguard Islam around the world." I asked, "Do you feel at ease now? Now that citizenship and marriage are defined in Pakistan with an explicit declaration of non-Ahmadi belonging?" He did not say anything.

IV.

The cricket match was scheduled for Shadman Park, and a group of us players arrived early. As the pitch was being readied, some of us were sitting under a tree, making small talk. I was the youngest on my team, and a player from the opposing team asked me if I had ever been to Shadman before. I had. I told him I studied nearby at FC College. He nodded. Others around us were talking about the national team and their recent match in the West Indies. "Did you know that this park was once Lahore's Central Jail?" he asked me. I did not understand what he meant. "The main jail where the British kept all their prisoners was exactly where we are now sitting," he said. "That way," he gestured, "was the jail for women, and beyond that was the mental hospital. And that way," he pointed toward the head of the wicket just as our team captains gestured us to come, "was where Bhagat Singh was hanged by the British. Pigs!" He spat on the ground. I was taken aback by his vehemence, but more so by my ignorance. Who was Bhagat Singh? Why did the British murder him? But then the game started, and all other thoughts vanished.

That there was a colonial Central Jail with a panopticon structure right next to the Cantonment made perfect sense, though it had never occurred to me before. The jails had disappeared when the Lahore Development Authority tore them down and replaced them with a residential and commercial colony in the late 1950s and 1960s. The effort was part of the implementation of the new

Figure 6.3. "Satnam Sri Vahiguru" Sikh *haveli* (2011)

Lahore master plan of 1951, which built new settlements between and across the old city and the colonial city: Samanabad,
Gulberg, Iqbal Town, Wahdat Colony, Garden Town, New Garden Town, Gulshan-e Ravi, and more.

The extent of my ignorance went far beyond my imagination. I
did not know that by the turn of the twentieth century, Lahore

was the global center for anti-colonial struggle. The deputy commissioner of Lahore was convinced that behind every Sikh turban was a revolutionary, that every Arya Samaj meeting was a terrorist meeting, and that every printing press was printing seditious material. His daily reports, in 1909, were full of descriptions of seizures of pamphlets on making bombs and open talk in the streets of assassinating Europeans.

I did not know about Lal Chand Falak (1887–1967), who was arrested in 1917, charged with sedition, and sentenced for four and half years of hard labor in Kala Pani (Andaman Island). Falak lived in Gawalmandi neighborhood in Lahore, and ran the Vande Mataram Book Agency, which published, among other things, a biography of Bal Gangadhar Tilak in Urdu and a series of publications by Lala Har Dayal (1884–1939) advocating for revolutionary struggle in support of independence. Falak also published the pamphlet *Jail khanay ki Kahani, Political Qaidiyon ki Zubani* (The Stories from Within the Jail as Told by Political Prisoners), which included excerpts by Tilak, Gandhi, Lala Lajpat Rai (1865–1928), and others extolling their bravery and resistance to the British overlords. Lajpat Rai, who practiced law in Lahore, had recently been arrested and deported to Mandalay Fort prison (in Burma). The colonial state seized this publication.

I did not know about Bhai Parmanand (1876–1947)—a graduate of D.A.V College in Lahore who later finished his MA from Punjab University in 1902. He wrote *Tarikh-e Hind* (History of Hindustan) among other histories (of Punjab, Rajasthan, Maharashtra), many of them also confiscated by the colonial state for carrying seditious anti-colonial messages. He, along with Har Dayal, took that message to San Francisco, California, and Astoria, Oregon. In Astoria, they co-founded the Hindustan Ghadar Party (Revolutionary Party of Hindustan) in May 1913. They published a news pamphlet, also called *Hindustan Ghadar*, and distributed it freely to the hundreds of Panjabi millworkers and farmhands who had arrived in the Pacific Northwest just a few years earlier. The aim was to unite with Germany and overthrow colonial rule in India. A date was set—February 21, 1915, according to the colonial investigators—to return from the United States and Canada and begin the revolution.

The Americans and the British crushed the nascent revolution. There were mass arrests in the United States, and those who had made it back to India, mostly on Japanese ships, were arrested (sometimes killed) on arrival. Prosecutors launched massive prosecutions against the arrested suspects, called the Lahore Conspiracy Case (1915–16). The first cases resulted in at least forty-two executions, and a series of punitive laws were passed—the 1915 Defence of India Act and the 1919 Rowlatt Act. Hundreds of young Indians were tried, convicted for alleged robberies, raising funds for workers and peasants, or attempts to derail trains, murder colonial officers and occupy Panjab. Those not killed were shipped to the Andaman Islands. The colonial state raided houses, presses, hostels, and dormitories. They coerced men into becoming informants. The First Lahore Conspiracy Case trial was followed by a "supplemental" case—these were mass prosecutions in which defendants were charged and judged as a collective group—and the San Francisco Conspiracy Case (1917–18). The punishment for sedition was death.

The Rowlatt Act prompted protests across Panjab, including a *hartal* strike launched by Gandhi. In early April 1919, Muslim, Sikh, and Hindu artisans came out in the streets of Lahore to protest. The colonial army, afraid of this "Danda Fauj" (Army bearing sticks), fired upon them, killing twenty.[10] The same excuse (of a marching "Danda Fauj") was used by Brigadier-General Dyer when he opened fire on a crowd of protestors in Amritsar, on April 13, 1919, killing almost 400 Panjabis. That event became known as the Jallianwala Bagh Massacre.

The British massacre of civilian protesters in Jallianwala Bagh prompted a renewed fight for independence across India. In Lahore, in particular, it reignited the question of whether or not there should be an armed struggle. Lala Lajpat Rai continued to critique the colonial state after the end of World War I. At Bradlaugh Hall, his lectures and classes attracted a new generation of young Panjabi students, including Bhagat Singh. Bhagat Singh took part in the formation of the Naujawan Bharat Sabha (Young India Association) and the Hindustan Socialist Republican Association.

I did know that Bhagat Singh, alongside his co-revolutionaries, was suspected of assassinating two police officers, John Poyantz Saunders and Chanan Singh, in December 1928 very near Government College. I did not know that the revolutionaries' actions were a response to the death of Lala Lajpat Rai. On October 30, 1928, Lala Lajpat Rai participated in a street protest in Lahore against the Simon Commission—an all-British MP collective aimed at figuring out the future for constitutional rule in British India. To quell and disperse the protesters, the superintendent of police ordered their dispersal using baton strikes. Lajpat was seriously injured and died two weeks later. Saunders was killed outside the district police office. The next morning a circular printed by the Hindustan Socialist Republican Army, written in English, was posted around Lahore: "J. P. Saunders is dead! Lala Lajpat Rai is Avenged!"

Their "direct political action" would continue. Bhagat Singh was arrested in April 1929 after he detonated a bomb in the Delhi legislative assembly—some were injured. He was taken back to Lahore and put on trial alongside ten others. He continued to resist, hoping to use the publicity of the trial and the courtroom to spread his message of freedom, but the colonial state succeeded in muzzling much of it. He was hanged alongside Shivaram Raj Guru and Sukhdev Thapar on March 23, 1931.

It was not just that I knew so little about Bhagat Singh. It was that I knew so little about revolutionary Lahore. I had no idea how many Lahoris had written seditious materials and revolutionary poems, passed out bomb-making pamphlets, and stood and listened to lectures on equality and freedom in dim halls and on street corners. The armed struggle for independence had happened on the same streets of Lahore that I was walking around, and I had no clue about any of it. The material for understanding this past had also vanished, either into Gurmukhi or into books published in India that were censored in Pakistan.

In 2011 a vigil was held at Shadman Chowk to recognize and rename the site after Bhagat Singh. A few speeches were made. The Punjab Government listened, and in 2012 it announced that Bhagat Singh would be memorialized in Lahore. Almost immediately, there were protests. The government rescinded the decision. Some years later, the Punjab Civil Secretariat inaugurated an exhibition for Bhagat Singh inside their building (colloquially known as Anarkali's Tomb), safe from public in that secure government facility. The senior government official giving the tour paused at the official death certificate of Bhagat Singh, remarking about March 23, It is good we celebrate that date as 'Pakistan Day' to celebrate the passing of the Lahore Resolution. Otherwise these activists will want it to be Bhagat Singh Day. He chuckled.

"The resolution was actually passed on March 24, 1940," I pointed out to him.

"Still, why would we celebrate Bhagat Singh?" he quipped. "He was a communist."

The reason the partitioned city cannot access these histories of dissent and resistance is that they aren't labeled as "revolutionary" or "anticolonial." Instead, they are labeled "Sikh" or "Hindu," and such a label takes away the histories' capacity to exist both in contemporary time and historical time. Bhagat Singh, born a Sikh, became an atheist, and now both his name and his ideologies make him an outsider to the civic infrastructure of the city in which he gave his life. The city was already purged of all such names. A statue of Lala Lajpat Rai (The Great Patriot) once stood outside Government College (in Gol Bagh). It was moved to Shimla, India, in 1948. The presses that printed revolutionary material are also gone, as are the words and deeds of Bhagat Singh.

V.

Figure 6.4. Stairs leading to an entrance to Lahore Fort (Shahi Qila) (2015)

I hid *Dast-e Saba* (Wind's Hand, 1952). I read it deep into the afternoon when everyone else was asleep. It opens: "Why grieve even if the wealth of pen and tablet are stolen / for I have dipped my fingers in my heart's blood / what matters that a seal is placed on my tongue / for I have put my tongue in every link of the chain." The poet who wrote this words, Faiz Ahmed Faiz, had recently died. I did not read much poetry, but I was introduced to Faiz and Saʿadat Hasan Manto in the same breath earlier that summer, in 1985, as "forbidden texts": the first was a communist and the second was obscene. I was keen to immediately get my hands on both. Faiz came first via *Dast-e Saba*.

The slim volume, with a cardboard cover, begins with a preface. Faiz writes that a poet's task is not merely to observe the world, but to show that world to others and to struggle in that world. There can be no tranquility in the poet's gaze, nor any distance between the world and the poet. The preface is dated September 16, 1952, and signed, "Central Jail Hyderabad." Faiz was imprisoned in the "Rawalpindi Conspiracy Case." He spent much of those four years of imprisonment between Hyderabad, Sahiwal, and Lahore, where he was kept in the "Bomb Ward." The barracks was constructed specifically for Bhagat Singh by the British. Faiz would later also spend time in the dungeons of Lahore Fort, where another prison existed specifically for political prisoners. Faiz called it the "famous urban concentration place."[11]

He wrote two volumes of poetry during his imprisonment. His next published volume of poetry, *Zindan Nama* (Prison Book, 1956), was written while in Montgomery Jail, Sahiwal, and in Central Jail, Lahore. That was the second book I purchased. I copied into a notebook all twenty-one poems from the two volumes, each of them explicitly marked with a month, year, the name of the prison, and the name of the city. The result was my own small replica of Faiz's prison notebook.

Faiz was arrested at his home in Lahore on March 9, 1951, for taking part in a conspiracy of army officers and communists to overthrow the government of Prime Minister Liaquat Ali Khan. At the time of his arrest, Faiz was the editor of a very successful daily newspaper from Lahore, *Pakistan Times*. He was also a decorated soldier, a lieutenant colonel, in the British army. He was part of a coterie of writers and poets who were "progressive" or "leftist." He was one of the most prominent cultural intellectuals in the country, at that point only four years young.

The state claimed that the conspiracy was motivated by either Pakistan's inaction in Kashmir or the prime minister's visit to the United States. The state charged fifteen individuals with treason and prosecuted them in a court in Hyderabad Sind. During the trials, on October 16, 1951, Liaquat Ali Khan was assassinated. Faiz was released in April 1955, although he, like the nation, would face further political turmoil. Six prime ministers had come and gone by October 1958, after which there followed a long decade of military rule under General Ayub Khan. The country broke into two, and a prime minister would be hanged by another military dictator. Faiz, his health compromised during the long prison sentence, lived mostly in exile, first in London and then in Beirut. His name, and fame, would grow such that he has become synonymous with a sense of dignified resistance against tyranny anywhere.

Faiz's own preface for *Dast-e Saba* does not comment directly on his imprisonment. For *Zindan Nama*, two essays bring his daily life in prison to light, both written by his co-accused in the Rawalpindi Conspiracy Case, who are also his dear friends. The first essay, by Sajjad Zaheer, is titled "Sar-e Aghaz" (In the Beginning), and the second, by Muhammad Ishaq, is "Rudad-e Qafas" (Prison Tale). Sajjad Zaheer, one of the founders of the Progressive Writers' Movement, was a writer, poet, and, at the time of his arrest, the general secretary of Pakistan's Communist Party. Major Muhammad Ishaq had known Faiz since Amritsar, where Faiz had been a teacher before coming to Lahore, and would go on to create the Mazdoor Kissan (Workers and Peasants) Party in Lahore. Ishaq writes of the intense public opinion that was mobilized against Faiz and the other accused. There was talk of having executions without trials, and a special military tribunal was set up to prosecute the accused.[12] Yet even as the men were moved cellblock to cellblock, from court to prison, there were poetry gatherings, salons, and readings, which were made open to all.

Pakistan was always the topic of conversation.[13] Faiz was in Lahore during the tumult of Partition. "He often spoke about witnessing how the warriors and heroes of each side had destroyed humanity," Ishaq writes. "He was overcome by emotion and would stop speaking. In my opinion, he saw atrocities at such a level that he was unable to bring them to verse. It may be that he finds a time to write a novel or drama on this tragedy of Panjab." Every time there was turmoil on the streets, new prisoners were brought to the jail. During those four years, Lahore was teeming with protests for anti-Ahmadi laws, against Urdu as the sole national language, for a constitution, and all of them infused Faiz's poetry.

Faiz's imprisonment was certainly not unique. Many who were arrested and imprisoned were asking for democracy. Qamar Yorish, an organizer for workers' rights and a writer, was picked up while at his job at the Railway Colony in 1959 for plastering posters that read "Azadi Kahan Hai?" (Where Is Freedom?) all over the city—to protest Ayub Khan, recently made dictator of Pakistan. Yorish's account of his imprisonment and torture in Lahore Fort, *Shahi Qila Se Jail Tak* (Lahore Fort to Jail), was published in 1972. In it, Yorish details his twelve-by-twelve-foot underground cell that had no light, no air, and a small, iron-barred door.[14]

Yorish tries to use his nails to scratch his name into the walls where Faiz Ahmed Faiz, Sibt-e Hasan, Ahmad Nadim Qasmi, Major Ishaq, and countless others had been imprisoned and tortured. We all know the stories of what happens underneath this Mughal fort, Yorish tells his jailers in a cheeky retort. He is beaten with clubs. A particularly grim episode highlights the vestiges of history even in a torture chamber. The state-appointed torturer asks Yorish to share his genealogy going back to his great-great-grandfather. Yorish tells him that Amritsar, his ancestral home, is now in India and he does not have access to any such information. He can only tell him the name of his grandfather, and even sharing that detail risks divulging information about his family, his caste, and his kin network. The torturer smirks and continues to beat him up.[15]

Faiz may not have been tortured under Lahore Fort, but he certainly breathed the air of those cells whose floors were stained with the blood and sweat of the tortured and the torturers—both groups citizens of the new independent nation. Major Ishaq observed that Faiz never wrote about the violence he witnessed in Lahore during Partition. This violence underneath the already blood-soaked and partitioned city was not that much different.

An unfinished poem, "Zindan ki aik Subah" (A Prison Morning), from *Dast-e Saba* gives us insight:

A gong strikes far, the listless feet began to move
to the beat, as if starved from long yellow afternoons
the terrorizing, roaring wails of the imprisoned begin
to awaken those still walking arms in arms
with intoxicating winds full of dreams
they awaken the poisonous secret calls of this jail
far a door opens, another closes
far a chain slithers, cries out loud
far a knife enters the heart of a lock
a door hits its head again and again
as if to awaken all from a dream
[to see] jinns draped in iron and steel
in whose grip cry night and day
the delicate fairies of my listless days and night.[16]

The yellow of the prison morning stays with Faiz as he moves from his prison cell out onto the streets of Lahore. There are no poems dated between March 28 and April 15, 1954, as during this span Faiz was being moved from Lahore to Sahiwal. But he memorialized his city in another fragmentary poem, "Ay Roshnion kay Shehr" (O City of Lights), a deeply tragic vision of the city: here his city appears shrouded in colorless grief, immobile under a roar of grief that rises and falls. Faiz recalls those renowned lights of the city, now bereft of their glow, and labels it as a city of exiles:[17]

Today my heart is troubled
O city of Lights
Will this night of bloodshed turn away forever all desire
May your lovers be protected, tell them
to turn up the flame when they light the candle tonight.

Paradoxically, the image of Faiz that I grew up with, one that
was popular in the 1980s, was of a romantic poet, who spoke in
defiance but whose verses were devoid of explicit political content,
and certainly free of horrifying bathos. But when I read *Zindan
Nama* for myself, I found Faiz giving testimony for a Lahore that
never forgot its violent rupture, and that continued to revisit that
rupture by foisting it upon its people. Reading Faiz was like being
slowly suffocated. The oxygen of daily life and truth turned poisonous gas.

VI.

Obscenity was a big concern for the new state in the immediate aftermath of 1947. The most frequent target of state persecution was a small, sickly writer known for his short stories and his small successes in All India Radio and Hindi cinema, Saʿadat Hasan Manto (1912–55). Manto was prosecuted before and after Partition for writing "obscene" fiction, as were his publishers in Lahore for publishing him. The first time Manto was put on trial was in 1942, for a short story, "Kali Shalwar" (Black Trousers), published in Lahore's *Adab-e Latif* monthly.[18] Then, in 1944, he was charged again, this time for two stories, one called "Bu" (Smell), also published in Lahore, and the other called "Dhuvan" (Smoke). One of his codefendants was Ismat Chughtai, charged with obscenity for her short story "Lihaf" (Blanket).

Manto's next trial was held in the newly independent Lahore, for his story "Thanda Ghosht" (Cold Meat), published in March 1949 in the magazine *Javaid*. After that trial, his stories "Khol Do" (Open It) and "Uper, Neechay aur Darmayan" (Up, Down and In Between) also prompted accusations of obscenity. His fifth and final trial took place in 1952. Manto was frequently found guilty, fined, imprisoned, and bailed out, with his sentences eventually overturned by the district-level courts. The charges were based on instances of sexual innuendo or coarse language. The defense often included other writers, such as Ahmad Nadim Qasmi, Faiz Ahmed Faiz, and Sufi Tabussum, who sometimes

Figure 6.5. Grave of Sa'adat Hasan Manto (2023)

testified that Manto's work was not obscene and sometimes conceded that he should have used other, less obscene, words in his works.

The obscenity, though, lay elsewhere. "Do not say a hundred thousand Hindus and a hundred thousand Muslims have died; say two hundred thousand human beings have died. And the big tragedy is not that two hundred thousand human beings have died, the real tragedy is that neither the killers nor the killed are in any ledger," says Mumtaz, Manto's Muslim character in the short story "Sahaey" (Support), as Mumtaz announces his intent to migrate from Bombay to Lahore.[19] This particular tale, often read as Manto giving his own reason for migrating from Bombay, pivots around four male characters—three Hindus and one Muslim. Juggal, one of the Hindus, receives a note that his uncle has been killed in a riot in Lahore. He contemplates, out loud, what would happen if the riots spread to Bombay. "I am thinking . . . maybe I will kill you." he tells the one Muslim friend, Mumtaz. The far-off violence needed or deserved a nearer retribution, Juggal imagines. But in fact, they are all confused. None of them is sure why Hindus and Muslims are killing each other, nor why they are supposed to kill one another. The characters decide that perhaps putting distance between each other is the best thing to do, and the Muslim friend leaves for Lahore from Bombay—as Manto did. The impetus for Manto, as for his fictional self, was the obscene violence consuming the subcontinent.

Manto was born and raised in Amritsar (where a portrait of Bhagat Singh hung on his wall). In 1936, after spending some time in Lahore trying to make a living as a journalist, he moved to Bombay. From there, he moved to Delhi to work for All India Radio, and then back to Bombay. He wrote plays, short stories, and film scripts. By the time he migrated to Lahore, seven collections of his short stories and four of his plays had been published. He was a known and respected figure. Partition unmoored it all. In Lahore, Manto writes as if in a fugue state.

Manto describes Lahore's refugee camps in his short story "Khuda ki Qasam" (By God). Set in March 1948, it describes the city filled with people with swollen stomachs from lack of food and water. "Who owns [the air] that is in those swollen stomachs? Pakistan or Hindustan?" Manto asks.[20] The story concerns the search for "abducted" women. Who were these women? Who abducted them? The narrator finds himself unable to restate or comprehend the

stories that he is hearing from the survivors. The chaos of the refugee camps mirrors the confusion of the narrator and the story.
Someone tells him of a search party across the border to retrieve
their *moti* (pearls, referring to the abducted women). Which pearls,
the narrator wonders, native or foreign? Violence clouds everything,
makes everyone unknowable.

The narrator stands in a busy public square in Lahore in "Sau
Kandal Power ka Bulb" (100 Candlepower Bulb). The short
story concerns the change in Lahore's urban fabric as a result of
Partition. The town square that was once the life of the town a
mere two years ago, when the narrator last visited, is now desolate
and filled with broken-seeming people milling around in torn
clothes. What a strange storm, he remarks to himself, that has
blown everything away, even the color of the buildings. "Human
beings killed human beings, raped women, but they also did the
same to the dry wood and bricks of all these buildings. He had
heard that in this storm women had been stripped naked, their
breasts cut off. But every building around here is also naked and
ripped up."[21] Amid the denuded buildings, the violated people
wander aimlessly, lacking emotions. The narrator attempts to save
a woman from being sold for sex and fails.

"Sarak kay Kinaray" (At the Street's Edge), another short story,
ends with a news item from Lahore of an abandoned newborn
baby girl recovered by the police. Someone had tried to strangle
the child and leave her exposed to the elements. She was found
barely alive, a beautiful child with blue eyes. The story is written as
a monologue from the perspective of the mother from whose
arms this child was forcibly removed. She has no power left to
resist or complain. All the atrocities are public, in view of everyone, and no one is able to stop them. Manto does not portray the
violence as outside the realm of human agency, but rather the op-
posite: he understands that there is a great deal of intimacy between the violence and the people; they are after all friends and
neighbors.

Most haunting (and considered "obscene") in Manto's accounts of Partition's violence, is his collection *Siyah Hashiye* (Dark Marginal Notes, 1948). This collection was also censored and banned. It is made up of a series of entries spanning a single page, some of them only a paragraph long, each with a short title—almost an archive of news items. Each of the entries describe a moment of violence during the upheaval of Partition in Lahore. The collection's dedication reads, "For the man who when describing his killings said: 'When I killed an old lady, I felt I was murdered myself.'"[22] The tone is dark, sad, biting.

In one entry, "Ta'vun" (Compliance), a man guides a rampaging mob to ransack his own house. In another, "Kasr-i Nafsi" (Inconvenience or Mental Anguish), a train is stopped and the adherents of the "other religion" are taken out and killed with swords and guns. The rest are fed milk and fruits by militia organizers. As they feed those left unharmed, they perform hospitality by declaring that their offerings are unbecoming to the guests only because they were too late in finding out about the train's arrival to their town. The incongruity between such a declaration and the massacre lingers with the reader. In this story, shops are destroyed and people are mistakenly killed, but outward social mores remain sacrosanct.

Such are the portraits of Partition in Lahore. Manto's narrators struggle to comprehend what is happening around them. Manto writes as a reporter invited to the end of times, jotting down fragments of speech, and describing the dark serendipity of fate and the sheer impossibility of escape. In this context, the post-Partition obscenity charges against Manto make little sense. The real absurdity was in the Lahori courtroom, where the witnesses for the prosecution described the nakedness of his prose, where the defense claimed that a particular word or two had been taken out of context, where the judge cited American case law on pornography, where the main focus was obscenity and not the bloodshed that imbues every single sentence Manto had published.

Manto's short story "Thanda Ghosht" (Cold Meat) is set inside a small hotel room, where Kalwant Kaur receives her lover, Isher Singh. Upon entering the room, Singh wearily rests his short sword next to the door. He has been killing and looting. In previous meetings he had returned with gold for her. This time, he seems haunted and preoccupied. Kaur attempts to seduce him, counting on their familiar courtship rituals. She fails. Suspicious that he has been with another woman, Kaur questions him, threatening him with his own sword. Mutely, he nods, confirming her suspicions. In a rage, she strikes him repeatedly. He makes no attempt to stop her, letting the sword cut into his body. Finally, with his dying breath, he confesses that after killing six men, he abducted a beautiful young girl. He carried her away on his shoulder with the intent of raping her. He then laid her down by the riverbed, but upon touching her, he realized that she was dead. She was, he says, cold meat. The story ends with Kaur's hand on Singh's hand, which is cold as ice.

The aftermath of violence also frames the story "Khol Do." It opens in a refugee camp in Lahore, where a train from Amritsar has arrived. One of the passengers is an elderly man by the name of Sirajuddin. He wanders for ten days, crying out the name of his abducted daughter, Sakina. He has already witnessed Sakina's mother, his wife, being disemboweled, and the image remains with him as he searches desperately for his daughter. All he has of hers is her *dupatta* (scarf). Meanwhile, teams of young male volunteers are routinely crossing the border to try and rescue women. He describes Sakina's face and beauty to them. They promise him they will find her. Many days pass. Sirajuddin keeps searching. He comes across the same group again and asks them about his daughter. They assure him that she will be found. That evening, a girl is found unconscious next to the railway tracks. Sirajuddin follows the crowd bearing the girl to the hospital. As the room empties and the light is turned on, Sirajuddin recognizes his daughter and yells her name, telling the doctor that he is the father. The doctor is convinced that the girl is dead. He asks someone to open the window. This is the story's final sentence: "Sakina's dead body shivers. Her lifeless hands move to untie her trousers and push them off. The elderly Sirajuddin screams with joy. 'Alive! My daughter is alive!' The doctor is drenched in embarrassment from head to toe."

In "Khol Do," Manto indicts the Lahori *razakars* (volunteers)—paramilitary wings of the Muslim League but also wings of other social and political parties—for the violence in the riots and the sexual violence against women. In many of his stories, the only characters who appear unmoored from the ethical landscape are the *razakars*. In other words, Manto does not blame the Sikh, Muslim, or Hindu communities. Rather, it is the *razakars*, the organized and armed militias, whom Manto specifically highlights as worthy of blame. They are also the inheritors of the new state, in which the obscenity trials are held.

The so-called obscenity trials over "Khol Do" or "Thanda Ghosht" or "Uper, Neechay aur Darmayan" eschew any acknowledgment of the violence that Manto describes in his stories, the violence that everyone inside that Lahore courtroom themselves witnessed or heard testimonies about. Nowhere in the court proceedings, in the witness statements, or the court judgments themselves is there any mention of the obscene violence that had consumed Lahore.[23] Nor in the records of the court proceedings is there any discussion of the tragic violence portrayed in the very text of "Thanda Ghosht." There is only commentary on its supposed sexual language, which Kaur uses to entice her lover, or in Manto's brief descriptions of their failed lovemaking. Any reader of the story, then or now, could not miss the graphic description of Partition killings. From the very beginning of the story, Manto makes clear that, outside that hotel room, the killing and looting has continued for days and days. Those assembled in the Lahore courtroom, including Faiz Ahmed Faiz, Shorish Kashmiri, and Ahmad Nadim Qasmi, had themselves witnessed or heard testimonies of such violence on their own. They said nothing about it. The state that was prosecuting this short story for obscenity certainly did not say anything about it. There was a staunch refusal to acknowledge what Manto was forcing them to read: a graphic depiction of a man confessing to killing, and a woman killing a man with a sword.

VII.

I was convinced, in 1984, that a femicide was happening in the country. The newspapers were filled with accounts of women raped, abducted, disfigured, attacked with swords, guns, or acid, murdered, burned to death. I had begun keeping a notebook in mid-1983 on violence against women, organizing information gathered from the three newspapers that were delivered to our house: *Daily Jang*, *Nawa-i Waqt*, and *Dawn*. The first two were local Urdu papers and the last was an English-language national newspaper. It was a small notebook of around 250 sheets of graphic paper, and by 1984 it was almost full.

The entries were organized by date, location, newspaper, and headline. For example, "April 21, Lahore, *Jang*, 19-year-old *dosheeza* (girl) killed by exploding cooking burner"; or "November 11, Multan, *Dawn*, School Principal kills herself by kerosene." The stories were very similar. There was always an exploding burner. There was always kerosene oil. There was always mention of a newlywed or a marriage proposal. The victims were always dead by the time the authorities arrived. No one was ever apprehended or convicted.

In a survey of two hundred women in Lahore (a hundred students and a hundred women working outside the home) conducted in March 1984, 95.5 percent reported being victims of sexual harassment, including "crude, vulgar, and cowardly" verbal and physical harassment.[24] These everyday crimes, each containing many layers of violence, were part of the national news cycle. One notable example was an incident in Nawabpur, near Multan, in early April 1984, in which women and girls from a family were forcibly stripped, beaten, and paraded through the streets at gunpoint by a group of powerful men, most of whom were land-owners and bureaucrats.

In this city of beginnings, there are two that matter here. The first is the beginning of resistance, against the patriarchal colonial state and then the matricidal and patriarchal nation-state. This was the history that was explained to me by the brave feminists who were fighting the military dictatorship in 1980s Lahore: the All Pakistan Women's Association, founded by Begum Ranʿa Liaquat Ali Khan in 1948 in Karachi; the women of Dhaka who led the protests for inclusion of Bangla in 1948–52; the Democratic Women's Association in 1952; the United Front for Women's Rights in 1955; the Federation of University Women in 1956; the Women's Front and Shirkat Gah in 1975; the Pakistan Women Lawyers' Association in 1980; the Women's Action Forum in 1981; and more in the years that followed.

Women publicly mobilized for greater equity in their personal and public lives and across all classes in Lahore and Karachi. They organized against the dictatorship of Ayub Khan. Their pressure led to the passing of the Muslim Family Laws Ordinance of 1961, which protected women's rights in marriage, custody, inheritance, and divorce and which made polygamy difficult by requiring the consent of the first wife and approval of a community council. They would continue to organize against the second military dictator, Zia ul Haq, who was stripping minorities and women of their rights of under the guise of Islamization.

The second beginning is in Lahore in 1941. This was also told to me, but this time by an elder in my own family. It begins when a journalist, Abu'l ʿAla Maududi (1903–79), established Jamaʿat-i Islami as a grassroots proselytizing collective. Islam, in Maududi's estimation, was exclusively a religion whose central purpose was conversion. In his prolific writing career in the 1920s and 1930s, his reading of history, the Qur'an, and theological writings convinced him of the centrality of *dawah* (invitation) for the Muslim *ummah* (a global political community). Importantly, conversion was not meant just for non-Muslims but those who were already Muslim and needed to be "converted" to the true path of the religion. It is this radical path of refashioning modern Muslims that would lead Maududi to attain global fame, as one of the most important revivalists of Islam, alongside the Egyptian Sayyid Qutb (1906–1966) and the Iranian 'Ali Shar'iati (1933–1977).

After 1947, Maududi and the Jama'at mobilized to shape the contours of the new state as a proper Islamic one. The organization motivated its followers to publicly protest any recognition of Bangla language at the national level and any participation in public and religious life by members of the Ahmadiyya, and to call for the curtailing of women's rights and, later, for the propagation of jihad in Afghanistan. Over his political life, Maududi was arrested, put on death row, and nearly assassinated, and his organization was banned from public activities by various Pakistani governments. Yet he continued to gain in stature and public prominence from 1948 onward.[25] By the time of his death, Maududi had indeed shaped Pakistan according to his particular ideas.

Pakistan, though created *for* Muslims, was not an *Islamic* state, according to Maududi. The laws, the office holders, the public spaces, the rights and responsibilities of the citizen—in other words, *everything*—needed to be constructed according to his particular understanding of Islam. He was key in reigniting the Khatm-e Nabuwwat (Finality of Prophethood) movement in 1948 and mobilizing against the state's perceived reluctance to enact a theologically orthodox form of government. The Muslim Family Laws Ordinance of 1961 was a clarion call for Maududi to redouble his fight against communists, secularists, and feminists. The struggle was against the state in Pakistan but also, just as significantly, against the people of Pakistan.

A belligerent nationalism came to his rescue. The 1965 war with India reaffirmed to the public that there was a stark conflict between Islam and Hinduism. Maududi's Jama'at would spin the creation of Bangladesh as a clearing away of "bad" Muslims. The ascendance of another military dictator, General Zia ul Haq, in 1977 opened for the Jama'at real possibilities for converting Pakistan into an Islamic state. Zia came to power through a coup and almost immediately imposed martial law on the country in July 1977. The deposed prime minister, Zulfiqar Ali Bhutto, was arrested on murder charges and taken to Lahore in September 1977. Whereas Zia's focus was the persecution of the supporters of Bhutto's Pakistan People's Party (PPP), the Jama'at's focus was, as it had always been, Islam and the women of Pakistan.

Zia announced, in February 1979, his "Enforcement of Hudood Ordinances," which prescribed public stoning, flogging, and amputation for crimes such as drinking and selling alcohol, theft (of goods, cattle, or property), adultery, any sexual relations outside of marriage, and rape. He had Zulfiqar Ali Bhutto hanged on April 4, 1979. He instituted the public flogging of PPP supporters in Lahore and drove them into exile. He also began to publicly punish women. The Federal Shariat Court was created in 1980, and in 1981 he announced the formation of a Majis-e-Shura (Advisory Council), which was modeled on the Jama'at. It demoted the value of a woman's testimony (in some cases) to half that of a man. A charge of rape required four male witnesses in good standing who could testify to the act of penetration. A woman accuser, failing to prove her rape allegation, could be prosecuted as an adulteress or slanderer. In July 1983, a legally blind eighteen-year-old girl, Safia Bibi, was sentenced to fifteen lashes in public after her landlord and his son were acquitted of the charges of raping her. She was pregnant at the time of her sentencing.

Zia gave a new directive, expressed as "Chadar aur Char diwari" (Covered and within Four Walls), as the new orientation for the Pakistani woman. She was to appear in public only with her head covered or in a hijab, and her life was restricted to inside the house. Public flogging stations were set up at major intersections in the city. Maududi's proxies, men like Israr Ahmed (1932–

2010), preached misogyny on national television. All female anchors were ordered to wear head coverings. Zia issued a mandate for the segregation of the country's higher education system, and new women-only universities were founded. The Soviet invasion of Afghanistan in 1979 opened Pakistan as a staging site for a U.S.-armed Afghan guerrilla force called the "Taliban" (Students), which would be trained and deployed from Pakistan. These Taliban attended schools in Pakistan taught largely by the Jama'at. The theological formulation for a sanctioned jihad against the USSR was based largely on Maududi's works. After so long in the wilderness, it was all coming together for the Jama'at.

In 1981, a series of changes to testimony and evidence laws were announced under the "Law of Evidence Act." The Women Lawyers' Association and Women's Action Forum tried to submit a petition to the Lahore High Court on February 12, 1983. Some two hundred women and supporters proceeded on foot toward the court building on Mall Road. They were met by a police contingent that first hemmed them in and then began to attack them with batons and tear gas.

The poet Habib Jalib, who had become a particularly vocal critic of autocracy since penning his revolutionary verses against Ayub Khan in 1962, was also caught up in the violence ("that light which burns only in palaces / that caters to the happiness of a few alone / that which was raised in shadows of compromise / that constitution, that morning without light / I do not recognize, I do not know").[26]

Photographs of women being beaten by policemen on a main boulevard of Lahore, their faces covered in blood, announced to the country that these draconian laws could and must be challenged. That these were "elite" or recognizable women with prominent fathers and husbands was a major factor. That they were lawyers, doctors, teachers, and other professionals was also important. These women were collectively standing up against the police state.

As the "Movement for the Restoration of Democracy" spread, Zia ul Haq was forced to lift martial law in 1985. Zia had already banned all student unions (they remain banned to this day). He was fully aware of the potential threat of politically aware women to his dictatorship, especially women from the middle and upper-middle classes. The Jamaʿat agreed. The political positions of both Zia and Jamaʿat would be defined largely by misogyny. By the late 1990s, most of these politically aware women would be ideologically converted to the Jamaʿat's vision of Islam by new preachers, such as Farhat Hashmi, who preached a domestic life for all women.

The main gate of the high school I attended opened onto the road that led directly to Lahore Airport. A number of times, we were ushered out of our classes, handed paper flags, and organized into queues at the side of the road, in anticipation of the moment when the presidential jeeps and limousines would rush by. I had a memory of seeing Zia ul Haq drive by in a car, but I am now certain that it's a false memory. There is a real memory, however, of when Benazir Bhutto was allowed to return to Pakistan. She landed in Lahore and passed by the front of our school's gate with her caravan of supporters. The daughter of the late Prime Minister Zulfiqar Ali Bhutto, she had been imprisoned in solitary confinement and then exiled. In April 1986, she returned to Pakistan. It was a Thursday, and by the time we got out of school, she had already gone past our intersection. It reportedly took her ten hours to reach Minar-e Pakistan, where she addressed a crowd of hundreds of thousands. For me, that moment of seeing her was electrifying.

In my final year of high school, I had been going to Shirkat Gah to listen in on lectures on women's rights, entrepreneurship, crafts. There was a small library and I read a few of their publications. I never told anyone there about my notebook, but at one gathering I finally learned why so many women were killed by kerosene. A standard part of a woman's dowry was a small portable *chola* (burner), which usually took a 16-ounce bottle of kerosene to ignite and remain lit. The newlywed whose dowry was examined the morning after she arrived in her wedded home was acutely at risk. Her father may have promised things in the dowry that were not there. Or her in-laws might be dissatisfied with the goods and gold her family had raised. Whatever the affront, the newlywed, clad in long, flowing bridal wear, was tasked to make breakfast that first morning or to take over all of the cooking for her husband. All that infinitely flammable fabric just needed one spark.

6

PLACE: WALKING LAHORE

This book began in another book. It was early in 2009, and I was in Lahore browsing a long row of books displayed on the pavement of a busy thoroughfare. The swarms of passing bicycles, rickshaws, and cars made lingering difficult but not impossible. I moved slowly, my eyes scanning the titles. All the books were secondhand and were often wrapped in brown paper, especially if they had racy covers.

From among the books by Danielle Steel and Harold Robbins, I picked up an oversize volume rebound in a dark black cloth. *Tahqiqat-e Chishti* (Chishti's Researches) by a Maulvi Nur Ahmad Chishti Lahori. It was a reprint (or rather, a "photostat" copy) of a lithograph, published by the oldest printing house in Lahore, Koh-i Noor. I opened the text at random to find a description of a walk from Lahore Gate to the Shalimar, which the author took on the occasion of the annual Mela Chiraghan. He describes a crowd of hundreds of thousands walking, celebrating, and enjoying this three-day-and-night-long public celebration. The language was ornate Urdu, with Persian and Panjabi verses and phrases mixed in.

I turned to the front of the text and found the author's bio. He was an employee of the British state in Lahore, and it seemed that the work was commissioned and written in the 1860s. The subject of Chishti's "researches" was Lahore itself. This was an exciting find. Later, I found several properly published reprints of the text and even a two-volume critical edition published in 1964 by the Punjabi Adabi Academy. I discovered the popularity of the text among scholars of Lahore, aficionados of urban history, and people who study Sufis and sacred sites and more.

I purchased the book on the side of the road, and since I was standing by Delhi Gate of the Walled City (I assumed this was the Gate of Lahore that Chishti had described), I decided to walk to the shrine of Madho Lal Hussain. It took about two hours because I got lost a couple of times and lingered to talk to some people whom I had asked for directions. The destination was more or less a straight line due east from the gate, but the road wandered slightly north, past the messy traffic in Misri Shah, the overflowing shops on Ghoray Shah road, the housing colony of UET (University of Engineering and Technology), the solemn tomb of Mir Naimat Khan (one of Shah Jahan's commanders, and a monument I had never seen before), a locked cemetery (that no one could tell me anything about), and finally to the shrine of Madho Lal Hussain.

For much of the way, I walked on the street itself, keeping an eye on traffic (there was no sidewalk). When, following directions, I ventured into dense, residential areas, I got "looks," and hurried through those narrow lanes with my eyes down. It was breathtaking when the narrow street suddenly opened up to reveal a magnificent lime-washed structure with ancient trees and a small group of worshippers chatting over chai in the courtyard. I sat with them to learn about the history of the Sufi buried there and what happened there nowadays. We talked about the annual Mela Chiraghan, which was now rarely ever celebrated outside the walls of the shrine. I found the walk, but also the connection of the walk to a nineteenth-century text, exhilarating.

Reading *Tahqiqat* led me to many more walks. It also became a guide to other texts—mostly about monuments and shrines in Lahore—from the nineteenth and early twentieth century. I became deeply enmeshed in this corpus of writing Lahore. The germ of an idea began to take shape. How would I "update" *Tahqiqat* by revisiting those same neighborhoods, monuments, and sites and thinking about how they had changed over the 150-plus years? However, the more I read the text, the more I realized that Chishti was not simply talking about the city as a collection of monuments or gardens. He was invested in the social and sacral relationships that formed the network of his Lahore. His book was a sacral geography of the city that emphasized the meaning his contemporaries had embedded into their surroundings. The only way to update *Tahqiqat* was to begin thinking through the cultural and social relationships that form contemporary Lahore. I decided to begin by walking specific neighborhoods and trying to glimpse the idea of the city from those vantage points.

I had read Robert Walser, Walter Benjamin, Georg Simmel, Georges Perec, Marcel Proust, Virginia Woolf, and Jean-François Augoyard. I loved the medievalist walkers-in-the-ruins, like Arnaldo Momigliano and Michel de Certeau. I was also aware that the twentieth century's walker-theorists had never ventured into the corners bearing colonialism's shame. Walking, valorized as a way to think about the European or American city, also hid its relationship with colonialism. Sailors were the imagined or celebrated "forefathers" of "discovery" and "exploration"—the Christopher Columbuses and the Vasco da Gamas and the James Cooks. But really, when it comes down to it, colonialism's history is formed not by the "discovery" of any landmass alone; rather, and more consequentially, it is formed by the walkers inland and across: Cabeza de Vaca, Gaspar da Cruz, Thomas Coryat, Henry Blount, William Moorcroft, Richard F. Burton, T. E. Lawrence, and Wilfred Thesiger, among others.

These men, as Coryat described himself, were the "walker forwards on-foot."[1] They were walking in order to describe, to explore for state or commerce, the first steps of colonialism. They carried colonial power—its capitalist engine, its all-seeing eye—in their feet, and they narrated the "East" for the sedentary scholars of London and mapped it for the military men in the

colony. Their texts circled the globe such that by the early twentieth century their "ethnographic" gaze could uproot families and
products from Asia and Africa and bring them to the Exhibition
Halls of Paris, Chicago, St. Louis, or New York, where white families could walk and "see" what they had read about.

Thomas Coryat (ca. 1577–1617) died in Surat from dysentery.
His book, published posthumously, describes his walk from London to Ajmer, via Lahore, and farther to Surat. Coryat wanted a
letter of introduction to Tamerlane from the Mughal king Jahangir. A courtier and a wag, Coryat thought it would be his
ticket to riches and fame in London. He learned four languages
(Italian, Turkish, Persian, and what Europeans at that time erro-
neously called "Arabian") and spent more than three years walking
from Jerusalem to Aleppo, then across Central Asia to the "goodly
city of Lahore in India, one of the largest cities in the whole
universe."[2]

It took him ten days to travel from Lahore to Agra on a paved
and shaded road he says was unparalleled in the known world.
Lest his London colleagues look askance at such praise, he adds
that on the left side of the road is a mountain, and the inhabitants
of this mountain "observe a custom very strange, that all the
brothers of any family, have but one and the self-same wife: so
that one woman sometimes doth serve 6 or 7 men."[3] This, he
helpfully notes, is something Strabo had written about in the beginning of the first century. For Coryat, the immutable landscape
of the East was dotted by deviant women. Once he got to Ajmer,
he managed to speak with Jahangir, who tossed him some money
(the equivalent of ten pounds, Coryat says) as appreciation for
walking so far from London. Coryat notes that this entire exchange was done in secret from the English ambassador, Thomas
Roe, who had been waiting for an audience this whole time. Coryat was the walker as entrepreneur.

Two hundred years later, a veterinarian employed by the East
India Company, William Moorcroft (1767–1825), walked across

much of Panjab, Afghanistan, and Ladakh, and spent some time in Lahore curing Raja Ranjit Singh of some stomach ailment in 1820. He took the opportunity to sketch and describe how artisans made Kashmiri rugs and carpets. The sketches would provide the EIC the wherewithal to establish their own factories. But Moorcroft was officially looking for horses to breed locally for the British war campaigns in India. Of his sojourn in Lahore, he noted with derision the "whores": "In general they are well dressed, have a profusion of ornaments, have good complexions but I am sure none that would have been considered beautiful when compared with women of this class in Europe, although the manners of the former have in them nothing offensive to decency."[4] His main takeaway was that the British should colonize the decadent kingdom of Panjab with its rich waterways and its beautiful city.

Such is the colonial inheritance of walking in the colony. Where walkers in Paris, Berlin, London, and New York see the urban fabric as a palimpsest, its layers there to peel back, the colonial walkers break the city into portions that can be owned, or improved, or saved, or condemned. Where sexuality is alluring in the European metropolis, it is degenerate in the colonial city. This literature on walking only exposes to our contemporary gaze the violence inherent in the act of an outsider prying open the city.

My grandfather was a walker. A farmer, he walked across partitioned Punjab in the autumn of 1947. When settled by the new state in the planned farms of Montgomery District (later Sahiwal), he walked daily from his *gobar*-thatched (dried cow dung mixed with straw and mud) home to his little piece of farmland. When I was young, he visited Lahore but with great unease, as if the brick-and-cement city clawed at his ankles. I remember his walking stick and I remember him vanishing every morning, early, for a walk from which he would return just as my mother's irritation was reaching its breaking point. "He can't just sit still. Look at his feet now all covered in dirt, mud, and who knows what," she would tell me. I remember holding his walking stick and trying to imagine how amazing a walk would be with its weight in my hand.

The first time I imitated my grandfather's long walk must have been around 1986 or 1987. I walked out of my home in a straight line, across what was then farmland to the haphazard *mohalla* lanes with their open-sewer brackets, and onto the main road that came to a sudden intersection colloquially called a *joray pull* (a short road over an open-air water canal that became a sewer). The crossroads was where two different worlds met—one clean, organized, richer; the other dusty, jumbled, and poorer. To the left were army garrisons, the Cantonment, and the former airport, and straight ahead was a very busy bazaar. I kept walking in a straight line, letting the dirt accumulate on my shoes, jumping over piles of garbage, standing water, bricks, until my path eventually turned right and led me to Lahore Railway Station. It was not a very long walk—around two hours—but not an easy one. The route flowed with tongas, carts, rickshaws, bicycles, cows, scooters, motorcycles (the Honda CD70), donkey carts, goats, minibuses, buses, trucks, and the occasional car. I walked, or bicycled, or took a passenger van that way hundreds of times during my college years. The Canal Road became another "walk" that I routinely did to get to FC College. My walking was, however, an unusual habit.

Lahoris only walked in processions. There were two main categories of procession: the "march," which can be a political rally or a protest, and the shorter funeral/marriage procession. Other than that, the walker remained a figure defined by class, caste, and privilege. Those who walked, walked for work and for a living. Men, usually two or more together, could walk in parks, some major streets, and in the markets and malls. Women could do the same as long as they were suitably accompanied (that is, with a male walker). They could never walk alone or even in a pair with another woman.

Walking in Lahore over the many years of the research for this book meant being asked hundreds of times: Where are you going?

Sometimes I would have an answer, but often I did not. In one particular case, I was escorted at gunpoint out of a residential colony because I had unwittingly walked in the street behind an important politician's house. My bearded male appearance afforded me some protection and access, but the main problem was always apparent: no one walked alone.

Walking in Lahore is a transgressive act if you are not from the working class, the poor, or the unhoused. Outsiders to any neighborhood are frowned upon. They can be followed, queried, asked to leave, outright ignored, and occasionally worse. If your eyes were only cast right ahead of the next step to avoid a pile of shit, a puddle, a sewage drain, a piece of garbage, you would miss the three-tiered houses leaning forward—the first tier cement, the second exposed brick, the third wood. Ornate woodwork jutting out in the *cortiço* alleyways.

Thus, the development of "Heritage Walk," in the *androon shahr* (Walled City) is a curious new phenomenon. These are largely chartered buses and multi-seat rickshaws, dressed up (in truck art) to look like the tongas of yore, that carry (mainly) Lahori "tourists" around some segments of the Walled City. Outside the "restored" areas, walking in the Walled City remains a challenge. Nor is it any easier in the new colonies or the more upscale neighborhoods.

The colonies of DHA are vast concrete jungles with no crosswalks for pedestrians, and foot-high "sidewalks" that even an able-bodied person would need to jump to get on. Those who walk are domestic workers. There is absolutely no infrastructure for them. One summer, over the course of a three-mile walk and with the temperature more than 100 degrees Fahrenheit, I spotted exactly one bench and no shade or water. Lahore itself is surrounded by a new ring road, new underpasses, and four-lane highways. None is passable by foot. There are footbridges that are two stories high and require immense physical strength to navigate. Walkers have broken small corridors into the cement, and families risk their literal lives running across four lanes of high-speed traffic.

The nineteenth- and twentieth-century works from Lahore that I read paint a different picture. Lahore was once a city full of walkers, with walking a particularly favorite pastime for the literati and the intellectuals. A. Hameed in his memoir gives a beautiful rendering of walking in the Walled City in late 1949:

> The walls of the city were already gone but a garden surrounded the extent of the [old] city. Walking through the garden, you saw the tall houses, with the peaks of rooftop coverings and bamboo curtains on the outsides of the windows. I would leave Misri Shah from the One-Gap Bridge and walk from garden to garden until Lohari Gate, seeing the trees, people-watching, some sitting and reading *Hir*, some listening to *qissa* [epics]. From Lohari Gate, I would cut across the flower shops into Anarkali bazaar, on my way to my destination, the Pakistan Tea House. But sometimes, I would go to the Urdu Publishers or New Publishers and I would turn from Lohari Gate toward the Circular Garden behind Mori Gate [now demolished]. Watch the Wrestlers training in the *akhara* out to the School Library. This walk was very calming with so many wonderful and heart-warming scenes.[5]

By 2011, much of this had changed. The gardens have disappeared. Only five of the thirteen gates remain. The "Walled City" is now a restoration project with international sponsors. There is a "food street" with garish, candy-colored homes turned into restaurants. Official tours have been launched to show visitors the sights and sounds of the dense quarters. Many of the residents have moved out to DHA or beyond.

Lahore is not a walking city.

I.

Figure 7.1. West bank of Ravi River (2012)

I could barely see him. His body was coiled into a tight bundle. Sunrise was imminent. We had arrived an hour or more earlier, in near pitch darkness, and he sat facing the waters of Ravi River, rocking his body back and forth, intoning at a rapid rate the verses given to him by his teacher. Gul had agreed to my presence here just the night before, when we had met at the maulana's evening gatherings. The maulana had informed us that this young man wishes to possess a jinn (a supernatural spirit made of fire), and among all the maulana's followers, he works the hardest toward that goal.

The maulana had called him a "young man," but Gul was barely fifteen years old. He repaired tire punctures at a busy street corner near Gol Bagh, behind the Badshahi Mosque. The tires of passing motorbikes or bicycles were easily damaged by the abundant nails, glass shards, steel filings, and sharp pebbles generated by the construction along Ravi Road.

Gul worked every day, charging ten or twenty rupees to fix each puncture.

Every morning around 5:30, he set up shop by the side of the road. He had with him two metal canisters—one shallow and one deep, both filled with water—a reasonable amount of rubber, a large iron pair of scissors, one soldering kit, one manual press, and two manual air pumps. Every evening, at 7:30, he would pack his belongings up in plastic sheeting and two buckets. Usually, he ate only once a day, after evening prayers. Sometimes he slept in a nearby mosque, sometimes at the warehouse in the Walled City where his father was a guard, sometimes at his brother's hut in a *katchi abadi* some two miles away.

The day we spent together, he ate lunch only because I purchased it for the two of us. When he had a moment, I asked him what he would do with a jinn. "I will be stronger and able to fix more punctures. From the jinn you get lots of strength," he said, grinning. "You do not feel hungry or if you do, the jinn brings you the most expensive food you cannot imagine. The jinn keeps the police away." A traffic policeman, I learned, was a particular nemesis and routinely stopped by to harass or goad Gul. After a pause, Gul said, "The jinn would be mine and no one else could take me away."

To those who ask, the maulana, Gul's spiritual guide, routinely provided verses, ritual prayers, stones, inscribed magic squares, and special scents or oils, which aided in possessing or controlling the jinn. He did warn them, as I myself heard him do, that this is an arduous undertaking—this task of controlling a jinn—and it was highly unlikely any of them would succeed without years of incredible fortitude and perseverance. He also warned them away from "charlatan" guides who do black magic. He was guiding them on a more spiritually serene pathway.

The gathering at the maulana, late after the last prayer of the night, was stoic and committed. But even in this group, the slim-framed Gul stood out for his drive. He had persisted for many months. He had learned by heart a 101-verse incantation, in which every verse started with the Arabic letter *jeem* (also the first letter of the word jinn). He recited the incantation at nearly impossible speed, in one breath, whenever prompted. The circle showed its appreciation.

Gul is a refugee. He was born somewhere outside Jalalabad, in Afghanistan, and is only comfortable speaking in Dari. His father and several brothers, now scattered around the city, came to Lahore in the mid-2000s. The family was part of refugee migrations that followed the U.S. occupation of Kabul in 2002. He was seven or eight when he arrived, he tells me. He has had to work daily since then, sleeping in mosques, in seminaries, or on the street. He worked for a bread maker, and after that, for a car mechanic. It took him two years to raise enough money to buy the tools for his puncture stop. He took out a loan and he is still in debt. He told me that a jinn had possessed his eldest brother, who was now addicted to opioids and cough syrup (Tyno). The brother slept in a nearby public park.

After a year of Gul attending the evening circle, the maulana gave him the instructions for the ritual to capture a jinn. The ritual can only be performed on the banks of the river Ravi at the first light of dawn. One's feet are to be enveloped in the dark smelly mud of this still, corpulent river, and they must remain silent throughout.

Once Gul finished and packed up his work, we went to the nearby mosque for his evening prayers and meal. We walked toward the riverbed, with his bicycle in his hands. We darted across the six lanes of the Ring Road, hoisting his bike over our heads and climbing through the broken-through cement divider. On the other side, we walked along the river, past small parcels of farmland lying fallow. I was careful, or so I imagined, to avoid the shit and rotting dog corpses, but it was in vain. Once we reached the spot where Gul would sit, I smelled shit everywhere, but especially on me.

I had never seen the river from this vantage point, nor at this time of the night. I had never been so close to the still water. I was one of the millions who simply drove across the Ravi on our way in or out of Lahore. There was little to see in any event. The river itself was partitioned, the control of it given to India in 1960 under the Indus Basin Treaty. Ravi was an inert presence, barely moving in any direction. It was mostly a place for buffalo and shallow boats. At some point in the past, fish were caught here and served in Lahore. Many fried fish joints still called themselves Ravi, but this is now merely a historical or aspirational reference. The river is mostly a mixture of toxins, industrial sludge, and human waste pumped into it by three large viaducts. We walked for slightly more than an hour.

Lahore had received many waves of war refugees—the first in 1947, the next one in 1971—but the first major influx of refugees from Afghanistan entered Lahore in the early 1980s after the Soviet invasion. I grew up with many refugee children my age, who, rather than being in school with me, worked as menial laborers or as unskilled apprentices. Still, I had never before spent extended time with someone displaced and living in Lahore. I had a comfortable home and was kept sequestered from the city. I had also never spent time chasing jinn.

Sitting on the banks of the Ravi, Lahore felt surreal. In the dim light, I could see Prince Kamran's *baradari* (pavilion) to the north, on the other side. What used to be the western bank of the Ravi, across from Lahore, is now a small island. Zahiruddin Babur and his army camped there on their way to destroying Lahore. Around 1530, at that same site, Babur's son Kamran built this pavilion with a recreational garden. On my last visit, I found it partially wrecked, with walls covered in graffiti (mostly people's first names and whomever they loved). The imagined once-beautiful hallways, supported by twelve pillars, were occupied by passed-out or drugged Lahoris. In that night, it looked eerie and a relic of a time much older than the early sixteenth century—as if it was occupied by actual jinn, above time and place.

Gul had been silently reciting his incantations when he suddenly stopped rocking. The sun had almost made visible the waste surrounding us. Gul sat straight-backed, quiet, eyes nearly shut. Then they spoke. They told me that they were a jinn who had taken possession of Gul and that they felt very disrespected by our meager attempts at exerting power over them. Unprepared for any dialogue with a being of fire, I demurred and said that we meant no disrespect and perhaps we can make an offering to help alleviate this situation. A long silence ensued. I asked if there was something they could share about themselves. *I am as old as Lahore.* We were lucky that they were a Muslim jinn and, hence, willing to forgive this transgression.

Another long silence. I kept my eyes on Gul, hoping that this wouldn't end in a medical emergency, and that no one would find us here sitting in the muck. When Gul finally came to, he had no clear recollection of what had happened, and seemed very disappointed that the ritual had been unsuccessful. We walked back in silence. Back at the Ring Road, there was a canteen and a small market. I gave him enough money to buy food and some chicken meat as an offering. We parted ways. I had not asked him if he would try the ritual again.

On my walk back from the Ravi, my mind was occupied by time. What did time mean for this young man, raised on the streets of Lahore, victim to its cruelties, prejudices, abuses, and neglect? As a war refugee, he had no legal or civic rights in the city. He had no documentation. He lived and worked in the shadow of the Badshahi Mosque and the Walled City. Many of the motorcycle tires he mended came from the oldest continuously habituated neighborhoods of Lahore. He was surrounded by material vestiges of the *longue durée*. Yet he was also removed from that history by birth, language, ethnicity, and class. The jinn was as old as Lahore, but Gul's Lahore was only eight years old.

Lahore is a city of variable timescapes. The location of the medieval city on the banks of the Ravi is one indication of temporal disharmony. The medieval settlement, sometimes called "Purana Shehr" (old city), sometimes "Androon Shehr" (inner city), most often the "Walled City," forces a temporal disharmony with the surrounding cement and concrete. The oldest buildings, oldest doors, oldest graves, and oldest trees exist in the middle of shops, warehouses, and parking blocks. Each historical site is embedded in a geography of contemporary Lahore without calling attention to itself. There are rarely any informative signs for them. They are rarely landmarks on Heritage Walks, which are confined to a very small part of the city. They are rarely afforded any archaeological protections from civil or state agencies. Yet their presence resets time for those who recognize them.

For Gul, Lahore is new and without a living past. He was displaced by war, but he has also seen war in this city of refuge. Some of the oldest sites of Lahore were hit by suicide bombers. I had met Gul just a short few months after one such bombing at the thousand-year-old Data Darbar—one of the oldest, and holiest, sites in the city. The fabric of Lahore was riven with terror and Gul cast in the midst of it. The evening circle with the maulana was a refuge, an opportunity to lose oneself in scripts, chants, and memories of someone else. I understood Gul's quest for a jinn as a means of seeking from Lahore a solace from war, hunger, and hate—a sanctuary that would become his home.

II.

The young woman was hired by an NGO to do a household survey of residents about women's education. She had recently finished a BA from National University of Sciences & Technology Lahore and was planning on taking the exam to become a chartered accountant. She carried a clipboard, two pencils, and a stack of cheaply printed questionnaires with seven questions arranged in three columns. She agreed to let me shadow her and her team. Three of them would arrive in the neighborhood, Garhi Shahu, by nine in the morning, and divide up the streets for the morning's work. The routine was to knock on the door, ask the residents if they would consent to a short interview, and then give them a ballpoint pen as a small token of appreciation in return for answers to the seven questions.

It was risky work. Across Pakistan, polio vaccination campaigns faced deadly violence, especially for women. It was also grueling work, walking ten or more miles a day in oppressive heat. Mostly the conversations among the team were limited to quips about the houses and their residents. Only a few days later did the woman who led the team reveal, rather hesitatingly, that she also had another side business. She sometimes sold the women she met via the survey some commodities—lipsticks, perfumes, bangles. I reassured her that I had no problem with her side business and would not inform her NGO. We continued our walk. "Since you are writing a book, I also sell books," she said.

Figure 7.2. Schoolboy looking at books (2022)

There were two sets of paperbacks, palm-sized and wrapped tightly in newspaper and a thick rubber band. *Sham'a Beauty Parlor*, *Maa Bachahy ki bemariyan* (Mother and Child Illnesses), *Tum Mille SMS* (Finding You SMS [text messages]), *Israr-e Palmistry* (Secrets of Palmistry), *Kokha Pandit: Lazzatul Nissa*

(Urdu translation of *Kamasutra*), and *Pur Taseer 'Amaliyat* (Effective Actions). The last one featured the image of a pregnant woman in a corner of the cover. The booklet contained spells, chants, and lists of abortifacient plants and herbs. "There are many women who really want help with either getting pregnant or getting rid of their pregnancies," she said.

She opened her backpack to remove another plastic-wrapped bundle. *Mukammal, Asli Kala Jadoo* (Complete, Authentic Black Magic), *Bangal ka Kala Jadoo* (Black Magic of Bengal). "These are very popular," she said. I offered to purchase a couple of copies. Some sample advice: "Immediate Love: On a Saturday, at ten in the morning when the Sun enters Cancer, write this on a silver sheet with an iron pen and immediately throw in a river. If no river, a well. The beloved will immediately be overcome with love and appear before you. This is a tried and trusted."[6] We began to walk again. I asked if the women who purchased these pamphlets also sought professional help. There are usually numbers listed on these pamphlets.

I called one of those numbers—a WhatsApp number. Instead of a ringtone, he had changed his cell to play the call to prayer, which boomed disconcertingly loud on my speakerphone. The man who answered, Dogar, after a bit of hemming and hawing, agreed to meet. His shop was in Urdu Bazaar but he lived near Garhi Shahu. We made an appointment. Over the next few days, he sent me tens of messages, all small JPEG advertisements for his books. Some were illustrated, some claimed Egyptian knowledge, some Chinese knowledge, but the vast majority touted Brahminical and/or Bengali hidden sexual knowledge.

Lakshmi and Hanuman, who among the deities were the most revered for their control over the realms of money, luck, and the underworld, featured prominently in the advertisements. Some of the 'amaliyat (actions or mantras) books used Islamic idioms, replacing Lakshmi and Hanuman with the Prophet Suleiman or words from the Qur'an. Sometimes, in the same text, both Brahminical and Islamic sources of control were provided with their recitation protocol. It was curious that in a city so determined to erase anything—scripts, languages, structures, ideas—that was Hindu or Bengali, here were hundreds of text messages presented without comment.

We met in front of Shimla Pahari (Simla Hill), where the Lahore Press Club is situated. For a while, we talked about me. Dogar inquired, with some genuine concern, about my heart and my loins and gave me recommendations of books as well as names of herbs and tonics (he helpfully suggested he procure them for me). After a while, I turned the conversation to his other customers and also to the reasons why these books of black magic were so popular. We walked into the maze of streets so narrow that motorcycles could barely pass through, let alone carts.

"Ours is a very old business," Dogar said. "Do you remember the Bangali 'Amil who used to have his name stenciled all over the city?" Dogar and I were roughly the same age, and I certainly did remember. "See, that Bangali 'Amil was the son of a famous Lahori 'Amil, who came from a long line of ascetics who controlled jinn and 'afrit [roughly, demonic beings]."

"They were from Bengal?" I asked.

"Yes," he replied, "So this is a durable line of 'Amils with genuine power. Our business is *genuine*." He emphasized the word. "We only reproduce these authentic books, and I ask a college student to make drawings. They are major sellers. We also do exam cheat-sheets, curriculum summaries, guidebooks, and medical textbooks."

We found ourselves in front of Bibi Pak Daman. I had not intended to be here, but the tight, busy lanes had inexorably moved us toward the shrine. The lane that led us there was full of open shops with many of the iconic ingredients for the annual *ta'zia* procession. Bibi Pak Daman, one of the oldest spaces of veneration in the city, is the shrine to six women who reportedly came to Lahore in the mid-seventh century after the Battle of Karbala, where the Prophet's grandson was killed by the Umayyad caliph. The women, one or all of whom are understood to be related to the

Prophet, lived and prayed in the wilderness after coming to Lahore, and were fearful of their modesty being revealed to non-Muslim eyes. They prayed to God to protect their honor and were swallowed up by the ground, leaving only some of their modesty fabric above the earth. Shrines were built around their last resting place. The site, one of the oldest in Lahore, was a place for veneration for both Muslims and Hindus. The women's legend contains an echo of the *Ramayana*, which ends with the earth swallowing up Sita.

The vast majority of those who come to the shrine to pray and pay their respects are women. They come to seek relief from pain or to have a wish fulfilled, and tend to be from the working classes. Upon approaching the doorway, they often touch or kiss the doorframe. Toward a corner is a place to light the ritual *diya* (small wick lamp)—first in mustard oil and, after the wish is fulfilled, in unadulterated ghee. The mesh wire enclosing the grave sites are laden with small locks of hair, each representing another wish (some would have tied a length of red string or fabric). The ash from the incense sticks and the oil residue from the lamps is then either tasted or smeared on one's forehead.

I mentioned to Dogar the many *satiyan* (sites of veneration of women being swallowed by the earth) I had seen in Sind. Many women from Karachi and Hyderabad visit these sites for blessings and wish fulfillment. Dogar reminded me that there were only a few places left in Lahore where women can have direct access to divine intervention. As part of a new practice, many shrines now keep women segregated from the sacral centers. Bibi Pak Daman was still a place in Lahore where women could come and go easily and with confidence.

"With our books, our customers can get such intercession at home," said Dogar. He was a consummate salesperson. "They are another way for the ladies to have their wishes for a happy home or male child or to seek protection from a mother-in-law. There are hidden powers all around us. Sometimes you only need to do the proper meditation and labor. They will find their heart's desires."

I promised to visit his shop and purchase some of his books, and we parted ways. I continued to walk around the shrine complex and the adjacent graveyard. A short lane carried me to an angular street that led to the Mayo Road. At the juncture is a curiously open space, with some tree cover and the remnants of a structure visible on the ground. I linger there to ask someone if it used to be a temple. It was.

When I began to walk in Lahore, I also began to document the prevalence of pulp books aimed at women and at men that were sold on the street and from the back of carts, as well as in drugstores and bookstores. The majority of wall advertisements in the city were for a "German Clinic" that promised cures for "manly disease" (erectile dysfunction). But there were also advertisements for purveyors of occult and black magic on city walls and in WhatsApp groups. It would continue to surprise me the degree to which these ads were grounded in the vocabulary and syntax of Hinduism or "Bengal."

In Lahore, the words "Hindu" or "Bengali" were generally recognized as curse words and derogatory terms. The long-standing prejudices that imagined Bengal as a site of deviance, wanton sexuality, and polytheism played an important role in making the hidden visible. But in these advertisements, the slur became the marker of deviant authenticity for the paying customers. In the imagination of the customers, the profane (Black magic, "Bengal") was imagined as untamed, beyond the purview of sanctioned spaces, which police and surveil women, keep them out of the shrine and out of sacred spaces, or only allow them in at certain times. There is thus a real advantage to imagining a more direct pathway via secretive acts, phrases, and tokens.

The pulp books offer another script for the city. They exist often at the feet of the buyer, resting on a sheet of plastic or propped up against a wall. The vast majority of passersby pay no heed. But some do. And some bend to pick up a book and buy it. How to make someone fall in love? How to make a husband stop beating you? How to control a household? How to do anything when you have so little control? The city offers up a pathway. It is, without any question, a false hope. If the men and women follow through and contact the so-called expert, they risk being taken in by hucksters, charlatans, and convicts, and robbed directly or indirectly. Almost everyone knows this. The pulp books offer a slightly less dangerous avenue. You are, after all, in charge of executing whatever formula is listed for your wish fulfillment.

III.

My earliest walks in Lahore were on the one-lane road that led from Joray Pull to Sadr Bazaar. First came Murghi Khana (Chicken Shack, presumably named after the Veterinary Research Institute set up there after 1947), after which came a long stretch of open fields where we played cricket and where the annual *mela* was set up. Next came the Officers Colony and finally the round-about of Sadr. Much of this patch of Lahore was agricultural land, except for the *qabaristan* (cemetery) at one end by the rail-way tracks. The tonga that operated along that stretch stopped after the evening prayers, which would thus necessitate a long de-tour through open fields and past packs of dogs.

Many years later, I was interviewing an old man who used to have a barber chair under a bare *taali* tree (Indian rosewood) at the far end of this road. He told me stories of possessions and of *chalawa* (poltergeists) and *churail* (female demons) who ensnared young men walking that stretch of the Cantonment. The land-scape around us had become alien to the memories he described—all of the agricultural land now gated colonies, requisitioned and granted to retired middle-rank army, air force, and navy officers.

"Why did there used to be so many *hawai* [invisible or super-natural] beings?" I asked him. He pointed to a closed metal gate in an inordinately high brick wall across the road. "The Christian cemetery," he said. The remark, though driven by his prejudice

Figure 7.3. A Christian shrine (2014)

toward Christians, still opened my eyes. Even though I had lived nearby and played across this narrow street, I did not know that there was a Christian cemetery there.

On one occasion, I saw the metal gate unlocked, so I entered the cemetery. A large enclosure full of ancient trees and graves, it was a serene space. I introduced myself to the *gorkan* (gravedig-ger). Masih had grown up in a small Christian neighborhood far-ther east. He was in his mid-sixties with a thin mustache and a kind demeanor. "As long as we can remember, we have lived in Lahore. We used to be near Krishan Nagar [now Islampura], but were driven out after Partition. I am responsible for the widow of an older brother, and I have three daughters. They work as maids in DHA. My brother used to work in LDA as a street sweeper."

"My grandfather was a *gorkan*," he continued, "and I have al-ways been here, taking care of our ancestors in this graveyard. It is the largest cemetery. We serve Khyber Colony, Ghausia Col-ony, Sarkari Lines Kachhi Abadi, Karachi Mohalla, and Ghazi Colony. We even have some *gora* [English] sahibs here. There are several other graveyards for Christians in Lahore—a small cluster of colonial-era graves near the shrine of Miyan Mir, another near Ravi. Many of the employees at large Muslim cemeteries, usu-ally gravediggers, are also Christian, but we cannot be buried there." He carefully walked with me, pointing out specific graves and their inhabitants. "We have an 'urs here on 28th of December and prayers are made for the many buried."

Just a year before this conversation, on March 9, 2013, some two to three thousand Lahoris stormed Yohanabad (Joseph Colony)—a small strip of a Christian neighborhood—and burned over 150 homes and two churches. The mob destroyed nearly the entire colony. The crowd had been "angered" by reports of blas-phemy. Such violence against individual Christians was routine in Pakistan. But this violent mob had acted as though they were trying to purge them from the city. Even the politicians, usually ready with a pious platitude when another victim of vigilante vio-lence becomes news, were shocked at this rampage.

Given such acute risk, I was grateful to Masih for trusting me. I politely inquired about his life as a working-class, lower-caste Christian in Lahore. What about his daughters? Does he feel safe in his own Lahore? Masih was contemplative. "They," he gestured vaguely, "think we are a threat. Who are we to threaten anyone?

We are poor, *miskin* [helpless]. My eldest daughter, she takes a rickshaw to work, but sometimes it gets late, so she has to walk out of the DHA colony to catch a bus. Sometimes that bus does not run or does not pick her up. She walks or she sits somewhere safe and I go on a bicycle to get her. She cannot just walk alone."

The eldest daughter, Sakina, agreed to meet me if I came to the DHA colony when she was heading home. Her employer's house was in the new frontier of the DHA development, which crept toward the eastern border region of Lahore. Much of this new-fangled colony was empty. All it contained was a network of roads, the ubiquitous green electricity hub box, and four-story cement buildings standing by themselves like weed flowers amid concrete. I had the address and arrived earlier than our appointed time so I could take a walk there.

The DHA houses are huge, with a clashingly unique visual language. Think baroque, or rococo, or any confusion of loud shapes, distinct at the level of each individual home. Their florid, shiny fronts and their high metal gates are perfectly hidden if seen from a car. But on foot, you can see the back and the sides of these freestanding homes. A feature that stands out is the narrow, cork-screw metal staircases, winding from the ground up to the second floor. This is the "servants' entrance," a means for the domestic labor to enter and exit the house. Usually there is a "dirty kitchen," which is only for the domestic labor. There are also small, bare barracks-style living quarters for the guards or staff that stay on the premises. As you walk through the home, the staircases illustrate how caste separation was built into the architecture.

After we met, Sakina and I walked for nearly two hours before we were able to get a rickshaw that took us to her home. She had been working as a domestic worker since she was eleven. During our walk, she told many stories of kind employers, but the ones I remember were her stories of violence, of beatings, of not being paid what she was due, of being accused of stealing. She spoke about the risk of losing her job were her employers to discover her religion or the restrictions placed on her in terms of rooms that are

off limits. Upper-caste Muslims understood her body to be un-
clean and impure, and while it was perfectly acceptable for domestic workers to clean the shiny marble verandas or the
bathrooms of these palatial homes, they were not permitted to
come inside. She never hid her religion, but she also never announced it.

She was married and had two children of her own. Her husband, an addict, had disappeared a while back. Then, at one point
after she had returned home from work, she told her family *mujh
par bhi ziadati hui* (I was also transgressed against).[7] With her
family around, now, as she narrated the story, I could feel the
shame of her family but also her bravery and defiance. Sakina
mentioned that she loves cooking and, as she grows older, would
much rather work in the kitchen. She said so wistfully, perhaps in
recognition of the limits imposed upon her.

In Lahore, sanitation workers and cleaners are usually Christian
and non-Muslim.[8] These laborers live in temporary and unse-
cured housing without the protection that comes with owning
property or land, without utilities or access to social and welfare
facilities, and certainly without any public recognition of their
existence. Many of the colonies where they live are densely packed
and removed from public view by imposing city infrastructure
such as overpasses, concrete walls, and gates (this is also true for
the Muslim working class). By design, the sight lines of the city
exclude those who clean, cook, and provide services for the middle
and upper classes of the city. There are no age or gender identity
protections, and certainly no protections against religious dis-
crimination. The two or three spectacular colonial-era churches
aside, much of Christian Lahore is found only in small, un-
marked single rooms in narrow corridors that are impenetrable to
outsiders. The same is true of the only existing temple in the city.

I went to high school at the Cathedral School in Cantonment.
A new branch of the long-standing school on Mall Road, it was
opened in the early 1980s. During my years there, we did not even
have a fully completed school building. The principal, S.K. Dass,

opened every morning with a rousing speech on self-discipline, on being a good citizen, and on neatness and cleanliness. He ended with the hymn "We Shall Overcome," which we all sang together. Our playground was the St. Mary Magdalene Church. On Sundays, when some of us gathered for a cricket match, we cheered our teachers and staff who were dressed in their Sunday best for Mass.

After the many assassinations, riots, and acts of arson, Lahore's minority faith communities fear their own city and its inhabitants. They remain out of sight for their own safety. Lahore is not just a city divided by religion and class, but social and public spheres also have been, and remain, segregated. The rare presence of a solitary Christian or Hindu member in either the National or Provincial Assembly—or, even rarer, of a Christian or Hindu member of the national cricket team marks the absolute erasure of such citizens from the everyday life of the city and the country.

Lahore's *shamshan ghat* (cremation grounds) on the Ravi have disappeared. The graveyards are segregated. The poorest and the most dispossessed live at the mercy of exigencies of the state. Every public space teems with specifically Muslim (and specifically sectarian) declarations of piety. The most hidden parts of Lahore are where the non-Muslim Lahoris live. They are also the most powerless. All of the one hundred suspects arrested for the destruction and burning of Yohanabad in 2013 were acquitted and released in 2017.

IV.

At the east end of Mall Road is a complex that now hosts the Al-falah Theater (formerly Cinema Hall) and a small mosque. The Punjab Assembly sits across the street, while the famous Faletti's Hotel is around the corner and the WAPDA building looms in the foreground. A preacher begins delivering a sermon at the mosque after the last prayer of the day. He is young, tall, and broad-shouldered with a long beard. He is always dressed in all white with a tight white *topi* (skullcap). His oratory skills are impeccable. He speaks in a lilting cadence, slow and measured. That night his sermon is about the responsibilities of a just ruler. It is a particularly sophisticated discourse with citations from medieval and modern jurists and theologians. The well-heeled congregants nod in appreciation. After the sermon ends, a small group coalesces around the preacher, bowing and kissing his hand. He is gracious, attentive and speaks a word or two in the ear of each supplicant.

The mosque is now empty and only five people remain. I am sitting at a slight distance, with my aching back against a pillar. One by one, men approach him and he whispers to them. I see him put his hand on their head and sometimes on their chest. Around ten o'clock, he is finally free, and we walk out together from the mosque. "Did you recognize the last one?" he asks me. I did not. "That was the corps commander of Lahore," he says with a smile.

Wasif migrated to Lahore only a few years ago to open up a residential office for his Sufi order. At the time Lahore was reeling from bomb blasts, and there were security checks at seemingly every crossroads. By the time I met him, he was starting to be recognized as a charismatic figure in Lahore, though unattached to any existing religious or political party. I met him because I was interested in figuring out the landscape of sacral politics in Lahore and was shuttling between a number of new connections. He was introduced to me as a particularly magnetic new presence.

The sacral landscape of Lahore was shifting. More of the intelligentsia and the well-off of the city were moonlighting as spiritual and religious guides. A senior economics professor at Government College University held theological discussions at his home with a bevy of students and colleagues. Many of the younger students were devotees of the professor. Another dynamic young professor (a PhD student in Islamic studies in Berlin) was the CEO of a prominent degree-granting religious institute. The institute, which was segregated by gender, had a four-year curriculum offering diplomas that promised BA equivalency. The monthly fees were robust. The young professor was very popular among students. There was also a loose social circle of extremely wealthy women (most were wives of active duty or retired senior military officials) who hosted meetings that streamed the sermons of Farhat Hashmi (the founder of Al-Huda Institute, who was devoted to a literalist reading of the Qur'an), followed by a discussion. There was a study group on *Kashf al-Mahjub*, which met every other Thursday. Among all these new purveyors of faith, I found Wasif the most striking.

I accompanied him as much as I could or was allowed. He ran a publishing house, which issued a monthly magazine and published books. He wrote a book every other month on some theological or social issue. He also reissued existing books on history, religion, Sufism, science, and medicine, with his commentary attached as a preface. He was credited as an author on more than 250 titles. He also had a pharmacy with a *Yunani* (Greek) medical center, where herbs and roots were transformed into homeopathic pills to soothe a crying baby, or enlarge a penis, or cure diabetes, or beat cancer. He solicited letters from his readers, which were then converted into advice columns and published in a journal, alongside recipes for homemade medicine. His recorded sermons were streamed on YouTube, Facebook, Instagram, and Twitter. A group of young men acted as his social media team, his advance team, his security, and his screeners.

Like a latter-day Dale Carnegie, his sermons and presentations put a heavy emphasis on self-making, self-fashioning, and self-empowerment. He avoided anything that might provoke controversy. It was not that he was apolitical, but I certainly never heard him mention anything about the country's politics or its politicians. He focused on explaining the ways in which one could become a better person and a better Muslim. That better self would be aided by reading his self-help manuals and purchasing his medicines. He did not spew hatred of any one religion or sect, but propounded a more ecumenical, capitalist way of thinking. Work hard, pray harder.

His followers tended to be wealthy. They liked his newest model Toyota HiAce, his spectacularly white outfits, and his shiny silver watch. He appreciated their ostentatious homes, where he was welcomed, and where he loudly validated their birthright to this wealth. "God provided all this for you," he told them. "Take from God without hesitation because he is giving." I recognized his pitch from the churches and the prosperity gospel of the early twenty-first century United States, but I had never encountered it in Lahore.

The parade of military officers in his seminars and gatherings also made sense. Just as he made the rich feel better about their wealth, he made the military men feel better as well. He absolved them from all the guilt of taking so much in a land where so many had so few resources. It was all God's bounty, meant for those who worked hard. And who worked harder than the military men? The elderly that sat with him also wanted to feel better about their wealth. The young who came to him also wanted to get rich quickly. He helped them with his direct-action religiosity: "God's bounty"—he repeated these two words many hundreds of times—"will give you this material advantage." Everyone loved this for themselves.

Wasif once allowed me to sit in on his session with a group of high-ranking military men. One of them, a very highly ranked officer, had back pain and was there to seek relief. The rest had more esoteric problems. I was introduced as a professor teaching in the United States, which garnered no interest from any of them. Wasif gave the man in pain a recitation and also began to chant something while putting his hand on his back. A few minutes later, he pronounced the man cured. The man rose up and stretched forward and backward and then did a quick, sharp salute. "You are a miracle maker," he said, and bowed. Wasif put his hand on my chest. "Can you feel the heat of this power?" The rest of the military men appeared jealous.

Nur Ahmad Chishti's *Yadgar-e Chishti* (1858) entails a description, more than ten pages long, of the class of mullah (preachers) in Lahore. He describes them with a proverb: *charagh talay andhera* (there is darkness underneath the lamp). Those who may encourage others to do good are themselves not good people.[9] Chishti criticized the men who gained only a little knowledge by reading the Qur'an and then became mediators and conduits of information for everyday Lahoris. He mocked the mullahs and their solemn bearing. Mostly, he told his Lahori readers to stay away from them. Much of early twentieth-century poetry, especially that of Muhammad Iqbal, would continue to deride the everyday preacher.

Yet, after Partition, like all other things, this too changed. There was a surfeit of men in the public sphere with grand titles, usually self-taken, such as mufti, maulana, and *hazrat*. They were touted as highly learned theologians, jurists, and spiritual leaders.

They also became political leaders. Maulana Maududi was the epitome of this shift, as he moved from a journalist to a respected commentator on the Qur'an to a political actor fighting the state over the future direction of Pakistan. The Islamization of society necessitated new leaders who could act as the proper Muslim leaders. This did not preclude civilian or military leaders such as Zulfiqar Ali Bhutto or Zia ul Haq from shrouding themselves in pious garb. But the real power was with the preachers-turned-political rulers. I remember, in 1989, Maulana Tahir-ul Qadri at the head of a massive political rally in Lahore announcing his creation of a new political party, Pakistan Awami Tehreek, because the Prophet had come to him in a dream and asked him to do so.

Lately, Wasif's followers number more than 7 million on Facebook, and the "mullah capitalism" model dominates the city and the country. "Modern" religious schools led by Ivy League or Oxbridge PhDs in Islamic studies have been established all over the city. They cater to the upwardly mobile, lower-middle class. The segregated schools are often the only educational outlets for working-class women whose families would otherwise deny them an opportunity to leave the household. Meanwhile, a healthy roster of men and women with access to gnostic knowledge are available to the rich and the discerning. The theosophists of yore would feel right at home in the current social climate in Lahore, where conversations often turn to transmissions from the hidden beings living in the Himalayas.

A number of women preachers, most of them partially based in the UK or the United States or Canada, have their own brands of self-help religiosity. Instagram reels dominate this sacral space with sermons and sound bites forwarded via WhatsApp or shared on Facebook. There is now a higher value placed on being veiled in public or *umrah* and hajj trips, or conspicuous displays of Qur'anic verses and modern art in the foyers of homes. The upper-middle class and affluent believers in Lahore enjoy having direct access to these preachers. The value is in having Wasif visit their homes for gatherings, in visiting the economics professor's living room for his seminars, and in collectively sharing testimonies of miraculous spiritual and financial growth over a sermon from Farhat Hashmi. The sacral landscape of Lahore divides itself along class and sectarian lines but unites in its veneration of consumption.

V.

Malik is an old *surkha* (meaning "leftist," it translates literally to "red") in Lahore and reminds me very much of a teacher I had in college who used to run a public access program on "common" persons' complaints against the state. Malik is voluble and empathetic. He used to run a small publishing house that he had to shut down in the late 1980s after a string of police actions against him. He converted it into a smaller bookstore, but he still publishes a few textbooks and some manuals of calligraphy. He sits in his small shop in Urdu Bazaar and insists on only speaking Punjabi.

The first time we met, he quizzed me on my knowledge of the Punjabi poet Ustad Daman (1911–84). I confessed that I did not know much at all about him. "He was born just there," Malik gestured, "right behind Lahori Gate." With a chiding glance, he recited Daman: *Pakastan makan ik ban gya aye / vassan sadh uttay, randhay chor haitan* (Pakistan is a house such that / the holy live upstairs and the thieves below). Ustad Daman is a link to a Lahore that no longer exists, one that goes all the way to Data Sahib and ends at Waris Shah's *Hir.* This is the Lahore that defies authority, that celebrates love, that knows only the pleasure of a well-recited verse. Punjabi Lahore. Sikh Lahore. Hindu Lahore. *Sharabi* (drunk) Lahore.

Suitably chastened, I purchased Ustad Daman's *diwan* and tried my best to decipher his Punjabi. *Waghay nal Atari di nain*

*takkar / na Gita nal Qur'an di aye / Nain kufr islam da koi jag-
hra / saari gal iay naf'ay nuqsan di ay* (Wagah [Pakistan] has no
conflict with Atari [India] / Nor Gita has any with the
Qur'an / there is no enmity between belief and unbelief / all of
this is about profit and loss).[10] Daman's visceral critique of the
landed elite, the military, and rentier state was exhilarating to
read. In one poem, "Vicho Vich Khai Jao" (Keep Stealing from
Within), he lacerates the "traitors" of the nation who ask for the
departed colonial rulers to come back after they (these nationalist
leaders) had already broken up the region's nations and partitioned the land. "Keep crying and keep stealing, keep eating, and
keep complaining. The people are starving and you keep on stuff-
ing yourself with Qorma and Pulao. The uncle gives to the
nephew, who gives to the uncle in this patronage system. Go va-
cation in Muree and tell the population to protest on Kashmir
Road. Tell us that alcohol is banned and go stock your cellars
with it."[11] I had not even imagined such clearly articulated
resistance poetry was openly available during Zia's military
dictatorship.

I often took walks with Malik in and around the old city. He
knew everyone but was also reticent in introducing me to people.
I imagine this was because of my limited knowledge about the
things he cared about: Punjabi, the left, and resistance in Lahore.
I used the walks as opportunities to learn about the writers, poets,
and political workers who resisted the military regime. We read
poet and literary historian Tabassum Kashmiri's (b. 1940) long
poem *Nohay Takht Lahore day* (Dirges of Lahore City), published
in 1985:[12]

No longer in the veins of this city
is blood
[it] is full of poison
fire
there is no blood
glowing forge

red hell
a spreading
rivers of sand
descending
jungles and jungles
in the face of this city
there remain no dreams
no flower in dreams
all dreams have melted and scattered
all dreams burnt in the red forge
and become ash
and the ash scattered.

Malik taught me that the hanging of Zulfiqar Ali Bhutto in 1979 and the subsequent declaration of martial law challenged an entire generation to register their protest in word and deed. Lahore was a key site for resistance. Malik praised the work of poet Fahmida Riaz (1946–2018), who was prosecuted by Zia ul Haq and went into exile in India. As a response to Zia's campaign against women in the public sphere, she published *Chadar aur Char Divari* (Veil and Four Walls), which included this searing poem, "Kaali Chadar" (Black Sheet):

Respected Sir, what can I do with this black sheet? Why are you granting it to me with such magnanimity?
   I am not in mourning such that I wear this
   to show my sorrow and pain to the public
   . . .
   Respected Sir, there is a dead body lying in your esteemed home
   Who knows rotting for how long?
   It begs mercy from you
   Sir, please do this one thing
   Do not give me this sheet
   Put this black sheet on this naked dead body in your home.[13]

We spent some time with the rage of Sara Shagufta (1954–84) and her "Mein Nangi Changi" (Am Better Naked, 1983): "I will burn the rivers / burn shadows / burn my doll / I will burn in the fire with my doll / Fire better Naked."

Malik took me on walks in Garden Town, Shadman Colony, Green Town, Sherpao Colony—we walked the resistance in Lahore. He recited the Punjabi poet and author Fakhr Zaman, who began his "Mera Shahr Lahore" (My City Lahore, 1987) with the line, *meray shehr Lahor nun kis di nazar lagg gaye aye* (who has cursed Lahore, my city?). Zaman writes, "I cannot bear to look at my city anymore. In place of the smile on its face, there is a grim line of dried blood. The light from its eyes has drained drop by drop and instead is black glaucoma." After lamenting the city's eyes, Zaman laments its forehead, its hands, and its feet. The city of beauty is now bitter and broken and covered in blood. Lahore is a prisoner awaiting death. In 1978, four of Zaman's Punjabi books (two novels and two essay collections) were seized and banned by the military regime.

One afternoon, Malik asked me if I wanted to visit his home in Green Town. I had never been and I happily agreed. When we met behind Walton Grounds, I did not know that an eleven-mile walk lay ahead of us. The purpose of the Green Town walk was to learn more about Lahore's rapidly deteriorating water supply. Almost all of Lahore's wastewater flows into the Ravi—ten sewage drains and five industrial waste drains. The Ravi cannot sustain any aquatic life due to this pollution. Untreated wastewater seeps into the ground, contaminating the water table. Three of the open-air drains (Baba Sabu, Hadiara, and Gulshan-e Ravi) cut through much of Lahore's southwest section. Malik's idea in picking one of these "tributaries" was to follow it from a spot right behind the Packages Mall for about eleven miles until it joined the Hadiara drain. Along the way, we would pass by Green Town.

Almost the entire way, we walked along a one-way road, which had no sidewalk and little shade, as well as a mind-numbing stench. Green Town, halfway through our walk, was another planned housing scheme with very little greenery. As we walked, the stench became more and more unbearable. Who writes about this stench of Lahore? Those who live here cannot stop smelling it. Those who don't live here never come here. Those who come here speed through in their cars. The stench reminded Malik of the stench that the resistance poetry of the late 1970s and 1980s often invoked—that of the rotting body politic. Here is the stench of a decaying city. The city builds overpasses and ring roads to help those with cars fly over these places. Even the affluent suburbs of DHA use a sewage-filled moat to demarcate the haves from the have-nots.

Malik was fond of those who resisted the imposed order. "Remember Dulla Bhatti," he asked. Dulla rode against the great Mughal Akbar Badshah. They got him and hanged him here in Lahore. Near Landay Bazaar. He is buried in the Miyani Qabaristan. A real Panjabi hero, a people's hero. I mentioned that there is no record of any such figure in *Akbarnama*, the history of Akbar's time written by Abu'l Fazl. "Why would there be?" Malik retorted. "Why would they register the imperial army's defeat from a small-time Rajput?"

Dulla Bhatti (ca. 1547–89) was celebrated by Muslims and Hindus alike. In popular tellings, he stood up to the emperor and saved the honor of a Hindu girl. Shah Hussain himself came to see Dulla before his hanging by the Mughal army. Hussain prophesized the end of all who participated in the hanging—and it transpired exactly as he said it would. The rich called Dulla a dacoit and a thief, but he was a true figure of resistance. Malik was certain that Dulla represented the true spirit of the Panjab—someone who was independent and fearless and who loved his people.

Some of this memory of Dulla survives in Pindi Bhattian, roughly eighty miles northwest of Lahore. There he was better known as a popular folk hero who robbed the rich to give to the poor. A number of Punjabi films, and plays, depicted his life, which extolled his championing of the poor. They played to packed houses in Lahore. Malik had attended a number of meetings of the Dulla Academy in Lahore and made me promise that I would do the same. I never did, but I did visit Miyani cemetery to locate Dulla's grave. It is a recent construction, having been "discovered" in 1943.[14]

We never made it to the Ravi in that walk. The heat got to both of us. Later, I picked up the walk at the Hadiara drain and walked from there to the Ravi. That proved to be an even more difficult walk. There was only a tiny dirt pathway, and the drain itself was the size of a two-lane highway. Soon the way was blocked by a heavy industrial area, so I turned back. "This was a city of red roses / a city of fertile gardens / a city of tall trees / a city like gold and silver / a city like diamonds and pearls / a city of red rubies / a city of shiny indigo / a city of beautiful indigo / in the burning noon of this city / in the sharp taste of this city / in the fast heat of this city / the blue of the eye has melted / the indigo of the city has dissolved / the eyes of the city are now at a boil."[15] I recited Tabassum Kashmiri as a dirge.

VI.

Figure 7.4. A pathway toward Punjab farmland (2023)

I can remember particular trees from bicycle rides in Lahore as a teenager, but I do not remember when I began taking pictures of them. Dead or alive, barren or flowering, whole or shattered, trees seemed to be the only witnesses left in Lahore. The old homes, *havelis*, shrines, and monuments are almost uniformly denuded of tiles (when not "restored"), but the trees that stood near those structures were almost as old or older. I cherished them. I collected them as markers of stillness that captured something of the city itself. The oldest ones, which were two hundred or more years old, were most abundant in the colonial gardens, but you could find remarkably old mango, banyan, *chinar, kikar, peepal, shisham* trees scattered in nooks around Lahore. One of my favorites, in Cantonment, perished in a bomb attack in 2009, its trunk split in two. Many of the trees I photographed came with stories offered by those who live near or in the shade of those trees.

Serendipity, or trees, brought Hafiz and I together. I was taking a photo of a tree behind the Punjabi Adabi Academy offices, having gone there to purchase a few books. Hafiz saw me take a picture and put his hand on the tree trunk. *Iko farash zamin da sara, iko maihna tarwat / bootay, rukh zamin par jitnay, sabhan vich tafavat* (There is only one ground to this earth, and the rain that falls is the same / but the plants and trees which grow are distinct), he recited. A verse by Hazrat Miyan Muhammad Baksh from his *Saif ul Malook*, it speaks of our universality and also our diversity, Hafiz explained to me with a smile.

Miyan Muhammad Baksh (1830–1907) wrote *Safr al-Ishq* (Journey of Love), famously known as *Saif ul Malook*, in 1862. His was a Panjabi telling of an epic romance known throughout the lands bordering the Indian Ocean. Thus, *Saif ul Malook* is an incredibly worldly tale. It goes from Ghazna to Khurasan to Damascus to Cairo to islands in the Indian Ocean to Istanbul and farther afield. The epic, particularly the Baskh rendition, combines the home and the world in an intimate way, linking ideas, textiles, poetic traditions, beliefs, and faiths across a vast expanse of geography.

We began walking, and we talked as we went. He was a "Hafiz"—a designation usually reserved for those who memorize the entirety of the Qur'an. In his case, as a devotee of Panjabi poetry, he had memorized vast swaths of material that I only barely recognized. His father, he told me, was from a small village near the current international border east of Lahore. He

grew up with the Panjabi verses of Guru Nanak, Bulleh Shah
(ca. 1680–1757), Waris Shah (ca. 1722–98), and Baksh. Hafiz and I
discussed *Saif ul Malook* many times over our next meetings.

It is a self-aware text. There are three nested framing stories in
Saif ul Malook. Within each, there is an "author" given the task of
writing a particular story, and the full plot of the tale is revealed
once the listener has heard all three. In the first story, Baksh's
Sufi master asks him to write a story of unparalleled love. The
second is set in the court of Mahmud (of Ghazni), where his minister, Hasan Maimandi, is tasked with narrating this story. That
frame opens in the court of Prince Saif ul Malook's father in
Cairo, where the story of the prince's future life is narrated by
astrologers and fairies.

It is such a delightful beginning, pushing the bardic voice back
in time until it melds seamlessly within the tale itself. Hafiz delighted me with his recitations of the moment in Damascus when
the story of *Saif ul Malook* is read out loud: *Jaan Sultan Damashq
Shahr da parhan laga aihia qissa / sun sun kanbay rukh chaman day,
lay halat da hissa* (When the Sultan of Damascus began to read
this tale / the trees in the garden began to tremble as they heard
the happenings).[16]

Sitting with Hafiz opened up other texts and other ways of
looking at Panjabi literary history. He was particularly fond of
the many versions of the romance *Hir Ranjha*. Hafiz invited me
to his village, where he said he would recite the entirety of Waris
Shah's *Hir* (roughly seven thousand verses). I was delighted to
accept. It was early evening when Hafiz sat with twelve or so men
on a platform built around an old tree. A small battery powered
the microphone on a short stand. Around the platform were gathered families seated on small plastic chairs or on the ground. The
sweet smell of the warm late-summer evening lingered. The recitation was not accompanied by any instrument, although a *ban-
suri* (side-blown bamboo flute) joined now and then.

Hafiz's voice was sonorous, and he stretched *nee*, the ending
syllable of many of the quatrains: *qiran al-sa'adin divan-e hafiz*

shirin khusrauan likh sawarian nee. I had read *Hir*, often in fragments and often in Urdu translations, but listening to it recited, I
heard it as if for the first time. I heard Pratik, Persian, Arabic, and
Panjabi words, phrases that were taken from other texts, meanings that only became clear when the rhythm of the poetry made
those meanings explicit.

The story of Waris Shah's *Hir* is a simple tale of lovers met, lovers torn apart, and love lost. Ranjha (birth name Dheedo) is the
youngest of a Jat landed family from Takht Hazara (near Sargodha). Without much ambition and taunted by his sisters, he
leaves home to find his path in life and reaches the banks of the
river Chenab. He has no money to buy his fare to cross the river
but is taken across for free out of the kindness of Luddan, the
boatsman. On the other side of the Chenab, the exhausted Ranjha
falls asleep. He is awakened by Hir, who is the reigning beauty of
Sayal. They fall in love at first glance. Hir advises Ranjha to seek
employment with her father as a buffalo herder so they can be
close to each other.

Hir convinces her father to hire Ranjha, and Ranjha becomes a
buffalo herder for the household. But Hir's uncle, Kedoo, finds out
about their romance and tells the family, and Ranjha is dismissed.
After the buffalo refuse to go to pasture without him, the family
is forced to convince Ranjha to come back to their house. As a
precaution, Hir is engaged to another man, despite her protests.
Ranjha refuses to run away with her. Hir, during the marriage
ceremony, publicly declares that she will only marry Ranjha, but
she is forcibly married off.

Then, Ranjha and Hir meet and Hir makes him promise that he
will help her escape. Ranjha becomes a yogi and eventually makes
his way to Hir's new home. Along with Hir's sister-in-law, they
contrive a story in which Hir is bitten by a snake and only Ranjha
can save her—thus bringing him back into the household. Then
the lovers elope but they are captured, and Hir is returned to her
new home. Ranjha curses the village, which burns down, and
Hir's parents agree to let Hir and Ranjha get married if he can

bring a proper wedding party. Shortly after Ranjha leaves the village to go and satisfy the parents' request, Hir is poisoned and dies. Ranjha, when he finds out, cries out and dies.

Hafiz lingered on the *saropa*—the description from head to toe of Hir's beauty as seen by Ranjha. A major component of any *kaviya* (poetic composition), the *saropa* is a place for the poet to showcase their imaginative skills and their use of simile and metaphor. When Ranjha first lays eyes on Hir, Waris Shah begins to describe her face as if it were the moon, the braids of her hair as if they were strands of the night, her eyes daffodils, her eyebrows the arches of Lahore. Waris continues to expand the scope of the *saropa*: her chin hearkens to *vilayat* (the lands beyond the seas), her skin is fair as if she were from Kashmir, her stature from China, her calves like apples from Balkh, the red of her lips like the red after the massacres in Urdu Bazaar. We laughed in pure delight. It is hard to capture how beautiful these places were in our minds when they were sung out loud in the Punjabi dusk.

Waris Shah's *Hir* is a love story that does not hide lust, nor does it shy away from describing physical, visceral beauty. When Hir and Ranjha arrange for a moment of joy, Waris renders it voluptuously with images of flowing water and breathless air. Nor does Waris Shah protect the sanctity of those who profess to be pious believers while standing in the way of pure love. Kaidoo, Hir's uncle, who is the villain of the tale, is beaten by Hir's women companions for informing on Hir to her mother, but also for being a voyeur and a sexual predator. They describe in detail how he touches them, smells their garments, grabs their thighs and backs, exposes himself, and gratifies himself when he corners them alone. *Waris Shah miyan mard sada jhotay, runaan sachiyan, sachh kiya tar dey hoo* (O Waris Shah, men are always liars and women truthful, how are you now finding truth?).[17] Each of these verses brought cheers and salutations when Hafiz sang them.

The night ended, and those of us leaving the village made our way to our various forms of transportation. I felt intoxicated by the recitation (there is a lot of intoxication in *Hir*), and I was trying to make sense of why this fabulous literary culture was so marginal to my life in Lahore. I had heard Attaullah Esakhelvi's rendering of *Hir*—the soundtrack to my youth riding public transport. But I had understood very little of it—not in terms of its language, but in terms of its cultural register and its invocations to higher powers, as much to Krishna as to Khizr.

Listening to Hafiz, I realized that this work of stupendous beauty captured that very spirit of Lahore that I kept looking for. I do not mean the physical city, though Lahore is mentioned numerous times in the text, but rather the spirit that Partition tore asunder—a living, breathing, embedded sense of the land and its people. Waris Shah's *Hir* was very particular in its embeddedness, even as it moved across all known spaces.

Panjab was shaped by the flow of five rivers—the Jhelum, Chenab, Ravi, Sutlej, and Beas—as they rush helter-skelter across the wide plains to merge with the Indus. *Hir*, a tale about farmers, cattle herders, and landowners, is also a tale about itinerancy, about movement, about worlds that cannot be separated. Hafiz mentioned Baba Farid Ganjshakar (1179–1266), buried in Pakpattan, who walked to Baghdad, Jerusalem, Mecca, and Ghazni; and Makhdoom Jahaniyan Jahangasht (1308–84), buried in Uch Sharif, who went to Mecca, Rome, and China, who circumambulated the world, and who is Ranjha's patron saint.

I mentioned to Hafiz many others who wrote verses that embedded themselves s across the subcontinent—such as Dnyaneshwar (1275–96), Lal Ded (1320–92), Chaitanya (1486–1533), Mirabai (1499–1570), Dadu Dayal (1544–1603), Kabir (1440–1518), and Surdas (1478–1581). We talked about Guru Nanak. In all of this movement is a genuine love for those you leave behind, and return to, but also those you meet and fall in love with and fight to be with. That spirit seemed alien to me in my disrupted city—the one in which you fight to be apart, and do not fight to be together.

VII.

Migration is a heavy burden. Generational migration, even more so. I am a migrant, so was my father, and so were his parents. My mother's parents were also refugees to Lahore. Some of these migrations were the result of the cleaving apart of the subcontinent and some the result of economic precarity. In that generation of refugees, there was the need to move without much, to put down shallow roots, to remember even less than you possess, and to keep moving and hoping for a more durable future for the next generation. Lahore became a city of refugees and migrants in 1947, and it has never stopped being that. People moved from rural to urban areas, fled from the wars in Afghanistan, and migrated to and from the Gulf for work. These many migrations made up the constant change in the city.

Riaz manages a bank in Samanabad, in southwestern Lahore, which services a predominantly Gulf-employed clientele. He loves his job. Riaz's own family, he told me with some pride, was one of the earliest to seek employment in the Gulf. "My great-grandfather went to Kuwait early in 1920. He was first employed as a ship loader and then found work on the port in Kuwait. His brothers, my grandfather, his sons—we have been connected to the Gulf for a hundred years." Riaz himself worked in Saudi Arabia as an accountant in the early 2000s.

We were sitting in his glass cubicle on the second floor of the bank branch. During our conversation, he was constantly fielding

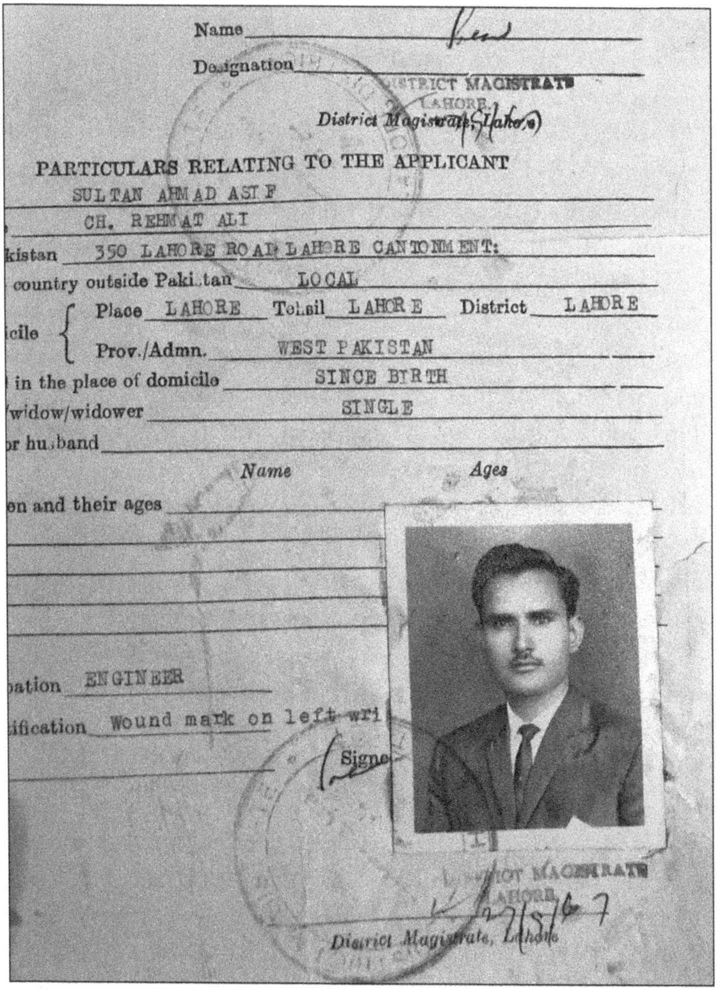
Name
Designation
DISTRICT MAGISTRATE
LAHORE.
District Magistrate, (Lahore)

PARTICULARS RELATING TO THE APPLICANT
SULTAN AHMAD ASIF
CH. REHMAT ALI
kistan 350 LAHORE ROAD LAHORE CANTONMENT:
country outside Pakistan LOCAL
Place LAHORE Tehsil LAHORE District LAHORE
icile
Prov./Admn. WEST PAKISTAN
in the place of domicile SINCE BIRTH
/widow/widower SINGLE
or husband
Name Ages
en and their ages
pation ENGINEER
ification Wound mark on left wri
Signe
DISTRICT MAGISTRATE
LAHORE
27/9/67
District Magistrate, Lahore

Figure 7.5. Domicile certificate for Sultan Ahmad Asif, dated September 27, 1967 (2021)

phone calls, requests for signatures, and deposits of large stashes of cash, which needed his stamp. Another six or seven customers were seated around us, listening and participating in the conversation. "If you sit here for a while, you will meet all the old customers," he said. "People who have been working in the Gulf since the early 1970s, they are retired now and their sons are where they used to work!" He got a large laugh.

I shared with them that my father was also part of the same cohort. He was given a passport and work authorization as a skilled laborer in the Gulf under the government of Zulfiqar Ali Bhutto. After his elementary school education in a small village in Sahiwal, my father wanted to become an engineer, but lacked the resources and funds to do so. Three years at a polytechnical institute enabled him to be certified as an electrical technician and join the Military Engineer Services. He moved to Lahore in 1965, and before he took the job in the Gulf in 1975, he survived on short-term contract work.

Being an "on-site" worker in the Gulf was physically grueling. Over the next twenty-five-plus years he worked for the government's electrical planning department. For the last fifteen of those years, he was alone without his family. When I was conducting interviews for this book, I asked him to speak with me as well. He demurred but wrote a five-page memoir that covered his life. The first sentence reads: "Slavery is a curse but People of the Third World adore it." He went on:

> They sell their freedom, Prestige, dignity, identification in exchange of Dirham, Dinar and Riyals. They get bonded labour entry visa after paying millions of rupees. They sell their property, life savings to pay the agents. Some risk their lives to enter G.C.C. [Gulf Cooperation Council] countries through launches, ferry and unlawful means of conveyance. Some get killed. Some enter prisons. We hate to work hard in our country.[18]

He described his various positions, and how over nearly thirty years he received no benefits, no retirement funds, and only one pay raise. He wrote about the harsh conditions for the unskilled workforce: "The conditions of the housemaids and domestic workers. Drivers are very poor and they are maltreated, abused and punished to establish their [the ruling elite's] supremacy. They are so cruel in certain circumstances."[19]

One of Riaz's customers, born in the immediate aftermath of Partition, went to the Gulf as a construction worker in the mid-1970s. He echoed these views. He worked mainly on U.S. air bases, building barracks, aircraft hangars, and kitchens. "I was able to get much of the men in my family employed in different roles. It is a difficult life," he said, as this labor is dependent on the *kafala* system—a client-sponsored visa regime that binds workers to an individual citizen. "Many of us had taken debts or paid intermediary advance monies to go to Dubai or Kuwait or Saudi Arabia. There was little freedom of movement and no opportunity to change employment." He mentioned the names of relatives or friends who died working in construction sites.

Riaz, his joviality unmatched, interjected. "Look at all these housing colonies all around Lahore. These are all because of this labor. Lahore is transformed over and over because of remittances. It is true. Even outside of the large homes in DHA and other expensive colonies that cater almost universally to overseas Pakistanis, the neighborhoods of Lahore are physically transformed by remittance capital. The lanes and streets that had two-story homes (often mixed usage with a commercial space on the ground floor) have transformed into four- or five-story homes, bulging wider as they go higher."

After his shift ended, Riaz and I took a walk in Samanabad. He often visits the homes of his customers in cases where he needs a signature from a senior or just to keep in touch with them. A residential colony, Samanabad came into being in the 1960s, but much of the infrastructure here now looks and feels much older. We turned off the broad commercial street into a purely residential one with three- and four-story houses on both sides. The "new" additions to the homes were easy enough to spot—the upper floors would still be exposed cement or colored differently. Some were burnished with glazed tiles and chrome-plated windows on the second floors. In some instances, the yellowish old

Lahore houses peeked through here and there. "You can always guess when the son is married and moves upstairs with the wife," Riaz laughed.

"Come this way, let me show you something" he said, briskly leading the way down a short alley and turning right. Nestled between four looming homes was a Mughal-era monument. Shaped like the Chauburji, it was likely a pavilion of a garden that once existed here. Now, the site was a dump. The houses in the vicinity used it for their everyday refuse. Seeing me step toward the structure, Riaz stopped me. "It is pure filth; your shoes and clothes will be ruined," he said. I insisted on climbing over the broken bricks to see it from the inside. The glazed tiles had been scratched off, the sun-baked bricks exposed. Part of the roof had collapsed, and one of the adjacent houses had hooked a clothes-line across it, on which sheets were drying. The names of young men in the neighborhood were carved into the monument. There was a flight of steps, but it did not feel safe to go up them. The steps were covered in feces.

I came out and saw a young man sitting on his bike. I asked him if he knew about this monument, how old it was, or who constructed it. He shrugged and said no, but someone had told him that it was a Mughal building. It was not Islamic, so the authorities should not maintain it. Confused, I asked him what he meant. "It's not a mosque, is it?" he asked with some irritation.

Riaz and I continued walking. He offered to walk with me to the tomb of Zeb 'un Nisa', which was only a few lanes away. When we reached it, we found the structure barricaded by a tall iron fence. A couple of cars were parked inside. The entirety of it had been whitewashed recently. "They will be restoring it and I think it will be amazing," Riaz said.

Itinerancy and migration have ripple effects across time. My father, once he left his village in Sahiwal, was loath to discuss that life. Though we visited my grandfather's village often, there was no "history" there either. My grandfather had only migrated in 1947, and their ancestral village was now on the other side of the border. I have vague memories of sitting under a tree as a child, listening to the *gurgurgurgur* of my grandfather's hookah as the village elders spoke. Were they reciting *Hir* or *Sassi*, or talking about the watering schedule from the colonial-era canal to the post-Partition small allotment of land where he grew grain? I do not know and my father never told me. He wanted instead to make a new life in the city of Lahore. Thus, Lahore's past, and my grandfather's village's past, are equally inaccessible. They lie beyond the links of the migratory chains, each adding a layer of amnesia, all necessarily violent.

Land developers have built new colonies for richer expatriates. Paragon City, Bahria Town, and Eden Towers are gated communities that offer the latest amenities in shopping malls and restaurants, and come with replica models of monuments from around the world—an Eiffel Tower here, a Pisa tower there. The lanes in these communities are numbered. The houses are beautiful (according to their tastes). Cars are numerous and shiny. There are large central mosques, bigger than any for miles. There are no crumbling monuments and certainly no claim toward any past. Instead, it is the once-promised future realized. Much of this capital is overseas and much of the investment is simply in land.

Lahore is a place to park capital in the form of built homes in safeguarded colonies. The political volatility of Islamabad, the constant crisis of a megacity like Karachi are absent from Lahore. The gated communities offer a stability that is marketable and replicable. The residential "colonies," embedded as they are in their own ecosystems of leisure, security, food, and entertainment, have little reason to look to "Lahore." Erstwhile smaller cities of the Punjab, such as Gujranwala, Faisalabad, Multan, and Sargodha, are filled with the same colonies and the same housing-plot infrastructures.

The migrations of my father bookend a certain history of Lahore. He was a migrant to Lahore, and then he was a migrant from Lahore. I cannot say that he *was* of any one place where he lived for an extended period in his life—the village in Sahiwal, the city of Lahore, Doha—as these were all semi-impermanent spaces for him. The military and the Gulf were the two possible points of departure for generations of men in Lahore, and both these systems worked on the basis of remittance, of being "away." My father, away from Lahore, sent remittances to the city that was always there for him, even if, for most of his life, he was not there.

Afterword

Figure 8.1. Ferrying across River Ravi (2023)

He said he was born on the river and had spent his whole life ferrying people and goods across the, at most, chest-high, sludge-inflected, water. For a small fee, paid to the Lahore Municipal Trust, he was rowing me across to Kamran's *baradari*. "Watch out, that you do not get any drop of water in your eye or on your skin. You will get a rash," he warned, as I watched small figures silhouetted on the bridge above us drop plastic bags of meat into the river—buzzards swooping in to try and retrieve fat and flesh for their own consumption. To give to the river, for the river to grant one's hopes, was once done at the shore with the offerings placed in small containers made of leaf and bark, and a *diya* (light) affixed. The ritual offering was generally made at the break of dawn. Now, the residents of Lahore can only stand on a bridge, pinned to the railing by fast-moving traffic, and toss their offerings into the river. To my left, giant machines were dredging up the shore soil, in preparation (so they announced in 2020) of a new futuristic residential colony called "World's Largest Riverfront City" with "ten million residents." The glossy videos and press releases on the website of the new "Ravi Urban Development Authority" promise a bright future with a sustainable greenbelt where now exists a dead and partitioned river.

There are many Lahores. There is the Lahore of the calligrapher who was also a saint and who taught most of the Khattat (writers) of Urdu Bazaar, and at whose grave visitors leave bamboo pens and inkpots as offerings. There is the Lahore of the painter of film posters whose art used to grace the entire outer facade of a two-story cinema hall and who now paints portraits of *pehlawans* (wrestlers). There is the Lahore of the land records, written in Persian *shikasta* script dating back to Sikh rule, that have been locked away in small, square cubbyholes behind a wood-paneled door inside the Punjab Records Archive. There is the Lahore of particular foods or particular kite-makers or queer and trans families or communists and labor activists and a million other things.

There is the Lahore of colonial urban planners laying out Cantonments across the subcontinent. There is the Lahore of Aurangzeb's dam, which saved thousands after the river destroyed nearly everything. There is the Lahore of Akbar. There is the Lahore of monumental temples. There is the Lahore of two generations of Afghan war refugees. There is the Lahore of the film industry that starts, and stops, and starts, and is shut down, converts to theater, and starts, and starts again. There is the Lahore of each of the hundreds of thousands who left Lahore.

Those many Lahores are not in this book, although I spent years learning about them and trying to bring them to life for myself. They are not all here because my intention was to tell one particular story of Lahore. This story was about the self-city-citizen triad, caught in the vortex between memory and history. The existence of those other Lahores helped me figure out the Lahores that *are* in this book. Their absence, like a darker shadow, brings these Lahores into relief.

There is a melancholy about this version of Lahore—about what happened to it, what could have happened to it and did not, and what will happen and what we'd rather did not happen at all. The city disrupted is a city melancholic. Yet the melancholia is only partially true. The many Lahores I have sought to capture in the book are also cities of survival, of joy, of deep learning, of embodied pieties, of embedded selves. These Lahores are made of everyday resistances and defiance. They are the Lahores of dissenters and protesters, the Lahores of myth-busters.

If a city can be in exile from itself, Lahore is it. Whenever I have met people who carry memories of Lahore, whether in their own self or in the memories inherited from their parents, I have found kinship, love, and smiles. Each of these conversations have hovered around this book for over a decade, and I hope what they hold in their memories corresponds with what is in this history.

I am unsure how Lahore will survive the coming disruption just as I am unsure how any of us, no matter where we live on this planet, will survive. This is a common global struggle to sustain ourselves in the face of brutal capitalism, unchecked nationalism, and a devastated natural environment. To write Lahore, as I learned in the writing of this book, is also to work toward its next flourishing.

Acknowledgments

I am profoundly indebted to, and grateful for, all who have given material, intellectual, and emotional support to this project over the last fifteen years.

Lahore: Shaista Ahmed Asif, Mukarram Ahmed, Junaid Ahmed, Talal Ahmed, Sonia Kashmiri, Umar Kashmiri, Zahid Munir, Irfan Waheed Usmani, Mubarak Ali, Arif Muhammad, Farida Shaheed, Neelam Hussain, Nighat Said Khan, Nyla Naz, Faizan Ahmad, Hala Malik, Aleena Afzaal, Afzaal Ahmad, Ammad Ali, Tasleem Ahmed Kayani, Samina Rahman, Laeeque Ahmed, Ziaullah Khokhar, Wajahat Baig, Faraz Anjum, Naimat Khan, Hassan Jawed, Samreen Shahbaz, Heer Cheema, Mahnoor Jalal, Arif Mahmood, Bilal Tanweer, Maryam Wasif Khan, Ali Raza.

Karachi: Sohail Sanghi, Hoori Noorani, Aslam Khwaja, Akbar Zaidi, Marvi Mazhar, Shaheen Aunty, Asghar Soomro, Tahira Khan.

New York City: Maha Shaista Ahmed, Kavi Kashmiri Ahmed, Shahnaz Rouse, Hasan Mujtaba, Karl Jacoby, Mae Ngai, Frank Guridy, Sarah Haley, Lawino Lurum, Brascia Auden, Amy Chazkel, Vishakha Desai, Samantha Feng, Michael Aden, Richard "Ricky" Rodriguez, Marwa Elshakry, Adam Kosto, Kavita Sivaramakrishnan, Anupama Rao, Shana Redmond, Ali Karjoo-Ravary, Beeta Baghoolizadeh, Eilleen Gillooly, Sheldon Pollock, David Lelyveld, Kitty Ahmed, Aamir Naveed, Madiha Tahir, Kathryn S. Poots, Karuna Mantena, Eric Beverley, Mana Kia, Kamini Masood, Abebe L. Tessema, Tessia De Mattos, Meenakshi

Gupta, Saeeda Islam, Delara, Soraya, Robeson, Talal Asad, Rebecca Goetz, Sarah Neilson, David Emmanuel, Gaiutra Bahadur, Mahmood Mamdani, Mira Nair, Naib Mian, Jyothi Nathrajan, Gia Gonzales, Brian Baughan, Benjamin Woodward.

Chicago: C.M. Naim, Muzaffar Alam, Rochona Majumdar, Whitney Cox, Rajeev Kinra.

Minneapolis: Rupa Mitra.

Delhi & Kolkata & Accra & Kampala & Zoom & WhatsApp: Shahid Amin, Partha Chatterjee, Sarover Zaidi, Anubhuti Maurya, Sanjiv Saraf, Sarnath Banerjee, Stephen Willis, Gianni Sievers, Ritu Menon, Samia Khatun, Takiywaa Manuh, Nur Sobers-Khan, Andrea Cassatella, Prachi Deshpande, Cyrelene Aboah-Boampong, Maidul Islam, Rajarshi Ghosh, Christophe Jaffrelot, Hasan Jawed, Dana Sajdi, Leela Gandhi, Judy Loeven, Vazira Fazila-Yaqoobali Zamindar.

NYC & Cambridge, MA: Durba Mitra.

Notes

Introduction

1. Stuart Hall, *Familiar Stranger: A Life Between Two Islands* (Durham and London: Duke University Press, 2017).

1. City

1. James Mallinson, *Messenger Poems by Kalidasa, Dhoyi & Rupa Gosvamin* (New York: New York University Press, 2006).

2. Kanhaiya Lal Hindi, *Tarikh-e Lahore* (Lahore: Majlis Taraqi Adab, 1992), 202.

3. Mufti 'Aliuddin and Mufti Khairuddin Lahori, *'Ibratnama*, ed. Muhammad Baqir (Lahore: Punjabi Adabi Academy, 1961), 59.

4. 'Ali ibn Julugh Farrukhi, *Divan-e Hakim Farrukhi-e Sistani*, ed. Dabir Siyaqi M. (Tehran: Chapkhana Vazarat-e Italat o Jahandari, 1976), 151–52.

5. Mas'ud Sa'ad Salman, *Diwan-e ash'ar-e Mas'ud Sa'ad Salman*, ed. Mahdi Nuriyan (Isfahan: Intesharat-e Kamal, 1985), 1: 212.

6. Ibid., 2: 689.

7. *Divan-e Ma'sud Sa'ad Salman* (Tehran: Intisharat-e Gulshana, 1983), 636–53.

8. Mahmud Lahori, *Mahmudnamah* (Lucknow: Naval Kishore Press, 1886), 4.

9. Claude Lévi-Strauss, *Tristes Tropiques* (Paris: Plon, 1955), 41–43.

10. Ibid., 42.

11. Samuel Purchas, ed., *Hakluyts Posthumous or Purchas His Pilgrimes*, vol. 4 of 20 (1625; repr., Glasgow: James MacLehose & Sons, 1905), 52–57.

12. Ibid., 54.

13. Ibid., 57.

14. Ibid., 57.

15. Faletti's Hotel, *Lahore; a Brief History and Guide. With notes on the Darbar Sahib* (Lahore: Civil and Military Gazette, 1913), 98.

16. 'Ali ibn 'Usman Hajweri, *Kashf al-Mahjub*, ed. Ahmad Ali (Lahore: Islamia Steam Press, 1923), 2.

17. Ibid., 6.

18. Ibid., 32–41.

19. Linus Strothmann, *Managing Piety: The Shrine of Data Ganj Bakhsh* (Karachi: Oxford University Press, 2016), 91–98.

20. Tara Chand and M. Riza Jalali Na'ini, eds., *Sakinat al-awliya* (Tehran: Mu'assasah-e Matubu'ati-e Ilmi, 1965), 98.

21. Jeet Singh Sateel, *Kalam-e Nanak* (Lahore: Punjab Heritage Foundation, 2001), 993.

22. Ibid., 543.

23. Ibid., 329.

24. Sayyid Abu Talib Mir 'Abidini, ed., *Divan-e Zeb'un Nisa' Mukhfi* (Tehran: Amir-e Kabir, 2001), 69.

25. Chandar Bhan Brahman, *Chahar Chaman* (New Delhi: Iran Culture House, 2007), 131–32.

26. 'Abd al-Hamid Lahori, *The Badshah Namah*, vol. 2., ed. Kabir al-Din Ahmad and Abd al-Rahim (Calcutta: College Press, 1867), 414.

2. History

1. H.R. Goulding, *Old Lahore: Reminiscences of a Resident* (Lahore: Civil and Military Gazette Press, 1924), 93.

2. Julius Bryant, "The Careers and Character of 'J.L.K,'" in *John Lockwood Kipling: Arts & Crafts in the Punjab and London*, edited by Julius Bryant and Susan Wever (New Haven: Yale University Press, 2017), 46.

3. Sara Suleri, *Meatless Days* (Chicago: University of Chicago Press, 1989), 54.

4. Ibid., 54.

5. Ibid., 123.

6. Ibid., 122.

7. Ramesh Chandra Sharma and Amit Mukerji, "A Contemporary Account of Lahore in the Early Seventeenth Century," *Proceedings of the Indian History Congress* 53 (1992): 205–10.

8. Nur Ahmad Chishti, *Yadgar-e Chishti* (Lahore: Majlis Tariqi-e Adab, 1975) 110–11.

9. Ibid., 152.

10. Kanhaiya Lal Hindi, *Tarikh-e Lahore* (Lahore: Majlis Taraqqi-e Adab, 1977), 47.

11. Ibid., 79.

12. Syed Muhammad Latif, *Lahore: Its History, Architectural Remains and Antiquities* (Lahore: New Imperial Press, 1892), 157.

13. Syed Muhammad Latif, *History of the Panjab from Remotest Antiquity to the Present Times* (Calcutta: Calcutta Central Press, 1891), x–xii.

14. Ibid., 264.

15. Pran Nevile, *Lahore: A Sentimental Journey* (Bombay: Allied Publishers Ltd., 1993), 56–57.

16. Ibid., 70–72.

17. Ibid., 106.

18. Ibid., 97.

19. Som Anand, *Batain Lahore ki* (New Delhi: Maktaba-e Jamia, 1981), 18.

20. Ibid., 27.

21. Ibid., 166. A very similar anecdote is narrated by anthropologist Talal Asad, who after Partition was a young child living with his family in Model Town. He recounts overhearing a group of *gundas* (goons) describe a killing of a Hindu after asking him if he was circumcised. Personal correspondence, New York, July 13, 2023.

22. Kirpal Singh, *Select Documents on Partition of Punjab, 1947: India and Pakistan* (Delhi: National Bookshop, 2005), 218–19.

23. Ibid., 21.

24. A. Hameed, *Lahore ki Yadain* (Lahore: Sang-e Meel Publications, 2000), 82.

25. Ibid., 87.

26. Ibid., 89–90.

27. Ibid., 103.

28. Ibid., 105.

29. Ibid., 131.

30. Santosh Kumar, *Lahore Nama* (New Delhi: Vibha Publisher, 1983), 51.

31. Ibid., 44.

32. Ibid., 35.

33. My gratitude to the family of Aamir Naveed for sharing this letter. It was written to Naveed's father in 1947, by a relative who had recently migrated to Lahore from Sultanpur Lodhi (current-day Punjab, India). In

July 2023, the family discovered this collection of letters in an unopened trunk in Lahore.

34. P.C. Joshi and Dhanwantri, *Bleeding Punjab Warns* (Bombay: New Age Printing Press, 1947), 10.

35. Ilyas Chattha, "Competition for Resources: Partition's Evacuee Property and the Sustenance of Corruption in Pakistan," *Modern Asian Studies* 46, no. 5 (2012): 1185.

36. Fikr Taunsvi, *Chhatta Dariya* (Lahore: Naia Idarah, 1948), 21.

37. Ibid., 27.

38. Ibid., 40.

39. Gopal Mittal, *Lahore Ka Jo Zikr Kiya* (New Delhi: Maktaba Tehrik, 1971), 116.

40. Tausnvi, *Chhatta Dariya*, 154.

41. Santosh Kumar, *Lahorenama* (New Delhi: Vibhai Publishers, 1983), 22.

42. Ibid., 27.

43. Ibid., 57.

44. Muhammad Baqir, *Lahore: Past and Present* (Lahore: Panjab University Press, 1952), ii.

45. Ibid., 11.

46. Ibid., 205.

47. Ibid., 243.

48. Muhammad Tufail, ed., *Naqoosh: Lahore Number*, no. 92 (February 1962): 16.

49. Tables 1 and 1A, *First Census of Pakistan 1951: Urban and Rural Population and Area*. Karachi: Office of the Census Commissioner, Government of Pakistan, Ministry of the Interior, 1952): 38–49.

50. Housing and Physical Planning Department, *Master Plan for Greater Lahore* (Lahore: Government Printing, 1973), 3.

51. Ibid., 48.

52. Muzaffar Abbas, Shinobu Kazama, and Satoshi Takizawa, "Water Demand Estimation in Service Areas with Limited Numbers of Customer Meters—Case Study in Water and Sanitation Agency (WASA) Lahore, Pakistan," *Water* 14 (2022): 2197.

53. Lahore Development Authority, *Integrated Master Plan for Lahore—2021*, vol. 1 (Lahore: National Engineering Services, 2004).

54. Viqar Ahmed, "Lahore Walled City Upgrading Project," in *Reaching the Urban Poor: Project Implementation in Developing Countries*, ed. G. Shabbir Cheema (Boulder, CO: Westview Press, 1986), 45–61.

3. Nation

1. Partha Chatterjee, *The Nation and Its Fragments: Colonial and Postcolonial Histories* (Princeton, NJ: Princeton University Press, 19993), 14.

2. R.E.M. Wheeler, *Five Thousand Years of Pakistan: An Archaeological Outline* (Karachi: Zaki Sons Press, 1992), 5.

3. Ibid., 64.

4. Ibid., 78.

5. Ibid., 128 (emphasis in original).

6. Ibid., 66.

7. Department of Archives, *Annual Report* (Islamabad: Govt of Pakistan, 1974). Also see, Syed Jalaluddin Haider, Archives in Pakistan, *Journal of Archival Organization*, 2, no. 4 (2004): pp. 29–52.

8. G.W. Leitner, *Sinin-e Islam: Arab ki Tarikh-e Ayam-e Jahalat say Ikhtatam-e Khanadan-e Abbasiya Tak* (Lahore: Indian Public Opinion, 1871).

9. M.H. Azad, "Zaban-e Urdu," in *Maqalat-e Azad* (Lahore: Majlis Taraqqi-e Adab, 1978), 154–68.

10. See Farina Mir, *The Social Space of Language: Vernacular Culture in British Colonial Punjab* (Berkeley: University of California Press, 2010), 33.

11. Ishtiaq Husain Qureshi, *Afkar o Azkar: Daktar Ishtiaq Husain Quraishi ke muntakhab maqalat, khutbat, mushafahat, aur nashri taqarir ka majmu'ah* (Karachi: Muqtadirah Qaumi Zuban, 1981): 50–51.

12. Ibid., 142–43.

13. I.H. Qureshi, *Education in Pakistan: An Inquiry into Objectives and Achievements* (Karachi: Ma'aref Limited, 1975), 166.

14. Mohammad Moazzamuddin, *Ikramnama* (Delhi: Educational Publishing House, 2010), 30–31.

15. S.M. Ikram, ed., *Saqafat-e Pakistan* (Karachi: Publication Institute, 1956), 11.

16. K.K. Aziz, *The Coffee House of Lahore: A Memoir 1942–57* (Lahore: Sang-e-Meel Publications, 2007).

17. Javid Iqbal, *Ideology of Pakistan and Its Implementation* (Lahore: Sh. Ghulam Ali and Sons, 1959), 68.

18. Aziz, *Coffee House*, 38–39.

19. K.K. Aziz, *Pakistan's Political Culture: Essays in Historical and Social Origins* (Lahore: Vanguard Publishers, 2001), 361.

20. K.K. Aziz, *Autobiography*, vol. 1, *1927–48* (Lahore: Izharsons Printers, 2006), 617–19.

4. Memory

1. Ritu Menon, *India on Their Minds: 8 Women, 8 Ideas of India* (New Delhi: Women Unlimited, 2023), 19.

2. Qurratulain Hyder, *Aag ka Darya* (Delhi: Urdu Kitab Ghar, 1984), 378–79.

3. Mukhtar Masood, "Minar-e Pakistan," in *Aawaz-e Dost* (Lahore: Naqoosh Press, 1973).

4. Jamiluddin Ahmad, ed., *Some Recent Speeches and Writings of Mr. Jinnah* (Lahore: Sh. Muhammad Ashraf, 1942), 154.

5. Ibid., 150 (emphasis added).

6. Tassaduq Hussain Raja, *Nasim Hijazi: aik mutala'ah* (Lahore: Qaumi Kutub Khana, 1987), 309.

7. *The Times of India*, March 29, 1926, and April 7, 1927.

8. Office of the Director of Public Instruction, *Report on Native Papers Published in the Bombay Presidency: For the Week Ending 20th May 1905* (Poona: Government Central Press, 35).

9. Government of Pakistan, Ministry of Education, *Report of the Commission on National Education* (Karachi: Government of Pakistan Press, 1960), 283.

10. B.R. Ambedkar, *Annihilation of Caste* (Bombay: B.R. Kadrekar, 1936).

11. Mukhtar Ahmed Matin, *Tarikh-e Jattan* (Rahim Yar Khan: Roznamah Shahadat, 1986), 240.

12. Asghar Ali Chaudhry, *Tarikh-e Ara'in* (Lahore: Ilmi Kitab Khana, 1963), 41.

5. People

1. Zamir Niazi, *The Press in Chains* (Karachi: Royal Book Company, 1986), 190.

2. Dayal Singh Public Trust Library, *Handwritten Catalog*, n.d., final page.

3. Qudratullah Shahab, *Shahabnama* (Lahore: Sang-meel Publications, 1987), 1096.

4. Ibid., 1151.

5. Ibid., 103–4.

6. Ibid., 247–58.

7. Ibid., 130.

8. See Fazle Haque, "Quaid Azam Chand Anmol Yadain," *Mahnama Nazria Pakistan* 11, no. 8 (Lahore: Shahid Rasheed Publishers, 2011): 28–30.

9. Qureshi, Mushtaq Muhammad, "Ki Muhammad se wafa tu nay," *Daily Jang*, January 1, 2011, pg. 6.

10. David Hardiman, *The Nonviolent Struggle for Indian Freedom, 1905–19*. (London and Oxford: Oxford University Press, 2018), pg. 171.

11. Faiz Ahmed Faiz, "About Myself and What I Have Been Up To . . . ," in Sheema Majeed, ed., *Culture and Identity: Selected English Writings of Faiz* (Karachi: Oxford University Press, 2005), 61.

12. Estelle Dryland, "Faiz Ahmed Faiz and the Rawalpindi Conspiracy Case," *Journal of South Asian Literature* 27, no. 2 (Summer/Fall 1992): 175–85.

13. Faiz Ahmad Faiz, *Zindan Nama* (Lahore: Maktaba-e Karavan, 1956), 45–47.

14. Ibid., 39.

15. Ibid., 50–52.

16. Faiz Ahmad Faiz, *Dast-e Saba* (Lahore: Maktaba-e Karvan, 1952), 68.

17. Faiz Ahmad Faiz, *Zindan Nama* (Lahore: Maktaba-e Karavan, 1956), 82.

18. Brij Paremi, *Sa'adat Hasan Manto: Hayat aur Karname* (Srinagar: Mirza Publications, 1982).

19. Sa'adat Hasan Manto, *Khali Botalain, Khali Dabbay* (Lahore: Al Bayan, 1950), 23–37.

20. Sa'adat Hasan Manto, *Sarak kay Kinaray* (Lahore: Naya Idarah, 1961), 129.

21. Ibid., 113.

22. Sa'adat Hasan Manto, *Siyah Hashiya* (Lahore: Maktaba Jadid, 1948).

23. Anis Nagi, *Sa'adat Hasan Manto kay Muqadamat* (Lahore: Daniyal, 1999).

24. Ikramul Haq, "Sexual Harassment of Women": Revealing Survey," *Dawn*, March 16, 1984. Clipping from *ASR Violence Women 1984–1996_NC_1409*, Government College University Library.

25. Syed Abul A'la Maududi, *Jama'at-i Islami kay 29 Saal* (Lahore: Ja'amat-Islami Pakistan Publications, 1970).

26. Among the women were Farida Shaheed, Hina Jilani, Asma Jilani née Jahangir, Neelam Hussain, Madeeha Gauhar, and Lala Rukh. Neelam Hussain, who directs the Simorgh Women's Resource and Publication Center in

Lahore, spoke with me about her memories of participating in the presidential campaign of Fatima Jinnah, the violent creation of Bangladesh, and the 1983 protest march on Mall Road and being baton-charged by the police. Farida Shaheed founded the Shirkat Gah Women's Resource Center as well as the international network Women Living Under Muslim Law, and spoke about the Ayub Khan regime and utilizing quantitative research as a shield and a weapon against the rampant misogyny of military dictators. The keeper of much of this archive is Nighat Said Khan, who founded the Applied Socio-economic Research (ASR) Institute of Women's Studies in Lahore and expressed her organization's absolute commitment to education and training for women in key social sciences, though stressed that this work needs to prioritize storytelling and partnerships. I want to thank all of these fierce feminists for their lifelong struggle and for speaking with me about this period and their participation in the women's rights movement.

6. Place

1. Thomas Coryate. *Thomas Coriate traueller for the English vvits : greeting : from the court of the Great Mogul, resident at the towne of Asmere, in easterne India* (London: W. Iaggard and Henry Featherston, 1616), 19.

2. Ibid., 13.

3. Ibid., 18.

4. Gary Alder, *Beyond Bokhara: The Life of William Moorcroft* (London: Century Publishing, 1985), 238.

5. A. Hameed, *Lahore ki Yadain* (Lahore: Sang-e Meel Publications, 2000), 155.

6. *Bangal ka Kala Jadoo* (Sialkot: Shama News Agency, n.d.), 13.

7. In colloquial Urdu, the word *ziadati* is often used as a euphemism for sexual violence or rape.

8. Arya Indrias Patras, *Swept Aside: A Story of Christian Sweepers in Lahore* (Lahore: Folio Books, 2023), 83.

9. Chishti, *Yadgar-e Chishti*, 170.

10. Javaz Jaffri, ed., *Kulliyat-e Ustad Daman* (Lahore: Punjab Institute of Language, Art & Culture, 2018), 42.

11. Ibid., 69–70.

12. Tabassum Kashmiri, *Nauhe takht Lahaur ke: EK tavil nazm* (Lahore: Misbah Sanz Publishers, 1985), 13–14.

13. Fahmida Riaz, *Four Walls and a Black Veil* (Karachi: Oxford University Press, 2004), 95–97.

14. Asad Salim Shaikh, *Dulle di bar: Pindi Bhatiyan aur gird o navāḥ kī tarikh* (Lahore: Izharsons, 1999), 50.

15. Tabassum Kashmiri, *Nauhe takht Lahaur ke*, 107.

16. Mian Muhammad Baksh, *Saif ul Malook* (Karachi: Anjuman Taraqqi Urdu Pakistan, 1990), 73.

17. Shaikh Abdul Aziz, *Hir by Syed Waris Shah* (Lahore: Panjab Adabi Academy, 1960), 157, 159.

18. Sultan Ahmed Asif, "Expetriates [*sic*] in Qatar," unpublished memoir.

19. Ibid. Also see Manan Ahmed Asif, "The State Shall Remain Nameless," in *The State*, vol. 4, *Dubai*, ed. Rahel Aima and Ahmad Makia (Sharjah: Rami Farook, 2013).

Bibliography

'Abbas, Muzaffar, Shinobu Kazama, and Satoshi Takizawa. "Water Demand Estimation in Service Areas with Limited Numbers of Customer Meters—Case Study in Water and Sanitation Agency (WASA) Lahore, Pakistan," *Water* 14, no. 14 (January 2022).

'Abbas, Syed Faizan. *Hamara Dharampura (Mustafabad)*. Lahore: Lahore Shanasi Publications, 2019.

'Abbasi, Syed Ahmed. *Jinnat kay Saath: Case Studies*. Karachi: Book Time, 2016.

'Abidini, Sayyid Abu Talib Mir, ed. *Divan-e Zeb'un Nisa' Mukhfi*. Tehran: Amir-e Kabir, 2001.

Abu-Lughod, Janet L. "The Islamic City—Historic Myth, Islamic Essence, and Contemporary Relevance," *International Journal of Middle East Studies* 19, no. 2 (May 1987), 155–76.

'Adib, Yunus. *Mera Shahr Lahore*. Lahore: Aatish Fishan Publications, 1992.

Ahmad, Faizan. *Lahore by Metro*. Lahore: La Topical, 2021.

Ahmad, Ishfaq. *Zikr-e Shahab*. Lahore: Urdu Science Board, 1989.

Ahmad, Jamiluddin, ed. *Some Recent Speeches and Writings of Mr. Jinnah*. Lahore: Sh. Muhammad Ashraf, 1942.

Ahmad, Muneer. *The Civil Servant in Pakistan*. Karachi: Oxford University Press, 1964.

Ahmad, Syed Jaffar. *Mahnat Kashon kay Naam Shairi*. Karachi: Mass Printers, 2012.

———. *Challenges of History Writing in South Asia*. Karachi: Mass Printers, 2013.

Ahmed, Viqar. "Lahore Walled City Upgrading Project." In *Reaching the Urban Poor: Project Implementation in Developing Countries*, edited by G. Shabbir Cheema. New York: Westview Press, 1986.

Akbarpuri, Ghafil. *Sultan Mahmood Ghaznavi, aik Tarikh, aik Navil.* Lahore: Alasar Publications, 2010.

Akhtar, Jamil, ed. *Zindagi-nama Qurratulain Hyder.* New Delhi: Qaumi Council Baray-e Farugh-e Zuban, 2014.

Alder, Gary. *Beyond Bukhara: The Life of William Moorcroft.* London: Century Publishing, 1985.

'Ali, Munshi Syed 'Abbas. *Qissa-e Ghamghin.* Edited by Satish Chandar Misra. Baroda: Maharaja Siyajirao University of Baroda, 1975.

Ambedkar, B.R. *Annihilation of Caste.* Bombay: B.R. Kadrekar, 1936.

Ameenuddin, Qaisar. *Lahore Tujhe Salaam.* Lahore: Alhaq Publishers, 2002.

Amrohi, Raees. *Jinnat.* Karachi: Welcome Book Depot, 2013.

Anand, Som. *Baten Lahore ki.* New Delhi: Maktaba-e Jami'ah, 1981.

Anwar, Ajaz. *Old Lahore.* Lahore: Al-Musawwar Printers, 1996.

———. *Na'en Reesan Shahr Lahor Diyan.* Lahore: Ahsan Tariq Printers, 2011.

Anwar, Khurshid. *Qurratulain Hyder kay Navilon mein Tarikhi Sha'ur.* New Delhi: Anjuman Taraqqi-e Urdu, 1993.

'Arif, Anwar. *Soresh Kashmiri: Savanih o Ifkar.* Lahore: Masood Printers, 1969.

Ashar, Meera. "Thriving on the Margins of History: Engaging with the Past in the Vernacular," *History and Theory* 60, no. 4 (December 2021): 59–73.

Asif, Manan Ahmed. "The State Shall Remain Nameless." In *The State,* vol. 4, *Dubai.* Edited by Rahel Aima and Ahmad Makia. Sharjah: Rami Farook, 2013.

———. *A Book of Conquest: The Chachnama and Muslim Origins in South Asia.* Cambridge, MA: Harvard University Press, 2016.

———. *The Loss of Hindustan: The Invention of India.* Cambridge, MA: Harvard University Press, 2020.

Awan, Mohabbat Husain. *Tarikh Khulasatul Awan.* Karachi: Idarah Tahqiq al-Awan Pakistan, 2016.

Azad, M.H. "Zaban-e Urdu." In *Maqalat-e Azad.* Lahore: Majlis Taraqqi-e Adab, 1978.

Aziz, K.K. *Some Problems of Research in Modern History.* Lahore: Ferozsons Ltd., 1967.

———. *Pakistan's Political Culture: Essays in Historical and Social Origins.* Lahore: Vanguard Publishers, 2001.

———. *Autobiography*, vol. 1, *1927–48*. Lahore: Izharsons Printers, 2006.

———. *A Journey into the Past: Portrait of a Punjabi Family, 1800–1970.* Lahore: Vanguard Publishers, 2006.

———. *The Coffee House of Lahore: A Memoir 1942–57.* Lahore: Sang-e Meel Publications, 2008.

———. *The Pakistani Historian.* Lahore: Sang-e Meel Publications, 2009.

Aziz, Shaikh Abdul. *Hir: Syed Waris Shah.* Lahore: Punjabi Adabi Academy, 1960.

Baig, Mirza Shahid Rizwan, Rao Qasim Idrees, and Hafiz Muhammad Usman Nawaz. "A Critical Analysis of Legal Framework Relating to Defence Housing Authority in Pakistan Vis-à-Vis the Goal of Housing for All as Envisaged by UN Habitat Agenda," *Pakistan Social Sciences Review* 4, no. 2 (June 2020): 883–94.

Baihaqi, Abu-'l-Fazl Muhammad. *Tarikh-e Baihaqi.* Tehran: Chapkhanah-e Bank-e Milli-e Iran, 1945.

Baksh, Miyan Muhammad. *Saiful Malook.* Edited by Shafi Aqeel. Karachi: Anjuman-e Taraqi Urdu Pakistan, 1990.

Bangal ka Kala Jadoo. Sialkot: Shama News Agency, n.d.

Baqir, Muhammad. *Panjabi Qissay Farsi Zuban mein.* Vol. 2. Lahore: Panjab Adabi Academy, 1960.

———. *Lahore: Past and Present.* Lahore: Panjab University Press, 1952.

———. *Ahval o Talimat Shaikh Abu'l Hasan Hajveri Data Ganj Baksh.* Lahore: Idarah Tahqiqat-e Pakistan, 1989.

Bashir, Muddasir. *Itahasik Lahore.* Lahore: Sanjh Publications, 2018.

Bava Dayal. *Kala Jadoo.* Huzdar: Nasib Gul Book Center, n.d.

Benjamin, Walter. *Berlin Childhood Around 1900.* Translated by Howard Eiland. Cambridge, MA: Harvard University Press, 2006.

Bergson, Henri. *Matter and Memory.* Translated by N.M. Paul and W.S. Palmer. New York: Zone Books, 1991.

Bernier, François. *Suite Des Memoires Du Sieur Bernier, Sur L'Empire Du Grand Mogol.* Paris: Chez Arnout Lees, 1672.

———. *Travels in the Mogul Empire, A.D. 1656–1668.* Edited by Vincent A. Smith. London: Oxford University Press, 1916.

Beveridge, Henry, and Alexander Rogers. *The Tuzuk-e-Jahangiri: Memoirs of Jahangir.* 2 vols. Lahore: Sang-e-Meel Publications, 2001.

Bhatti, Abdul Jalil. *Shibli ki Tarikh Navisi: Aik Tajziati Mutta'ila.* Multan: Bahauddin Zakariya University, 1998.

Bhatti, Amjad Ali. *Ustad Daman: Shaksiyat aur Fann*. Islamabad: Pakistan Academy of Letters, 2009.

Blount, Henry. *A Voyage into the Levant*. London: I.L. for Andrew Crooke, 1636.

Brahman, Chandar Bhan. *Chahar Chaman*. New Delhi: Iran Cultural House, 2007.

Brown, Giles T. "The Hindu Conspiracy, 1914–1917." *Pacific Historical Review* 17, no. 3 (1948): 299–310.

Bruce, J.F. *A History of the University of the Panjab*. Lahore: University of Panjab, 1933.

Bryant, Julius, and Susan Weber, eds. *John Lockwood Kipling: Arts & Crafts in the Punjab and London*. New Haven: Yale University Press, 2017.

Bulleh Shah. *Kalam-e Baba Bullhe Shah*. Lahore: Kamal Academy, 2006.

Burton, Richard F. *First Footsteps in East Africa; or, an exploration of Harar*. London: Longman, Brown, Green and Longmans, 1856.

Butt, M. Abdullah. *Tipu Sultan*. Lahore: Qaumi KutbKhana, 1940.

Butt, Waqas H. *Life Beyond Waste: Work and Infrastructure in Urban Pakistan*. Stanford, CA: Stanford University Press, 2023.

Cabeza de Vaca, Alvar Núñez. *Naufragios de Alvar Nuñez Cabeza de Vaca, y Relacion de la jornada, que hizo a la Florida con el adelantado Panfilo de Narvaez (1542)*. Madrid, 1749.

Canetti, Elias. *Crowds and Power*. New York: Continuum Publishing, 1962.

Chatterjee, Partha. *The Nation and Its Fragments: Colonial and Postcolonial Histories*. Princeton Studies in Culture/Power/History. Princeton, NJ: Princeton University Press, 1993.

Chattha, Ilyas. "Competitions for Resources: Partition's Evacuee Property and the Sustenance of Corruption in Pakistan," *Modern Asian Studies* 46, no. 5 (September 2012): 1182–211.

Chaudhry, Ali Asghar. *Tarikh-e Sindh ka Gumshuda Baab, yani Qaum-e Arain ka Tarikhi Pasmanzir*. Hyderabad: Mansoor Press, 1971.

———. *Tarikh Arain: Mujahid Azam Hazrat Muhammad bin Qasim kay Rufqa yani Shami Mujahideen kay halat par mushtami*. Lahore: Ilmi Kitab Khana, 1977.

Chaudhry, F.A. *Ab wo Lahore Kahan?* Lahore: Combine Printers, 2009.

Chishti, Nur Ahmad. *Tahqiqat-e Chishti*. 2 vols. Lahore: Punjabi Adabi Academy, 1964.

———. *Yadgar-e Chishti*. Lahore: Majlis Taraqqi-e Adab, 1975.

Coryate, Thomas. *Thomas Coriate traueller for the English vvits: Greeting. From the court of the Great Mogul, resident at the towne of Asmere, in easterne India*. London: W. Iaggard, and Henry Fetherston, 1616.

Cruz, Gaspar da. *Tractado em que se côtam muito por estèso ab cousas da China*. Lisbon: Andrés de Burgos, 1569.

Dadi, Iftikhar. *Lahore Cinema: Between Realism and Fable*. Seattle: University of Washington Press, 2022.

———, ed. *Lahore Biennale 01: Reader*. Milano: Sira Editore, 2022.

Dani, Ahmad Hasan. "Archives—Its Place in the Cultural Heritage of a Country," *Pakistan Archives* 1, no. 1 (January–June 1984).

Dehlavi, Hasan Nizami. *Ahval-e Jang Muhammad bin Qasim*. Delhi: Army Barqi Press, 1927.

———. *Hindustan mein Islam kyon kar Phela?* Delhi: Army Barqi Press, 1926.

Department of Archives. *Annual Report*. Islamabad: Govt of Pakistan, 1974.

Dheer, Kaiwal. *Mein Lahore Hoon: Lahore ki Tarikhi, Saqafati, Sayasi, aur Adabi Dastaviz*. Lahore: 'Ilm o Irfan Publishers, 2021.

Dryland, Estelle. "Faiz Ahmed Faiz and the Rawalpindi Conspiracy Case," *Journal of South Asian Literature* 27, no. 2 (1992): 175–85.

Edwards, Holly. *Of Brick and Myth: The Genesis of Islamic Architecture in the Indus Valley*. Karachi: Oxford University Press, 2015.

Faiz, Faiz Ahmed. *Salaiban Meray Dareechay Mein: Ayam-e Aseeri kay 135 Khatoot*. Karachi: Pak Publishers Ltd., 1971.

———. *Zindaan Nama*. Lahore: Maktaba Karawan, 1952.

Faiz, Alys. *Dear Heart—to Faiz in Prison (1951–1955)*. Lahore: Ferozsons Ltd., 1985.

Faletti's Hotel. *Lahore: A Brief History and Guide with Notes on the Durbar Sahib*. Lahore: Civil and Military Gazette, 1913.

Faqir, Muhammad Faqir. *Kulliyat-e Bulleh Shah*. Lahore: Panjab Adabi Academy, 1960.

Faridabadi, Syed Hashmi. *Ma'athir-e Lahore*. Lahore: Idarah-e Saqafat-e Islamia, 2011.

Farrukhi, 'Ali ibn Julugh. *Divan e Hakim Farrukhi Sistani*. Tehran: Chapkhana Vizarat-e Itla'at o Jahangardi, 1995.

Fauq, Muhammad Din. *Hazrat Data Ganj Baksh, Savanh 'Umri*. Lahore: Book Home, 2007.

————. *Akhbar Navison kay Halaat.* Lahore: Matbua Rafai Aam Steam, 1916.

Frembgen, Jürgen Wasim. *"We Are Lovers of the Qalandar": Piety, Pilgrimage, and Ritual in Pakistani Sufi Islam.* Karachi: Oxford University Press, 2011.

Gandhi, Supriya. *The Emperor Who Never Was: Dara Shukoh in Mughal India.* Cambridge, MA: Harvard University Press, 2020.

Gauhar, M. Ramzan. *Shahabuddin Gauri.* Lahore: Maktaba-e Gauhar, 2010.

Geddes, Patrick. *Cities in Evolution: An Introduction to the Town Planning Movement and to the Study of Civics.* London: Williams & Norgate, 1915.

Ghafarullah, Muhammad Sayeed. *Divan-e Mukhfi.* Kanpur: Matbua Mujeedi, 1930.

Ghaffar, Huma. *Pakistan mein Tarikh navisi ka tajziati Muttaila: Ishtiaq Husain Qureshi, Aziz Ahmad, Sheikh Muhammad Ikram.* Karachi: Pakistan Study Center, 2016.

Ghaznavi, Qamar. *Naseem jo Hijaz se chali (Shaksiyat o Fann).* Lahore: Peace Publications, 2015.

Glover, William J. *Making Lahore Modern: Constructing and Imagining a Colonial City.* Minneapolis: University of Minnesota Press, 2008.

Goulding, H.R. *Old Lahore: Reminiscences of a Resident.* Lahore: Civil and Military Gazette Press, 1924.

Groote, P.D., R. de Jonge, J.B.R. Dekker, and J. de Vries. *Urban Planning in Lahore: A Confrontation with Real Development.* Groningen, University of Groningen, 1988.

Grunebaum, Gustave von. "The Structure of the Muslim Town." In *Islam: Essays in the Nature and Growth of a Cultural Tradition.* London: Routledge, 1961.

Gundapur, Sardar Sher Muhammad Khan. *Tarikh-e Khurshid Jahan (Tarikh-e Pashtun).* Karachi: Shaikh Shaukat Ali and Sons, 1979.

Haider, Syed Jalaluddin. "Archives in Pakistan," *Journal of Archival Organization,* 2, no. 4 (2004).

Hajweri, Abu'l Hasan 'Ali. *Kashf al-Mahjub.* Tehran: Kutab Khana Tahuri, 1979.

Hameed, A. *Lahore ki Yadain.* Lahore: Sang-e Meel Publications, 2000.

Haq, Ikramul. "Sexual Harassment of Women: Revealing Survey" *Dawn,* March 16, 1984. Clipping from *ASR Violence Women 1984-1996_NC_1409.* Government College University Library.

Haq, Zia ul. *Address to Nation, Rawalpindi, 24 December, 1981.*

Haque, Fazle. "Quaid Azam Chand Anmol Yadain," *Mahnama Nazria Pakistan* 11, no. 8. Lahore: Shahid Rasheed Publishers, 2011.

Hardiman, David. *The Nonviolent Struggle for Indian Freedom, 1905–19.* London and Oxford: Oxford University Press, 2018.

Haroon, Anis. *Kab Mahkay gi Fasl-e Gul.* Karachi: Mass Printers, 2016.

Hasan, Mumtaz, ed. *The Adventures of Hir & Ranjha.* Karachi: Lion Art Press, 1966.

Hijazi, Nasim. *Pakistan Se Diyare Haram Tak.* Gujranwala: Publication Club, 1960.

———. *Muhammad bin Qasim.* Lahore: Jahangir Book Depot, 2002.

Hindi, Kanhaiya Lal. *Tarikh-e Lahore.* Lahore: Majlis Taraqqi-e Adab, 1992.

Hourani, Albert H., and S.M. Stern, eds. *The Islamic City.* Philadelphia: University of Pennsylvania Press, 1970.

Housing and Physical Planning Department, *Master Plan for Greater Lahore.* Lahore: Government Printing, 1973.

Husain, Tasadduq. "The Spiritual Journey of Dara Shukoh," *Social Scientist* 30, nos. 7–8 (July–August 2002): 54–66.

Hyder, Qurratulain. *Aag ka Darya.* Delhi: Urdu Kitab Ghar, 1984.

———. *Kar-e Jahan Daraz Hai.* Delhi: Educational Publishing House, 2003.

———. *Sita Haran.* Lahore: Sang-e Meel Publications, 2008.

Ikram, S.M. *Aab-e Kausar.* Lahore: Ferozsons Ltd., 1965.

———., ed. *Saqafat-e Pakistan.* Karachi: Idarah Matbuat-e Pakistan, 1964.

Ikram, S.M., and Percival Spear, eds. *The Cultural Heritage of Pakistan.* London: Oxford University Press, 1955.

Indian Universities Commission: University of the Punjab Part I. Abstract of Evidence. Simla: Government Central Printing Office, 1902.

Iqbal, Javid. *Ideology of Pakistan.* Lahore: Ferozsons Ltd., 1971.

Iqbal, M. *Education in Pakistan.* Lahore: Aziz Publishers, 1977.

Ishaque, M. *Four Eminent Poetesses of Iran.* Calcutta: Baptist Mission Press, 1968.

Jaffar, S.M. *A Guide to the Archives of the Central Record Office, NWFP.* Peshawar: Government Printing and Stationery, 1948.

Jaffri, Aftab Ra'is Ahmad. *Syed Ra'is Ahmad Jaffri, Shaksiat aur Fann.* Karachi: Rais Ahmad Jaffri Academy, 1970.

Jaffri, Javaz, ed. *Kulliyat-e Ustad Daman*. Lahore: Punjab Institute of Language, Art & Culture, 2018.

Jaffri, Rais Ahmad. *Shahabuddin Ghauri*. New Delhi: Kitabistan, n.d.

Jafri, Jawaz. *Kulliyat-e Ustad Daman*. Lahore: Punjab Institute of Language, Art & Culture, 2018.

Jalal, Ayesha. *The Sole Spokesman: Jinnah, the Muslim League, and the Demand for Pakistan*. Cambridge, UK: Cambridge University Press, 1994.

———. *The Pity of Partition: Manto's Life, Times, and Works Across the India-Pakistan Divide*. Princeton, NJ: Princeton University Press, 2013.

Jalalpuri, Ali Abbas. *Maqamat-e Waris Shah*. Lahore: Kitab Numa, 1972.

Jawed, Hasan, and Muhsin Zulfiqar. *Suraj pay Qumand: National Student Federation ki Kahani, karkunon aur waqi'at ki zubani*. 3 vols. Karachi: Sawera Publications, 2017–2021.

Jodidio, Philip, ed. *Lahore: A Framework for Urban Conservation*. Munich: Prestel Verlag, 2019.

Joshi, P.C., and Dhanwantri. *Bleeding Punjab Warns*. Bombay: New Age Printing Press, 1947.

Kashmiri, Soresh. *Pas-e Divar-e Zindan*. Lahore: Chattan Publishers, 1971.

Kashmiri, Tabbasum. *Nohay Takht Lahore kay: Aik Tavil Nazm*. Lahore: Misbah Sons Publisher, 1985.

Kerr, Ian J. "Bombay and Lahore. Colonial Railways and Colonial Cities: Some Urban Consequences of the Development and Operation of Railways in India, c. 1850–c.1947," *II Congreso de Historia Ferroviaria Aranjuez* (2002).

Khalid, Haroon. *Walking with Nanak*. New Delhi: Westland Books, 2016.

———. *Imagining Lahore*. Delhi: India Viking, 2018.

Khalid, M.B. *Qudratullah Shahab kay saath Ayvan-e Sadr mein Sola Saal*. Lahore: Ahmad Publications, 2009.

Khalid, Muhammad Mateen, ed. *Shaheedan-e Namoos-e Risalat*. Lahore: 'Ilm o Irfan Publishers, 2003.

Khalid, Saifullah. *Shahab Beynaqab*. Lahore: T&T Publishers, 2003.

Khan, Ahmad Yar. *Jinnat kay Darbar Mein*. Lahore: Maktaba-e Dastan, 2010.

Khan, Annie Ali. *Sita Under the Crescent Moon: A Woman's Search for Faith in Pakistan*. Mumbai: Simon & Schuster India, 2019.

Khan, Hakim Syed Wazir Ali. *Miratul Hind*. Quetta: Qureshi Publications, 1988.

Khan, Liaquat Ali. *Pakistan: The Heart of Asia*. Cambridge, MA: Harvard University Press, 1950.

Khan, Maryam Wasif. *Who Is a Muslim? Orientalism and Literary Populisms*. New York: Fordham University Press, 2021.

Khurradadhbih, Abu'l Qasim. *Kitab al-Masalik wa-l-Mamalik*. Edited by M.J. de Goeje. Leiden: E.J. Brill, 1967.

Khwaja, Aslam. *People's Movements in Pakistan*. Karachi: Kitab Publishers, 2016.

Kipling, John Lockwood. *Lahore as It Was: Travelogue, 1860*. Lahore: National College of Arts Publication, 2002.

Kuldip, R.K. *Waris Shah: 1730–1790*. Calcutta: Intertrade Publications, 1971.

Kumar, Santosh. *Lahore Nama*. New Delhi: Vibha Publications, 2002.

Kunjahi, Sharif, Sajjad Haider, and Muhammad Asif Khan. *Waris Shah: Zindagi aur Zamana*. Islamabad: Alhamd Publications, 1990.

Lahore Development Authority. *Integrated Master Plan for Lahore, 2021*. Lahore: National Engineering Services Pakistan, 2011.

Lahori, 'Abd al-Hamid. *The Badshah Namah*. Edited by Kabir al-Din Ahmad, 'Abd al-Rahim, and W. Nassau Lees. Calcutta: College Press, 1867.

Lahori, Mufti Khairuddin, and Mufti 'Aliuddin. *'Ibratnama*. 2 vols. Lahore: Punjabi Adabi Academy, 1961.

Lakhnavi, Syed Agha Mehdi. *Shahzadi Zebun-Nissa*. Karachi: Jamiat Khuddam-e 'Uza, 1977.

Lal, Chaman. "Revolutionary Legacy of Bhagat Singh," *Economic and Political Weekly* 42, no. 37 (2007): 3712–18.

Lapidus, Ira. *Muslim Cities in the Later Middle Ages*. Cambridge: Cambridge University Press, 1984.

Latif, Syed Muhammad. *Lahore: Its History, Architectural Remains and Antiquities*. Lahore: New Imperial Press, 1892.

———. *Tarikh-e Panjab ma' Halat-e Shahr Lahore*. Lahore: Sang-e Meel Publications, 1982.

———. *History of the Panjab from Remotest Antiquity to the Present Times*. Calcutta: Calcutta Central Press, 1891.

Lawrence, T.E. *Seven Pillars of Wisdom: A Triumph*. Middlesex: Penguin Books, 1922.

Leaning, Jennifer, and Shubhangi Bhadada, eds. *The 1947 Partition of British India: Forced Migration and Its Reverberations*. New Delhi: Sage Publications India, 2022.

Leitner, G.W. *Sinin-e Islam: Arab ki Tarikh-e Ayam-e Jahalat say Ikhtatam-e Khanadan-e Abbasiya Tak*. Lahore: Indian Public Opinion, 1871.

———. *History of Indigenous Education in the Panjab: Since Annexation and in 1882*. Patiala: Languages Department Punjab, 1971.

Lévi-Strauss, Claude. *Tristes Tropiques*. Paris: Plon, 1955.

Majeed, Sheema, ed. *Culture and Identity: Selected English Writings of Faiz*. Karachi: Oxford University Press, 2005.

Malik, Abdul Rauf. *Surkh Siyasat*. Lahore: Jamhoori Publications, 2017.

———. *Syed Sajjad Zaheer: Marxi Danishvar aur Communist Rahnuma*. Lahore: Jamhori Publications, 2012.

Malik, Muhammad Latif. *Auliya-e Lahore*. Lahore: Sang-e Meel Publications, 1962.

Mallinson, James. *Messenger Poems by Kalidasa, Dhoyi & Rupa Gosvamin*. New York: New York University Press, 2006.

Manto, Sa'adat Hasan. *Sarak kay Kinaray*. Lahore: Naya Idarah, 1961.

———. *Khali Botalain, Khali Dabbay*. Lahore: Al Bayan, 1950.

———. *Siyah Hashiya*. Lahore: Maktaba Jadid, 1948.

Manucci, Niccolao. *Storia do Mogor or Mogul India, 1653–1708*. 4 vols. Translated by William Irvine. London: John Murray, 1907–1908.

Marçais, Georges. *Mèlanges d'histoire et d'archèologie de l'occident musulman*. Alger: Impr. Officielle, 1957.

Marçais, William. "L'Islamisme et la vie urbaine," *L'Académie des Inscriptions et Belles-Lettres, Comptes Rendus* (January–March 1928): 86–100.

Marh, Bhupinder Singh. *Geomorphology of the Ravi River*. New Delhi: Inter-India Publications, 1986.

Masood, Mukhtar. *Aawaz-e Dost*. Lahore: Naqoosh Press, 1973.

Massanet, Jules. *Le Roi de Lahore: Opéra en 5 actes*. Paris: 2e série, 66e année, N° 19, 12 Mai 1877.

Massignon, Louis. "Les corps de métiers et la cite Islamique," *Revue Internationale de sociologie* 28 (1920): 473–87.

Mas'udi, Abu al-Hasan. *Muruj al-Dhahab wa-Ma'adin al-Jawahar*. 2 vols. Beirut: Daar al-Kutub al- 'Ilmiyya, 1985.

Matin, Mukhtar Ahmed. *Tarikh-e Jattan*. Rahim Yar Khan: Roznamah Shahadat, 1986.

Maududi, Syed Abul. *A'la. Jama'at-i Islami kay 29 Saal*. Lahore: Ja'amat-Islami Pakistan Publications, 1970.

Mehta, Ved. *Daddyji*. New York: W. W. Norton & Co., 1972.

Menon, Ritu. *India on Their Minds: 8 Women, 8 Ideas of India*. New Delhi: Women Unlimited, 2023.

Miéville, China. *The City & the City*. New York: Ballantine Books, 2009.

Mill, James. *The History of British India*. 2 vols. London: Baldwin, Cradock, & Joy, 1817.

Ministry of Education, Government of Pakistan. *Action Plan for Educational Development, 1983–88*. Islamabad: Pangraphics, Ltd. 1984.

———. *The Education Policy, 1972–1980*. Islamabad, 1972.

Mir, Farina. *The Social Space of Language: Vernacular Culture in British Colonial Punjab*. Berkeley: University of California Press, 2010.

Mittal, Gopal. *Lahore Ka Jo Zikr Kiya*. New Delhi: Maktaba Tehrik, 1971.

Moazzamuddin, Mohammad. *Ikramnama*. Delhi: Educational Publishing House, 2010.

Moffat, Chris. *India's Revolutionary Inheritance: Politics and the Promise of Bhagat Singh*. Cambridge: Cambridge University Press, 2019.

Morrison, Toni. "Racism and Fascism," *Journal of Negro Education* 64, no. 3 (Summer 1995): 384–85.

Mufti, Masood. *Lamhay: Mashriqi Pakistan kay Akhari Dinon ki dairy-1971*. Lahore: Naqoosh Press, 1978.

———. *Do Minar*. Karachi: Oxford University Press, 2020.

Mukammal Asli Kala Jadoo. Lahore: Hameed Book Depot, n.d.

Mumford, Louis. *The City in History: Its Origins, Its Transformations, and Its Prospects*. New York: Harcourt, Brace & World, 1961.

Munir, Munir Ahmed. *Mit-ta Huwa Lahore*. Lahore: Aatish Fishan, 2018.

Nagi, Anis. *Sa'adat Hasan Manto kay Muqdamat*. Lahore: Daniyal, 1999.

Nagi B.A. *Jinnat ka Beta*. Lahore: Ilm o Irfan Publishers, 2010.

Naim, C.M. *Urdu Crime Fiction, 1890–1950: An Informal History*. Hyderabad: Orient Blackswan, 2023.

Nanda, B.R., ed. *The Collected Works of Lala Lajpat Rai*. 4 vols. New Delhi: Manhar, 2004.

Naqvi, Syed Faizan Abbas, ed. *Qademi Lahore Guide, 1909*. Karachi: Fiction House, 2020.

National Archives of Pakistan. *Annual Report for the Year 1974*. Islamabad: Department of Archives, 1974.

Naz, S.M. *Lahorenama*. Lahore: Maqbool Academy, 1992.

Nevile, Pran. *Lahore: A Sentimental Journey.* Bombay: Allied Publishers Ltd., 1993.

———. *Lahore: A Sentimental Journey.* Lahore: Ilqa Publications, 2016.

Niazi, Zamir. *Hikayat-e Khunchakan.* Karachi: Fazli Sons, 1997.

Niazi, Zamir. *The Press in Chains.* Karachi: Royal Book Company, 1986.

Noe, Samuel V. "Old Lahore and Old Delhi: Variations on a Mughal Theme," *Ekistics* 49, no. 295 (July/August 1982): 306–19.

Nomani, Shibli. *Sawaneh Zaib-Un-Nisa Begam.* Lucknow: Darul Nazar Press, n.d.

Office of the Director of Public Instruction. *Report on Native Papers Published in the Bombay Presidency: For the Week Ending 20th May 1905.* Poona: Government Central Press, 1905.

Ogden, Johanna. "Ghadar, Historical Silences, and Notions of Belonging: Early 1900s Punjabis of the Columbia River," *Oregon Historical Quarterly* 113, no. 2 (Summer 2012): 164–97.

Onians, Isabelle. *What Ten Young Men Did by Dandin.* New York: New York University Press, 2005.

Pakistan Historical Records and Archives Commission. *Proceedings of the Meetings of the Second Session Held at Peshawar, February 1954.* Karachi: Government of Pakistan Press, 1957.

———. *Proceedings of the Meetings of the Third Session Held at Karachi, 1955.* Karachi: Government of Pakistan Press, 1958.

———. *Proceedings of the Meetings of the Fourth Session Held at Karachi, 1959.* Karachi: Government of Pakistan Press, 1959.

———. *Proceedings of the Meetings of the Fifth Session Held at Dacca, 1970.* Karachi: Government of Pakistan Press, 1970.

Paremi, Brij. *Sa'adat Hasan Manto: Hayat aur Karname.* Srinagar: Mirza Publications, 1982.

Pasha, Kyla, and Salima Hashmi, eds. *Two Loves: Faiz's Letters from Jail.* Lahore: Sang-e Meel Publishers, 2011.

Patel, Alka. *Iran to India: The Shansabanis of Afghanistan, c. 1145–1190 CE.* Edinburgh: Edinburgh University Press, 2022.

Patras, Ayra Indrias. *Swept Aside: A Story of Christian Sweepers in Lahore.* Lahore: Folio Books, 2023.

Perec, Georges. *An Attempt at Exhausting a Place in Paris.* Translated by Marc Lowenthal. Cambridge, MA: Wakefield Press, 2010.

Pervaiz, Syed. *Habib Jalib: Ghar ki Gawahi.* Karachi: Maktaba Daniyal, 1994.

Pinault, David. *Notes from the Fortune-Telling Parrot: Islam and the Struggle for Religious Pluralism in Pakistan*. London: Equinox Publishing Ltd., 2008.

Pirenne, Henri. *Medieval Cities: Their Origins and the Revival of Trade*. Princeton, NJ: Princeton University Press, 1925.

Purchas, Samuel. *Hakluyts Posthumous or Purchas His Pilgrimes*. Glasgow: James MacLehose & Sons, 1905.

Puri, Harish K. "Revolutionary Organization: A Study of the Ghadar Movement," *Social Scientist* 9, no. 2/3 (1980): 53–66.

Qadeer, Muhammad A. *Lahore: Urban Development in the Third World*. Lahore: Vanguard Books, Ltd. 1983.

———. *Lahore in the 21st Century: The Functioning and Development of a Megacity in the Global South*. Oxon: Routledge, 2023.

Qasmi, Ali Usman. *The Ahmadis and the Politics of Religious Exclusion in Pakistan*. London: Anthem Press, 2014.

Qudsiya, Banu. *Mard-e Abraisham*. Lahore: Sang-e Meel Publications, 2019.

Qureshi, Ishtiaq Hussain. *Afkar o Azkar: Daktar Ishtiaq Husain Quraishi ke muntakhab maqalat, khutbat, mushafahat, aur nashri taqarir ka majmu'ah*. Karachi: Muqtadirah Qaumi Zuban, 1981.

———. *The Pakistani Way of Life*. London: William Heinemann, 1956.

———. *Education in Pakistan: An Inquiry into Objectives and Achievements*. Karachi: Ma'aref Ltd., 1975.

———. *Aspects of the History, Culture and Religions of Pakistan*. Bangkok: SEATO Publications, 1961.

———. *Akbar: The Architect of the Mughal Empire*. Karachi: Ma'arif Ltd., 1978.

———. *The Administration of the Sultanate of Delhi*. Karachi: Pakistan Historical Society, 1958.

Qureshi, Mushtaq Muhammad. "Ki Muhammad se wafa tu nay," *Daily Jang*, January 1, 2011.

Rahi, Aslam. *Nishapur ka Shaheen: Aik Azeem Tarikhi Navil*. Lahore: Maktaba al Quresh, 1980.

Rahman, 'Atiq. *Incyclopedia Tar'ikh-e Lahore*. Lahore: Nazir Sons Publishers, 2003.

Rahman, Syed Mueenul, ed. *Muhammad Naqoosh*. Multan: Karavan-e Adab, 1983.

Raja, Tasadduq Husain. *Naseem Hijazi, aik Muta'illah*. Lahore: Qaumi Kutab Khana, 1987.

Rasheed, Mamoonur, Sajid Rashid Ahmad, and Rashid Saleem. "Building a Geodatabase for Parcel and Cadaster Mapping and Add-Ins Development: A Case Study for Defense Housing Authority (DHA), Lahore, Pakistan," *Journal of Geographic Information System* 7 (2015): 588–97.

Rehman, Hafizur, ed. *Resistance Literature*. Islamabad: Pakistan Academy of Letters, 1995.

Report of the Commission on National Education, Government of Pakistan, Ministry of Education, January-August 1959. Karachi: Manager of Publications, 1960.

Riaz, Fahmida. *Four Walls and a Black Veil*. Karachi: Oxford University Press, 2004.

Riaz, Riaz Ahmad. *Ibn Insha: Ahval o Asar*. Karachi: Anjuman Taraqqi Urdu, 1988.

Ross, E. Denison. *Tarikh Fakhruddin Mubarakshah Marvar-rudi*. London: Royal Asiatic Society, 1927.

Sabri, Maqsood Ahmad. *Tazkira Aulia-e Pothohar*. Rawalpindi: Hashmi Publishers, 2010.

Sadiqian, Muhindhakt, and Abu Talib Mir 'Abidini, eds. *Divan Zebun-Nissa Mukhfi*. Tehran: Amir Kabir, 2002.

Saeed, Ahmad. *Lahore aik Shahr-e Be-Misaal*. 2 vols. Lahore: Punjab University Press, 2022.

Saeed, Muhammad. *Lahore: A Memoir*. Lahore: Vanguard Publications, 1989.

Salim, Ahmad, ed. *Lahore: 1947*. Lahore: Sang-e Meel Publications, 2003.

Salman, Mas'ud Sa'ad. *Divan-e Mas'ud Sa'ad Salman*. Tehran: Intisharat-i Gulshani, 1983.

Saqi, Jam. *Baatain Hamari Yaad Rahain Gi!* Karachi: Fiction House, 2018.

Sateel, Jeet Singh. *Kalam-e Nanak*. Lahore: Punjab Heritage Foundation, 2001.

Shackle, Christopher. "Punjabi in Lahore," *Modern Asian Studies* 4, no. 3 (1970): 239–67.

Shahab, Qudrutullah. *Shahabnama*. Lahore: Sang-e Meel Publications, 1987.

Shahzadi, Warda. *Qissa Nashiran-e Lahore Ka*. Lahore: Nigarishat Publishers, 2020.

Shaikh, Asad Salim. *Dulle di bar: Pindi Bhatiyan aur gird o navah ki Tarikh*. Lahore: Izharsons, 1999.

Shaikh, Maqsood. *Muhammad bin Qasim: Azeem Muslim Fatih*. Lahore: Ilm o Irfan Publishers, 2010.

Sharar, Abdul Halim. *Asrar-e Darbar-e Harampur*. Lahore: Alhamra Publications, 2000.

Sharar, 'Abdulḥalīm. *Malik al-'Azīz Virginā*. Āgrah: Bālkishn Mashīn Pres, 1940.

Sharma, Ramesh Chandra, and Amit Mukerji. "A Contemporary Account of Lahore in the Early Seventeenth Century," *Proceedings of the Indian History Congress* 53 (1992): 205–10.

Sharma, Sunil. *Persian Poetry at the Indian Frontier: Mas'ud Sa'ad Salman of Lahore*. Delhi: Permanent Black, 2000.

———. "Forbidden Love, Persianate Style: Re-reading Tales of Iranian Poets and Mughal Patrons," *Iranian Studies* 42, no. 5 (December 2009): 765–79.

Sheikh, Abdul Majid. *The Probable Origins of Lahore and Other Narrations*. Lahore: Sang-e Meel Publications, 2019.

Sheikh, Atique Zafar. "Development of Archival Institutions in Pakistan," *Pakistan Archives* 8, no. 1–2 (January–December 1991).

Shikoh, Dara. *Sakinatul Auliya*. Edited by Tara Chand and Syed Muhammad Reza Jalali Nai'ni. Delhi: Ilmi Publishers, 1969.

Siddiqi, Hamid Afaq. *Lahori's Padshahnamah (1592–1638)*. 2 vols. Delhi: Idarah-e Adabiyat-e Delhi, 2010.

Siddiqi, Sadiq Husain. *Sultan Muhammad Gauri: Aik Islami Tarikhi Navil*. Lahore: Maktaba al Quresh, 1991.

———. *Muhammad bin Qasim, aik dilkash Tarikhi dastan*. Lahore: Maktaba al Quresh, 1997.

Siddiqi, Shahid. *Potohar: Khita-e Dilruba*. Jhelum: Book Corner, 2022.

Siddiqui, Iqtidar Husain. "The Thirteenth and Fourteenth Century Farmans Concerning the Conduct of the Governors in the Sultanate of Delhi," *Proceedings of the Indian History Congress* 49 (1988): 211–19.

Siddiqui, Salma. *Evacuee Cinema: Bombay and Lahore in Partition Transit (1940–1960)*. New Delhi: Cambridge University Press, 2022.

Sidhwa, Bapsi, ed. *City of Sin and Splendour: Writings on Lahore*. New Delhi: Penguin India, 2005.

Simmel, Georg. "The Metropolis and Mental Life." In *On Individuality and Social Forms*, edited by Donald N. Levine. Chicago: University of Chicago Press, 1971.

Sindhu, Liaqat Ali. *Lahore ki Khoj*. Lahore: Takmil Printing Press, 2019.

Singh, Bawa Satinder, ed. *The Letters of the First Viscount Hardinge of La-hore to Lady Hardinge and Sir Walter and Lady James, 1844–1847*. London: Butler and Tanner, Ltd., 1986.

Singh, Ganda. *Private Correspondence Relating to the Anglo-Sikh Wars*. Patiala: Sikh History Society, 1955.

———. *Seditious Literature in the Panjab*. Patiala: Punjabi University Publication Bureau, 1988.

Singh, Munshi Ghulab. *Sair-e Lahore*. Karachi: Fiction House, 2020.

Singh, Pashura. "Speaking Truth to Power: Exploring Guru Nanak's Bābar-vānī in Light of the *Baburnama*," *Religions* 11, no. 328 (2020): 1–19.

Singh, Surinder. "Darul Sultanat Lahore: The Socio-Cultural Profile of an Urban Centre (1550–1700)," *Proceedings of the Indian History Congress* 54 (1993): 287–96.

Sohadravi, Kamran Azam. *Awan Qabail*. Karachi: Fiction House, 2020.

Sohal, Sukhdev Singh. "Pangs of Partition: Lahore in 1947," *Proceedings of the Indian History Congress* 63 (2003): 1066–73.

Sökefeld, Martin, and Christopher Moss. "Teaching the Values of Nation and Islam in Pakistani Textbooks," *Internationale Schulbuchforschung* 18, no. 3 (1996): 289–306.

Strothmann, Linus. *Managing Piety, the Shrine of Data Ganj Bakhsh*. Karachi: Oxford University Press, 2016.

Suleri, Sara. *Meatless Days*. Chicago: University of Chicago Press, 1989.

Suvorova, Anna. *Lahore: Topophilia of Space and Place*. Karachi: Oxford University Press, 2011.

Taj, Syed Imtiaz Ali. *Anarkali*. Lahore: Sang-e Meel Publications, 2012.

Talbot, Ian. "A Tale of Two Cities: The Aftermath of Partition for Lahore and Amritsar, 1947–1957," *Modern Asian Studies* 41, no. 1 (2007): 151–85.

Talbot, Ian, and Tahir Kamran. *Colonial Lahore: A History of the City and Beyond*. Karachi: Oxford University Press, 2017.

Tasavur, Tasleem Ahmad, ed. *Shahabnamay: Qudratullah Shahab kay Khattut*. Lahore: Suraj Publishing Bureau, 1996.

Taunsvi, Fikr. *Chhatta Dariya*. Lahore: Naia Idarah, 1948.

Tavernier, Jean-Baptiste. *Les Six Voyages de Jean-Baptiste Tavernier ecuyer Baron D'Aubonne qu'il a fait En Turquie, en Perse, et aux Indes*. Paris: Chez au Palais, 1676.

Thesiger, Wilfred. *Arabian Sands*. London: Longmans, 1959.

Trouillot, Michel-Rolph. "The Odd and the Ordinary: Haiti, the Caribbean and the World," *Vibrant: Virtual Brazilian Anthropology* 17 (2020).

Tufail, Muhammad, ed. *Lahore Number*, no. 92 (February 1962).

Ullah, Inayat. *Chardiwari ki Duniya*. Lahore: 'Ilm o Irfan Publishers, 2008.

Umar, Mumtaz. *Naseem Hijazi ki Tarikhi Navil Nagari ka Tahqiqi aur Tanqidi Tajzia*. Karachi: Anjuman Taraqqi-e Urdu, 2004.

Vatuk, Ved Prakash. *Ghadr Party's Lahore Conspiracy Case 1915 Judgment*. Meerut: Archana Publications, 2006.

Waheed, Sarah Fatima. *Hidden Histories of Pakistan: Censorship, Literature, and Secular Nationalism in Late Colonial India*. Cambridge: Cambridge University Press, 2021.

Walser, Robert. *Berlin Stories*. Translated by Susan Bernofsky. New York: New York Books Classics, 2012.

Walzer, Richard, ed. *Al-Farabi on the Perfect State*. Oxford: Clarendon Press, 1985.

Waraich, Malwinderjit Singh, and Harish Jain. *First Lahore Conspiracy Case: Mercy Petition*. Ludhiana: Unistar Books, 2010.

———. *Ghadr Movement Original Documents-Judgements*. Ludhiana: Unistar Books, 2012.

Weber, Max. *The City*. Translated and edited by Don Martindale and Gertrud Neuwirth. New York: The Free Press, 1958.

Wheeler, Mortimer. *My Archaeological Mission to India and Pakistan*. London: Thames and Hudson, 1976.

Wilson, Horace Hayman, ed. *Travels in the Himalayan Provinces of Hindustan and the Panjab; in Ladakh and Kashmir; in Peshawar, Kabul, Kunduz, and Bokhara by William Moorcroft and George Trebeck, from 1819–1825*. London: Murray, 1841.

Yorish, Qamar. *Shahi Qila se Jail Tak*. Lahore: Dabistan Publishers, 1987.

Zeb'un Nisa', Begum. *Divan-e Mukhfi*. Lahore: Matbua Islamiya, 1912.

Zuberi, Hilal Ahmad. *Afkar o Azkar: Daktar Ishtiaq Husain Qureshi*. Karachi: Muqtadra Qaumi Zuban, 1981.

Index

Aag ka Darya 164–165
Abbasid caliphate 132, 194, 214
Abbott, James 212
Abdali, Ahmad Shah 61
Abu-Lughod, Janet 17
Accra 8
Adi Sri Guru Granth Sahibji
  (Nanak) 49–50
Agra 39, 41, 66, 81, 272
Agra: Historical and Descriptive 81
Ahmad, Mirza Ghulam 231,
  237–238
Ahmad, Ashfaq 224, 227, 239
Ahmadiyya movement 227, 231,
  237–240, 263
Ahmed, Giasuddin 144
Ahmed, Israr 264–265
Aibak, Qutbuddin 117, 167,
  176–180, 183, 192
Aitchison, Charles 129
Aitchison College 129
Jalaluddin Akbar (emperor)
  29–32, 41, 59, 67, 71, 75,
  80–81, 116, 132, 149, 306,
  322
Alam Ara (1931) 87
Alfalah Theater 296

Ali, Mubarak 120, 158, 161
Aligarh University 141, 171, 173
All India Muslim League 124,
  147
All India Muslim Students
  Federation 193
All India Radio 253, 255
All Pakistan History Conference
  143
All Pakistan Women's Associa-
  tion 262
Amritsar 8, 45, 91–92, 97, 109,
  231, 237, 244, 249–250,
  255, 258
Anand, Som 88–89, 166
anglophone 17, 161
Anjuman-e Himayat-e Islam 207
Anjuman-e Nao Musalmanaan-e
  Sind 207
Anjuman-e Punjab 129–130
Anarkali 28–33, 67
Anarkali (film) 32
Anarkali (play) 32
Anarkali bazaar 17, 27–28,
  32–33, 74, 79, 97, 99–100,
  153, 156, 176–177, 180, 192,
  231, 276

Anarkali's Tomb (Punjab Archives) 27–28, 30–32, 56, 118, 122, 246

anti-colonial 87, 143, 173, 193–194, 198, 207, 221, 243, 246

Anwar, Ajaz 93–94

Arabic 7, 54, 65, 81, 118, 129–130, 132, 137–140, 143, 146, 149, 188, 197, 199, 202, 207, 213–214, 279, 311

Ara'in community 104–105, 196, 211–216

Arc de Triomphe 113

archives 5–7, 12, 14, 27–29, 115, 118, 122–126, 128, 133, 140, 154, 156, 194, 213, 215, 257, 322

Arya Samaj 193, 207–208, 211, 231–232, 243

Augoyard, Jean-François 271

Alamgir Aurangzeb 44, 53, 55, 59, 80, 94, 173, 201–202, 322

Awami League 144, 187

Ayaz, Malik 21–23, 26, 167

Tomb of Malik Ayaz 21, 25–26

Ayub Khan 69, 124, 143–144, 154, 170, 176–178, 196, 224, 228, 239, 249–250, 262, 265

Azad, Muhammad Hussain 130, 137–139,

Aziz, Khurshid Kamal 120, 124–125, 152–156, 160

Baba Farid (Fariduddin Ganjsha-kar) 40, 49–50, 131, 313

Zahiruddin Babur 47–48, 58, 173, 280

Baburvani verses 47–48

Badr Se Batapur Tak 186

Badshahi Mosque 1, 17, 51, 77, 79, 171, 278, 281

Badshahnama (Shah Jahan) 59–60

Baghbanpura 74–75, 139

Bagh-e Anarkali (the Pomegran-ate Gardens) 41

Bagh-e Jinnah 61

Baihaqi 66–67

Baksh, Miyan Muhammad 309–310

Baloch, Nabi Bakhsh 132

Baluchi 139, 143, 209

Baluchistan 124, 138, 157, 239

Bangla (language) 118, 131, 136, 138–139, 143, 145, 151, 154, 174, 209, 262–263

Bangladesh (previously East Pakistan) 69, 88, 116, 120, 122, 124–125, 138, 144–145, 153, 167, 174, 179, 188, 209, 239, 264

Bangladesh independence 144, 153, 188

Bengali (culture, identity) 116, 145, 188, 285–286, 288

Baqir, Muhammad 103–105, 107

Basant (Kite Flying) festival 80, 85, 220

Basantnagar 75

Beas 50, 313

Begumpura 87

Benjamin, Walter 271
beri tree 42
Bernier, François 28, 67
Bhagatpura 139
Bhagwan Das 136, 152
Bharata 94, 164
Bhattachariya, Santosh Chandra
   144
Bhoray Shah 75
Bhutto, Benazir 39, 266
Bhutto, Zulfiqar Ali 39, 153, 215,
   233, 239–240, 264, 266,
   300, 304, 316
Bibi Pak Daman 56, 286–287
Bibi Taj 42
Bikramjit (ruler) 81
blasphemy 218–219, 233–234,
   292
"blasphemy laws" (Pakistan) 219,
   233–234
Blount, Henry 271
Bogra, Muhammad Ali 196
Bombay (now Mumbai) 8, 32,
   148, 194, 207, 255
Boundary Commission 91
Bowen, George 231
Bradlaugh Hall 244–245
Bulleh Shah 140, 310
Bureaucrats
   Chishti, Nur Ahmad 71–76
   Ikram, S.M. 147–151
   Kanhaiya Lal Hindi 77–83
   Shahab, Qudratullah 223–228
   Syed Muhammad Latif
      77–83
Burton, Richard F. 271

Cantonment (neighborhood) 2,
   45, 85, 95, 109, 111–112,
   127, 134, 190, 241, 274, 290,
   294, 309
Capitalism 152, 271, 298, 300,
   328
Central Jail (Lahore) 241, 248
Chachnama 207, 209
Chadar aur Char Divari (Veil and
   Four Walls) 264–265, 304
Chaitanya 49, 313
Lal Chand Falak 243
Charsada 116
Chattan 237–240
Chatterjee, Partha 115, 167
Chauburji (Four Pillars) 52–57,
   318
Chaudhry, Ali Asghar 214–216
Chauhan, Prithviraj 173, 179
Chenab 50, 311, 313,
Chishti, Nur Ahmad 31, 73–76,
   138, 166, 269–271, 299
Choudhry, Faustin Elmer "F.E."
   101
Chughtai, Ismat 253
Civil and Military Gazette 101,
   105
Civil Secretariat 28, 122, 246,
Clark, Henry Martyn 231
The Coffee House of Lahore: A
   Memoir 1942–57 152, 155
colonial 5, 13, 17–18, 28–29, 31,
   54, 56, 58, 61, 68–73, 77–78,
   80–82, 85, 91, 104–105,
   115–116, 118–119, 122–123,
   125, 127, 129, 131, 133,

colonial (cont.)
136–139, 143, 148–149,
156–158, 167, 176, 192, 195,
199–201, 204, 208–209,
212–213, 215, 231–232,
241–245, 262, 271, 273, 292,
294, 303, 309, 319, 322
colonization 17–18, 67, 70,
129–130, 139, 143, 167, 199,
200–202, 209, 212, 273
Communism 85, 87, 99, 112, 145,
154–155, 246, 248–249, 263,
322
Cooperative Model Town Society
85, 87, 89, 99, 109, 111,
127, 166
Coryat, Thomas 67, 271–272

da Cruz, Gaspar 271
Dadu Dayal 49, 313
Raja Dahir 197–198, 205,
209
Daily Inqilab 229
Daily Jang 218, 224, 233–234,
261
Daily Khilafat 194
Daman, Ustad 302–303
Dandin 14
Dani, A.H. 132
Dara Shikoh (Mughal heir-
apparent) 31, 38, 41, 43–45,
54–55
Darul Uloom Nadwatul Ulama
193
Dasakumaracarita (What Ten
Young Men Did) 14

Data Darbar (or Data Sahib)
34–35, 39–40, 50, 105, 282,
302
Data Ganj Baksh (see also:
al-Hajweri, 'Ali al-Jalabi
al-Ghaznavi) 34–35, 39, 105,
131
Daudpota, U.M. 209
D.A.V College 100, 243
Dawn 224, 261
de Certeau, Michel 271
decolonization 4
Lal Ded 49, 313
de Vaca, Cabeza 271
Defence Housing Authority
(DHA) 62, 111–113, 125,
275–276, 292–293, 306, 317
Defence of India Act 237, 244
Delhi 8, 15, 39, 47–48, 50,
66–67, 71–72, 109, 122–124,
138, 141–143, 163, 173,
178–179, 183, 193, 203,
207–208, 245, 255
Devanagari 107, 134, 139–140,
151
Dhaka (Dacca, pre-1982) 49, 124,
131–132, 138–139, 144, 150,
187, 207, 262
Dil Gudaz 203
Dina Nath Temple 79, 113
Divan-e Mukhfi 54–55
Dnyaneshwar 49, 313
Dogra, Hira Singh 86
Dow, Alexander 200
dowry 266–267
Dowson, John 104

dreams 6, 8, 9, 36, 38, 41, 43, 177, 181, 183, 225, 233, 251, 300, 304

Dulla Bhatti 306

Dyal Singh Trust Library (previously Dyal Singh Public Library) 122, 221–222

East India Company (EIC) 29, 67–68, 73, 76, 104, 121–122, 129, 158, 173, 199–200, 207, 272–273

Elliot, Henry M. 104

Lord Ellenborough 199–200

Embree, Ainslie T. 151

Esakhelvi, Attaullah 313

Evacuee Trust Property Board 111

Faisalabad 319

Faiz Ahmed Faiz 248–253, 259

Faletti's 31, 152, 296

al-Farabi 65

Al-Faruq 202

Fazl, Abu'l (historian) 67, 306

feminism 220, 262–263

Ferozsons 152, 192, 221

Fikr Taunsvi 100

Finch, William 30–31, 67

Firishta (historian) 180, 200–201

Firuz Shah Tughluq 194, 201

Five Thousand Years of Pakistan: An Archaeological Outline 115

Forman Christian College (FC College) 129, 153, 221, 241, 274

Fughan-e Dilli (1863) 15

Gandapur, Sardar Sher Muhammad Khan 213

Garhi Shahu 75, 283, 285

Gauhar, M. Ramzan 180

Gauri I (missile) 182

Gauri, Shahabuddin 117, 172–173, 180–182, 192, 194–195, 201, 210, 212–213

Gawalmandi 85, 92, 243

Geddes, Patrick 4

Ghalib (poet) 147, 148

Ghauri, Iftikhar Ahmad 132

ghazal 25, 54, 71

ghazi 168, 195, 229–230, 235

Ghiyasuddin 179

Ghulam Jilani 61–62

Gibbon, Edward 68, 200–201

Gilani, Abdul Qadir 43

Gol Bagh 246, 278

Government College 129, 147, 153, 224, 245–246, 297

Grand Trunk Road 1, 109, 181

Griswold, Hervey DeWitt 231

Gujranwala 319

Gulberg 161, 242

Gulberg Scheme 110

Gurdwara, Sunehri 94

Gurdwaras 79, 94, 140, 174

Gurmukhi 107, 131, 138–140, 246

Guzishta Lucknow 203

Hadiara drain 305, 307

Hafiz (poet) 147, 310

hajj 228, 300

Hajjaj bin Yusuf 194, 195

al-Hajweri, ʿAli al-Jalabi al-
Ghaznavi 35–39, 44
Hali, Altaf Hussain 15, 202
Hameed, A. (Abdul) 91–94,
224, 276
Hamid Gul, General 196
Hamza, Amir 151
Hanuman 94, 285
Haq, Zia ul 39, 111, 153–154,
157, 159, 188, 198, 205,
215–216, 220, 224, 227, 233,
240, 262, 264–266, 300,
303–304
Harappa 115–116
Harbanspura 139
Lala Har Dayal 243
hartal 244
Hashmi, Farhat 266, 297, 301
Herder, Johann Gottfried 68
"Heritage Walks" 275, 282
"Heroes of Islam" (poster) 206
Heroes of Islam 161, 168, 183,
185–186, 193, 199, 201,
205–206, 210, 212
Aibak, Qutbuddin 176–183
Araʾin community 211–216
Gauri, Shahabuddin
176–183
ʿIlm Din 229–235
Mahmud Ghaznavi, Sultan
184–189, 199–204
Qasim, Muhammad bin
184–189, 190–198, 199–204,
205–210
Hijazi, Nasim 191, 193, 195–199,
204, 225

Hikayat (magazine) 184–185, 191,
236, 240
al-Hilal (magazine) 195
Hindu 13, 30, 44, 48, 68, 72–83,
87, 88–107, 113, 116,
118–120, 130, 132–134,
136–137, 142, 145, 150,
155–159, 165–166, 168,
172–174, 177, 179, 186–187,
193, 197, 199–201, 205,
207–208, 211–212, 225–227,
229, 231–232, 244, 246,
254–255, 259, 286–288, 295,
302, 306
Hindu Mahasabha (political
party) 174, 207–208
Hinduism 44, 133, 154–155, 174,
197, 205, 208, 231, 264, 288
Hindustan 15, 24–25, 28, 30, 37,
47–49, 66–67, 71, 75, 85, 87,
131–132, 136, 149, 163–167,
172, 174, 178–179, 183, 195,
197, 200, 202–203, 208, 237,
243, 245, 255
Hindustan Socialist Republican
Association 245
Historians
Ali, Mubarak 157–161
Aziz, Khurshid Kamal
152–156
Baqir, Muhammad 103–107
Ikram, S.M 120, 132, 147–153
Qureshi, Ishtiaq Husain
141–146
The History of India, as Told by Its
Own Historians 104

History of the Moorish Empire in Europe 201–202

Hitti, Philip K. 131–132

Hotchand, Seth Naomul 157–158

Hourani, Albert 17

Al-Huda Institute 297

Hudood Ordinances 264

Hunterwali (1935) 87

Hussain, Madho Lal 46, 74–76, 79–80, 105 158, 270

Hussain, Muhammad Bashir 132

Shah Hussain (see also Hussain, Madho Lal) 46, 74, 140, 306

Hyder, Qurratulain 163–169

Hyderabad 8

Hyderabad (Sind) 159, 163, 207, 248–249, 287

Ibratnama 21

Icchra 43, 75, 87, 99

The Ideology of Pakistan and Its Implementation 154

Ikram, S.M. (aka Shaikh Muhammad Ikram) 120, 132, 147–153

'Ilm Din 229–232

Ilmi Kitab Khana (publisher) 215

Inayatullah 184–189

independence 76, 101, 119, 122, 133, 138, 144, 147, 153, 155, 156, 188, 234, 243–245

    Bangladesh independence 144, 153, 188

India Office Library 121–122

Indian Civil Services (ICS) 147, 224

Indo-Pak war of 1965 213, 263–264

Indus Basin Treaty 280

Integrated Master Plan for Lahore (2004) 112–113

Iqbal, Javed, Justice 154

Iqbal, Muhammad 21, 25–26, 118, 147, 153–154, 157, 194, 218, 229, 233–234, 237, 299

Islam 15, 17, 25, 35, 44, 65, 75, 93, 100, 116–118, 125, 130–133, 143, 145, 146, 149–151, 153–155, 165, 168, 171, 174, 180, 185–186, 188, 192–193, 195–198, 201–203, 205–209, 216, 219–222, 231, 233–234, 236–238, 240, 262–264, 266, 285, 300, 303, 318

Islamabad 125, 181, 319

Islamia College 129, 196

Istiqlal (journal) 227

Jaffar, S.M. 132

Nuruddin Jahangir (emperor) 29–32, 56, 59, 80, 131, 272

Jalandhar 25, 92

Jalandhari, Hafiz 107, 176

Jalandhari, Muhammad Akbar Ali 214

Jalib, Habib 265

Jallianwala Bagh Massacre 244

Jama'at-i Islami (Islamic Organization), or Jama'at, for short 188, 196, 208–209, 216, 220, 233, 238, 262–266

Jamia Millia Delhi 193
Janamsakhi 48
Jaswantlal, Nandlal 32
Jat-Pat Todak Mandal 211–212
Jauhar, Maulana Muhammad
  Ali 194
Javaid 253
Jenkins, Evan 91
Jhelum 50, 179, 181, 313
jihad (only ital. in first instance)
  37, 150, 198, 215, 263, 265
Jilani (née Jahangir), Asma
  220–221
Jinnah, Muhammad Ali (Quaid-
  e-Azam) 29, 125, 138–139,
  142, 152, 157, 172–173, 194,
  229, 232–233
joray pull (term for intersection)
  274
Joray Pull (neighborhood) 290
*Journal of the Pakistan Historical
  Society* 131
*Journal of the Punjab Historical
  Society* 130
journalists 85–87, 91–92, 99, 106,
  118, 123, 149, 154, 160, 168,
  193–197, 208, 219, 237, 255,
  262, 300
Juzjani (historian) 183

K. Asif 32
Ka'aba 38, 221
Kabir 49, 313
Kabir, M. 132
Kalichbeg, Mirza 209
Kalidasa (poet) 14

Mirza Kamran 42, 58–59, 280
Kamran's *baradari* (pavilion) 42,
  58–59, 280, 321
Kanhaiya Lal 21, 31, 47, 77–78,
  80
Karachi 124, 131, 139, 142–143,
  158, 196, 213, 215, 224, 262,
  287, 319
Kardar, A.H. 175
Kartarpur 49
Kashf al-Mahjub (Rendering of
  the Veil), *Kashf*, for short
  35–36, 38–39, 44, 297
Kashmiri, Shorish 186, 237–240,
  259
Kashmiri, Tabassum 7, 303, 307
Kashmiri, Zaheer 155
katchi abadi (urban village) 110,
  112, 278, 292
kavya (lyric poem) 14, 16, 18
Khair, Abul 144
Khairi brothers 174
Khan Bahadur (title) 81
Khan Research Lab 181
Khan, Abdul Qadir, Dr. 180–
  182, 196, 240
Khan, Abu'l Hasan Asif 59
Khan, Ayub 69, 124, 143, 154,
  170, 176–177, 196, 224, 228,
  239, 249–250, 262, 265
Khan, Begum Ran'a Liaquat Ali
  262
Khan, Liaquat Ali 141, 248–249
Khan, Mir Naimat 270
Khan, Sa'adullah 20
Khan, Sikander Hayat 88

Khan, Syed Ahmad (1817–98) 72, 118, 202
Khan, Wazir 41, 190
Khan, Yahya 144, 239
Khan, Yar Muhammad 132
Khana, Qaumi Kutab 193, 196
Khatm-e Nabuwwat (Finality of Prophethood) 234, 237–240, 263
Khilafat Movement 193–194, 208
Khol Do (Manto) 106, 253, 258–259
Khusrau 67
Kinnaird College for Women 129
Kipling, John Lockwood 68, 86
Kipling, Rudyard 68–69, 86
Kohistan 196
Krishan Nagar 85, 292
Kumar, Santosh 94, 101

Lahore
    Aitchison College 129
    Alfalah Theater 296
    Anarkali bazaar 17, 27–28, 32–33, 74, 79, 97, 99–100, 153, 156, 176–177, 180, 192, 231, 276
    Anarkali's Tomb 27–28, 30–32, 56, 118, 122, 246
    Tomb of Malik Ayaz 21, 25–26
    Badshahi Mosque 1, 17, 51, 77, 79, 171, 278, 281
    Baghbanpura 74–75, 139
    Bagh-e Anarkali (the Pomegranate Gardens) 41

Bagh-e Jinnah (see also Lawrence Garden) 61
Basantnagar 75
Begumpura 87
Bhagatpura 139
Bibi Pak Daman 56, 286–287
Cantonment (neighborhood) 2, 45, 85, 95, 109, 111–112, 127, 134, 190, 241, 274, 290, 294, 309
Central Jail (Lahore) 241, 248
Chauburji 52–57, 318
Civil Secretariat 28, 122, 246
Cooperative Model Town Society 85, 87, 89, 99, 109, 111, 127, 166
Data Darbar (or Data Sahib) 34–35, 39–40, 50, 105, 282, 302
D.A.V College 100, 243
Defence Housing Authority (DHA) 62, 111–113, 125, 275–276, 292, 293, 306, 317
Dina Nath Temple 79, 113
Dyal Singh Trust Library (previously Dyal Singh Public Library) 122, 221–222
Faletti's 31, 152, 296
Ferozsons 152, 192, 221
Forman Christian College (FC College) 129, 153, 221, 241, 274
Garhi Shahu 75, 283, 285
Gawalmandi 85, 92, 243
Gol Bagh 246, 278

Lahore (cont.)

Government College 129, 147, 153, 224, 245–246, 297

Grand Trunk Road 1, 109, 181

Gulberg 161, 242

Gurdwara, Sunehri 94

Hadiara drain 305, 307

Harbanspura 139

Icchra 43, 75, 87, 99

Islamia College 129, 196

Jat-Pat Todak Mandal 211–212

Joray Pull (neighborhood) 290

Kamran's *baradari* (pavilion) 42, 58–59, 280, 321

Kinnaird College for Women 129

Krishan Nagar 85, 292

Lahore Railway Station 97, 182, 192, 194, 274

Lakshmi Chowk 84, 94

Landay Bazaar 306

Lawrence Garden (see also Bagh-e Jinnah) 61, 85

Lorang's 152

McLeod Road 98, 169, 192, 212

Medical School (Lahore) 78, 80

Melaram Building 85

Minar-e Pakistan 170–173, 192, 266

Minto Park 87, 171, 173–175

Miyan Mir's Shrine 42, 45–46, 292

Miyani Sahib graveyard 74, 229

Mozang 75, 87

Multan Road 56

National College of Arts 1

National University of Sciences & Technology (NUST) 283

Navakot 54

old city (Lahore) 1, 3, 11, 17, 20, 50, 74–75, 78–79, 85, 90, 93, 95–97, 99, 101, 109, 112–113, 139, 242, 270, 275–276, 278, 281–282, 303

Patiala Ground 169, 184, 236

Qila Gujjar Singh 75

Race Course Park (aka Jilani Park) 62

Raja Teja Singh Temple 79

Rajgarh 139

Guru Ram Das Asthan 79

Ramnagar 85, 139

Rang Mahal 20–21

Ravi 1, 12, 22–23, 50, 53–54, 58, 60, 63, 82, 99, 111, 164, 171, 242, 277–282, 292, 295, 305, 307, 313, 321–322

Sadr 98, 121, 134–135, 290

Sadr Bazaar 121, 290

Samadhi of Ranjit Singh 51, 77, 113

Sant Nagar 85

Shah Alami 78, 92

Shalimar Garden 53, 58–62, 67, 74–75, 105, 269

St. Mary Magdalene Church 205, 295

Tomb of Aibak 117, 176–178, 180, 183, 192

University of the Punjab (also Punjab University) 103, 129, 138, 243

Urdu Bazaar 169, 192, 206, 285, 302, 312, 322

Walled City (see also old city) 1, 11, 20, 74–75, 78–90, 96–97, 109, 112–113, 270, 275–276, 278, 281–282

Walton Grounds 305

Wazir Khan Mosque 79

Well of Raja Dina Nath 113

Yohanabad (Joseph Colony) 292, 295

Lahore Cantt Cooperative Housing Society 111

Lahore Chronicle 81

Lahore Conspiracy Case 244

Lahore Development Authority (LDA) 111, 241

Lahore ki Batain (Talking about Lahore) 88

Lahore ki Ghazal 71

Lahore ki Yadain (Memories of Lahore) 91–92, 276

Lahore Master Plan (1951) 242

Lahore Railway Station 97, 182, 192, 194, 274

Lahore Resolution 88, 171–174, 246

Lahore Urban Development and Traffic Study 111

Lahori, Abdul Hamid 59–60

Lahori, 'Aliuddin 21, 72

Lahori, Khairuddin 21, 72

Lahori, Mahmud 25

Lajpat Rai 243, 244–246

Lakshmi 94, 285

Lakshmi Chowk 84, 94

Landay Bazaar 306

Lapidus, Ira 17

Latif, Syed Abdul 31

Latif, Syed Muhammad 77, 81–83

Lawrence Garden (see also Bagh-e Jinnah) 61, 85

Lawrence, Henry 129

Lawrence, John 61, 105, 129

the Left (politics) 152, 220–221, 248–249, 302–303

Aziz, Khurshid Kamal 152–156

Ali, Mubarak 157–161

Faiz Ahmed Faiz 247–252

Manto, Sa'adat Hasan 253–260

Singh, Bhagat 241–246

Women's Action Forum 261–267

Leitner, Gottlieb W. 129–132, 137–138

Lévi-Strauss, Claude 27–28

Lorang's 152

Lucknow 8, 49, 193, 203–204, 207–208

Lyallpur 147, 231

Mabadi' ara'ahl al-Madinah al-Fadilah 65

Madhubala 32

Mahmud Ghaznavi, Sultan 21, 23, 25, 117, 167, 179, 184, 210, 212

Mai Baghi 75

Majlis Ahrar-ul Islam 237–238

Majma-ul Bahrain (Conjunction of the Two Seas) 44

Makhdoom Jahaniyan Jahangasht 49–50, 313
Maktab Islamabad 196
Mangla Dam 181
Manto, Sa'adat Hasan 106, 248, 253–260
Manucci, Niccolo 67
Marçais, George 17
Marçais, William 17
Mardana 48–49
Masood, Mukhtar 170, 180
Massignon, Louis 17
Master Plan for Greater Lahore (1966) 110, 113
    Lahore Master Plan (1951) 242
    Lahore Urban Development and Traffic Study (1980) 111
    Integrated Master Plan for Lahore (2004) 112–113
Matba'i Koh-i Noor Press 72–73, 269
Mau'dudi, Abu'l 'Ala (also Maulana Maududi) 196, 238, 262–265, 300
Mazdoor Kissan Party 249
McLeod Road 98, 169, 192, 212
McLeod, Donald 212
Mecca 44, 49, 194, 313,
Medical School (Lahore) 78, 80
Medina 49, 65, 194
Meghaduta (Cloud Messenger) 14, 16
Mela Chiraghan 74, 79, 140, 220, 269–270
Melaram Building 85
Memon community 213

Mercantile Press 148
Minar-e Pakistan 170–173, 192, 266
Ministry of Information and Broadcasting 148, 150, 224, 228
Lord Minto 173–174
Minto Park 87, 171, 173–175
Mirabai 49, 313
Mirchandani, Sita 163–164
Mirza, Iskander 224
Mittal, Gopal 100
Miyan Mir 31, 42, 45–46, 292
Miyan Mir's Shrine 42, 45–46, 292
Miyani Sahib (graveyard) 74, 229
Moenjodaro 17, 116
Mohani, Hasrat 233
Momigliano, Arnaldo 271
Montgomery, Robert 129, 212
Moorcroft, William 67, 271–273
Movement for Restoration of Democracy 159, 266
Mozang 75, 87
Mudabbir, Fakhrudin Mubarak-shah 25, 104, 140, 178
Mufti, Mumtaz 196, 224, 227
Mughal 8, 20, 22, 30–32, 38, 43, 47, 51, 53, 56, 58–60, 62, 67, 72, 75, 80, 106, 117, 122, 136, 150, 159, 165, 173, 201, 250, 272, 306, 318
    Jalaluddin Akbar 29–32, 41, 59, 67, 71, 75, 80–81, 116, 132, 149, 306, 322

Aurangzeb 44, 53, 55, 59, 80, 94, 173, 201, 202, 322

Zahiruddin Babur 47–48, 58, 173, 280

Dara Shikoh (Mughal heir-apparent) 31, 38, 41, 43–45, 54–55

Nuruddin Jahangir 29–32, 56, 59, 80, 131, 272

Nur Jahan 59

Shah Jahan 20, 41, 44, 53, 56, 59–60, 62, 75, 80, 270

Mirza Kamran 42, 58–59, 280

Zeb'un Nisa' 53–55, 59, 318

Mughal-e-Azam 32

Muhammad, Malik Ghulam 224

Multan 17, 25, 50, 81, 104, 109, 150, 178–179, 261–262, 319

Multan Road 56

Munshi Muhammad Azim 81

Munshi Syed 'Abbas 'Ali 15

Murat-Khan, Nasreddin 171

Musharraf, Pervez (General) 180

Muslim Family Laws Ordinance of 1961 262–263

Mirza Muzaffar Ahmad 239

Nadir Shah 15

Nadira Begum 31, 45

Nagari (see also Devanagari) 136, 145

Guru Nanak 47–51, 75, 310, 313

Naqoosh 105–106, 192, 240

Narain Das Bhagwan Das 152

Narain, Brij 100

nasta'liq 203

National College of Arts 1

National University of Sciences & Technology (NUST) 283

Naujawan Bharat Sabha 245

Navakot 54

Naval Kishor Press 193

Nawa-i Waqt 224, 261

Nevile, Pran 88

Nizami, Khwaja Hasan 208

Nizami, Tajuddin Hasan 178, 180

Nomani, Shibli 193, 199, 202, 204

Shah Noorani 40

Noreen, Asiya 234

North West Frontier Province (NWFP) 124, 138, 157

Nur Jahan 59

Nur Jehan (singer) 32

old city (Lahore) 1, 3, 11, 17, 20, 50, 74–75, 78–79, 85, 90, 93, 95–97, 99, 101, 109, 112–113, 139, 242, 270, 275–276, 278, 281–282, 303

On Heroes, Hero-Worship, & the Heroic in History 201

One Thousand and One Nights 93

Orme, Robert 68

Pahlavi, Muhammad Reza Shah 105

Pakistan Awami Tehreek 300

"Pakistan Defence Officers Housing Authority Order" 111

Pakistan Historical Records and Archives Commission 124
Pakistan Historical Society 131–132
Pakistan People's Party 233, 264
Pakistan Studies 119, 154, 205
Pakistan Women Lawyers' Association 262, 265
Panjab (place; also Punjab) 13, 28–29, 47, 50, 53, 61, 68, 72, 78, 81, 88, 91, 93, 96, 99, 101, 105, 109, 122, 124, 127–129, 136–138, 153, 156–157, 164, 179, 206–207, 209, 211–213, 217–218, 227, 231, 234–235, 243–244, 246, 250, 273, 296, 306, 308, 312–313, 319
Panjab Historical Society 127, 130
Panjab University Historical Society (previously Panjab Historical Society) 130–131
Panjabi (identity/culture; also Punjabi) 91, 155–156, 168, 206, 243–245, 302, 305–306, 309–310
Panjabi (language; also Punjabi) 7–8, 11, 50, 69, 94, 117–118, 132, 136–140, 143, 151, 154, 156, 160, 231, 269, 302–303, 305–306, 309–311
Parmanand, Bhai 243
Partition 8, 13–14, 18, 32, 51, 61, 69, 76, 85, 88, 91–92, 94–96, 99–102, 104–105, 107, 109–110, 117–118, 121, 123, 126, 131–132, 138–139, 142, 148, 150–151, 154, 161, 163–166, 168, 174–175, 187, 205, 209, 212, 220, 224, 227, 236–237, 246, 250–251, 253, 255–257, 259, 273, 280, 292, 299, 303, 313, 317, 319, 322
Pashto (language) 117, 139
Pataudi, Sher Ali Khan 182–183
Patiala Ground 169, 184, 236
pehlawan (wrestler) 24, 93, 106–107, 203, 276, 322
Perec, Georges 271
Persian 7, 14–15, 29, 31, 35, 47, 53–54, 65–66, 69, 73, 78, 81, 103, 122, 127, 129–130, 132, 136–140, 143, 145, 147, 149, 154, 174, 179, 188, 199, 202, 207, 213–214, 269, 272, 311, 322
Perso-Arabic 117, 136, 138, 145, 151, 154
Peshawar 17, 49, 124, 131, 150, 193, 215
Pind di Kuri (1935) 87
Piper "PA-28" Cherokee 1
Pirenne, Henri 17
poetry 16, 22–24, 46, 54, 137, 147, 248, 250, 299, 303, 306, 309, 311
Poets
Baksh, Miyan Muhammad 309–310
Bulleh Shah 140, 310
Daman, Ustad 302–303

Lal Ded 49, 313
Faiz Ahmed Faiz 248–253, 259
Fikr Taunsvi 100
Ghalib 147, 148
Hafiz 147, 310
Hali, Altaf Hussain 15, 202
Hussain, Madho Lal 46,
    74–76, 79–80, 105 158, 270
Iqbal, Muhammad 21, 25–26,
    118, 147, 153–154, 157, 194,
    218, 229, 233–234, 237, 299
Jalandhari, Hafiz 107, 176
Jalib, Habib 265
Kabir 49, 313
Kalidasa 14
Kashmiri, Tabassum 7, 303, 307
Mohani, Hasrat 233
Riaz, Fahmida 304
Sa'ad Salman, Mas'ud 15,
    23–25, 71, 140
Shagufta, Sara 305
Surdas 49, 313
Zeb'un Nisa', Begum 53–55,
    59, 318
Political Action
    Lahore Conspiracy 241–246
    Rawalpindi Conspiracy
        247–252
    San Francisco Conspiracy
        Case 244
    Women's Action Forum
        261–267
Postans, Thomas 200
postcolonial 4, 6, 8, 18–19, 39,
    115, 131–132, 158–159
Potohar Plateau 172, 181

Prakrit 127, 131–132
precolonial 68, 126
Print culture
    Chattan 236–240
    Hikayat 184–189
    Kohistan 196
    Naqoosh 103–107
Prithvi I (missile) 181–182
Progressive Writers' Movement
    249
Prophetic Pakistan 219, 228
Punjab Archives 27–29
Punjab Records Archive 122,
    322
Punjab Textbook Board 144, 155,
    168, 205, 210
Punjabi Adabi Academy 76, 269,
    309
Purchas, Samuel 31, 67

Qadri, Mumtaz 235
qasida (panegyrics) 15, 22
Qasida-e Shahrashob 15
Qasim, Muhammad bin 146,
    149–150, 167–168, 180,
    183–185, 188–189, 195,
    197–198, 201, 203, 205–210,
    212–213, 215
qaum (nation) 213–214
Qila Gujjar Singh 75
Qissa-e Ghamgin (A Tale of
    Sorrow) 15
Qudsia, Bano 224, 227, 239
Qur'an 53, 118, 130, 140, 171,
    201, 215, 219, 226, 263, 285,
    297, 299–300, 303, 309

Qureshi, Ishtiaq Husain 120, 141–146, 153, 210, 234
Qutb, Sayyid 263

Race Course Park (aka Jilani Park) 62
Radio Azad Kashmir 227
Radio Pakistan 228
Rahman, Fazlur 115–116, 131
Rahman, Mujibur 144, 187
Raikes, Charles 72
Raja Teja Singh Temple 79
Rajatarangini (Stein) 129
Rajgarh 139
Rajpal, Mahashe 231–232
Ramayana 14, 163–164, 167, 208, 287
Raja Ram Chand 75
Guru Ram Das Asthan 79
Ramnagar 85, 139
Rang Mahal 20–21
Ranjit Singh 45, 50–51, 61, 73, 75, 77, 79, 80, 104, 113, 137, 273
Ravi 1, 12, 22–23, 50, 53–54, 58, 60, 63, 82, 99, 111, 164, 171, 242, 277–282, 292, 295, 305, 307, 313, 321–322
Rawalpindi 105, 181, 196, 248–249
Rawalpindi Conspiracy Case 105, 248–249
razakar 92, 259
Rehman Baba 40
Report of the Commission on National Education 210

Riaz, Fahmida 304
the Right (politics)
Baqir, Muhammad 103–107
Chattan 236–240
Hijazi, Nasim 190–198
Ikram, S.M. 147–151
Inayatullah 184–189
Kashmiri, Shorish 186, 237–240, 259
Mau'dudi, Abu'l 'Ala (also Maulana Maududi) 196, 238, 262–265, 300
Qureshi, Ishtiaq Husain 141–146
Shahab, Qudratullah 223–228
Roe, Thomas 272
Rowlatt Act (1919) 244

Sa'ad Salman, Mas'ud 15, 23–25, 71, 140
Sacral Figures
Ayaz, Malik 20–26
Data Ganj Baksh 34–40
Guru Nanak 47–51
Miyan Mir 41–46
Sadr 98, 121, 134–135, 290
Sadr Bazaar 121, 290
Sahiwal 216, 248, 251, 273, 316, 318–319
Saif ul Malook 151, 309–310
Saigal, K.L. 86–87
Sakhi Sarwar 40
Sakinat ul Auliya (Calmness of the Saints) 41, 43–44
Salam, Abdus 210

Samadhi of Ranjit Singh 51, 77, 113
Samanabad Scheme 110
San Francisco Conspiracy Case 244
Sanskrit 14, 37, 81, 129–131, 136–140, 145
Sant Nagar 85
Mirza Sauda 15
Saunders, John Poyantz 245
Scott, Samuel Parsons 201
Section 295A (of Indian Penal Code) 232
Section 295C (of Pakistan Penal Code) 233–235
Sehwan Sharif 40, 50, 164
Mirza Shabbir Baig Sajid 236–237, 240
Shadbagh Scheme 110
Shagufta, Sara 305
Shahab, Qudratullah 196, 223–228, 239
Shahabnama 224–227
Shah Alami 78, 87, 92
Shah Jahan 20, 41, 44, 53, 56, 59–60, 62, 75, 80, 270
shaheed 183, 229–230, 235
Shahi Qila Se Jail Tak 250
shahr ashob (city disrupted) 15–16, 18, 23, 203
Shaikh Ghulam Ali & Sons 192–194
Shalimar Garden 53, 58–62, 67, 74–75, 105, 269
Sharar, Abdul Halim 193, 199, 202–204, 208

Shar'iati, 'Ali 263
Shi'a 25, 73, 150
shikasta (script) 322
Shirkat Gah 220, 262, 266
Shivaji Day 207–208
Shivaram Raj Guru 245
Siddiqui, Syed 233
sifat (qualities) 24
Sijzi, Mu'in al-Din Hasan (Sufi Chishti order) 39, 174
Sikh 13, 29, 45, 47, 50–51, 72–76, 79–83, 86–88, 90–92, 94, 96–103, 105–107, 113, 118, 120, 137, 155–156, 174, 176, 213, 221, 227, 236, 242–244, 246, 259, 302, 322
Simmel, Georg 4, 271
Simon Commission 245
Sind 41, 49, 117, 120, 124, 138, 145–146, 149, 157–160, 164, 168, 195, 197–198, 203, 207, 209–210, 213–214, 231, 249, 287
Sindhi (culture) 139, 209
Sindhi (language) 117–118, 139, 143, 209
Singh, Bhagat 87, 220–221, 241, 245–246, 248, 255
Singh, Chanan 245
sira 202
Sistani, Farrukhi 22
Socialism 174, 245
Sohni Mahiwal 87
Somnath (temple) 200
St. Mary Magdalene Church 205, 295

Stein, Marc Aurel 129
Stiffles 152
Struggle of Independence:
 Photograph Album,
 1905–1947 101
Sufi 24, 35–41, 43–44, 46, 50,
 54, 59, 73–76, 118, 149, 174,
 181, 208, 214, 270, 297, 310
Prophet Suleiman 285
Suleri, Sara 69–70
Sunni 25, 73, 133, 150, 161, 171,
 206, 216, 226
Surdas 49, 313
Sutlej 50, 313

Tabla Shah 75
Tafazzul Husain Kaukab 15
Maulana Tahir-ul Qadri 300
Tahqiqat-e Chishti (Chishti's
 Researches) 73–74, 76,
 269–271
Tahrik Takmil-e Pakistan 186
Taj, Imtiaz Ali 32
The Talisman 202
Tarikh (journal) 160, 200
Tarikh Awkhai Memon Biradari
 213
Tarikh-e Ara'in 215
Tarikh-e Baihaqi 67
Tarikh-e Hind 243
Tarikh-e Jatan 213
Tarikh-e Lahore 78
Tarikh-e Panjab (History of
 Panjab) 78
Tarikh-e Pashtun 213
Tarikh-e Sind 203

tariqa 43
tariqat (knowledge of the path) 36
Taseer, Salman 217, 219, 234–235
Tavernier, Jean-Baptiste 28, 67
tawa'if 79, 86
"terrorism" 4, 17, 87, 112, 243
Thanwi, Ashraf Ali 233
Thapar, Sukhdev 245
Thesiger, Wilfred 271
Tilak, Bal Gangadhar 207, 243
Timurid dynasty 47
Tiwana, Khizr Hayat Khan 88
Tomb of Aibak 117, 176–178,
 180, 183, 192
trees 42–44, 52, 60, 136, 181,
 276, 282, 290, 307–308, 319
Tufail, Muhammad 105–106

Uch Sharif 25, 39, 49–50, 66,
 178–179, 207, 313
udasi (exile) 48–49
Umar Baba 40
Hazrat 'Umar bin Khattab' 202
Unionists 85, 87
University of the Punjab (also
 Punjab University) 100, 103,
 122, 127, 129, 131–132, 138,
 141, 148, 243
Urdu Bazaar 169, 192, 206, 285,
 302, 312, 322
'urs (pilgrimage and gathering)
 45–46, 292
Uttar Pradesh 193, 207, 231

Vande Mataram Book Agency
 243

victory towers 171, 173, 175
von Grunebaum, Gustave 17
von Ranke, Leopold 202

Shah Waliullah Dehlawi 150
Walled City (see also old city) 1,
    11, 20, 74–75, 78–79, 90,
    96–97, 109, 112–113, 270,
    275–278, 281–282
Walser, Robert 271
Walton Grounds 305
Waris Shah 140, 153, 156, 302,
    310–313
Wasif Ali Wasif 224, 227
Water & Power Development
    Authority (WAPDA) 110
Water and Sanitation Agency
    (WASA) 110, 296
Wazir Khan Mosque 79
Well of Raja Dina Nath 113

West-östlicher Diwan (1819) 201
Wheeler, Robert Eric Mortimer
    115–117
Women's Action Forum 262, 265
Women's Front 262
Woolner, Alfred 127–131

Yadgar-e Chishti 73, 76, 299
Yaum al Fath (Victory Day) 207,
    209
Yohanabad (Joseph Colony) 292,
    295
Yorish, Qamar 250

Zaheer, Sajjad 249
Zaidan, Jurji 194–195
Zaman, Fakhr 305
Zamindar 194, 237
Zeb'un Nisa', Begum 53–55, 59,
    318

About the Author

Manan Ahmed Asif is an associate professor of history at Columbia University. He is the author of *A Book of Conquest* and *The Loss of Hindustan* and founder of the *Chapati Mystery* blog. He lives in New York.

Publishing in the Public Interest

Thank you for reading this book published by The New Press; we hope you enjoyed it. New Press books and authors play a crucial role in sparking conversations about the key political and social issues of our day.

We hope that you will stay in touch with us. Here are a few ways to keep up to date with our books, events, and the issues we cover:

- Sign up at www.thenewpress.com/subscribe to receive updates on New Press authors and issues and to be notified about local events
- www.facebook.com/newpressbooks
- www.twitter.com/thenewpress
- www.instagram.com/thenewpress

Please consider buying New Press books not only for yourself, but also for friends and family and to donate to schools, libraries, community centers, prison libraries, and other organizations involved with the issues our authors write about.

The New Press is a 501(c)(3) nonprofit organization; if you wish to support our work with a tax-deductible gift please visit www.thenewpress.com/donate or use the QR code below.